D0202139

THE SOCIAL PSYCHOLOGY
OF GENDER

TEXTS IN SOCIAL PSYCHOLOGY
Susan T. Fiske, *Series Editor*

Social Cognition: Understanding Self and Others
Gordon B. Moskowitz

The Social Psychology of Gender:
How Power and Intimacy Shape Gender Relations
Laurie A. Rudman and Peter Glick

THE SOCIAL PSYCHOLOGY OF GENDER

How Power and Intimacy Shape Gender Relations

Laurie A. Rudman
Peter Glick

Series Editor's Note by Susan T. Fiske

THE GUILFORD PRESS
New York   London

© 2008 The Guilford Press
A Division of Guilford Publications, Inc.
72 Spring Street, New York, NY 10012
www.guilford.com

All rights reserved

Paperback edition 2010

No part of this book may be reproduced, translated, stored in a retrieval
system, or transmitted, in any form or by any means, electronic, mechanical,
photocopying, microfilming, recording, or otherwise, without written permission
from the Publisher.

Printed in the United States of America

This book is printed on acid-free paper.

Last digit is print number: 9   8   7   6   5

Library of Congress Cataloging-in-Publication Data

Rudman, Laurie A.
   The social psychology of gender: how power and intimacy shape gender
relations / Laurie A. Rudman, Peter Glick.
      p. cm. – (Texts in social psychology)
   Includes bibliographical references and index.
   ISBN 978-1-59385-825-4 (hardcover: alk. paper)
   ISBN 978-1-60623-963-6 (paperback: alk. paper)
      1. Interpersonal relations.   2. Intimacy (Psychology)   3. Sex role–
Psychological aspects.   4. Social psychology.   I. Glick, Peter.   II. Title.
   HM1106.R83 2008
   305.301–dc22

                                                            2008006887

To Bob, for his unstinting love and support
–L. A. R.

To my mom, Betty Udman Glick,
and her daughters, Amy, Anne, and Sarilyn,
who taught me to respect as well as love
competent women
–P. G.

About the Authors

Laurie A. Rudman, PhD, is Professor of Psychology at Rutgers, The State University of New Jersey, in New Brunswick, New Jersey. Her research interests are intergroup relations and implicit social cognition. The author of more than 40 professional publications, she is currently associate editor of *Personality and Social Psychology Bulletin*. Her honors and awards include the National Research Service Award from the National Institutes of Health and (with Eugene Borgida) the Gordon Allport Prize from the Society for the Psychological Study of Social Issues. Dr. Rudman is an honorary Fellow of the American Psychological Association, the Association for Psychological Science, and the Society of Experimental Social Psychology, for which she currently serves on the Executive Committee. She also serves on the Advisory Council for the National Science Foundation and is a representative on the board of the Federation of Behavioral, Psychological, and Cognitive Sciences. Dr. Rudman has served as an expert witness in several workplace discrimination cases.

Peter Glick, PhD, is Professor of Psychology and the Henry Merritt Wriston Professor in the Social Sciences at Lawrence University in Appleton, Wisconsin. His research focuses on prejudice and stereotyping, particularly ambivalent prejudices. Along with Susan T. Fiske, he won the Gordon Allport Prize for developing the theory and measurement of ambivalent sexism. The Ambivalent Sexism Inventory has since been administered to tens of thousands of people in over 25 nations. These cross-cultural studies have shown that subjectively benevolent, but traditional, beliefs about women are associated with hostility toward nontraditional women, and with actual gender inequality. Dr. Glick is on the editorial boards of four professional journals and has been elected a Fellow of the American Psychological Association, the Association for Psychological Science, and the Society for the Psychology of Women. He is also on the Executive Councils (and a Fellow) of the Society of Experimental Social Psychology and the Society for the Psychological Study of Social Issues.

Series Editor's Note

Launching a series requires pioneering crafts to sail first, and this book, the second in the Texts in Social Psychology series, helps set its course. The series aims to chart the broad expanse of social psychology, including all our central destinations, through the eyes of expert, exciting explorers.

Laurie A. Rudman and Peter Glick's deft, yet comprehensive, treatment of the social psychology of gender represents just what I had hoped for. Provocative but professional, engaging but expert, the chapters cover every standard topic in gender courses, and then some. The chapter organization works equally well for a course or for a professional who is catching up. Bringing in everyday examples and news stories, as well as popular culture, the book also describes research examples and methods throughout. This is fully engaged science at its best.

Rudman and Glick organize their text around the twin themes of dominance and interdependence. This goes beyond traditional views of gender relations as yet another intergroup encounter, so readers will appreciate just how different this intimate interaction really is. Intriguing topics include the nature–culture tension, development of voluntary gender segregation, stereotype accuracy, why gender stereotypes are uniquely prescriptive, self-stereotyping, how to overcome backlash, and meditations about romance amid dominance. This text provides new vistas on familiar topics and new routes to explore. Bon voyage!

SUSAN T. FISKE
Eugene Higgins Professor
Princeton University

Preface

About the Book

Each of us interacts on a daily basis with both women and men. From personal experience, we all know a tremendous amount about gender relations, although often what we know is implicit, something we cannot fully articulate. This book aims to help readers look at this well-trod territory with fresh eyes, providing conceptual tools as well as a foundation of empirical facts about gender. Although some of this material may confirm common sense, we hope that this book will do much more than that. Indeed, the success of the book can be judged by how many times you, the reader, thinks "Ah, so *that's* why ..." as you experience a moment of insight into otherwise puzzling events in your own life. In other words, although the gender-related phenomena discussed here may be highly recognizable, the purpose of this book is not merely to describe but to explain and make sense of people's daily experiences with gender, using the scientific tools of social psychology.

Put more boldly, we hope that students who read this book will see their social world in new ways. Although this book reflects our underlying commitment to and concern with equality, the main aim here is intellectual rather than political, to reveal just how intriguing, complex, and strange gender phenomena are. For example, have you ever considered how your attitudes toward the other sex have changed during the course of your life? Many people spend their childhood largely indifferent to or actively avoiding members of the other sex, only to later want their most intimate, closest relationship to be with a person from this previously ignored or dreaded group. Or have you considered the seemingly contradictory ways that society treats men and women? On the one hand, women are relatively scarce at the highest levels of power and leadership, often viewed or portrayed as sexual objects, and consigned to enact feminine ideals that lead them to labor more on behalf of others than for their own status and independence. By these standards, women are oppressed. But what about the facts that women are stereotyped more positively than men, that they are currently doing better in high school and college than young men, and that men genuinely report tremendous affection for women? By these standards, women are thriving and valued. Gender relations defy simple, overgeneralized narratives about oppression (the "battle between the sexes") or rosy platitudes about how love conquers all; instead, they embody all sorts of apparent contradictions. Nonetheless, some basic social psychological principles about gender, based on contemporary theories and research, can help to resolve this confusing picture, making sense of its underlying patterns.

Research on the psychology of gender has exploded since the 1970s. However, social psychological investigations of gender relations developed primarily in two separate areas: prejudice and close relationships. Prejudice researchers treated sexism as though it were just another type of prejudice (like racism or homophobia), driven by an underlying antipathy toward women. For the most part, this research focused on negative stereotypes of women and resistance to giving them equal rights and roles. By contrast, relationship researchers emphasized romantic attraction and interdependence, focusing on the factors that draw women and men together into loving, intimate relationships. These two approaches painted very different, seemingly incompatible, pictures of male–female relations. However, since the mid-1990s, a second wave of research has revolutionized the field's appreciation of the complexities and subtleties of relations between the sexes, and has begun to bridge the gap between the approaches taken by prejudice and close relationship researchers. This book is very much conceived in the spirit of this integrated view of gender.

In particular, the central aim of this book is to show how two basic aspects of gender relations—male dominance and intimate heterosexual interdependence—combine to foster complex and ambivalent relations between and attitudes toward men and women. These basic facts about the structure of gender relations help to make sense of many otherwise apparently contradictory observations, from which an impressive number of implications for how people conceive of men's and women's traits, roles, and behavior follow. This approach also emphasizes the uniqueness of gender relations. No other two groups have experienced such persistent differences in power and status coupled with such deep and intimate interdependence. In the past, gender relations have been inappropriately shoehorned into existing paradigms (e.g., if prejudice is an antipathy, sexists must be overtly hostile toward women). Only recently have the unique qualities of gender relations begun to be understood and investigated.

We aim, then, to present the "cutting edge" of gender research. But we also have diligently attempted to present this work in a highly accessible way. It should take no prior scientific training to understand this book. Further, although our claims are based on evidence, we have tried to avoid merely compiling a list of facts about gender. Instead, we hope that each chapter reads a bit like a story, with a coherent set of identifiable themes. We intend this not to be a dry textbook but rather fun and engaging reading that, at the same time, does not "dumb down" the research and illuminates the complexity of the subject. Our intended audience includes students in undergraduate and graduate courses on gender, the psychology of women, women's studies, and social psychology. But we hope that this book will prove equally accessible to a general audience of people interested in gender issues while doing sufficient justice to the current state of the field that researchers seeking an overview on gender relations will also find it useful.

Finally, although, as stated previously, our main aim is intellectual, no book on gender can avoid a political dimension. We do not pretend to be apolitical, but we have attempted above all to be balanced and to let the empirical data, not wishful thinking, guide our conclusions. That said, this book reflects a commitment to gender equality (which we hope is a noncontroversial position in the minds of most readers) and, therefore, emphasizes the challenges that women face as they strive for gender parity and that both sexes face as they strive toward harmonious and equitable relations.

About the Authors' Collaboration

We initially met at a conference in Toronto in 1997 and began plotting our first research collaboration within an hour. Both of us were experienced gender researchers with keen interests in bridging the gap between research on sexism and close relationships. When Susan T. Fiske asked us to write this volume for the Texts in Social Psychology series, it was an offer we could not (and did not want to) refuse. This book is very much a joint product of the two authors.

Acknowledgments

First, we owe Susan Fiske an enormous debt for providing us with a rich and rewarding opportunity and for her generous editorial assistance throughout the process of writing this book. We are also deeply indebted to Alice Eagly for her valuable insights and comments on an earlier version of the book. More generally, we wish to acknowledge how much both Susan and Alice have influenced and supported each of us throughout our careers, as colleagues, collaborators, first-class scientists, role models, and supportive friends.

We are also grateful to Julie Phelan for her assistance with Chapters 7 and 8 and her constructive comments on every page. We thank Corinne Moss-Racusin and Natasha Quesnell Theno, who made many helpful suggestions for each chapter. Additionally, the many graduate students who participated in the 2007 Summer Institute in Social Psychology (SISP) course on gender (taught by Peter Glick and Alice Eagly) provided an invaluable sounding board for the penultimate draft of this book. The SISP course, in turn, was sponsored by the Society for Personality and Social Psychology and supported by a grant from the National Science Foundation. We also thank Leslie Trudell for her tireless help compiling the many references for this work. We acknowledge the support of National Science Foundation Grant No. BCS-0417335 to Laurie A. Rudman during the preparation of this volume.

Last, but not least, we wish to thank our respective spouses, Robert Jorissen and Karen Carr Glick, for their many insightful conversations about gender and for helping us appreciate the very best aspects of relations between the two sexes.

LAURIE A. RUDMAN
PETER GLICK

Contents

CHAPTER 1

Understanding Gender

Try casually scanning newspaper articles for a week or two with an eye toward assessing the current state of gender relations. This exercise will as likely lead to confusion as insight, with one article seeming to contradict the next. For example, in the Business pages, you might find any number of feature stories profiling female executives, something unheard of not so long ago. But turn the page and you may well find an article documenting the stubborn persistence of the "glass ceiling." In 2005, the profiled female CEO would have been one of only eight to lead a Fortune 500 company (Catalyst, 2006).

In the Nation section, an article cites disturbing evidence that boys currently perform significantly worse overall than girls in high school and college, earning lower grades and dropping out at a higher rate (Lewin, 2006). A conservative editorial columnist cites these data as evidence that "reverse discrimination" increasingly targets boys while girls unfairly benefit (Brooks, 2006). But another article shows that, among adult men and women, men still make markedly more money and that past progress toward closing the gender gap in pay has stalled or even reversed in recent years (Leonhardt, 2006). Even though boys currently perform worse than girls in school, in the job market power and resources still seem to flow more toward men than women.

An obituary of the pioneering feminist Betty Friedan marvels at the doors she helped to open, freeing young women from traditional notions of "femininity." Yet months later, in a Sunday magazine article, a prominent journalist anguishes about her own young daughter's fanatical attraction to "Princess culture," those ubiquitous dolls, accessories, and fashions marketed to girls that have become increasingly popular, generating billions of dollars in business (Orenstein, 2006). The journalist openly worries about how her daughter's fascination with "playing Princess" might curtail her aspirations by leading her later to abandon personal ambition in favor of "waiting for my Prince to come." A later article reveals how it is increasingly popular for women to bring their young daughters with them for spa treatments (Rosenbloom, 2007) and "Club Libby Lu" advertises its own "sparkle spa experience" and products aimed at its 6- to 12-year-old clientele whom they label as "very important princesses" (see *www.clublibbylu.com*).

Finally, the Sports section devotes more coverage than ever before to women's sports, reflecting both a shift in attitudes and government laws that mandate equal opportunity for female athletes in high schools and universities. Yet men's sports still dominate, especially at the professional level. A front page article reveals an interesting symptom of ambivalence about female athletes. It describes conflict among female cheerleaders and female athletes in high schools that now require cheerleaders to perform their routines at girls' as well as boys' team sporting events (Hu, 2007). Both the cheerleaders and the female athletes seem upset. For the cheerleaders, it means extra work, rendering them less available for travel to the boys' games (which they seem to value as more important), and some report that cheering for other women makes them feel "odd." The female athletes, in turn, view the cheerleaders as projecting a conventionally feminine and constrictive image that conflicts with their vision of the competitive female athlete. School administrators counter by pointing out the athleticism of the cheerleaders' routines. In the end, everybody seems uncomfortable about this juxtaposition of old and new feminine ideals.

The apparent contradictions in these and many other newspaper articles related to gender reflect, in part, conflicting contemporary political viewpoints. They also represent a complex and confusing reality in which every current seems to have a cross-current, every change seems to evoke a backlash. A student on the debate team assigned to argue that "there has been a steady march of progress toward gender equality, which will be completely achieved in the near future" would have no difficulty creating a compelling narrative. For example, who can doubt that our grandmothers had many fewer career and relationship choices than women do today? Yet another student assigned to the opposing side could amass a host of facts suggesting that progress toward gender equality has often been superficial or uneven, and that past gains have now stalled or even begun to reverse.

This book will not provide a definitive answer to this complicated debate. However, it will offer a set of conceptual tools to help you better understand the bewildering complexity of gender relations. We will provide ways of thinking about the apparent paradoxes of gender relations that will help cut through some of the clutter. To do so, we focus on fundamental social psychological forces that have long shaped (and continue to shape) how people conceive of men and women as well as how the sexes relate to each other. Although research on gender is still young, having begun in earnest in the 1970s, researchers have learned a tremendous amount in the past 35 years about how gender colors almost every aspect of daily life.

Brief Overview of the Book

This book examines how gender affects people's social lives from childhood onward, focusing on how women and men relate to each other. We cover a variety of domains in which gender relations occur, ranging from the schoolyard to the workplace to heterosexual romance. Our approach, however, is not simply to cover a set of topics but to provide a set of principles that lends coherence to an otherwise confusing picture.

To begin, the current chapter reviews the long-standing nature–culture debate. Evolutionary and cultural approaches will both figure prominently throughout this book. These approaches, however, have often been viewed in the past as oppositional. Some have argued that the psychology of gender is fixed as a result of inherent, evolved sex differences. Others have viewed gender as a wholly arbitrary cultural construction based on rules about masculinity and femininity determined only by history, not biology. We seek to transcend simplistic debates about whether gender is more conditioned by nature or by culture by detailing a "third way"–the social structural approach (Eagly, 1987)–which has the potential to incorporate and envelop insights from both evolutionary and cultural theories.

Chapter 2 considers in more detail how the unique structure of gender relations, with its unusual combination of dominance and intimate interdependence, creates a fundamental ambivalence toward both sexes. For instance, although many cultures devalue women in a variety of ways, women also commonly elicit affection, adoration, and protection from men; and although men may automatically be accorded more status and authority than women, stereotypes generally characterize men more negatively than women. We show how these ambivalent reactions result from two structural facts: (1) men's power and social dominance coupled with (2) intimate interdependence between the sexes. Although male dominance tends to encourage hostility between the sexes, intimate heterosexual interdependence entwines men and women, blunts hostility with benevolence, and creates genuine feelings of love and affection between the sexes. Although preferable to hostility, some forms of subjectively benevolent feelings toward each sex, especially women, can have harmful effects, insidiously reinforcing gender inequality in surprising ways. Distinguishing benevolence that is patronizing and condescending from attitudes that are purely affectionate or loving constitutes one of the most difficult puzzles of gender relations.

Chapter 3 traces the curious journey that most people take from endorsing overtly hostile gender relations in early and middle childhood to experiencing much more complicated and ambivalent feelings in adolescence and adulthood. These emotional changes parallel changes in the structure of gender relations. Sex segregation in childhood typically gives way to intimate heterosexual relationships in adolescence, when, for most, sexual development changes indifference and animosity toward the other sex into heightened interest and attraction.

Chapters 4 and 5 detail how popular conceptions of masculinity and femininity affect women's and men's self-conceptions and behavior toward members of each sex. Chapter 4 covers the origins and content of "gender stereotypes," defined as beliefs that specific attributes characterize one gender more than the other. These beliefs show impressive consistency across cultures and across time and can be traced to men's and women's differing roles and status. Chapter 5 explains how gender stereotypes describe men and women, setting up differing expectations about their preferences, traits, and behavior. It also shows how gender stereotypes go further to prescribe how men and women ought to be, specifying gendered norms about appropriate behavior. Both the descriptive and prescriptive aspects of stereotypes have important implications for how individual men and women are perceived and treated differently based on their gender.

Chapters 6 and 7 reveal how gender stereotypes affect people's social interactions and their self-concepts. In Chapter 6, we examine the means by which gender stereotypes can create social reality because people often conform to gendered expectations (e.g., boys acting tough) to avoid being punished for failing to do so. These processes lead to a self-sustaining prophecy that allows stereotypes perpetually to regenerate. In Chapter 7, we describe both personal and social obstacles to thwarting stereotypes, emphasizing the unfavorable treatment that gender vanguards (such as female leaders) receive. Although men and women in many contemporary societies are allowed greater leeway in their behavior than in more traditional times, gender deviance still often elicits social rejection and punishment. This is often especially harsh toward boys and men (e.g., rejection of boys who are "sissies" and men who are effeminate).

Chapter 8 focuses on the workplace, juxtaposing the substantial gains that women have made with the obstacles that remain to be overcome. We apply principles from earlier chapters to understand the ways in which "old-fashioned" sexism has shape shifted to more modern forms of discrimination that maintain sex segregation in the workplace, despite the increasing number of women who have careers outside the home.

Chapters 9 and 10 examine heterosexual love and sex. In both chapters, we consider how popular cultural ideals about romance impose a restrictive set of norms on the conduct of intimate heterosexual relationships (e.g., requiring men to show off their talents and resources while women are passively wined, dined, and wooed). We attempt to distinguish love (transcendent feelings of passionate attraction and intimacy) from traditional ideals of romance that can act to reinforce inequality, for instance by insisting on feminine virtues of modesty and deference in order to attract a man. These cultural ideals can straitjacket both men and women by trapping them in predetermined relationship roles, reducing a couple's freedom to express their love and making it more difficult to achieve fulfilling sex lives.

Chapter 11 considers the link between gender and violence. We note how patriarchy elicits not only violence against women but also violence between men as they compete for status and resources. Statistically, men are by far the more physically violent sex, but male-initiated aggression, especially murder, much more frequently targets other men rather than women. To some extent, women are the protected sex, with boys and men being raised "not to hit a woman." In addition, common forms of couple aggression (e.g., throwing objects) show, at least in Western nations, a surprisingly high degree of gender parity. Yet when it comes to violence in relationships producing injuries, men are more commonly the culprits. Further, rape and sexual assault are almost wholly committed by men and primarily victimize women. Although women disproportionately fear assaults by strangers, they face much greater risk of assault from male acquaintances and intimates than from strangers.

Chapter 12 concludes by considering the advances industrialized societies have made toward achieving gender equality, the problems that remain, and the prospects for global change in a time of increasing disparity between more and less developed nations. We emphasize the accumulating evidence that gender equality is good for men as well as women and point to organizational, personal, and legal remedies that have the potential to promote progress.

Conceptual Approaches to Gender

No two human groups experience more constant social differentiation than men and women. Indeed, the first question people typically ask about a newborn is whether the baby is a boy or a girl. Of course, gender is rooted in biological sex categories, based on the genotype and genitalia one possesses when born. But many cultural constructions, such as gender stereotypes, are layered on top of this biological distinction. These cultural beliefs dictate the relative masculinity or femininity of a host of behaviors, traits, occupations, and roles. This book loosely follows the conventional distinction gender researchers make between the terms "sex" and "gender." When strictly referring to the biological categories of male and female we typically use the term "sex," and when referring more broadly to social constructions of masculinity and femininity, such as stereotypes and roles, we typically use the term "gender." This rule, however, is not hard and fast. For example, we sometimes use "gender" when referring to people's social classification of others as male or female because once an individual is categorized by sex, a variety of assumptions about gender (i.e., masculinity or femininity) automatically come into play. As a result, we frequently use "sex" and "gender" interchangeably when referring to the simple categorization of these two groups.

Avoiding Simplistic Essentialism

The sex versus gender distinction represents an attempt by theorists and researchers to try to avoid "essentializing" cultural conceptions of masculinity and femininity. "Psychological essentialism" is the tendency to view category members (e.g., all men or all women) as sharing deep, immutable properties that fundamentally determine "who they are" (Medin & Ortony, 1989; Yzerbyt, Rocher, & Schadron, 1997). In other words, essentialism views biological sex differences as strongly determining a host of psychological sex differences. Gender essentialists view differences in how women and men think, feel, and act as biologically fixed and immutable. As a result, they assume that new cultural conditions (e.g., the influx of women into the paid workforce) will not make men and women more alike.

Categories endowed with essences are viewed as "homogeneous, mutually exclusive, and unalterable" (Haslam, Rothschild, & Ernst, 2000, p. 114). Racial and other social groups have also historically been represented in these terms. For example, racists talk about race as "in the blood," and the "one-drop" rule labeled people as Black even if they appeared to be White. The Nazis used a similar rule to label people as Jewish during World War II, even if they had been raised as Christians. Nonetheless, compared with other social categories, people rate gender as more natural, immutable, discrete, and stable, in other words as more "essentialistic" (Haslam et al., 2000).

The jury is still out on the degree to which biological sex differences translate into psychological characteristics (as we note later). However, laypeople show an exaggerated tendency to essentialize gender that even the most biologically oriented psychologists would probably dispute. The perennial success of books such as *Men Are from Mars, Women Are from Venus* (Gray, 1992) reveals the widespread appeal of gender essentialism. The popularity of essentialist beliefs occurs for at least two reasons. First, gender relates to an underlying and (usually) clear-cut dichotomy between being female or male that is not the case for other social categories. For example, many African Americans may also have White ancestors and thus not be purely Black or White. Other important group memberships are based on beliefs and practices (e.g., being Christian or Muslim) that can change throughout one's lifetime. By contrast, women and men are more clearly and permanently biologically divided. Second, obvious physical differences underscore gender as a highly differentiated social category. Women have more salient reproductive sexual characteristics than men, whereas men are taller, stronger, and hairier and weigh more, on average, than women. Sex-linked physical attributes make gender a prime category for popular versions of essentialism.

For everyone, from kindergartners to adults at a cocktail party, essentialism provides a ready explanation for why people behave as they do: "He's a boy" or "She's a woman" often constitutes the only explanation people require (Gelman, Collman, & Maccoby, 1986; Yzerbyt, Rogier, & Fiske, 1998). Because it divides men and women into seemingly immutable categories, essentialism reinforces perceptions of the sexes as biological opposites, implying that when it comes to gender, nature conquers nurture (Gelman & Taylor, 2000; M. G. Taylor, 1996). Keep in mind as we review biological views about gender that evolutionary and biological influences are only part of a complex stew of ingredients that differentiate the two sexes.

Biological and Cultural Explanations

Essentialism remains an important undercurrent in nature–culture debates among gender theorists and researchers (see Eagly & Wood, 1999, Wood & Eagly, 2002, for insightful discussions). On one side, some evolutionary theorists view women and men as fundamentally different, both physically and psychologically, such as in their abilities, ways of thinking, and personalities. From this perspective, gender stereotypes (e.g., that men are analytical and women emotional) reflect inherent and stable sex differences that developed as adaptations that served to increase the odds of human survival.

By contrast, most cultural or social theorists view gender as a social construction, a product of cultural ideals about femininity and masculinity. Gender, of course, builds on the biological categories of female and male, but social constructionists tend to believe that biological sex differences affect only a limited number of physical traits (e.g., size, genitalia, and facial hair) and that psychological differences between the sexes are culturally created. Biological essentialism is anathema to social constructionists, who point out that variation within each sex on any specific characteristic remains much greater than the average difference between the sexes (Hyde, 2005). From this perspective, differences between men and women trace back to culture more than nature. These differences nevertheless become "real" because social forces compel men and women to enact or "perform" gender (and not because sex differences are deeply embedded in people's genetic codes).

In the remainder of this chapter, we first review the two poles of the nature–culture debate before introducing a social structural approach that can help to integrate both biological and cultural views. Indeed, although the nature–culture debate has often been viewed as an either–or proposition, many contemporary psychological theorists view biological and social explanations as compatible and complementary.

The Cultural Approach

The most prominent cultural theories and research on the psychology of gender emphasize gender socialization, the process by which girls and boys learn feminine and masculine identities (e.g., see C. L. Martin & Ruble, 2004). From infancy on, how people are treated depends on their sex. Nonetheless, socialization is not a passive process. Rather, as children learn gendered expectations, they also begin actively to "perform gender," trying to live up to society's predetermined gender ideals and stereotypes (processes we explore in detail in subsequent chapters). Thus, cultural theorists are social constructionists; they assume that cultural beliefs create most, if not all, observed sex differences in behavior as people act out cultural scripts assigned to their gender.

Social learning theory (Mischel, 1966) represents one influential cultural explanation of gender differences. Social learning theorists focus on modeling or observational learning, which refers to acquiring behaviors by observing how similar others, such as same-sex others, behave. Consistent with the social learning perspective, many studies demonstrate that children learn what it means to be male or female through observation. For instance, children are more likely to imitate the behavior of a person of the same sex as opposed to the other sex (Bussey & Bandura, 1999).

Cultural theorists (e.g., Bem, 1981) also emphasize how society communicates shared cultural ideals about how people of each gender ought to behave. These expectations range from the kinds and colors of clothes boys and girls should wear (e.g., blue vs. pink) to the kinds of activities (e.g., baseball vs. figure skating) and occupations (e.g., doctor vs. nurse) they should prefer. These gendered cultural ideals form coherent knowledge structures known as "gender schemas" that guide people's perceptions of self and others and their behavior and preferences and generally become the lenses through which people view their social world (Bem, 1981). Children quickly learn gender schemas, such as which toys they ought to prefer, and use this knowledge to understand other people and to inform their actions toward others. Gender schemas represent habits of mind that persist through adulthood. For instance, one might assume solely on the basis of their gender that a man probably prefers watching football over shopping, whereas a woman would likely prefer shopping.

Consider how cultural theorists might explain popular beliefs about sex differences by listing your own responses to the question, "What cultural forces or institutions account for the persistence of gender stereotypes?" We cannot enforce a brief pause here, but humor us—it will only take a few seconds for you to list a few things that most quickly come to mind.

Have you made a short list? If you have, we suspect it includes the media (e.g., television, movies, video games, the Internet), authority figures (e.g., parents and teachers), and peers as conduits of stereotypes. Why? Because the media, authority figures, and peers transmit cultural beliefs that affect children's socialization. If these cultural agents consistently reinforce messages about sex differences, they can at least partly account for the continuation of gender stereotypes. Also, because people adopt traits appropriate to their gender (i.e., attempt to live up to the stereotypes about their sex), gender socialization can precipitate actual sex differences in behavior. In turn, sex differences in behavior perpetuate the stereotypes by making them appear to be accurate.

There is no doubt that cultural influences are both important and ubiquitous. The next time you watch a television sitcom, go to a movie, or read a book, try to notice their heavy reliance on stereotypes to "tell a story." This shows how stereotypes allow people to communicate with each other in a kind of short-hand code that relies on culturally shared assumptions about gender. Television commercials (and the products they advertise) illustrate this phenomenon nicely. For instance, spend a day counting how many advertisements for cleaning products feature women versus men. An analysis of television commercials from the 1990s revealed that female characters tend to be shown in a family setting rather than at work in a paid job. And women depicted at work tend to hold service-oriented or clerical positions rather than high-status professional jobs; they also tend to lack authority and were frequently shown as sex objects (Coltrane & Adams, 1997).

The constant bombardment of such cultural images can influence viewers' gender attitudes. For example, men who viewed more "macho" (vs. androgynous) magazine advertisements subsequently evinced more traditional gender role attitudes (Garst & Bodenhausen, 1997). Among adolescent girls, those who watch more television also show more traditional gender role attitudes (Rivadeneyra & Ward, 2005), as do girls who frequently view music videos (Ward, Hansbrough, & Walker, 2005). Throughout this book, we describe the myriad effects that cultural forces, including the media, have on people's perceptions of gender.

But exclusively cultural explanations of gender tend to beg an important question: How did beliefs about what it means to be male or female get started in the first place? The cross-cultural ubiquity and consistency of beliefs about gender remain especially puzzling given the existence of few, if any, inherent psychological sex differences (see Hyde, 2005). In other words, if men and women are more similar than different, why do so many human cultures persistently view the sexes as different? And why do so many cultures tend to agree in their characterizations of the two sexes (e.g., viewing men as aggressive and women as warm)? In fact, evolutionary psychologists use cross-cultural consistency as a primary source of support for their suggestion that sex differences stem from different selection pressures that were first established in primeval environments.

The Evolutionary Approach

Based on Darwinian theory, the evolutionary approach emphasizes biologically based sex differences, not only in physical characteristics but in psychological traits, mental processes, and behavior (e.g., Buss, 2003). Like cultural theorists, evolutionary psychologists are concerned with the origins of gender differences, but their focus is on more distal, biological causes. Both schools of thought argue that past events continue to influence people today, but evolutionary theorists stress long-ago species adaptation, whereas cultural theorists focus on more proximate social forces. Moreover, evolutionary theorists uniquely rely on comparing people to animals because some of the basics of heterosexual reproduction, which are theorized to have created psychological and behavioral sex differences, ought to have had similar evolutionary influences across species.

When it comes to gender, evolutionary theorists suggest an alternative to cultural explanations. They contend that men and women fundamentally differ, in all sorts of ways, because of evolutionary biology. For instance, why are men stereotyped as aggressive and women as nurturing? Evolutionary theorists answer that these beliefs accurately reflect inherent sex differences. Men evolved to be competitive providers, whereas women evolved to be caregivers. The evolutionary approach generates controversy among gender researchers because it suggests an essentialistic view in which men and women fundamentally differ psychologically as well as physically. Although social as well as natural scientists generally accept Darwinian evolution as an explanation for how humans evolved over time, whether evolutionary pressures created significant biologically based sex differences in people's personality traits and behavior remains a matter of debate (see Eagly & Wood, 1999, Wood & Eagly 2002, or Hyde, 2005, for the more minimalist position and Buss, 2003, for the evolutionary argument).

The evolutionary argument about sex differences relies heavily on the process of sexual selection, as distinguished from the more familiar notion of natural selection. Evolutionary theory emphasizes that people must reproduce, not just survive, to pass on their genes. Survival to adulthood, of course, is essential for an individual to reproduce. But Darwin (1871) recognized that survival alone is not enough and that sexual reproduction is a tricky business that requires, among other things, the ability to attract mates. Darwin's sexual selection theory considers mating strategies, noting that possessing the traits potential mates find attractive increases an individual's chances of reproducing, making the genes for those traits more common in successive generations. If, in earlier stages of human evolutionary history, men and women began to select mates based on different traits, then sexual selection could have led to biologically based sex differences in personality and capabilities. These sex differences in psychological characteristics would, unless subjected to new selection pressures, persist to the present day.

Consider a nonhuman example. If peahens prefer peacocks with beautiful plumage, the more bedecked the male, the better his chances of reproducing. This kind of selection, repeated over many, many generations, can result in large differences between males and females. Peacocks became increasingly colorful because only the ones with colorful plumage attracted mates and passed on their genes, so that genes for drab plumage became deselected in males. In contrast, females retained their more modest coloring because peacocks did not restrict themselves to mating with the most ornate peahens. Subjected only to natural selection, the peahens' more modest coloring persists because it allows them to blend in with the underbrush, offering more protection from predators. Sexual selection, then, can work in a direction opposite to natural selection. The peacock's magnificent plumage makes it ungainly and potentially more vulnerable to predation; therefore, it would not occur through natural selection, commonly referred to as survival of the fittest. Of course, natural selection places limits on how ornate the peacock's plumage can get, but the peahen's preferences also represent a potent selective force. Similar examples occur in many other bird species, with males being more brightly or ornately plumed than females (e.g., the cardinals in your backyard).

But why did peahens and not peacocks become so choosy about their mate's superficial plumage? Darwinian sexual selection arguments (more fully developed by Trivers, 1972) rely on the notion that asymmetries in the mechanics of sexual reproduction lead to sex differences in mate preferences. The crux of the argument is that sperm is cheap and eggs are not. Consider this argument in a human context. Sexual access to a variety of women maximizes a man's potential reproductive success. If an individual man could attract multiple female sexual partners, he could potentially sire many children. Consider the potential reproductive abilities of an ancient male ruler who had a harem or a contemporary male sports or rock star with a large following of "groupies." Theoretically, a particularly attractive man could potentially sire thousands of offspring. By contrast, a woman's reproductive potential faces a sharp limit, no matter how many mates she can obtain. Each offspring requires at least a 9-month investment at considerable physiological costs to the mother. Across her life span, a woman might potentially give birth to a dozen or so children, but certainly not hundreds, let alone thousands.

According to Trivers (1972), because of differences in reproductive investment, women evolved a choosier mate selection strategy. As a result, men and women theoretically look for different kinds of traits in a mate. According to this evolutionary logic, women tend to desire a mate who appears not only "fit" (i.e., a survivor) but also able and willing to provide resources for offspring, thereby maximizing each one's survival potential. A man's social status and dominance hypothetically indicate his ability to provide, suggesting that he has the ability to outcompete other men for resources. Women's choosiness placed a selection pressure on men, increasing competition among them to demonstrate dominance and to amass the most resources. This argument has been used to suggest that, ironically, women's mating preferences result in the selection of genes that foster male dominance, which in turn results in the subordination of women, whom men exclude from this competition (Sidanius & Pratto, 1999; Smuts, 1995).

Evolutionary theorists further note that men face the particular problem of uncertainty about the paternity of a mate's offspring. Men hypothetically evolved to exercise control over their mates' sexuality so that they can have confidence that their mate has not had sex with anyone else (Daly, Wilson, & Weghorst, 1982; Smuts, 1995). Because of paternal uncertainty, men evolved to experience strong sexual jealousy and to engage in "mate guarding." The latter can be seen in various cultural practices designed to control women's sexuality, ranging from marriage (to ensure wives' monogamy) to female circumcision, which curtails women's sexual pleasure. According to evolutionary theorists, selection pressures toward male assertiveness, combined with those for mate guarding and control over female sexuality, explain men's tendency to dominate women as well as sex differences in traits such as aggressiveness (Buss, 2003, 2005).

So far, we have described an evolutionary account for human sex differences that could also be applied to other species. However, contemporary evolutionary theorists have provided more complex explanations that incorporate the unique properties of humans. In particular, they emphasize how humans' cognitive flexibility combined with openness to the influence of others enabled adaptation to different and rapidly changing environments (Caporeal, 2004). The human propensity to absorb social norms and culture makes good evolutionary sense because it enabled people to band together to survive and to pass on important knowledge, such as how to build tools (Caporeal, 2001). Moreover, our ability to form stable, interdependent groups affords a wide range of adaptive behaviors; to enhance group functioning, many roles are necessary. For example, not every male needs to be aggressive if he has other skills useful to the group.

As a result, very little human behavior is genetically preprogrammed; instead, malleability and openness to social and cultural influences distinguish humans from most other species. For example, females of most other species cannot choose when or whether to mate; when they are in estrus, their biology dictates it is time for sex. By contrast, humans' ability to choose a wide variety of behaviors, sexual and otherwise, makes us a divergent and diverse species. In popular culture, however, evolutionary explanations that take account of the interaction between biological predispositions and social environments tend to be rendered in a more simplistic, essentialistic manner.

Further, keep in mind that evolutionary theory does not imply that sex differences are either desirable or inevitable. The first false conclusion—that what is natural is also desirable—represents what philosophers term the "naturalistic fallacy" (Moore, 1903). This fallacy is quickly exposed when one substitutes "death and illness" for "sex differences": The former are certainly natural but not at all desirable. The unnatural eradication of devastating illnesses (e.g., smallpox) and the creation of living conditions and medical interventions that prolong life represent some of humanity's most prized achievements. To expose the second fallacy—that genetically influenced traits are inevitable or unaffected by social conditions—consider another example. Height clearly has a strong genetic component, but how tall an individual becomes also has a great deal to do with environment. A poorly nourished child may quickly lose the height advantage conferred by inheriting a genetic predisposition for tallness. If you have seen examples of clothing and armor from earlier eras, you know that they dramatically illustrate how environmental changes have affected this "biologically determined" trait. The increased height among people today reflects social changes that led to enhanced food production rather than further biological evolution. Thus, biologically influenced traits are still affected by environmental factors.

Nonetheless, if the sexual selection argument holds and some psychological sex differences are deeply embedded in human biology, not just human culture, important implications follow. Although evolutionary theorists acknowledge that environments significantly alter the expression of genes, they also view evolved characteristics as setting limits on environmental effects. For example, if boys and girls receive similar nutrition, genetic predispositions for sex differences in height will still lead, on average, to taller men. Similarly, if male dominance striving is coded in men's genes, efforts to create gender equality must work against psychological sex differences that continue to promote male dominance (see Chapter 2).

The Continuing Nature–Culture Debate

Evolutionary theorists support their views by pointing to cross-cultural consistencies in sex differences, which they view as incompatible with the cultural approach. For instance, an initial examination of men's and women's mate preferences in 37 nations suggested, as sexual selection theory predicts, that men and women focus on different characteristics when choosing mates (Buss et al., 1990), with women putting greater emphasis on a mate's earning potential (i.e., ability to obtain resources) and men putting more emphasis on potential mates' physical attractiveness.

A reanalysis of the same data (by Eagly & Wood, 1999) with an eye toward cross-cultural differences in mate preferences, however, suggests a social explanation for these gender differences. National indices of gender equality (e.g., gender similarities in health, standard of living, and occupational equality) significantly accounted for sex differences in mate preferences. Specifically, more egalitarian nations show reduced sex differences in preferences for mates with good earning potential. When women have few opportunities to gain resources on their own, they appear to seek such resources in their mates, but when women's status is higher this sex difference tends to dissipate (although not completely disappear).

These data still leave plenty of room for debate. Arguments over the degree to which gender-related phenomena show cross-cultural similarities (as evolutionary theory predicts) or differences (as cultural explanations imply) tend to have the quality of disagreements about whether a glass is half full or half empty. Further, evolutionary psychologists do not expect complete cross-cultural uniformity, noting that evolved predispositions respond to environmental triggers or circumstances. Thus, variations across cultures do not necessarily falsify the evolutionary approach. Nonetheless, evidence that mating preferences vary depending on the degree of gender equality in a society tends to undercut the evolutionary argument and to support cultural explanations.

Examining the cumulative research on sex differences in psychological traits and abilities also sheds light on the nature–culture debate. Meta-analyses—statistically based summaries of research findings—generally reveal small or nonexistent sex differences in psychological traits. Additionally, there tends to be much greater variation within each sex on any specific trait relative to between-sex differences (Hyde, 2005). Figure 1.1 illustrates how, even for traits in which modest sex differences have been found, the overlap between the sexes overwhelms

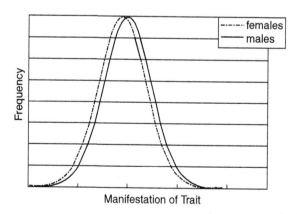

FIGURE 1.1. Graphic representation of a modest (typical) sex difference. From Hyde (2005). Copyright 2005 by the American Psychological Association. Reprinted by permission.

the average difference between them. The figure represents an approximately 0.20 standard deviation difference between average scores by men and women, which is typical of sex differences on many attributes, including spatial ability, moral reasoning, and self-esteem. From a practical standpoint, such differences are trivial compared with 85% overlap between the distributions for men and women. As a result, Hyde (2005) argues that the genders are far more similar than different, in contrast to popular conceptions.

Although many empirically investigated sex differences between men and women resemble Figure 1.1, Hyde's (2005) meta-analysis reveals two important exceptions to relative gender similarity, both of which support sexual selection theory. First, attitudes about casual sex sharply differ between men and women. Men, consistent with their small reproductive investment, evince much more interest in casual sex and have much lower standards for the characteristics of a casual sex partner compared with women. The second difference concerns same-sex physical aggression, which is much more prevalent in men than women (see Chapter 11), consistent with the notion that men have been selected to compete to gain the resources that will attract female mates. These differences, however, do not preclude cultural explanations. Sex differences in attitudes about casual sex may reflect adopting a cultural double standard that penalizes women, but not men, for promiscuity (Crawford & Popp, 2003). Similarly, differences in physical aggression may reflect cultural ideals of masculinity that value physical bravery and not letting others "push you around."

In short, when framed as an either–or dichotomy, the nature–culture debate seems never to end. Each approach has merits and weaknesses. The cultural approach shows how social conceptions of gender influence people's beliefs and behavior but may overemphasize social causes to the exclusion of biological differences, particularly those that pertain to reproduction. Biology does not consign men and women to different destinies, but it plays a role in the psychology of gender. On the other hand, although the evolutionary approach tells a plausible story about the distant origins of sex differences, its focus on primeval origins can make it difficult to put many of these hypotheses to rigorous empirical tests (cf. Buss, 2003; Kenrick & Simpson, 1997, for a refutation of this argument).

Throughout this book, we make extensive use of both cultural and evolutionary theories. However, we generally do so in the context of a social structural approach. Social structural theories have the advantage of addressing both cross-cultural similarities and differences in gender-related phenomena. Like cultural theories, social structural theories emphasize gender as a social construction, but with an important twist: They do not view social conceptions of gender as accidental products of specific cultural beliefs but rather as predictable consequences of how societies are organized. The remaining section of this chapter considers the distinct advantages of social structural theories.

A Third Way: The Social Structural Approach

Structural explanations suggest that the social positions of groups within society and the structure of intergroup relationships determine perceptions of and behavior toward members of differing social groups. "Social position" refers to the roles and occupations members of a group typically perform and their place in status and power hierarchies. The "structure of intergroup relationships" refers to how situational context shapes intergroup relations. For example, when groups vie for limited resources (e.g., land or water is scarce) or have incompatible goals, intergroup relations tend toward competitiveness. In contrast, when groups have little choice but to depend on each other to achieve shared goals (e.g., when groups must create alliances to defeat a common threat or enemy), cooperative intergroup relations occur. In short, power disparities and interdependence motives represent structural variables that permeate and inform all intergroup relations, including gender (S. T. Fiske, Cuddy, Glick, & Xu, 2002).

Structural variables play an important role in shaping gender relations, the content of gender stereotypes, and observed sex differences in traits and behaviors. Because structural explanations emphasize social causes, they fit under the general umbrella of social constructionism. But structural explanations can also complement and incorporate evolutionary theory. We consider a specific example of such integration in Chapter 2, which examines how evolutionary and social structural explanations can combine to explain the cross-cultural ubiquity of patriarchy.

Given that social structural explanations represent a kind of constructionist approach, how do they differ from cultural explanations? To some degree, the two overlap. Like cultural theorists, social structural theorists view socialization as an important mechanism that shapes men's and women's traits and behaviors. However, by focusing on the causal role of factors such as groups' relative positions in a status hierarchy, structural explanations do not merely describe the content and transmission of current gender beliefs, but can help to (1) explain the underlying origins and content of gender stereotypes as well as actual sex differences in traits and behaviors; (2) predict the degree of consistency versus variation in stereotypes and behaviors across cultures and historical periods; (3) explain when and why gender stereotypes become prescriptive ideals, not just expectancies, concerning how men and women ought to behave; and (4) span and interconnect various levels of analysis, from wider social conditions to intergroup behaviors to individual psychology. In the next section, we describe social role theory (Eagly, 1987; Eagly et al., 2000), the most influential social structural theory of gender, to illustrate these advantages of the structural approach.

Social Role Theory

Social role theory (Eagly, 1987) focuses on two social structural aspects of gender relations: a gendered division of labor and gender-based hierarchy (in which men generally have more status and power than women). The theory suggests that these structural factors determine the content of socially shared beliefs about men and women as well as observed gender differences in personality, skills, and behavior. We illustrate social role theory's insights, organized according to the advantages of social structural theories listed previously.

The Origins and Content of Gender Stereotypes and Sex Differences

Social role theory observes that roles generate specific demands for individuals to exhibit particular traits and behaviors. For example, women's long-standing child-rearing role requires nurturing traits and behaviors. The cultural assignment of women to a child-rearing role is rooted in reproductive biology, which ties women to bearing and nourishing infants. Social role theory suggests that such role segregation produces stereotyped expectations; for example, because of women's link to child rearing, people associate women with communal traits (e.g., helpful, nurturing, and kind). Similarly, social role theory attributes stereotypes of men as more assertive, competitive, and aggressive (i.e., more agentic) to their nondomestic work roles, which tend to require physical bravery and leadership skills.

Status differences between men and women reinforce these gender-stereotypical expectations. The two structural aspects of gender relations that social role theory identifies—division of labor and hierarchy—are closely related. Male roles typically accrue more status and provide greater opportunity to amass resources than female roles. Housekeeping and rearing children—traditionally women's work—do not confer prestige or significant amounts of money. The content of stereotypes of many low- versus high-status groups corresponds to the content of stereotypes of homemakers versus providers because the communal traits assigned to women are low-status traits, whereas the agentic traits assigned to men are high-status traits (S. T. Fiske et al., 2002; Ridgeway, 2001b). In other words, gender stereotypes strongly reflect status differences in men's and women's traditional social roles.

Social role theory posits that roles not only foster stereotypes about each sex but also help to create a corresponding reality. This occurs because (1) people are socialized to enact the traits demanded of roles their group typically occupies (e.g., girls are taught to be nurturing and are rewarded for acting this way), (2) people adopt traits associated with their social groups (e.g., girls and women are more likely than boys and men to define themselves in terms of nurturance), and (3) performing gender-linked roles increases the degree to which people exhibit the traits and behaviors these roles require (e.g., when women become mothers, the role elicits nurturing behavior).

Because social rewards and punishments provide incentives for people to act in line with expectations about members of their group, an individual may act in concert with gendered expectations even when this does not suit his or her personality. For instance, a woman might act in a nurturing way not because she wishes to but rather to avoid the sting of others' disapproval. The processes outlined previously serve to ensure that women and men do behave differently, which fosters a reality that matches gender stereotypes (Rudman & Fairchild, 2004; Swim, 1994).

The implications of social role theory for the content of gender stereotypes and for sex differences in traits and behaviors are clear. Social role theory suggests that cultural beliefs about women and men are not haphazard or arbitrary. From this perspective, cultural ideals of femininity and masculinity could have developed differently only if men's and women's social roles had been different. If, for instance, women and men contributed equally to child rearing and work outside the home, they would be perceived as having similar, not different, traits.

Consistency versus Variability across Cultures and Historical Periods

Social role theory has another important advantage over the cultural approach: It predicts when and why social changes should lead to changes in gender stereotypes and corresponding sex differences in traits and behaviors. If social roles determine both the content of stereotypes and differences in how men and women behave, then changes in men's and women's distribution into societal roles ought to either reinforce or diminish gendered stereotypes and behavior (Diekman & Eagly, 2000). For example, what would happen if men were just as likely as women to become stay-at-home parents? Social role theory would predict convergence between stereotypes about men's and women's nurturance. Further, the theory suggests that the actual traits men and women exhibit (e.g., being understanding, kind, and communal) would also converge as men began to respond to the demands of the child-rearing role. Similarly, if roles outside the home changed, such that women had full-time jobs that demanded "masculine" traits such as decisiveness and ambition, stereotypes of men as more agentic than women would disappear.

The influx of women into the paid workforce in the past several decades, therefore, provides a naturalistic test of social role theory. Women's participation in paid work outside the home has changed dramatically, but domestic roles have not; women remain the primary caregivers at home, even when employed (Bianchi, 2000), and still perform a disproportionate amount of household labor (Bianchi, Milkie, Sayer, & Robinson, 2000; Deutsch, Lussier, & Servis, 1993; see Chapter 8). In other words, women's roles have changed in some ways (more likely to be in the paid workforce) and not in others (remaining as primary caregivers). Social role theory, therefore, predicts that stereotypes of women ought to have changed in specific ways: Women should be stereotyped as becoming more agentic (e.g., ambitious, assertive) as a result of their participation in paid careers but should still be stereotyped as highly communal because of their continued role as child rearers. In contrast, because men's primary role as chief provider has remained constant, male stereotypes ought not to have changed. We consider evidence that supports these predictions in Chapter 5 (Diekman & Eagly, 2000; Spence & Buckner, 2000; Twenge, 1997a).

These same principles ought to apply to understanding cross-cultural similarities and differences in gendered stereotypes and behavior. We have noted that the cultural approach would predict greater variability in cross-cultural gender stereotypes than exists, while cross-cultural consistencies are used to support evolutionary theory. Social role theory can potentially address both consistency and change, explaining why women are cross-culturally viewed as, and probably are, more communal—they remain the predominant child rearers across cultures—as well as when and why gender stereotypes and behaviors change. In short, the ability of social structural theories to predict cross-cultural similarities and differences in gender stereotypes and behavior, as well as stability and change over time within the same society, represent distinct advantages of this structural theory.

When and Why Gender Stereotypes Become Prescriptive Ideals

Another advantage of structural approaches is that they help to explain why gender stereotypes are prescriptive, specifying the way men and women ought to act, as well as descriptive, specifying how men and women tend to act. Prescriptions have been referred to as "injunctive norms," or socially enforced expectations about how people ought to behave that elicit punishment when people do not conform (Burgess & Borgida, 1999; Cialdini & Trost, 1998). Social role theory suggests that role demands create gender prescriptions. When a society relies on a group-based division of labor, it has a stake in ensuring that people act in accordance to their roles. If people fail to enact their roles or to do them well, the normal division of labor becomes inefficient and unproductive. In a gender-traditional society, if women fail to nurture the children, who will raise them? If men do not succeed at work, how can they provide for their families?

Observing whether violating a stereotype results in anger, not just surprise, from onlookers illustrates whether a stereotype is prescriptive or merely descriptive. If people who deviate from the stereotype are rejected, then the belief functions prescriptively. Prescriptions pressure individuals to conform to their expected roles (Rudman & Fairchild, 2004). For instance, a man might decide not to quit his job to be a stay-at-home father for fear of others' disapproval or rejection. Gender prescriptions, therefore, create sex differences in traits and behavior even when individual men and women do not initially possess stereotyped traits. Further, such prescriptions create strong resistance to changes in gender roles, such as backlash toward working women as "bad mothers" (Cuddy, Fiske, & Glick, 2004). By contrast, aspects of stereotypes that are not role based, such as the stereotype that women like shoes, are unlikely to be highly prescriptive: People do not care so much if a particular woman is not "into shoes" but are more likely to condemn her for not being interested in raising children.

Spanning and Interconnecting Various Levels of Analysis

The final advantage of social structural theories concerns their ability to span and interconnect various levels of analysis, from wider social forces (e.g., labor divisions in society) to the psychology of the individual (e.g., an individual's preference for a gender-congruent occupation). Social structural theories can also connect evolutionary explanations with social structure, as Wood and Eagly's (2002) more recent biosocial theory does (see Chapter 2). For example, social role theorists reject the idea that evolution has created inherent sex differences in people's desire or ability to nurture. However, they posit that women's greater biological role in sexual reproduction indirectly created gender stereotypes of female nurturance and, as a result, corresponding social pressures on women to behave in a nurturing manner.

Social structural approaches are also well suited to incorporating cultural explanations. For instance, social role theory explains how social roles and gender hierarchy create shared, prescriptive cultural stereotypes of men and women that lead individuals to conform (e.g., to develop the skills, traits, and behaviors "appropriate" to their gender). These social pressures create real differences in male and female behavior across cultures and historical periods because women's biological role in reproduction consistently ties them to a child-rearing role.

In the next chapter, we consider another social structural theory of gender: ambivalent sexism theory. Although complementary to social role theory, ambivalent sexism theory more particularly focuses on how the structural factors of traditional male dominance and intimate interdependence between the sexes create ambivalent (i.e., both positive and negative) emotions and stereotypes toward each sex.

Chapter Summary

This chapter outlined the dispute between theorists and researchers who emphasize the role of culture versus the role of evolution in shaping gender relations and creating sex differences in behavior. This debate is often intense because, far from being an arcane academic matter, it has serious political consequences, including whether and how gender equality might be achieved. The cultural approach views gender as a social construction primarily shaped by social values and beliefs. Although gender is based on a biological dichotomy, cultural theorists view it as more of a social than a biological category. Further, these theorists view gendered beliefs as arbitrary cultural products, mere accidents of history and cultural development.

By contrast, the evolutionary approach emphasizes nature over culture, suggesting biologically based sex differences that result from human evolution. This approach focuses on sexual selection (i.e., how men's and women's mate preferences exerted selection pressures on the other sex). In particular, evolutionary theorists suggest that women's greater reproductive investment led them to prefer dominant, high-status male mates who appeared capable of amassing resources by competing successfully with other men. This, in turn, accounts for men's tendency to compete aggressively with other men and, because of nagging doubts about paternity, to attempt to control their female mates.

Social structural approaches offer a way of integrating cultural and evolutionary forces. By focusing on the relative roles and positions of groups in society and the conditions that shape intergroup relations, structural approaches offer unique insight into the origins of cultural conceptions of gender. This approach is also well suited to explaining similarities and differences in how gender functions over time and across cultures, based on differences and similarities in structural relations between the sexes. Social role theory, which focuses on gender roles (e.g., caregiver vs. provider) and status differences, has been the most prominent structural theory of gender. This theory has demonstrated how a gendered division of labor and gender hierarchy can account for prescriptive conceptions of gender and actual sex differences in behavior.

CHAPTER 2

Dominance and Interdependence

Imagine an alien planet populated by two intelligent species living together in a shared society, the "ehormbs" and the "jumeres," about whom we know very little. What we know is this: The ehormbs tend to be a bit larger than the jumeres and dominate the most powerful positions in society, allowing them to monopolize most of its wealth and resources. By contrast, the jumeres tend to fill lower status roles that the ehormbs do not care to perform. Given this information alone and asked to play "extraterrestrial sociologists" (a game Peter Glick has asked a number of student groups to play), people assume mostly hostile relations between the two alien species, with the ehormbs acting as arrogant and abusive overlords who view themselves as smarter and better and the jumeres reacting as potentially rebellious underlings who resent their ehormb masters. And how might the ehormbs behave toward the jumeres if they do rebel? Most participants assume that the ehormbs' response would be brutal, including the potential destruction of the jumeres. Similarly, were catastrophe to strike the planet and food to become dangerously scarce, students assume that the ehormbs would use their greater strength and power keep the resources to themselves, letting the jumeres starve.

25

Adding a second "fact" about these aliens changes things substantially. Imagine that the jumeres possess a pheromone that has a powerful, pleasurable narcotic effect. Jumeres secrete the pheromone through their skin when they have close bodily contact with an ehormb, producing a blissful high eagerly sought after by the ehormbs and experienced as pleasurable by the jumeres as well (and no, the pheromone cannot be produced artificially or packaged). Further, imagine that the pheromone is most powerful when the jumeres release it willingly (although they can also be forced) and that the deeper the green tint of the jumeres' skin, the stronger the pheromone's effect.

How might this pheromone change relations between the groups and the structure of their society (keeping in mind that the ehormbs still dominate)? This addition to the story produces considerably more complicated speculations about relations between the ehormbs and jumeres. Students still assume that the ehormbs view themselves as superior, but realize that the ehormbs now have a substantial stake in keeping the jumeres around. How might the ehormbs respond to a wholesale rebellion by the jumeres? Would they destroy them or engage in negotiation and appeasement (in addition to coercion)? Given the pheromone the jumeres possess, the equation shifts considerably toward negotiation rather than force. To keep the jumeres mollified, the ehormbs are likely to give a little (e.g., more pay, better working conditions) to get a lot (compliant pheromone suppliers). If food became scarce, would the ehormbs let all of the jumeres starve? Probably not. For the ehormbs, a genocidal attack on or complete neglect of the jumeres become unthinkable because the jumeres are too valuable a resource.

Although some students generate analogies to "White slavery" and rape in the ehormbs' treatment of the jumeres, given the pheromone's greater power when given willingly, most assume that overt enslavement of the jumeres would be avoided and enticement with resources would be preferred. Students quickly generate an alien version of marriage (sometimes including polygamy and harems) in which wealthy ehormbs entice the most intensely green-skinned jumeres to live with them. The interdependence of the two species (of the ehormbs on the jumeres' pheromone and of the jumeres on the ehormbs' resources) also sets up interesting competitions within each species. The ehormbs would probably compete with each other to amass more wealth and prestige in order to attract the greenest jumeres. The jumeres might develop a thriving cosmetics industry as they seek products to make their skin greener, using this as their ticket to nabbing a wealthy ehormb who will provide for them.

People who participate in this exercise begin to realize that the attitude of each alien group toward the other would be highly ambivalent. On the one hand, the ehormbs still see themselves as superior to the jumeres—as smarter, more powerful, and naturally deserving to be in charge—but they also have positive feelings toward the jumeres, especially those delightful greenest ones, who give them so much pleasure. Similarly, the jumeres resent the ehomrbs' greater power and resources (and the inevitable abuse of that power) but also admire the ehormbs for their achievements and are attracted the most successful ehormbs, who can serve as providers in exchange for the jumeres' pheromone.

This example works best in workshops not advertised as dealing with gender relations, so that it slowly dawns on participants what the example is really about. Readers of this book undoubtedly recognized from the beginning that the ehormbs and the jumeres (anagrams of *hombres* and *mujeres*) represent a caricature of relations between women and men. However imperfect the analogy may be, it nevertheless highlights a critical tension: In human societies, male dominance is prevalent but coexists with a high degree of intimate interdependence between the sexes.

Imagining our own world from an outside viewpoint, as if it were an alien society, enables a better appreciation of this odd combination of dominance and intimate interdependence in gender relations, a condition of social life that can be as invisible to people as water is to fish. Yet these two simple facts together have numerous and profound implications for gender relations, which explains why people are able to infer so much about the ehormbs and jumeres from such limited information.

The pheromone in the alien example is, of course, an analogy for sex. The intimate physical contact shared by men and women creates a potent bond. But to make the alien example match gender relations on our planet, other aspects of interdependence must be introduced. For example, the ehormbs would not be able to have children without the jumeres, the groups would be tied together in familial relationships rather than being separate species or races, and the jumeres would traditionally perform most child-rearing and domestic labor. These other elements increase the degree of interdependence between men and women and have additional implications for how each gender is perceived as well as how they relate to each other. These further points of contact reinforce the need for societies and people within societies to reconcile male dominance with intimate interdependence between the sexes.

Much of this book explores the myriad implications created by this curious combination of dominance and interdependence. Foremost among them is ambivalence (or mixed feelings) on the part of each sex toward the other. Ambivalence helps to explain many of the apparent contradictions that gender relations exhibit. For example, understanding how different circumstances activate dominance-related versus interdependence-related motives illuminates when negative and positive feelings toward each sex are elicited. Although ambivalence complicates matters, gender relations are not arbitrary but follow some predictable patterns.

In the current chapter we consider (1) how gender relations differ from other intergroup relations because of the unique amalgamation of male dominance and intimate interdependence; (2) evolutionary and social structural explanations for the origins of male dominance, including (3) the surprising ways in which human sexuality (the primary force for intimate interdependence between the sexes) may feed into male dominance; and (4) the ideological consequences of dominance and interdependence for traditional ideologies and ambivalent attitudes toward each sex.

Gender Exceptionalism

The opening example for this chapter illustrates how much gender relations differ from other intergroup relations. The history of relations between human groups that differ on the basis of ethnicity, race, tribal affiliation, or other cultural identities (e.g., religion) has spawned a litany of intergroup brutality, from wars of conquest (e.g., the European conquest of North America) to ethnic cleansing and genocide. Literally hundreds of millions of people have died from such intergroup violence. When groups do live in relative harmony, they nevertheless often maintain a significant degree of segregation, "sticking with" their own kind.

Gender relations present a striking exception. As Henry Kissinger pithily said, "Nobody will ever win the battle of the sexes. There's just too much fraternizing with the enemy." Men and women interact, usually harmoniously, on a daily basis. They do not live in segregated neighborhoods, even though, in some cultures, they do live relatively separate daily lives. The two sexes need each other to produce offspring, and virtually all cultures institutionalize heterosexual marriage, considering it an important, intimate bond, whether in monogamous pairs, polygamy, or, more rarely, polyandry. Examine the contents of the arts (e.g., in popular songs or plays) in any culture and it is likely that heterosexual love—both its joys and, when unrequited or interrupted, its pains—is one the most frequent themes.

The difference between gender and other intergroup relations can be illustrated by considering one of the first measures of prejudice, the Social Distance Scale (Bogardus, 1927). This scale assesses tolerance for various degrees of intimacy with members of another group. For instance, one might be content to have a member of another group as a coworker but be disinclined to socialize with them and completely unwilling to marry one. Marriage is viewed as representing the highest form of intimacy on the Social Distance Scale. The Social Distance Scale assumes that tolerance for higher levels of intimacy (e.g., marriage) emerges only after people develop tolerance for lower levels (e.g., working together).

Social distance measures simply do not work when assessing gender prejudice. Call to mind the most sexist, traditional man you know. Chances are that he is not too eager to work with women, especially a female boss, and that he prefers to socialize with men. On these lower levels of intimacy, he shows limited tolerance for women. But how would he react if asked, "Would you be willing to marry a woman (as opposed to a man)?" Presuming that the man you called to mind is heterosexual, he would find the question absurd and probably offensive. Sexist heterosexual men tend to idealize marriage with a woman as the highest form of intimacy and a central goal in life, even while believing that the two sexes should not mix in other, less intimate contexts.

This example illustrates that gender relations are not immune to discrimination and oppression, but that they encompass and reconcile dominance with intimate interdependence. Most men maintain subjectively positive attitudes toward women, seek intimacy with them, and idealize their "feminine" qualities; at the same time, women are generally accorded lower status, discriminated against in ways that foster continuing inequality, and often treated with hostility when they stray from traditional roles. Ample evidence documents the existence of male dominance, or patriarchy, but patriarchy cannot be properly understood without acknowledging that it has been profoundly shaped by, and may even have originated in, men's and women's sexual interdependence.

The Nature and Origins of Patriarchy

In Chapter 1, we briefly reviewed the evolutionary argument that men have been sexually selected to exhibit dominance, competing with other men and trying to control and restrict women. The evolutionary argument suggests that heterosexuality, the core of men's and women's interdependence, is also the root of patriarchy. Recall that evolutionary theorists view sexual selection—women's mate choices—as the source of men's drive to dominate. It is because women selected dominance seeking in men that men allegedly evolved to be more obsessed with status and dominance and more prone to violence. If this is so, heterosexual interdependence does not merely constrain the form male dominance can take but is its original cause.

Is Love a "Protection Racket"?

Locating the origins of patriarchy in women's mate choices may sound like blaming the victim, but at least one evolutionary theorist suggests that a female preference for dominant mates may have been developed as a self-protective response to violent male behavior, especially male sexual aggression (Smuts, 1995). The argument is based on comparisons with humans' closest primate cousins (chimpanzees, orangutans, gorillas) as well as the logic of sex differences in reproductive investment. Given that males' reproductive potential is limited only by access to fertile females, males hypothetically could achieve reproductive success through coercive sex (i.e., rape; see Thornhill & Thornhill, 1983). In fact, this appears to happen in chimpanzees as well as orangutans, for which sex and violence often go hand in hand. Males use aggressive displays to intimidate reluctant partners or even outright force to achieve copulation. A related form of violence is infanticide, in which a male chimpanzee will kill infants that have been sired by another male as a prelude to encouraging estrus in the female and subsequent investment in his *own* offspring.

What strategies might females develop to protect themselves from the threat of sexual coercion and the murder of their infants? Bonobos, commonly known as pygmy chimpanzees, illustrate one possible solution. This species is closely related to the chimpanzee and, like the chimpanzee, shares 98% of its genes and a common ancestor with humans (de Waal & Lanting, 1997). Bonobo females, as well as males, are not choosy when it comes to mating. In fact, bonobos treat sexuality as a casual part of social contact not only with members of the other sex but with members of the same sex (e.g., rubbing genitals and what has been termed "penis fencing" are common bonobo behaviors).

What are the consequences of this casual attitude toward sex? First, the lack of female choosiness avoids aggressive sexual coercion by males: Free love removes any reason for males to bully females for sex. Second, because any offspring might have been sired by any number of males, bonobos' promiscuous mating habits remove any incentive for males to engage in infanticide. (However, promiscuity also reduces male incentive for investing in offspring, and it is exclusively bonobo females that care for the young.) Third, because they do not need to compete for mates, male–male aggression is rare. In short, bonobos are a species that "substitutes sex for aggression" (de Waal & Lanting, 1997). It is probably no coincidence that bonobos have the most egalitarian social relations of our primate cousins. The bonds females form with each other and with their offspring lend them considerable social influence. The contrast between bonobo and chimpanzee societies is striking. Chimpanzees exhibit significant male dominance and aggression both among males (individually and between groups) as well as toward females.

Smuts (1995) argues that human females went down a different path to prevent male sexual coercion, seeking to bond with a particular male who serves as a protector from other males and a provider for her offspring. This strategy offers males the benefit of a higher degree of paternity certainty, as a result of monogamous pair bonding, in exchange for providing protection for their mates and greater parental investment in offspring. In this view, love is an adaptation that makes the system work, an emotional bond that motivates both parties to stick to their deal. Of course, for this strategy to work, females need to select their partners carefully, seeking a male who has the strength and status to be an effective protector but also the emotional wherewithal to stay with the relationship and be attached enough to the resulting offspring to be a willing provider.

There can hardly be a darker theory of the origins of human heterosexual love. Forget the idealization of romance. In this theory, romantic love between men and women has its distant origins in violent sexual coercion, infanticide, and a female strategy to avoid these perils. In short, love results from a "protection racket" in which men pose a threat to women that women solve by bonding with individual men. Despite such a dark theory of love's origins, however, the bonds of affection and love people experience are genuine and promote authentic caring for one's partner and children. Such a system has advantages for both sexes. Nonetheless, because this solution puts men in the position of being protectors and primary providers, it fosters and reinforces overall male dominance. Further, for women, the attractiveness of the trade-off relies, to some extent, on an undercurrent of threat—why else does one need a "protector"?—and dependence—who needs a provider if she can obtain sufficient resources for herself?

As Smuts acknowledges, this is a speculative account of the origins of human pair bonding, although it does yield some interesting, testable hypotheses, such as the way in which female–female alliances can also reduce the threat of sexual violence (see Smuts, 1995). Whether correct or not, the theory is certainly thought provoking. Later we review other evidence consistent with the idea that the threat men generally pose to women, ironically, leads women to turn to individual men for protection, ceding power to men in exchange for the promise of security.

Critiques of the Evolutionary Account of Patriarchy

Supporters of the evolutionary approach note that, historically and cross-culturally, men have been the dominant sex (Sidanius & Pratto, 1999). The ubiquity of patriarchy argues against purely cultural explanations. If male dominance results from historical and cultural development within separate, diverse societies, why is it so widespread? Cultural explanations would suggest that some societies ought to exist where women are the primary aggressors and warriors or have higher status and more power than men. This simply does not appear to be the case. Societies vary from relatively egalitarian to men having significantly more social status and power (Salzman, 1999). There appear to be no historical or contemporary matriarchies in which women dominate (Harris, 1993). Additionally, across cultures, physical aggression, whether interpersonal or between groups, is much more common among men than women (see Chapter 11), and men are more likely to endorse a social dominance orientation (an ideology that supports social hierarchy; Sidanius & Pratto, 1999).

Critics point out, however, that even if men are more prone to aggression and competition for status and resources, patriarchy may not have been the natural state of humans in the environment in which people evolved. Anthropological research shows that hunter–gatherer or foraging societies, which likely resemble the type of social environment within which humans evolved, tend to exhibit more egalitarianism than agricultural and industrial societies (Leacock, 1978). Indeed, such societies have less hierarchy overall. Further, in preagricultural societies, although men are more likely to hunt, women's gathering also constitutes a critical food source, giving women considerable control over important resources and, therefore, more power. If most of human evolution occurred in societies organized in this manner, the plausibility of the evolutionary account of patriarchy is diminished (Wood & Eagly, 2002).

Why might male dominance increase when societies develop agriculture? The likely answer is that the ability to grow and store foods (e.g., grains) creates surplus wealth and the possibility for large disparities in resources. In other words, storable wealth enables increased competition for resources and status. For sexual selection theorists, this represents a perfect example of an environmental trigger for the tendency toward male dominance: When there is more to compete for (e.g., resources that, unlike a hunter's catch of the day, do not soon spoil), men's tendency to aggressively compete is triggered. Furthermore, the increased complexity and density that societies achieve after they develop agriculture provides an environment in which male dominance potentially reaps tremendous genetic rewards. A man who controls ample lands and wealth can attract many women, giving him the potential to sire hundreds of offspring. Thus, sexual selection theorists argue that technological advances, like the development of agriculture, have simply given freer rein to an inherent male tendency (Sidanius & Pratto, 1999). However, the evidence that agriculture increased, or possibly even created, patriarchy illustrates the importance of culture, and the human technologies that make certain cultural arrangements possible, in shaping gender relations.

Moreover, some have questioned whether women really prefer dominant male mates. Recall that the sexual selection argument relies on the notion that women choose men who not only can protect and provide but who also signal a willingness to invest in their mate. Being a good provider does not necessarily involve being dominant but rather being competent. For instance, being a good hunter involves a variety of skills, such as tracking and, in humans, the ability to communicate and coordinate with others, because humans were most successful by hunting in cooperative groups. Competence and being socially cooperative (Caporeal, 2004) may have been more important than dominance in determining the ability to bring home the meat. Finally, evolutionary theorists also assume that women selected men who exhibited a willingness to provide resources to their mates and to work together as part of a child-rearing team. Such behavior might be characterized as being more "agreeable" than dominant.

Studies of American students' mate preferences have experimentally manipulated male targets' behavior to see whether women are attracted to men who exhibit dominance or to men who show exhibit agreeableness (Graziano, Jensen-Campbell, Todd, & Finch, 1997; Jensen-Campbell, Graziano, & West, 1995). In contrast to what evolutionary theorists have argued, Graziano and colleagues found that nice guys did not finish last in terms of their attractiveness as mates. In fact, although dominance exerted some appeal for women, agreeableness was a more powerful predictor of which men women rated as attractive. If women actually select more for agreeableness than for dominance, sexual selection cannot explain patriarchy. It is possible, however, that women select men who exhibit agreeableness toward their female romantic partners but dominance when competing with other men. This would help to explain why male–male physical aggression is by far the most common form of violence, a topic reviewed in more detail in Chapter 11.

Social Structural Accounts of the Origins of Patriarchy

In general, evolutionary psychology relies on speculative inferences about the social and physical environments in which people first evolved, leaving considerable room for alternative explanations. Wood and Eagly (2002) provide an integrative biosocial theory of sex differences, which developed as a supplement to social role theory. The biosocial theory assumes that while evolution has led to some physical differences between the sexes, such as men's greater size and upper body strength, selective pressures generally fostered psychological similarities, rather than differences, between the sexes.

This view is consistent with Caporeal's (2004) view that humans' evolutionary advantage rests on our sociality and flexibility. People evolved to work and live in groups, as a defense against being highly vulnerable, slow, poorly armed (e.g., no fangs or claws), naked animals. How did an animal with such an unimpressive physique manage to adapt to so many environments while its closest primate cousins (e.g., chimpanzees) did not? The answer is that humans developed more complex ways to communicate, allowing them to pass on knowledge and techniques (e.g., how to make a stone ax) crucial to adapting to changing environments. By being flexible and open to living in and learning from the accumulated experiences of groups, humans not only survived but thrived in widely varied environments, adapting more quickly to changing conditions than animals driven by fixed instincts. The secret to this adaptability is human's cognitive and social flexibility, allowing a tremendous variety in learned behavioral repertoires and social organizations depending on what works in any given environment. If so, the overwhelming selective pressures on all humans, both male and female, are to be flexible, sociable, and open to group influence. In this view, dominance is "a form of social action," emerging as a part of group dynamics, "rather than a persistent trait internal to the person" (Caporeal & Baron, 1997, p. 334).

Instead of assuming that sexual selection fostered male–female psychological differences in dominance, the biosocial theory assumes that physical differences between the sexes coupled with particular cultural developments sufficiently explain why patriarchy became prevalent. Specifically, Wood and Eagly (2002) focus on women's role in reproduction, as bearers of children and nourishers of infants, and men's greater upper body strength. In simpler societies, these differences did not create patriarchy given women's important role in gathering food, which can be accomplished with a child on one's back, and because the perishability of resources fostered sharing rather than hoarding. Differences in strength and reproductive roles, however, appear to have become very important once agriculture developed. Wood and Eagly argue that the confluence of physical sex differences with new forms of social organization and resource acquisition led to patriarchy.

Why? Agriculture promotes a more extreme division of labor between the sexes; women no longer forage and, therefore, lose direct control over an important set of resources. When society is organized so that women become more confined to domestic labor, they lose power and independence. Men, who are free from the restrictions of pregnancy and child rearing, can then begin to monopolize control of storable resources. This dynamic is illustrated by a modern Bedouin tribe in western Egypt, which experienced an increase in gender inequality when they ceased to be nomadic and settled down into permanent communities (Abu-Lughod, 1986). Once the tribe settled down, women became more restricted to a fixed domestic sphere, making them isolated and less influential.

In other words, the biosocial theory posits that because men are not tethered to domestic life by pregnancy and lactation, they are better positioned to reap the benefits of agriculture and, later, industry. Agriculture increases the wealth and complexity of societies, expanding social stratification or hierarchy (i.e., more extreme differences possible in power, wealth, and status develop). Additionally, the generation of surplus wealth and resources spawns conflicts between groups seeking to expand their resources (e.g., by taking over other groups' lands), leading to intergroup violence (see also Sidanius & Pratto, 1999). The warrior role, which throughout human history has been almost exclusively a male occupation, becomes another male route to power and decision-making authority. In addition, men's greater upper body strength is more suited to this role, at least when technologies are relatively simple (e.g., wielding a sword as opposed to launching a missile through the push of a button).

In sum, Wood and Eagly (2002) argue that men's greater strength and their lesser commitment to child rearing did not matter so much in the simple, relatively egalitarian, foraging societies in which humans evolved, but these differences fostered patriarchy once agriculture developed. Thus, cultural developments, rather than a sex-specific, evolved tendency to seek dominance, may explain the origins of patriarchy. Because powerful groups tend to endorse ideologies that further their power (Sidanius & Pratto, 1999), Wood and Eagly's view suggests that men's greater dominance orientation is a social consequence, rather than a biologically evolved cause, of patriarchy.

The debate about the origins of patriarchy, however, does not have to be viewed in either–or terms. Most evolutionary theorists agree that some types of social structures and cultural practices work to restrict or minimize male dominance (e.g., in societies with little surplus or where women have independent resources). Thus, patriarchy is not inevitable even if an innate male tendency toward dominance exists. Also, keep in mind that patriarchy does not just oppress women; male dominance also involves harsh, often violent, competition among men. In Chapter 11 we further explore the ways in which the oppression of women relates to male–male violence, often between male groups vying for status and resources. Patriarchy fosters the oppression of a variety of out-groups, defined along a large set of cultural lines (e.g., tribal, ethnic, religious, caste; Sidanius & Pratto, 1999).

Regardless of debates about evolutionary versus social structural causes of patriarchy, strong cross-cultural evidence indicates that (1) physically aggressive behavior toward members of the same sex is much more common among men than women (Daly & Wilson, 1994; Buss, 2005; Hyde, 2005); (2) men are more likely to embrace antiegalitarian ideologies that support patriarchy and other forms of social hierarchy, whereas women more frequently endorse attitudes and policies aimed at attenuating social hierarchies (Sidanius & Pratto, 1999); and (3) men tend to dominate positions of power (United Nations Development Programme, 2005). In today's world, patriarchy is more the norm than the exception.

Ideological Consequences of Male Dominance and Intimate Interdependence: Ambivalent Sexism Theory

Social structural facts have ideological consequences. Dominant groups are attracted to and propagate ideologies that justify their dominance as morally correct, and even members of subordinated groups may accept such ideologies. This contention can be traced back to Karl Marx and is reiterated in system justification theory, which has received empirical support (Jost & Banaji, 1994; Jost, Burgess, & Mosso, 2001). Similarly, social role theory posits that well-established status and role arrangements result in belief systems that help to maintain and defend their existence (Eagly, 1987).

Prejudice theories have tended to focus on hostile ideological justifications for social hierarchy, such as the belief in the inferiority of subordinate groups (see Jackman, 1994, for a critique of this approach). But, as the example that began this chapter illustrates, the combination of dominance with intimate interdependence that characterizes gender relations requires a trickier balance. Unmitigated expression of hostility toward women is not conducive to maintaining smooth functioning of heterosexual intimacy and cooperative interdependence. How do traditional gender ideologies balance the competing needs to justify male dominance while avoiding or at least limiting hostility and resentment, which might ruin intimate interdependence?

Ambivalent sexism theory (Glick & Fiske, 1996, 1999, 2001) explores how male dominance and intimate interdependence have shaped the content of traditional gender ideologies and their emotional tone. Specifically, this theory (1) details the content of socially shared ideologies that legitimize or justify traditional gender relations; (2) argues that these ideologies should be evident across cultures, because the underlying conditions that generate them exist across cultures; (3) explores the mixed emotions and attitudes that are associated with these ideologies; and (4) offers a set of self-report inventories to measure these attitudes.

Typical responses to the example with the ehormbs and jumeres that began this chapter nicely illustrate the basic contentions of ambivalent sexism theory. When given a version of the fictitious alien society where the ehormbs dominate but there is no interdependence between the groups, people assume mutual intergroup hostility. Specifically, people suppose that the higher status ehormbs feel contempt for the lower status jumeres, whereas the lower status jumeres view the ehormbs as arrogant and resent their power. Adding intimate interdependence, the pheromone the ehormbs crave, to the mix changes the situation, creating subjectively positive benevolent attitudes. For example, the higher status ehormbs have a stake in providing for and protecting the lower status jumeres; in turn, the jumeres may admire and appreciate ehormbs for their provision and protection. Because hostile and benevolent attitudes coexist, specific characteristics of a situation can bring out one or the other. For instance, an arbitrary use of power by a member of the high-status group would provoke resentment, whereas a protective act might yield gratitude.

The ambivalent content of ideologies about each sex is illustrated in the attitude inventories used to measure them: the Ambivalent Sexism Inventory (ASI; Glick & Fiske, 1996), which targets hostile and benevolent attitudes toward women, and the Ambivalence toward Men Inventory (AMI; Glick & Fiske, 1999), which assesses hostile and benevolent attitudes toward men. Items from the ASI and AMI are reproduced in Table 2.1 (for full versions of the scales, see Glick & Fiske, 1996, 1999, 2001).

Each inventory has a Hostile and a Benevolent Attitudes scale and covers three aspects of gender relations: power relations, gender roles and stereotypes, and intimate heterosexual relations (sex and romance). Each of these subdomains helps to generate or maintain male dominance and intimate interdependence. For instance, because traditionally female roles have lower status and less power, gender roles reinforce male dominance. At the same time, traditional gender roles complement each other (e.g., the male breadwinner and female homemaker) and form the basis of male–female interdependence.

Given the hostile and benevolent aspects of each inventory and the subdomains each scale taps, the ASI and AMI have complicated structures (readers interested in factor analyses of the ASI and AMI, which have been examined for a variety of nations, should see Glick et al., 2004, or Glick & Fiske, 2001). But researchers have focused mainly on participants' overall scores on the Hostile and Benevolent Attitude scales toward each sex (described next). Although the ASI was developed by considering men's attitudes toward women and the AMI by

TABLE 2.1. Ambivalent Sexism Inventory and Ambivalence toward Men Inventory Items

Hostile Sexism (toward Women):
- Women seek to gain power by getting control over men.
- Women exaggerate problems they have at work.
- When women lose to men in a fair competition, they typically complain about being discriminated against.
- Feminists are making unreasonable demands of men.
- Many women get a kick out of teasing men by seeming sexually available and then refusing male advances.
- Once a woman gets a man to commit to her, she usually tries to put him on a tight leash.

Benevolent Sexism (toward Women):
- Many women have a quality of purity that few men possess.
- Women should be cherished and protected by men.
- Every man ought to have a woman whom he adores.
- Men are incomplete without women.
- Women, compared to men, tend to have a superior moral sensibility.
- Men should be willing to sacrifice their own well-being in order to provide financially for the women in their lives.

Hostility toward Men:
- Men will always fight to have greater control in society than women.
- Even men who claim to be sensitive to women's rights really want a traditional relationship at home, with the woman performing most of the housekeeping and child care.
- Most men sexually harass women, even if only in subtle ways, once they are in a position of power over them.
- When men act to "help" women, they are often trying to prove they are better than women.
- Men act like babies when they are sick.
- When it comes down to it, most men are really like children.

Benevolence toward Men:
- Even if both members of a couple work, the woman ought to be more attentive to taking care of her man at home.
- Every woman needs a male partner who will cherish her.
- A woman will never be truly fulfilled in life if she doesn't have a committed, long-term relationship with a man.
- Men are mainly useful to provide financial security for women.
- Men are more willing to put themselves in danger to protect others.
- Men are more willing to take risks than women.

Note. Copyright 1996, 1999 by Peter Glick and Susan T. Fiske.

considering women's attitudes toward men, both inventories can meaningfully be completed by male and by female respondents.

Ambivalent Attitudes toward Women

The ASI's subscales tap hostile sexism (HS) and benevolent sexism (BS) toward women.* As evidenced by the items in Table 2.1, the emotional tone of HS compared with BS is quite different. HS items mainly reflect an overt justification of or attempt to preserve male dominance. Many HS items suggest a negative reaction to women's increasing power in society. Specifically, HS items have a strongly adversarial tone, viewing (at least some) women as seeking to gain power over men, decrying women who take on nontraditional roles (e.g., feminists, career women), and complaining about women who use sexuality to control men. By contrast, BS items celebrate intimate interdependence in a subjectively positive, even adoring, way. BS items characterize (at least some) women as wonderful but vulnerable creatures who need men's protection, extol the virtues of women who embrace traditional roles, and claim that every man requires a woman's love to be complete.

Research on people's spontaneous stereotypes of women supports the idea that HS taps subjectively negative and BS subjectively positive views of women. Glick et al. (2000, 2004) had people in various nations complete the ASI and later generate traits they associate with women. Participants then indicated how positive or negative each trait was; the average of these valence ratings formed an index of how positively or negatively respondents viewed women. BS consistently predicted more positive and HS more negative stereotyping of women.

Given that earlier definitions viewed sexism as an antipathy toward women, it is not surprising that HS correlates strongly with other measures of sexism, such as the Modern Sexism Scale (Swim, Aikin, Hall, & Hunter, 1995) and the Neosexism Scale (Tougas, Brown, Beaton, & Joly, 1995), both of which assess similarly hostile, but somewhat veiled, contemporary aspects of sexism. All of these scales (HS, Modern Sexism, Neosexism) tap antifeminist attitudes and denial that women are discriminated against and suggest a backlash toward changing gender roles (e.g., resentment of more women working in traditionally male occupations). HS also strongly correlates with measures of overtly traditional attitudes about women's roles, such as Spence and Helmreich's

---

*The terms "benevolent sexism" and "hostile sexism" will be referred to as "BS" and "HS," respectively, after their first mention in the text in this chapter.

(1972) Attitudes toward Women Scale, which has served as the standard measure of sexist attitudes for many decades, assessing belief in traditional gender norms (e.g., women ought not to use harsh language) and roles (e.g., women should not work outside the home).

What about BS? The BS scale has a markedly different tone from any other measure of sexism. Given that prejudice has long been defined as antipathy or dislike toward a group (Allport, 1954/1979), the term "benevolent sexism" itself may seem like an oxymoron. Increasingly, however, prejudice researchers have begun to recognize that prejudice is not a unitary antipathy and to acknowledge that paternalistic prejudices, such as BS, are not merely a disguised form of hostility. "Paternalism" refers to treating a group or an individual as a traditional father might treat a child; in other words, as incapable of fully governing or providing for themselves and as requiring the wise guidance, protection, and provision of an affectionate, superior benefactor.

Consider a relatively obvious example of paternalistic or patronizing behavior. Imagine a supervisor or a professor who treats you like a third-grader, "dumbing down" explanations of tasks or simply doing them for you, all the while patting you on the head and making comments that are the equivalent of "You tied your own shoes; good for you!" In such an obvious case, you would probably be angry because the treatment is condescending and assumes that you are incompetent.

Patronizing behavior, however, is usually much more subtle, so that people do not always know they are being patronized. To complicate things, the patronizer may feel genuine affection toward the target, treating her like a pet or mascot, just as one might love a particularly clumsy and not-too-bright pet dog or cat whose incompetence is endearing. Whether obvious or subtle, paternalistic treatment implicitly assumes that the patronized individual is incompetent. As a result, people can be damaged by others' patronizing behavior, especially when it happens at work (see Vescio, Gervais, Snyder, & Hoover, 2005), an issue explored in Chapter 8.

Paternalistic attitudes, such as BS, may seem trivial in comparison to hostile forms of prejudice. Women generally like men described as fitting a benevolent sexist profile and prefer them much more than men described as hostile sexists, although they like nonsexists best (Kilianski & Rudman, 1998). In some national samples, women endorse BS as strongly as or, in a few cases, even more than men do. In contrast, in every nation studied, women consistently endorse HS less strongly than men (Glick et al., 2000, 2004). Figures 2.1 and 2.2 illustrate HS and BS scores, respectively, across 17 nations, from data reported by Glick et al.

(2004). Figure 2.1 is organized so that nations are listed in descending order of men's HS scores. The later figures preserve the same order to make it easier to compare all of them.

If many women do not have a problem with BS, what is wrong with it? In addition to the underlying presumption that women are unable to protect or provide for themselves, BS represents a significant problem for achieving gender equality for the following reasons: (1) Individuals who endorse BS are also likely to endorse HS and other attitudes and ideologies that legitimize gender inequality; (2) Societies with the highest endorsement of BS show greater hostility toward women who enact nontraditional roles and have the least amount of structural gender equality (e.g., fewer women in positions of power); (3) because it seems "nice" and less objectionable than hostile gender prejudice, BS effectively undermines women's resistance to inequality; (4) women accept BS most strongly in those nations in which men are the most hostile, suggesting a protection racket in which women most seek men's benevolent protection in response to significant male threat. Next we review evidence for each of these points.

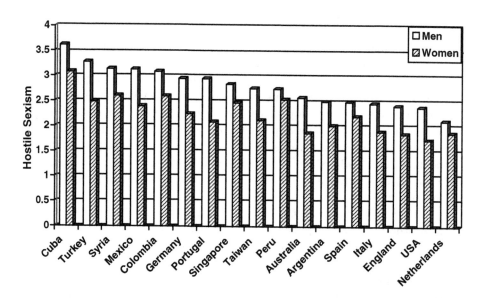

FIGURE 2.1. Hostile sexism scores across 17 nations. From Glick et al. (2004). Copyright 2004 by the American Psychological Association. Reprinted by permission.

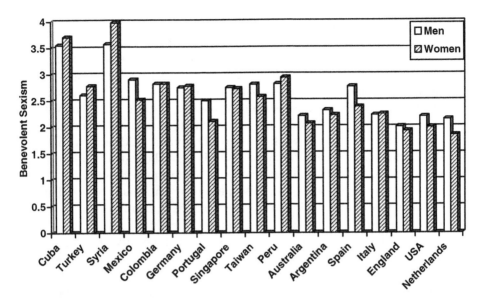

FIGURE 2.2. Benevolent sexism scores across 17 nations. From Glick et al. (2004). Copyright 2004 by the American Psychological Association. Reprinted by permission.

People Who Endorse BS Also Tend to Endorse HS

In two cross-cultural studies, one involving samples from 19 nations (Glick et al., 2000) and the other samples from 17 nations (Glick et al., 2004), individuals' scores on BS typically correlated moderately positively with their scores on HS. In other words, people who accept (as opposed to reject) BS are more likely to accept HS. Given that BS is a subjectively positive and HS a subjectively negative attitude toward women, one might expect the opposite to be true: That is, a benevolent sexist might be expected to express less, not more hostile, sexism. Indeed, the standard view of ambivalence by psychological theorists, going back to Freud, supposes that holding both positive and negative attitudes toward the same object creates uncomfortable mental conflict. By contrast, ambivalent sexists seem to be quite content to embrace both HS and BS; their positive correlation suggests that these attitudes are complementary, not conflicting.

The key to understanding the complementarity of HS and BS is realizing that they are two faces of the same sexist coin. Together, HS and BS pull off the tricky balance of justifying the coexistence of male dominance with intimate heterosexual interdependence, while making this seem like the most natural thing in the world rather than something contradictory and strange. In part, HS and BS are complementary because they target different types of women or different types of behavior that women may exhibit. HS expresses hostility toward women viewed as trying to usurp men's power. This includes feminists who allegedly want to wield power over men, women who complain about poor treatment at work, women who pursue traditionally male-dominated careers, and "temptresses" who use their sexual allure to control men. By contrast, BS is directed toward women viewed as fulfilling men's needs rather than challenging their status and power. This includes traditionally minded women, such as homemakers, who are viewed as pure and worthy of being put on a pedestal.

For instance, men's scores on HS predict negative stereotypes and emotions toward career women while their BS scores predict positive stereotypes and emotions toward homemakers (Glick, Diebold, Bailey-Werner, & Zhu, 1997). These attitudes are complementary because both reinforce traditional gender roles and power differences. The same individual who resents feminists and career women extols the virtues of stay-at-home mothers, sending the message that women should remain in their "proper" roles.

Societies That Endorse BS Also Endorse HS

Evidence that BS and HS complement each other also appears in cross-national comparisons. In research to date, nations where people score highly on BS have, without exception, also scored highly on HS. Using sample averages as the unit of analysis, the two large international studies described previously each found that HS and BS correlate extremely highly, at almost .90, whether one examines women's or men's average scores. In other words, if people in a nation strongly endorse BS, they also strongly endorse HS.

Why, at the societal level, are BS and HS so highly correlated? One answer lies in Jackman's (1994) insightful theory of paternalism. She argues that dominant groups prefer to justify their position through paternalistic ideologies, which serve several functions. First, it is flattering to view oneself and one's group as wise benefactors rather than as oppressors. Thus, White slave owners in the old South tended to characterize slavery as "beneficial" to enslaved Blacks, who would otherwise live like "primitives." Similarly, European colonialists viewed themselves as bringing the gift of civilization to "unenlightened" parts of the world, as benefactors who assumed the "White man's burden" of civilizing "savages."

Jackman further suggests that paternalism also placates and better controls subordinated groups. Imagine trying to control a subordinate on whose work you depend solely through hostile and punitive strategies. How effective would this be? Certainly, the threat of severe punishments, such as beatings, can motivate compliance, but it has other consequences as well: intense and unmitigated resentment. When subordinates have nothing to lose but their chains, they tend constantly to look for a chance to rebel or exact revenge. Ruling through fear, intimidation, and punishment is time consuming and labor intensive, requiring constant surveillance of underlings. In short, for dominants, overtly hostile oppression has a double disadvantage: Desired behaviors by subordinates only happen when they are closely watched and rebellion is an ever-present possibility.

Dominants can rule more effectively by acting in a paternalistic, rather than hostile, fashion toward subordinates. People who have few or no resources of their own may feel gratitude, rather than resentment, toward a powerful person or group that treats them tolerably well, especially because they have few alternatives. Jackman (1994) notes that paternalistic systems thrive by combining dominance with affection, fostering loyalties between members of low- and high-status groups. For example, the novel *The Kite Runner* (Hosseini, 2003) poignantly describes the affectionate bonds between a high-status Pashtun family in Afghanistan and their devoted, loyal, but lower status Hazara servants. The affection is genuine but infused with paternalism from the family and a corresponding deference on the part of the servants that both reinforce, rather than diminish, the status differences between them.

Because of the high degree of intimate interdependence between the sexes, it is not in men's best interests to be unremittingly hostile toward women. Furthermore, daily contact and heterosexual attraction foster authentic bonds of affection between the sexes. Although affection and dominance may seem mutually exclusive, traditional heterosexual romantic ideals comfortably combine the two (an issue we explore in greater depth in Chapter 9). Consider the romantically ideal man compared with the romantically ideal woman. Prince Charming is heroic, strong, decisive, and powerful; his princess is delicate, demure, and swept off her feet. In other words, images of dominant males and submissive females are integral to romantic ideology (Rudman & Heppen, 2003).

Can such paternalism exist without hostility? Jackman suggests that the potential for hostility always lies in the background of paternalistic dominant–subordinate relations. But this hostility may only emerge when the dominant power is challenged. Subordinates who comply with expectations to be deferent and accept their lot receive the rewards of affection and of resources trickled down from above. But when subordinates seek equality, opportunity, or power, paternalism can quickly turn ugly. As Jackman (1994) notes, this attitude is summarized by Charles V's strategy of ruling with "an iron fist in a velvet glove."

The iron fist–velvet glove combination explains the strong societal level correlation between BS and HS. In a society that strictly adheres to traditional gender roles and power relations, BS legitimizes these arrangements as beneficial to women, promising rewards of affection, protection, and provision to women who comply with traditional roles. HS targets women who reject traditional roles or who agitate for equal opportunities. Just as the proverbial donkey is best motivated to move by dangling a carrot in front of it and wielding a stick on its behind, BS is the carrot offered to women to accept their traditional place in society and HS the stick that punishes them if they fail to do so. Thus, HS and BS together form a system of incentives and punishment that is much more effective than either would be alone.

In fact, the societies that most strongly endorse BS and HS have significantly less gender equality on objective indicators. The United Nations Development Programme (*www.undp.org*) annually reports statistics that index gender equality in nations around the globe. The Gender Empowerment Measure (GEM) assesses the degree to which women have attained high-status, powerful roles in a nation, including the percentage of women in parliaments or senates (the bodies with the most political power) and the percentage of female business managers. Glick and colleagues (2000, 2004) have shown that, in cross-national comparisons, average BS scores negatively correlate with the GEM The same holds true for HS, and both effects occur whether one examines women's or men's average scores. In short, women have less actual power and status in nations where people most strongly endorse BS (or HS).

BS Undermines Women's Resistance to Inequality

BS is particularly insidious because it undermines women's resistance to social inequality. Recall that although women, as a group, consistently score lower than men on HS, they sometimes accept BS as much as men, and, in a few nations, even more than men. The subjectively favorable tone of BS and its promise to set women on a pedestal is, not surprisingly, much more attractive to women than an overtly hostile sexist ideology.

But once women buy into BS, they may be more accepting of other gender-traditional beliefs (e.g., that a woman's proper place is in the home). In the many national samples studied, Glick et al. (2000, 2004) repeatedly found that women's scores on BS showed stronger correlations with other gender-traditional attitudes (such as HS) than men's scores did. In other words, compared with other women, women who accept BS are more likely to embrace a whole set of beliefs that justify gender inequality. For example, a woman who accepts that (some) women ought to be "put on a pedestal" are likely to resent feminists, who may be seen as trying to upset the traditional trade-off between women and men, in which women remain in a more passive and dependent role in exchange for men's protection, affection, and provision. Believing that men will protect and provide for them, such women may be content with a subordinate, traditional role.

This idea is quite explicit among the Promise Keepers, an evangelical Christian movement oriented toward defining men's and women's proper roles in marriage. As one adherent put it, "A man should ... be willing to die for his wife. And if you have a man that is willing to do that for you, it would probably be a really good idea to subordinate yourself to that man" (Snowberger, 1997).

In fact, merely thinking about BS may lead women to view society as fairer. Jost and Kay (2005) asked male and female Stanford University students about the fairness of society as a whole. Typically, women, like members of other groups who have less power and status in society, rate society as less fair than men do. A simple manipulation altered this tendency. When participants responded to items from the BS scale before completing the social fairness measure, the usual gender gap disappeared, women rated society just as fair as men did. This occurred even when participants first completed both BS and HS items. By contrast, when they only saw items from the HS scale, women rated society as less fair than men did. These data suggest that BS has a causal role in convincing women to accept their traditional place in society. BS may "sweeten the pot" sufficiently that many women implicitly agree to trade personal power and status for men's affection and protection (see Chapter 9).

Protection Racket Revisited

Recall the theory reviewed earlier in this chapter that human heterosexual pair bonding evolved as a female strategy to avoid the threat of male sexual coercion and violence (Smuts, 1995). We labeled this vision, in which male threat causes women to seek male protectors, as a protection racket. Whether the evolutionary version of the protection racket idea is correct or not, cross-national comparisons of HS and BS scores provide evidence in favor of an ideological analog. Note in Figure 2.2 that the gender gap between men's and women's BS scores reverses in a few nations, with women outscoring men. The nations in which this reversal was statistically significant were precisely those in which men had the highest hostile sexism scores. This finding suggests that when men in a society are extremely hostile toward women who seek equality, many women counter by embracing BS, which elicits male protection. This represents a vicious cycle: The more men threaten women, the more women seek out men for protection (ironically) from other men. This effect replicated in two cross-national studies (Glick et al., 2000, 2004).

Finally, a study by Fischer (2006) showed that this effect can be reproduced for individual women. In a laboratory setting, women were told, based on a "national poll," that men have either generally hostile or favorable attitudes about women. When told that men were hostile, women countered by endorsing BS more strongly. This supplements the cross-national studies by showing a causal effect: When women are threatened with hostility from men, they seek to prop up traditional benevolent attitudes toward women.

In sum, BS is a particularly significant ideology given the subtle but powerful role it plays in perpetuating gender inequality. The idea that sexism usually combines HS with BS helps to explain what otherwise might appear to be attitudinal inconsistency, such as when a man evinces hostility toward female coworkers but protectiveness toward a wife or daughter. Later chapters expand on when, why, and toward which women benevolent versus hostile sexism occurs.

Ambivalent Attitudes toward Men

Ambivalent sexism theory suggests that, as a group, men are both resented and admired. The AMI, therefore, taps both hostile and benevolent attitudes toward men, covering the domains of power, gender roles and stereotypes, and heterosexual relations. The Hostility toward Men (HM) scale focuses on resentment of men's dominance and abuses of their power, especially when directed against women. This includes their alleged drive for dominance, perceived need for women to take care of them at home, and sexually harassing and domineering behavior in heterosexual relationships. In contrast, the Benevolence toward Men (BM) scale expresses favorable attitudes toward men as providers who deserve to be taken care of at home by a wife, extols male heroism, and suggests that a woman is incomplete without a man who cherishes and adores her. Mean scores on the two AMI scales from people in 17 nations (from Glick et al., 2004) can be seen in Figures 2.3 and 2.4.

Similar to ambivalent attitudes toward women, individuals' scores on the HM and BM scales correlate moderately positively, suggesting that hostility and benevolence toward men are complementary beliefs. Moreover, the AMI scales also correlate positively with HS and BS toward women, suggesting that ambivalent attitudes toward both sexes tend to go together as a package of traditional gender beliefs.

It is particularly interesting that HM, which assesses resentment of men's power, is correlated with BM and with traditional attitudes toward women. A scale that assesses resentment of men's power hardly seems to fit the category of gender-traditional beliefs because it would not seem to support gender hierarchy and traditional roles. A closer

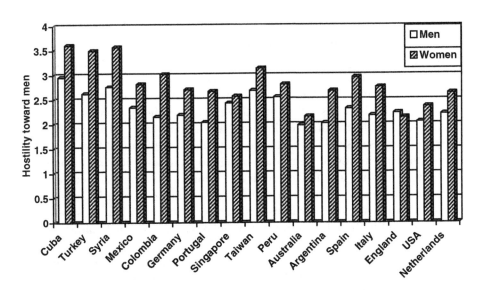

FIGURE 2.3. Hostility toward men scores across 17 nations. From Glick et al. (2004). Copyright 2004 by the American Psychological Association. Reprinted by permission.

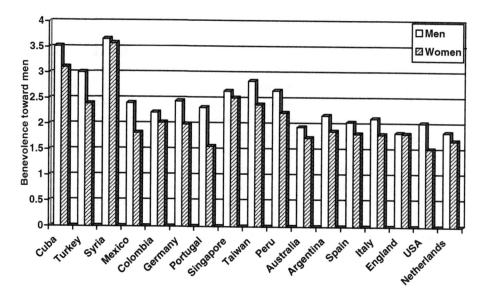

FIGURE 2.4. Benevolence toward men scores across 17 nations. From Glick et al. (2004). Copyright 2004 by the American Psychological Association. Reprinted by permission.

look at the content of HM, however, shows that it reinforces the idea that men will inevitably dominate, implying that there is little use in trying to change things. If so, HM is inimical to feminism, which generally assumes that change is possible. Theorists (e.g., Tajfel, 1981) have suggested that social change movements only develop when people in disadvantaged groups believe two things: (1) that the current hierarchy or system is illegitimate (i.e., immoral and unfair) and (2) that the current system is unstable (i.e., change is possible). Without the first belief, people cannot muster the moral outrage to band together, but without the second, they are unlikely to act: If things cannot be changed, why waste the energy? In support of this view, Thomas (2002) found that women who supported feminism scored lower on HM than those who did not. This directly contradicts popular stereotypes of feminists as having "anti-male" beliefs (Rudman & Fairchild, 2007).

Examples of an underlying hostility toward men in traditional gender beliefs can be found in *The Rules* (Fein & Schneider, 1995), a dating advice book that counsels women to have a manipulative orientation toward potential male romantic partners. Women are advised to "play hard to get," which is supposed to appeal to men's inherent desire to "conquer." Similarly, the popular radio pundit Laura Schlessinger (aka "Dr. Laura") instructs women to use their "feminine wiles" to "work their men" and to marry a good provider. This, in turn, allows women to fulfill their "feminine essence" by remaining in an exclusively domestic role and being "my kids' mom." The manipulative aspects of such advice suggests some degree of hostility toward men, coupled with a form of biological essentialism: that men "are the way they are" by nature. HM seems consistent with such advice as well as the adage that "boys will be boys." In other words, HM reflects the view that men naturally have unattractive traits (e.g., hypercompetitiveness) related to grabbing and abusing power but also suggests resignation toward such stereotypically male behavior as an unalterable fact of life.

Cross-national comparisons of average scores on the AMI scales further suggest that HM and BM represent complementary gender-traditional beliefs (Glick et al., 2004). Across nations, average scores on HM and BM were strongly correlated; nations in which people generally agreed with HM (i.e., evinced the most resentment of men's power) were also nations where people most strongly endorsed BM (i.e., believed that men are heroic providers who ought to be taken care of by women at home). Additionally, national averages on the AMI scales correlated strongly with national averages on HS and on BS. In other words, societies tend to embrace or reject the entire set of hostile and benevolent beliefs represented by the ASI and AMI scales.

As with HS and BS, cross-national averages on HM and BM, for both male and female respondents, negatively correlated with actual gender equality (as indexed by the United Nations' Gender Empowerment Index). Thus, nations where people most strongly endorse HM and BM have the least gender equality. Of particular interest is that men in the most male-dominated nations, in comparison to those in more egalitarian nations, were more likely to agree with statements that are hostile toward men.

If HM is a consequence of viewing men as designed to dominate others, traditional men's endorsement of HM makes sense. It reflects a macho male ethos in which being "bad" (e.g., callous, tough, dominant) is good (see Mosher & Sirikin, 1984). Consider macho images of the lone gunslinger, perfected by Clint Eastwood, whose attraction lies in his lack of charm, fierce independence, and unwillingness to back down from anybody. Such characters are most definitely not nice but represent a masculine ideal. In Chapter 4, we consider how stereotypes of men include traits that, although viewed as "bad," are valued because of associations with the ability to achieve status, respect, and power.

However, Figure 2.3 shows that it is women in gender-traditional nations who show the strongest endorsement of HM. They also score highly on BM, suggesting a great deal of ambivalence toward men. That is, women in gender-traditional nations appear both to resent men's power and admire them as providers who ought to be nurtured at home. These results fit with ambivalent sexism theory. Women in gender-traditional, as opposed to egalitarian, societies experience a higher degree of male dominance (eliciting HM) but also more dependence on men for resources, which they have little opportunity to secure on their own, and protection (fostering BM).

In sum, the structural factors of male dominance and intimate interdependence produce ambivalent attitudes toward both sexes. Although these attitudes, as assessed by the ASI and AMI, differ in terms of their subjective positivity or negativity and are directed specifically toward women or toward men, they form an interlocking set of complementary beliefs that support traditional gender relations and roles. Ambivalent attitudes toward women function to reward them with paternalistic benevolence for staying within traditional roles that support rather than challenge men's power but also to threaten women with hostility if they seek equality or power. Ambivalent attitudes toward men include a hostile depiction of men as arrogant dominators, an idea that, rather than posing a real challenge to their power and status, may reinforce the belief that they will always rule, alongside benevolent beliefs that men are heroes and providers who ought to be nurtured by women at home.

Chapter Summary

This chapter introduced a general theme that runs throughout this book, showing how the unique combination of male dominance and intimate heterosexual interdependence affects the way women and men are perceived and relate to each other. From the evolutionary perspective, male dominance reflects sexual selection; more specifically, it is viewed as the product of eons of women choosing assertive male mates who could provide for and protect their offspring. However, such female preferences may have developed as a self-protective response to the threat of violent male sexual coercion, leading women to form pair bonds with male protectors. Men, in exchange, gained more certainty about the paternity of their mate's offspring. In either case, evolutionary theories locate the origins of male dominance in sexual selection, linking heterosexual attraction, the primary motive for intimate interdependence between the sexes, to the ubiquity of patriarchy.

The evolutionary view is not without its critics. The biosocial theory of patriarchy does not assume that men were selected for dominance but rather that men were in a better position to monopolize positions of power once societies developed agriculture and industry. Because reproductive biology tied women to childbearing and, therefore, the home, men took over. The biosocial view gains credence from the observation that foraging societies, of the sort from which humans initially evolved, tend not to have much social hierarchy of any kind, including gender hierarchy. Rather, patriarchy seems to have emerged much more strongly after the advent of agriculture, which tied women to the domestic sphere and gave men more resources to compete over. Thus, patriarchy can potentially be accounted for without positing an innate male tendency toward dominance.

There is no dispute, however, that patriarchy today is prevalent across cultures or that heterosexual reproduction continues to foster intimate interdependence between men and women. This union of male dominance and heterosexual interdependence has profound implications for cultural gender ideologies. Ambivalent sexism theory explores these ideologies, which encompass both hostile and benevolent orientations toward each sex. BS is a subjectively positive but patronizing attitude toward women that rewards them for remaining in traditional roles, whereas HS is a subjectively negative attitude that punishes women who stray from the narrow pedestal that BS defines for women. The two work hand in hand to reinforce gender inequality, with BS playing a particularly insidious role by undermining women's resistance to male dominance. Ambivalent gender ideologies also target men. HM is subjectively negative in tone but implies that men are designed to dominate, whereas BM extols men as heroic protectors and providers. Both sets of ambivalent gender ideologies help to reconcile male dominance with intimate heterosexual interdependence, serving to perpetuate and reinforce gender inequality and traditional roles.

Although the twin facts of intimate heterosexual interdependence and male dominance represent common features of gender relations across cultures, there is one stage of life in which this combination does not hold: childhood. Chapter 3 considers the development of gender relations, including how and when children become aware of gender as an important social category and the curious journey most of us take from childhood hostility to adult ambivalence toward the other sex.

CHAPTER 3

Development of
Gender Relations

Think back to your most memorable birthday party during your elementary school years. Who were the guests? What activities did you do? If you have successfully reconstructed one of your early birthday parties, count the number of party goers who were boys versus girls. Were the guests primarily same-sex friends? Chances are that the degree to which you (as opposed to your parents) freely chose the list, most or even all of your guests were of the same sex as you.

The previous chapter stressed how gender relations have a unique dynamic in comparison to relations between most groups. More specifically, we have argued that an unusual combination of power difference and intimate interdependence combine in adult gender relations, creating both hostile and benevolent attitudes on the part of each sex toward the other. Although such ambivalence is a central theme of this book, relations between young girls and boys fundamentally differ from relations between adult women and men. Most likely, the vast majority of heterosexual adults who currently say they "can't live without them" once happily and voluntarily avoided members of the other sex like the plague. The plague metaphor is quite apt: Those fictional, gender-specific germs known as "cooties," although purely symbolic, are a serious business among children, constituting one way in which children enforce norms that minimize contact with other-sex peers. When cross-sex play occurs, it is often initiated by adults (e.g., teachers) who organize play in mixed-sex groups (Fabes, Martin, & Hanish, 2003) or, if child intiated, reinforces gender boundaries, such as through chasing games in which the whole point is to avoid physical contact with (or being "caught" by) a player of the other sex (Thorne, 1986, 1997).

In other words, ambivalence is largely absent in the behavior and attitudes of young girls and boys toward each other. Instead, indifference, even outright hostility, and overt discrimination between the sexes is quite common and tends to increase throughout childhood until puberty (C. L. Martin & Ruble, 2004; Powlishta, 1995b). Childhood gender relations more closely resemble the hostile relations that occur between competing groups or, too often, across social categories defined by differing ethnicities or religions. In part, this reflects children's cognitive and emotional development: Ambivalence requires a cognitive and emotional complexity of which young children simply may not be capable (C. L. Martin & Ruble, 2004). Additionally, however, many of the structural factors that influence adult gender relations, such as divergent roles, either are not present in childhood or have only indirect effects on children. As a result, charting the development of gender relations involves tracing not only developmental changes in the individual (e.g., increasing cognitive skills that affect the complexity of gender attitudes) but also structural changes in male–female relations.

This chapter follows the development of gender relations and gender identity from early childhood to puberty. Prominent developmental psychologist Eleanor Maccoby (1998, 2002) has aptly characterized childhood gender relations as "growing up apart" before later "coming together" (and this chapter owes a considerable debt to Maccoby's work). Childhood and adult gender relations are so dissimilar in terms of cross-sex intimacy that one might think that adults and children belong to different species. At the same time, continuities occur in how the two sexes are constructed by society and, importantly, by themselves. Although gender differences in toys, activities, and interaction styles can partially account for children's tendency to self-segregate and to strongly prefer their own sex, we underscore the importance of social identity processes for understanding these phenomena (see also Maccoby, 2002).

Gender Segregation

Gender segregation and hostility toward the other sex are the most prominent features of childhood gender relations. Partly as a cause, and certainly an effect, of childhood gender segregation, the social worlds of boys and girls differ so much that they have been characterized as "two cultures" (Maccoby, 1998). How gender segregated are the lives of young children? By the ages of 6 to 7 years, about 70% of unsupervised play by young children in preschool occurs in exclusively same-sex pairs or groups (Maccoby & Jacklin, 1987). In research involving hundreds of children in day care over several months, C. L. Martin and Fabes (1997) reported that not a single child spent 50% or more of his or her time in play that included members of the other sex.

Figure 3.1 presents the results of observations from more than 200 preschool- and kindergarten-age children (4-6 years old) at a university day-care center over the course of 3 years (Fabes et al., 2003). Although children spent a considerable amount of time in mixed-sex group play (which the day-care teachers deliberately encouraged), this typically occurred under adult supervision rather than when children freely chose partners. Girls most prefer same-sex pairs and boys most prefer same-sex group play. Pairing up with a member of the other sex

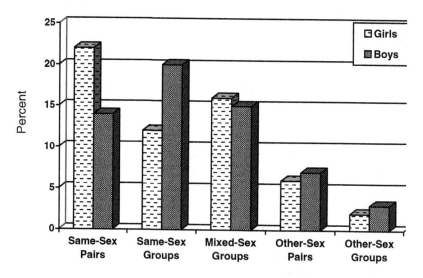

FIGURE 3.1. Percentage of time young children spent interacting with same-sex versus other-sex peers. Data from Fabes, Martin, and Hanish (2003).

is relatively rare, and playing with a group of exclusively other-sex peers (i.e., where the individual is the only boy or only girl in the group) is quite unusual.

Gender segregation begins early. Even before the age of 2 years, children show preferences for interacting with some peers over others, although at this stage play is typically "parallel" with children sitting side by side engaged in similar activities with little direct interaction (Howes, 1988). As infants, children do not show same-sex preferences, but at roughly 2 years most children begin to show a preference for same-sex peers (Fagot, 1995; LaFreniere, Strayer, & Gauthier, 1984; Maccoby & Jacklin, 1987). This preference intensifies throughout the early and middle childhood years, typically through age 11. Same-sex preferences occur among children interacting in groups as well as pairs. Children sometimes maintain cross-sex friendships they formed before the age of 2, but subsequent friendships almost exclusively occur with same-sex others. As children get older and group play (e.g., organized games such as kickball or team jump-rope) becomes more sophisticated and interactive, sex segregation becomes particularly strong.

Childhood segregation occurs in all of the societies where childhood play has been systematically examined (Whiting & Edwards, 1988), and children themselves actively prefer it (Maccoby, 2002). In playgrounds around the world, when their play is not organized and supervised by adults (i.e., when playmates are freely chosen), children typically congregate in same-sex pairs and groups (Fabes et al., 2003; Maccoby & Jacklin, 1987; Thorne, 1986, 1997; Whiting & Edwards, 1988). The societies in which childhood sex segregation has been documented range from gender-traditional to highly egalitarian, nonindustrialized to highly industrialized and include both Western and non-Western cultures.

In some cultures, sex segregation is imposed or encouraged by adults, but even in circumstances in which adults explicitly discourage sex segregation, children nevertheless develop and maintain it (Fabes et al., 2003; Maccoby, 2002). It seems that adults can easily reinforce sex segregation but have a much more difficult time curtailing it. Wellmeaning efforts by day-care workers, teachers, and parents to encourage cross-sex play are often met with children's resistance. For example, Maccoby (1998) describes how children managed to undermine the goals of a mixed-sex sports program. Even though girls and boys were on the same baseball team and the coach encouraged egalitarian treatment, the children quickly defined a "boys' bench" and a "girls' bench" on which they sat while waiting to bat. Unless sustained efforts are made, interventions designed to promote gender integration tend to have only temporary effects, with children segregating when left on their own (Bigler, 1999).

Effective interventions are possible. Strongly progressive schools that consistently reinforce egalitarian values and behavior can increase the amount of children's spontaneous cross-sex play (Thorne & Luria, 1986; Zammuner, 1993). Perhaps the consistency with which such schools promote egalitarian practices has a cumulative effect. Also, parents who send their children to progressive schools probably reinforce the message at home. In contrast, scatter-shot approaches to changing children's behavior tend to fail.

Additionally, some mixed-sex play occurs without adult intervention. For instance, children are more likely to engage in mixed-sex play in private settings where they do not have a large group of peers to choose from or to observe them crossing gender lines (Bannerje & Lintern, 2000; Gottman & Parker, 1984; Thorne, 1986). Some play occurs in mixed-sex groups. Individual boys and girls, however, rarely play with a group of other-sex children. The exceptions to the rule tend to flow in one direction, with some girls crossing over to play with the boys rather than individual boys playing with a female group. So-called tomboys may be tolerated as "one of the guys." These are usually highly athletic girls who enjoy and do well at competitive, physical games (Thorne, 1997).

A boy who crosses over to play with girls, however, elicits hostility from the girls with whom he seeks to play and, especially, from other boys who bully him for violating norms of masculinity. Boys learn early in life that they need to present themselves as masculine to be accepted by male peers. As young as 4 years of age, boys' toy and activity preferences become more "masculine" when they are playing with others as opposed to playing alone, suggesting awareness of masculine social norms (Bannerje & Lintern, 2000). Boys who fail to display masculinity are labeled as "sissies" and "babies" (Fagot, Rodgers, & Leinbach, 2000). This type of childhood taunting and teasing behavior has profound effects on its victims (see Archer & Coyne, 2005), bringing most children quickly in line with peer-approved behavior to avoid social rejection. Consider your own most painful memories of being rejected or taunted by peers and how it affected you. Such incidents often remain both vivid and painful even though they happened long ago (and rejection by peers for violations of gender norms, although it may become more subtle, does not end in childhood; see Chapters 6 and 7).

Mixed-sex interaction on the playground often involves teasing and taunting that merely reinforces the general rule of gender segregation. For instance, Thorne (1986, 1994) describes how boys stage "raids" on the girls to disrupt their games (e.g., by stealing their ball). Girls, in turn, may try to capture a boy and kiss him, which both groups treat as a taunt that transfers "cooties," not a reward. Such "border work" may sometimes be more playful than hostile, however, and children themselves often recognize that behavior couched as aggression (chasing, poking, pulling hair) can be masked expressions of cross-sex attraction, with considerable teasing about who likes whom (Schofield, 1981). At the same time, these interactions highlight gender boundaries: that boys and girls are separate, antagonistic groups and that heterosexual aggression is more socially acceptable among childhood peers than heterosexual attraction (especially having a boyfriend or girlfriend).

In short, children generally prefer to associate with same-sex peers. Further, absent sustained and consistent efforts, children resist adult interventions to encourage cross-sex play. Childhood gender segregation is not absolute, except in societies where adults impose such rules; but it is pervasive across cultures, an active choice that children make, and strongly enforced among children by punishing those who deviate from the norm.

The "Two Cultures" of Childhood

Segregation both allows and encourages girls and boys to develop separate social worlds or "cultures" characterized by different activities, interaction styles, and social rules. Over time, the more boys play with boys and girls with girls, the more gender typed their play activities become (e.g., more rough-and-tumble play by boys, more doll play by girls; Martin & Fabes, 2001). This suggests a socialization by peers concerning which activities are appropriate for members of each gender. Children quickly develop strong gender schemas (Bem, 1981, 1989), cognitive associations of different attributes, behaviors, objects, or social practices with "male" and "female." Schemas represent "knowledge structures" that guide how people perceive and organize the world as well as how they behave toward others. According to gender schema theory (Bem, 1981), children learn gender schemas from their social environments, but they also willingly adopt and exaggerate distinctions between the sexes. Gender schemas become part of self-identity, influencing children's preferences, attitudes, and behavior as they strive to act in socially appropriate "masculine" or "feminine" ways (Martin & Ruble, 2004).

Gender schemas associate maleness and femaleness with myriad different attributes, behaviors, and objects, defining "masculine" as rougher, tougher, and more active and feminine as nicer, softer, and more passive (see Martin & Ruble, 2004, for a review). This theme carries through to gender stereotypes applied to adults (see Chapter 4), including associating strength and power with men and warmth and nurturance with women. This general theme also emerges in the earliest associations children make with each sex, such as which toys are for boys and which are for girls.

Toy and Activity Preferences

In addition to sex segregation, another cross-cultural consistency in childhood behavior is the gendering of toys and activities (e.g., some toys are "for boys" and some are "for girls"). As toddlers, girls and boys begin to show differences in activity and toy preferences (Campbell, Shirley, Heywood, & Crooke, 2000; Fagot, Leinbach, & Hagen, 1986). Consistent with the general theme that boys are rougher and girls are sweeter, boys' toys (and masculine objects more generally) are hard and sharp, whereas girls' toys (and other feminine objects) are soft and smooth (Bem, 1981; Martin, 1999). Reactions to novel toys confirm that children do not merely learn by rote which toys are for boys and which are for girls, but extract general qualities that distinguish masculine from feminine. In other words, they have begun to learn a more general gender schema. In one study, researchers transformed a pastel "My Little Pony" by shaving the mane (a soft "girlish" feature), painting it black (a "tough" color), and adding spiky teeth (for an aggressive demeanor). Both boys and girls classified the altered pony as a boy's toy, and most of the boys (but not the girls) were extremely interested in obtaining one (Hort & Leinbach, 1993, cited in Martin, 1999).

Judging on the basis of children's preferences, however, many toys and activities are gender neutral. American children spend much of their time playing with gender-neutral toys (e.g., crayons) as well as gender-specific toys (e.g., trucks vs. dolls), but children rarely play with toys associated with the other sex, which happens for less than 5% of children's playtime (Fagot et al., 2000). Most likely, children have learned to avoid being seen playing with toys associated with the other gender (Bannerjee & Lintern, 2000). Thus, children not only segregate themselves by playing with same-sex peers but engage in different kinds of play within these groups.

Toy and activity preferences intersect. Both sexes play with minia-turized human figures that encourage them to engage in fantasy role playing. But as any boy will tell you, an action figure is most definitely not a doll and the two are used quite differently. As the name "action figure" implies, these are toys in which the play theme is both active and tough; aggression is a strong theme of boys' play (Flannery & Wat-son, 1993). Action figures represent the toughest male fantasy figures (e.g., superheroes and their arch enemies) or occupations (e.g., sol-diers), and not other highly male-dominated, but less tough, roles (e.g., engineers, senators, or computer scientists). In contrast, girls tend to stick to pretend play that involves domestic or school-related roles (McLoyd, 1983). The miniaturized human figures girls play with typi-cally include baby dolls or feminine icons such as Barbie. Barbie and her legion of imitators represent feminine ideals and encourage such activities as pretend shopping, grooming, and accessorizing. Girls' pre-tend play often includes assuming family roles, such as one playing the mother and another (or a doll) playing the baby, who has to be fed and rocked to sleep. These different forms of role-playing reinforce traditionally gendered adult roles and the enactment of stereotypically masculine traits among boys (physical toughness, leadership, assertive-ness) and stereotypically feminine traits among girls (gentleness, nur-turance, warmth).

Even before children are capable of the more sophisticated role playing that they use with action figures and dolls, they exhibit prefer-ences for different kinds of physical activity. As toddlers, boys (in com-parison to girls) show a stronger attraction to rough-and-tumble play (i.e., boisterous and more physically active play, such as wrestling). Even when playing with a gender-neutral toy, boys evince a rougher, more physical style, such as ramming into things or into other players during tricycle play (Dunn & Morgan, 1987). Similarly, when given a chance to play on a trampoline in same-sex groups of three children, boys tended to jump together while intentionally trying to bump into each other, whereas girls tended to take turns jumping separately (DiPietro, 1981). Sex differences in rough-and-tumble play have also been observed in other primates, such as chimpanzees, suggesting a biologically based sex difference (Meany, Stewart, & Beatty, 1985). Manipulations of pre-natal hormone levels in monkeys have been shown to affect preference for rough-and-tumble play. Female rhesus monkeys exposed to higher levels of testosterone in utero engage in more rough-and-tumble play than do control female peers (Goy, Bercovitch, & McBrair, 1988).

Interaction Styles

The differences in the content of boys' and girls' play are emblematic of stylistic differences in how boys and girls interact with their same-sex peers. Gender segregation allows boys and girls to develop different social norms and interaction styles, and their play styles reinforce those differences. Sex differences in aggression tend to emerge at about 3 years of age (a year or so after gender segregation begins). At 3 to 4 years of age, girls become less likely to engage in physical aggression, whereas boys become more likely to do so (DiPietro, 1981). Rough-and-tumble play among boys can devolve from good-natured roughhousing (much more common) into aggression (less common but more frequent among boys than girls). Boys tend to act more assertively than girls do, such as grabbing a desired toy from a peer rather than negotiating to share it (Serbin, Sprafkin, Elman, & Doyle, 1984). This assertiveness can also lead to male–male aggression; when one boy grabs a toy away from another, conflict can ensue (Fagot, Hagen, Leinbach, & Kronsberg, 1985).

Competition permeates many of boys'—more so than girls'—play activities. Boys are much more likely than girls to construct and engage in overtly competitive games (often between teams of boys). These include both simple physical challenges (e.g., races, seeing how far each one can throw) and more complex, organized games (e.g., pick-up football). Mostly, boys' play occurs without obvious hostility or aggression (Crombie & Desjardins, 1993). Nevertheless, boys evince much more concern with constructing explicit dominance hierarchies, establishing relative status among their same-sex peers through physical competitions (Omark, Omark, & Edelman, 1973). A greater male preference for group-based dominance hierarchies occurs in adults as well (see Chapter 11).

In contrast to boys' interaction style, girls tend to avoid open competition or aggression. Girls more frequently engage in cooperative exchanges with each other, negotiate sharing arrangements, and take turns without interrupting (Maccoby, 1998; Serbin et al., 1984). Although girls also establish status differences or dominance hierarchies, they tend to downplay this fact. Girls construct more subtle hierarchies based on social concerns rather than physical prowess. Just as status hierarchies are more covert among girls, so too is aggression. Although overt conflict and physical aggression occurs among girls less often than among boys, girls (more than boys) engage in what has variously been termed indirect, relational, or social aggression, such as undermining a peer's social status or relations with other peers (see Archer & Coyne, 2005, for a review).

This less overt type of aggression, often done behind the victim's back, includes socially undermining behavior such as spreading malicious rumors or trying to get friends to exclude a peer from group activities. More direct acts of social aggression include threatening to end a friendship if a peer does not do as one asks or criticizing another's appearance. Contrary to the rhyme that "sticks and stones can break my bones, but words can never hurt me," children rate social aggression as more psychologically painful than physical aggression (Paquette & Underwood, 1999), and being the victim of social aggression predicts future maladjustment (Crick, 1996).

Because social aggression is more subtle and verbal than, for instance, forcefully grabbing a toy or pushing another child, it does not emerge until about age 4. Evidence on the frequency with which girls versus boys engage in social aggression is mixed but seems to indicate a sex difference that peaks in adolescence. Further, social aggression, compared with physical aggression, is clearly the preferred mode of attack by girls, whereas the reverse is true of boys (Archer & Coyne, 2005).

In general, then, boys tend toward greater assertiveness, overt competition, and physically rough play in their interactions with same-sex peers, whereas girls develop a more considerate and cooperative style. Boys generally welcome their male peers' assertive and physical play, enjoying competitive and physical games, but male conflict can erupt into physical aggression. By contrast, girls' more polite, cooperative play and avoidance of physical aggression does not indicate an absence of hierarchy and conflict, which are expressed socially (e.g., through exclusion) rather than physically. For children of both sexes, interpersonal conflict with same-sex peers is painful, and both boys and girls prefer to avoid it. That is, boys generally prefer to compete in rule-governed games rather than in hostile brawls, and girls prefer to engage in cooperative play than to backbite. By contrast, children's attitudes about the other sex are often more overtly hostile, representing well-entrenched intergroup attitudes.

Not Just Segregation, but Hostility between the Sexes

Logically, boys and girls could inhabit mostly separate social worlds and not have significant intergroup animosity; separation might simply breed a "live and let live" attitude toward the other sex. This is not the case. As toddlers, children have already begun to develop derogatory attitudes toward peers of the other sex. Most adults know that if they ask a young boy or girl what he or she thinks about other-sex peers (or, if trying to be especially provocative, inquires about whether he has a girlfriend or she a boyfriend), a child will most likely respond with disgust and contempt (e.g., "Boys—yuck!").

Hostile childhood sexism is expected and treated quite differently than, for example, childhood racism. Imagine how most adults would react to a White child who blurted out "I hate Blacks." Most adults would be horrified and immediately deliver a serious lecture on the immorality of hating others because of their skin color, the history of racism, and how people of different races are all alike. By contrast, adults typically show benign amusement or weary acceptance of statements such as "I hate girls." When one of our young nephews recently chanted at a family gathering, "Boys go to college to get more knowledge, but girls go to Jupiter because they are stupider," the adults reacted with laughter. Even intense expressions of animosity toward the other sex tend to yield a chuckle and the sage observation that "someday you'll like them." Although many adults dismiss childhood sexism, it is a perfect example of hostile prejudice in which negative emotions and derogatory beliefs about the out-group generate discriminatory behaviors such as segregation.

Hostile Emotions

Prejudice is often defined in terms of emotional reactions to other groups, whereas stereotypes refer to beliefs about groups and their members (Allport, 1954/1979). Children show social emotions early in life, distinguishing between different types of people. For instance, even 1-year-olds show more positive emotional reactions to attractive versus unattractive adults (Langlois, Roggman, & Rieser-Danner, 1990). Although people often think of stereotypes (beliefs about groups' attributes) as a primary cause of prejudiced feelings toward others, children show intergroup hostility before they develop specific beliefs about other groups. For example, when young English children were asked about people of various nationalities, they agreed on one thing: that they liked some nationalities better than others. In this classic study, conducted in the 1960s (during the Cold War), English children generally viewed Americans as "better than" Russians. This consensus occurred long before children developed any specific stereotypes or beliefs about Americans or Russians. Older children might say that Americans are better because they are democratic, wealthy, and generous. Younger children simply felt that "Americans are good" but could not say why they thought so (Tajfel & Jahoda, 1966).

Similarly, young children express strong feelings about the other sex long before they can articulate reasons for their feelings. Boys and girls in kindergarten openly express hostility toward the other sex when asked how they feel about them (Powlishta, 1995b; Powlishta, Serbin, Doyle, & White, 1994). Further, children do not simply exhibit more favorable feelings toward their own sex (as in "Girls are okay, but I like boys better"); rather, each sex expresses active dislike of the other (e.g., "Boys are bad"). As with gender segregation, open hostility begins among toddlers and, if anything, intensifies until puberty (Yee & Brown, 1994).

Stereotypes

Young children do not hold complex gender stereotypes (associating specific personality traits with each sex), but they quickly and actively pick up "cues about gender—who should or should not do a particular activity, who can play with whom, and why girls and boys are different" (Martin & Ruble, 2004, p. 67). Even as toddlers, children associate different objects with the two sexes, such as dolls with girls, trucks with boys (G. D. Levy, Zimmerman, Barber, Martin & Malone, 1998). Gendered cognitive associations soon develop (about age 3) to include sex-specific activities, clothing, and adult jobs (e.g., firefighters are men and nurses are women; Fagot, Leinbach, & O'Boyle, 1992; Martin & Ruble, 2004; Ruble & Ruble, 1982). These associations reflect social realities: Boys and girls do often engage in different activities, play with different toys, dress differently, and see an adult world with many jobs almost exclusively occupied by men and others by women. So long as these social realities persist, children will naturally perceive them and, given their limited cognitive capacities, overgeneralize (e.g., assume that all firefighters are male). Further, as we review in Chapter 4, the media constantly reinforce gender stereotypes in advertising and programming. Thus, children inevitably pick up these stereotypic associations.

However, simply knowing the stereotypes does not necessarily indicate hostile gender prejudice toward the other sex (Bigler, 1997).

The development of personality trait stereotypes takes longer, but by ages 5 to 6 children have developed rigid gender stereotypes (Trautner et al., 2005). Personality trait stereotypes develop later because "traits" are sophisticated, inferred concepts. For instance, children might associate boys with "pushing" well in advance of conceiving of a trait labeled "aggressiveness." Of particular interest is that children's initial personality-based stereotyping of the other sex tends toward uniform hostility. In one study (Powlishta, 1995a), 8- to 10-year-old boys and girls rated various personality traits as masculine (associated with boys) or feminine (associated with girls) and also rated the favorability of each trait (its desirability vs. undesirability). Both boys and girls exhibited a strong in-group bias, claiming favorable traits for their own sex and assigning unfavorable traits to the other sex.

Children's early in-group favoritism partly overrides their tendency to embrace cultural conceptions of masculinity and femininity, as evident in Table 3.1, which provides children's masculinity–femininity ratings of positive traits. In this table, positive ratings indicate traits rated as more likely to be feminine (i.e., shown by girls), and negative ratings indicate traits rated as more likely to be masculine (i.e., shown by boys).

TABLE 3.1. Ratings of the "Masculinity" and "Femininity" of Positive Traits by Boys and Girls

Trait	Boys' ratings	Girls' ratings
Intelligent	−0.56	+0.67
Dependable	−0.46	+1.05
Sure of self	−0.77	+0.48
Sense of humor	−0.79	+0.29
Careful	−0.38	+0.88
Fair	−0.23	+0.90
Mature	−0.38	+1.29
Honest	−0.28	+1.21
Helpful	−0.10	+1.36
Independent	−0.18	+0.48
Ambitious	−0.31	+0.19
Daring	−1.77	−0.60
Strong	−1.74	−1.19
Polite	+0.10	+1.45
Shares	+0.21	+1.40
Soft hearted	+0.41	+1.60
Gentle	+1.07	+1.71
Affectionate	+1.28	+0.83

Note. Positive scores = more "feminine" and negative scores = more "masculine." Adapted from Powlishta (1995a). Copyright 1995 by Springer. Adapted by permission.

Although adults view "independent" and "sure of self" as stereotypically masculine, in Powlishta's (1995a) study, both boys and girls claimed these favorable traits more for their own sex. Similarly, "helpful" and "careful," favorable traits that adults would stereotypically view as more feminine, were claimed by both boys and girls to be more characteristic of their own sex. Cultural stereotypes were not completely ignored. For example, boys rated "independent" and "sure of self" as highly masculine, whereas girls rated them as only slightly more feminine than masculine. "Helpful" and "careful" showed the reverse pattern, with girls claiming them as highly characteristic of their sex and boys claiming them only slightly more masculine than feminine. Further, both sexes agreed that boys are more daring and strong, whereas girls are more polite, sharing, soft-hearted, gentle, and affectionate.

The pattern for negative personality traits was also somewhat group serving, as evident in Table 3.2. "Severe" is a negative viewed as more masculine by adults, but boys assigned it to girls (and girls to boys), and "dominant," a trait usually at the core of the adult male stereotype, was rated as gender neutral by girls. "Complains" and "nagging" are seen by adults as stereotypically female, but girls assigned the former to boys and saw the latter as gender neutral. Again, there was considerable agreement by both boys and girls on some traits. Boys were viewed as

TABLE 3.2. Ratings of the "Masculinity" and "Femininity" of Negative Traits by Boys and Girls

	Boys' ratings	Girls' ratings
Boring	+1.05	−0.55
Complains	+0.67	−0.33
Fickle	+0.77	−0.12
Nagging	+0.89	−0.05
Apathetic	+0.15	−0.95
Severe	+0.31	−0.24
Flirts	+0.43	−0.21
Stuck-up	+0.23	−0.31
Brags	+0.13	−0.79
Dominant	−0.54	0.00
Careless	−0.11	−1.02
Messy	−0.59	−1.52
Cruel	−0.67	−1.17
Fights	−1.38	−1.62
Loud	−0.54	−1.00
Crude	−1.07	−1.45
Sorry for self	+.067	+0.38
Cries	+1.29	+0.60

Note. Positive scores = more "feminine" and negative scores = more "masculine." Adapted from Powlishta (1995a). Copyright 1995 by Springer. Adapted by permission.

more likely to fight and to be loud, crude, messy, and cruel. By contrast, girls were seen as more likely to cry and to feel sorry for themselves.

Although we review gender stereotypes in much more detail in the next chapter, the study described previously is particularly revealing. Whereas adults' gender stereotypes assign both favorable and unfavorable traits to both sexes (i.e., indicate ambivalence), children's stereotypes are relatively more bipolar, favoring their own sex. The general rubric that children seem to exhibit when it comes to associating personality traits with either sex is "my sex = good, other sex = bad." Although a considerable degree of conventional sex typing occurs among children, they bend the stereotypes in ways that favor their gender in-group.

Important exceptions to the "my sex = good, other sex = bad" rule include traits that both boys and girls consistently classify as masculine—daring, strong, crude, loud, likes to fight—and others that they both classify as feminine—gentle, affectionate, cries easily, feels sorry for self (Powlishta, 1995a). These traits comport with observed sex differences in interaction styles and with the general gender schema that boys are "rougher" and girls are "nicer." These traits also cohere as well with adult gender stereotypes that cast men as less nice and more dominant and women as nicer but less assertive and more fragile. Apart from these exceptions, the negative stereotypes expressed by boys and girls are consistent with the hostile emotions and avoidant behavior children exhibit toward the other sex.

In sum, both children's emotions toward and stereotypes of the other sex reflect an overt and categorical hostility. Differing activity preferences, interaction styles, and identification with similar others may elicit some of this hostility. Further, the sex segregation that children initiate reinforces, as well as reflects, gender-based antipathy. But different activity preferences and interaction styles do not seem likely to account for the degree of active avoidance and hostility each sex exhibits toward the other. Moreover, this overt hostility somehow later transforms to considerably more complex and often pleasant cross-sex adult relations.

Explanations for Segregation and Hostility in Childhood Gender Relations

As with all gender-related phenomena, gender segregation and hostility in childhood have multiple causes. Early childhood research suggests that simple socialization accounts, in which children act as passive sponges that soak up the gendered rules of behavior and stereotypes of the wider culture, fail to capture how children actively construct their own social worlds (Martin & Ruble, 2004; Maccoby, 2002). Children often behave quite differently from what adults might prefer and show resistance to adults' influence attempts. We by no means dismiss the importance of socialization; children clearly pick up on and adapt to the gender roles and styles of behavior that adults model (Bussey & Bandura, 1999). At the same time, children are not empty receptacles into which adult attitudes are simply poured.

In this section, we highlight the ways in which sex differences in children's interaction styles foster sex segregation and how this, in turn, feeds into social identity processes (children's construction of group-based identities, norms, and affiliations based on sex category) that energize intergroup animosity. Finally, we consider how the social structural factors—male dominance and heterosexual interdependence—that create ambivalence in adult gender relations are much less prominent in childhood gender relations. These structural features of adult gender relations temper the expression of gender animosity; the absence of such mitigating factors in childhood allows antipathy freer rein.

Interaction Styles as an Initial Cause of Sex Segregation

Gender differences in toy use, activities, and interaction styles have been offered as one explanation for why boys and girls choose to segregate themselves along gender lines (Maccoby, 2002). For instance, if José likes rough-and-tumble play and Maria does not, they will soon learn that they are better off playing with different peers. However, most toy play is gender neutral and rough-and-tumble play constitutes only a minority of playtime among children, usually less than 10% of total play (Fagot et al., 2000).

Nonetheless, early childhood research shows that as toddlers, girls initially separate themselves from the boys rather than the reverse (Jacklin & Maccoby, 1978). Observational studies suggest that girls have difficulty dealing with boys' more physically assertive and less socially responsive interaction styles, such as grabbing a toy away from another child rather than taking turns (Maccoby, 1998; Serbin et al., 1984). Girls seem to find most boys annoying and frustrating to interact with because girls have a difficult time getting what they want and are unwilling to reciprocate boys' more aggressive style. In turn, boys find little advantage to adapting to girls' more cooperative style because this would involve giving up control. It is easier, when they have a choice, to play with others of the same sex whose styles are more likely to match their own.

Are gender differences in interaction styles a product of parental socialization? On the one hand, a review of the literature suggests that American parents treat male and female infants similarly on most dimensions, interacting with them with equal frequency and showing equal degrees of responsiveness, affection, and nurturance to sons and daughters (Lytton & Romney, 1991). On the other hand, parents do sex stereotype their infants. Parents of newborns described daughters as smaller, more delicate, and softer, whereas they saw sons as more robust, stronger, and more alert (Rubin, Provenzano, & Luria, 1974). Parents also interact differently with sons and daughters in some ways, roughhousing more with sons and discouraging their children from playing with "sex-inappropriate" toys, especially discouraging sons from playing with "girl" toys such as dolls (Siegal, 1987). Parents' degree of roughhousing, however, does not strongly predict children's subsequent behavior in free-play sessions (Maccoby & Jacklin, 1987). Studies that examine parents' interactions with their children may not fully capture the ways parents make gender salient, but the overall picture suggests more similarities than differences in how parents treat young daughters and sons.

Even if parents treated their sons and daughters identically, parental pressures may be overpowered by the influences of culture and peers. The assumption that parents represent the greatest influence in children's lives has been challenged by studies of peer influence (J. R. Harris, 1998). Strikingly, children raised by the same parents, on average, behave no more similarly to one another than pairs of children selected at random from the population (Plomin & Daniels, 1987), probably because siblings typically have different peer groups. Even among preschoolers, peers teach one another preferences for foods, games, and music. For older children, peer influence expands to affect habits (e.g., likelihood of smoking), activity preferences, clothing styles, and who is popular or an outcast. The nephew's ditty about "girls are stupider" came from his peers, not his parents. Thus, J. R. Harris (1998) argues that the strongest influence parents can have on a child (once basic survival and attachment needs are met) concerns their choice of neighborhood to live in, school to attend, and activities to join because these determine the child's peer group. From this perspective, parents play an important but largely indirect role in how their progeny develop. In other words, parenting styles are overpowered by the strong need that children have for peer acceptance and approval. Because children segregate into same-sex groups, they learn the ins and outs of their separate "cultures" from imitating same-sex peers.

Although differences in interaction styles may drive the initial impetus among children to segregate themselves by gender, they do not fully explain why children exhibit such strong group-based animosity. Girls may experience some animosity toward boys because they find them frustrating as interaction partners. The animosity, however, quickly becomes mutual, and boys soon enforce gender segregation even more strictly than girls (Maccoby, 1998). Understanding the process by which girls and boys develop such intensely antagonistic groups requires consideration of how children construct distinct and competitive social identities that contrast their own sex with its "opposite."

Social Identity Processes as a Source of Animosity between the Sexes

People readily form attachments to social groups and incorporate group memberships as part of their own self-image (Tajfel, 1981; Tajfel & Turner, 1979). Social identity refers to a group identity that has become part of one's self-concept. Social identities can include groups that individuals are born into (e.g., sex, ethnicity) or groups with which people choose to affiliate (e.g., identification with a sports team). Sex category ("I am a boy" or "I am a girl") is one of the earliest and strongest social identities most individuals form and developmental psychologists agree that social identity processes powerfully influence childhood gender relations (Maccoby, 2002; Martin, Ruble, & Szkyrbalo, 2002).

When a group membership becomes part of the self, self-esteem becomes linked to the status and success not only of oneself but also one's group (Oakes & Turner, 1980). To bolster self-esteem, people attempt to construct a positive group identity by viewing the in-group as better and more desirable than rival out-groups (groups to which the individual does not belong; Tajfel & Turner, 1979). When people are assigned to newly created groups, they allocate more resources to and express more liking for in-group compared with out-group members (Tajfel, 1981). Group membership, however, does not inevitably entail animosity toward the out-group. In the absence of conflict, people simply express a preference for the in-group. For instance, people in lab-constructed groups show reluctance to actively harm out-group members (e.g., by administering some sort of punishment) but are eager to allocate more resources to the in-group than the out-group (Brewer, 1999).

In-group preference, however, can quickly turn into hostility toward out-groups viewed as threatening the in-group's identity, status, or resources (Stephan & Stephan, 2000). The more intensely people identify with their group, the more they strive to construct and defend a positive image of the group. When another group threatens this image, hostility often ensues. Further, derogating out-groups is an easy way to gain positive in-group distinction (Oakes & Turner, 1980). Social identity theory also helps to explain why people have such strong motivation to conform to the accepted social practices of their in-groups. Groups construct shared norms, rituals, and values so that they will have a distinctive group identity. Individuals who identify with the group typically strive to behave in ways that gain the approval of other group members, thereby preventing rejection by their group (Tajfel & Turner, 1979).

Social identity processes, to a significant extent, drive childhood hostility toward the other sex (Maccoby, 2002; Martin et al., 2002). When children realize that there are two sexes and that they belong to only one of these groups, social identity theory predicts that they will seek to construct distinctive group identities and evaluate their sex more positively than the other. All of this occurs in service of feeling good about oneself.

The minimal condition required for children to form gendered social identities is the ability and propensity to categorize self and peers as boys and girls (Martin & Ruble, 2004). This ability, not surprisingly, occurs at about the same time that children begin to segregate by sex, between 2 and 3 years of age (Etaugh & Duits, 1990). Although gender segregation may begin (as a result of different interaction styles) even before children can reliably categorize peers or self by gender, the tendency to segregate no doubt gets exacerbated by children's developing gender identities.

As children get older, they increasingly organize their peer relations in terms of gender category membership. As a result, the sex of a peer becomes more than a cue for making satisfying interpersonal choices based on sex differences in play styles (e.g., With whom am I likely to have a pleasant interaction?). Instead, children construct intergroup boundaries between the sexes, and acceptance by one's same-sex group depends on avoiding members the other sex (or interacting with them in acceptable ways, e.g., taunting and teasing). The difference between interpersonal versus intergroup processes can be seen in children's differential willingness to cross gender boundaries in private versus in public. A neighbor of the other sex who has similar play preferences may be accepted as a playmate in private (a "home friend") but not in public (e.g., at school; Bannerjee & Lintern, 2000; Gottman & Parker, 1984; Thorne, 1986). Once these intergroup processes develop, most children conform to their gender group's norms. For many, this may comport happily with their personal preferences and a developing gender identity. For others, it may reflect a forced conformity aimed at avoiding social rejection. In either case, gender categorization governs children's social lives, becoming an extremely important cue about how, or even whether, to interact with a peer.

A number of reasons explain why gender represents such a salient or prominent category by which children classify themselves and their peers. First, adults make the boy–girl distinction salient, treating it as an important category to which each child belongs. After all, the first question typically asked about a new baby is whether it is a boy or girl. Even if boys and girls were treated similarly by adults in all other respects, categorization alone has been shown to initiate social identity processes. Gender categorization is reinforced by giving children sex-specific names, dressing girls and boys in distinctively different ways, and (in at least in some domains, such as the toys they are encouraged to play with) differential treatment of boys and girls by parents and other adults.

Second, children do not have many alternative social identities available to them. Ethnic and racial identities, for example, are realized later (Davey, 1977). Children also do not have occupational or social roles that might help to group themselves with some peers and distinguish themselves from others. Family affiliation may be learned early on but does not fulfill the same social functions as gender. Optimal distinctiveness theory (Brewer, 1991) suggests that people seek identities that simultaneously fulfill two needs: a desire to fit in with a group and to be individually distinctive. Among peers, gender is well suited to achieving optimal distinctiveness. Being grouped as similar to about half of one's peers and different from the other half offers the perfect mix of belonging and distinctiveness.

Third, although all group identities are a matter of social comparison—my group is defined as distinctive according to its differences from other groups—this comparative process may be intensified when there are only two groups. Social comparison processes make it likely that the two sexes will be viewed as polar opposites, as the popular phrase "the opposite sex" indicates. In other words, social norms about what it means to be a boy are, in large measure, defined against what it means to be a girl (and vice versa). For instance, boys are not supposed to cry; if they do, they may be accused of being like a girl. Indeed, for boys, being likened to a girl (a sissy or a "little girl") may be the worst insult male peers can hurl. Because gendered social identities revolve around this kind of opposition and each group wishes to construct a positive identity, the tendency to derogate the other sex is exacerbated.

Fourth, children treat gender identity as important because gender is a socially useful category for them. It not only corresponds to a distinction that adults define as important but (given early sex differences in interaction styles) serves as a cue for which peers are likely to be compatible playmates. If girls first choose to segregate because they find most boys' interaction style to be frustrating, then gender acts as a pragmatic cue, tipping off girls about which peers to avoid. In fact, girls seem especially wary of interacting with boys, as compared with girls, whom they do not know (Maccoby, 1998).

Social identity processes help to explain why gender segregation becomes so extreme and rigid (especially in public), the hostility expressed toward the other sex, and the resistance that children often show to adults who try to mitigate these tendencies. When strong group identities form, so too do powerful social and personal rewards for those who "fit in" with their groups and punishments for those who do not (Cialdini & Trost, 1998). As noted, group members strive to distinguish themselves from rival groups by developing distinctive norms and characteristics that "mark" group membership and by enforcing strict group boundaries (Tajfel, 1981).

Because children's cognitive and emotional make-up is less complex and more impulsive, once they latch onto gender group membership as important, it is not surprising that they are quite rigid in maintaining gender boundaries, adhere to their gender in-group's norms, and derogate their gender out-group. Chapter 2 noted how the structure of gender relations among adults prevents uniform hostility, primarily because the two sexes are intimately interdependent (which tempers adult gender hostility with benevolence). By contrast, the lack of interdependence between boys and girls allows unfettered competition and hostility.

In addition to lacking interdependence, childhood gender relations have less well-defined power relations. In childhood, boys' greater assertiveness largely gets neutralized by sex segregation and boys also do not have the occupational status and pay differences that, on the whole, benefit men over women. Both the absence of heterosexual intimate interdependence in childhood and the greater fluidity of power dynamics between boys and girls may increase childhood gender hostility.

Power and Status in Childhood

Power differences between men and women follow from differences in status and resources that accrue from segregated adult social and occupational roles, which are still evident even within relatively egalitarian cultures. But boys do not earn more money than girls or hold positions of greater authority in government, business, and religious institutions. Rather, children's main role as students, once they are old enough, is similar for both sexes (at least in more egalitarian societies).

This does not indicate a complete lack of power and status differences between the sexes in childhood. Because of the prevalence of gender hierarchy in adulthood, being male (even when young) constitutes a diffuse status characteristic (i.e., a marker of belonging to a high-status group; Ridgeway, 2001b). That is, boys have somewhat greater social status simply by virtue of being male. In some cultures, these status differences are quite significant and lead, even early in life, to role differences, such as girls being deemed unfit for school and instead trained at home to fulfill domestic roles (United Nations Development Programme, 2005). Even in gender-traditional cultures, however, girls are not necessarily encouraged to defer to boys until after they reach puberty. For instance, Bedouin girls begin to veil (a symbol of deference) only when they reach sexual maturity (Abu-Lughod, 1986). Also, boys may be expected to obey adult female authorities, primarily their mothers.

To some extent, boys' greater tendency toward aggressive rough-and-tumble play and direct aggression gives them more power in interactions with girls. Recall that boys tend to get their way (e.g., monopolizing a favorite toy) when interacting with girls. But segregation provides a simple solution to this problem, a means by which girls manage to short-circuit male dominance (Maccoby, 1998). Boys' physical assertiveness then becomes directed mostly at gaining status among male peers.

Further, to the extent that school performance confers status, girls currently tend to attain higher status than boys. As a group, in elementary and high school, girls currently outperform boys in their shared role as students (at least in the United States). Social commentators (e.g., Hoff-Summers, 2000; Brooks, 2005) have suggested that these effects reflect a worsening male disadvantage for boys and young men in American society. According to data from the U.S. Department of Education (see Peter & Horn, 2005), girls receive significantly higher grades than boys in high school, evince higher academic aspirations for their post-high school plans, and pursue college degrees at higher rates. The academic achievement advantage continues after high school, at least in terms of college enrollment and completion rates; more women are currently enrolled in college than men, and it is projected that in the year 2010 there will be 142 female college graduates for every 100 male graduates (Brooks, 2005).

Keep in mind, however, that this childhood and adolescent advantage for girls' academic performance coexists with continuing male advantage in the workplace: Immediately after receiving a bachelor's degree, men are more likely than women to be working full time and to earn more money (Peter & Horn, 2005). Further, men still monopolize the highest status positions, earn significantly more money, and are more likely to be promoted than women (Reskin & Padovic, 2002). To the extent that there is any female advantage in childhood, it appears to be countervailed in adulthood. How this transition occurs—from girls outperforming boys in school to men outearning women as adults—is considered in more detail in Chapter 8.

What consequences arise from a less clear-cut and stable gender hierarchy in childhood gender relations? Social identity theory (Tajfel, 1981) suggests that when groups have relatively equal status and power differences are not stable, competition is enhanced as each group tries to find a way of gaining positive distinction (to show that "we" are better than "them"). One way group members construct a positive group identity is to value domains where they experience an advantage (Tajfel, 1981). For instance, many boys begin to place a strong value on the toughness and athletic skills that they see as distinguishing their sex from girls. At the same time, they may devalue academic performance (a domain in which girls perform better) as a source of status among peers. These social comparison processes reinforce the development of separate male and female "cultures" in childhood.

By contrast, when segregated roles (e.g., the traditional division of labor with men as breadwinners and women as homemakers) create stable power differences, both dominant and subordinate groups try to avoid direct conflict (Jackman, 1994). Dominants find conflict more costly than placating subordinates, and most subordinate group members find it in their own best interests not to buck the system by initiating a fight they are likely to lose. Thus, the absence of clear-cut and stable power differences in childhood may exacerbate competition between the sexes compared with adult gender relations.

Interdependence in Childhood

Another reason for the antagonism of childhood gender relations is a lack of incentive for children to avoid hostility toward the other sex. Heterosexual adults have powerful reasons for trying to get along because they typically view having a psychologically and physically intimate, fulfilling and long-lasting relationship with a person of the other sex as a key to a happy life. Cross-sex attractions occur before puberty but generally elicit disapproval from peers and are not yet energized by intense sexual longings. Thus, most children happily confine themselves mainly to same-sex peer interaction and do not have much incentive to indulge any cross-sex attractions they experience.

Younger children do, however, possess the cognitive understanding that some day they will be adults and that adults are expected to be attracted to members of the other sex. This occurs after children achieve gender constancy (Kohlberg, 1966). Gender constancy is defined as the realization not only that "I am a boy/girl" but also that gender identity is a permanent feature ("I will grow up to be a man/woman"). The achievement of gender constancy has been put as late as 7 years of age (Kohlberg, 1966) to as early as 3½ (Bem, 1989). For girls, the idea that they will, in an imagined future, become intimately interdependent with men does not appear to be rejected given that their pretend play often includes romantic and domestic fantasies (Maccoby, 1998). For example, play with the perennially popular Barbie doll focuses on improving her appearance (grooming, dressing, accessorizing) as a means to attract her beau, Ken. This suggest that girls imagine a future in which they will be in love with a man, but the implications this may have for current peer relations (that a girl might "like" a specific boy) tend to be denied (Sroufe, Bennet, England, Urban, & Shulman, 1993). Girls' early romantic fantasies that "someday a man will provide for me" may, however, have lasting effects. Adult women who have implicit romantic fantasies of men as their protectors and providers have lower career aspirations, presumably because they expect to rely on a male provider (Rudman & Heppen, 2003). Thus, girls' romantic fantasies suggest one reason why their early advantage in academic achievement does not translate into a female advantage (or even equality) in adult occupational achievement.

In comparison to girls, young boys evince much less interest in fantasizing a future in which they will have a heterosexual romantic relationship. As noted, their pretend play typically involves aggressive and heroic male action fantasies that do not typically include romance (Flannery & Watson, 1993). Further, boys show greater vigilance than girls in avoiding any appearance of romantic attraction to female peers. Boys' acceptance of tomboys hinges on viewing them as "one of the guys" and not as potential romantic partners. Boys distinguish tomboys from girls, making these "buddy" relationships safe from the usual taunting than any hint of romance would evoke (Thorne, 1997).

In conclusion, even if they acknowledge a future in which they will have a cross-sex romantic attachment, most young children have no need for peers of the other sex. Children are typically able to find plenty of same-sex peers to associate with and have a number of reasons for not interacting with other-sex peers, including peers' general disapproval of cross-sex friendships and teasing about anything that resembles heterosexual romantic attraction.

As children move from early to middle childhood, gender segregation intensifies. For those who are primarily heterosexual, however, sexual attraction eventually leads to looking at members of the other sex not just as rivals but as objects of attraction. This is not the end of sex segregation, because friendships remain primarily with same-sex others (Bukowski, Gauze, Hoza, & Newcomb, 1993; Larson & Richards, 1991), but the tenor of cross-sex relations abruptly changes as pubescent sexuality develops. For individuals with a homosexual orientation, the situation differs. Although homosexual attraction does not motivate attraction toward members of the other sex, homosexual males may find greater acceptance among heterosexual female peers because girls and women express considerably less antihomosexual prejudice than boys and men (Herek, 2002; Kite & Whitely, 1996).

Puberty, then, represents a particularly interesting time to consider gender relations because, for most individuals, it marks the beginning of a transition from childhood segregation to adult togetherness. For heterosexual adolescents, the separate cultures of childhood have not prepared them particularly well for interacting with the other sex. The conflict between male and female styles can no longer simply be avoided by failing to interact once boys and girls come together in heterosexual relationships. Interdependence changes many things, including not only attitudes about and behavior toward the other sex but also power relations and self-identity. We consider these changes in detail in the later chapters of this book on love (Chapter 9) and sex (Chapter 10).

Chapter Summary

Gender relations among children fundamentally differ from those among adults. Adult men and women typically interact on a daily basis, often in intimate, interdependent relationships. By contrast, children's social world, to the extent that they control it, resembles a gendered version of apartheid in which segregation goes hand in hand with hostile intergroup attitudes. These adult and childhood differences indicate that gender socialization is not simply a matter of children mimicking adults' attitudes and behaviors; children construct their own social world and actively use gender as an organizing principle to do so. Children certainly pick up gender-related cultural values and images and make inferences about gender based on observations of the structure of adult society (e.g., noting that men and women often perform different roles and occupations). What children pick up from society and adults, however, is not passively adopted rather is, but actively used to inform their constructions of gendered identities.

Childhood sex segregation appears to have its roots in differing male and female styles of interaction that emerge early in life, with boys exhibiting a rougher, more aggressive, and competitive style in contrast to girls' more polite and cooperative mode of interaction. Even as toddlers, boys show greater insistence about getting what they want and girls, as a consequence, begin to avoid them. These interaction style differences appear to have a biological component but are also reinforced by parents' encouragement of boys to be rougher and tougher than girls. Avoidance of other-sex peers becomes mutual, and boys soon exceed girls in enforcing sex segregation. Egalitarian adults who attempt to tamper with these child-enforced norms quickly find the limits to their influence as childhood peer groups become much more important as a source of influence than adults.

Throughout middle childhood, segregation is accompanied by increasingly hostile attitudes toward the other sex. The intensity of this hostility cannot be fully explained by differing interaction styles and activity and toy preferences, which alone might breed aloof indifference. Rather, gender becomes an important, self-relevant social identity. Children's stake in gaining positive differentiation (group esteem) for their gender in-group fosters social comparisons in which each sex derogates the other. Masculine and feminine gender identities, initially constructed around the simple fact of group membership (e.g., "I am a boy"), develop into elaborate norms about masculinity (being tough, assertive, and competitive) versus femininity (being soft, gentle, and cooperative). Children, especially boys, who violate gender norms (e.g., by playing with toys considered to be inappropriate for members of their sex) may not only face the disapproval of adults but, more importantly for most children, painful rejection by their peers.

Once puberty arrives, however, attitudes about the other sex begin to change rapidly as, for most people, heterosexual attraction becomes energized by sexual desire. Although this represents a radical break from earlier attitudes toward the other sex, earlier habits of mind and behavior do not simply disappear. In the next two chapters, we focus on how gender stereotyping continues to affect gender relations in adulthood.

CHAPTER 4

Content and Origins of Gender Stereotypes

Consider women as a group: What personality traits are stereotypically associated with this category? (Note: You do not have to believe stereotypes are correct to know their contents, so please play along.) Write down the personality traits that most quickly come to mind as stereotypically feminine. Now write down the personality traits that most quickly come to mind as stereotypically masculine.

Because gender stereotypes represent a form of cultural knowledge to which everyone has repeatedly been exposed, this task should have been relatively easy. Even if you personally do not agree with a particular stereotype, like an advertising jingle you have heard too often, stereotypes tend to "stick in your head" (i.e., to be highly mentally accessible whether you like it or not). If you followed the instructions to list the stereotyped traits of women and men, look over the traits you produced for women. Typical traits you might have generated include empathy, warmth, kindness, and consideration for others' feelings. On the negative end, you may have produced traits such as overly emotional, dependent, and weak. In contrast, while you may have associated men with positive traits, such as competence and ambition, you may also have thought of negative traits, including arrogance, hypercompetitiveness, and insensitivity toward others. Keep the list you generated handy; we will come back to it later in the chapter.

These differences in how men and women are characterized have often been tied to agentic and communal dimensions, first offered by Bakan (1966) as two "fundamental modalities" by which people live. He defined agentic as a mode of being in which the individual focuses on achieving his or her own needs, whereas communal refers to living a life that connects to others. Stereotypes of men stress agency (e.g., looking out for oneself, seeking to fulfill one's own goals, being task oriented), whereas stereotypes of women emphasize communality (e.g., having consideration for others, seeking connections, exhibiting empathy and understanding).

This chapter expands on themes developed in prior chapters: the association of girls and women with gentleness, kindness, and softness (which are consistent with communal) compared with the association of boys and men with toughness, competitiveness, and assertiveness (which are consistent with agentic). In each case, the stereotype represents a trade-off between communality and warmth (stereotypically female but not male traits) versus agency and dominance (stereotypically male but not female traits). In short, men are stereotyped as "bad but bold" and women as "wonderful but weak." Although these stereotypes suggest greater liking for women, they accord men more respect, reinforcing gender differences in power.

More specifically, the current chapter covers (1) the content, origins, and cross-cultural consistency of gender stereotypes; (2) the evaluative aspects of gender stereotypes; and (3) how gender subtypes elaborate on and encapsulate exceptions to broader stereotypes of men and women. We focus on gender stereotypes as socially shared conceptions of women and men; in the chapters that follow, we will show how these cultural conceptions create gender-related expectations and ideals (Chapter 5) and how these ideals, in turn, pressure people to conform to gendered norms (Chapter 6).

Categorization and Stereotyping

Stereotypes are knowledge structures that associate members of social categories with specific attributes, which form the content of the stereotype. This chapter focuses on cultural stereotypes, stereotypes that are widely socially shared, at least in the sense that people within a society have a common understanding of the content of the stereotype. That is, if you compared how you responded to the requested listing of stereotypical traits of women and men, you would probably find that many others generated similar kinds of traits.

This does not necessarily mean that individuals agree with the stereotypes or see them as correct. Cultural stereotypes can be distinguished from personal stereotypes, which reflect more idiosyncratic personal beliefs. However, the fact that gender stereotypes (as illustrated later) have a high degree of social consensus (i.e., people agree about their general content) lends them credibility. People are often swayed by the logic that "if everyone agrees, it must be true," especially when it comes to perceptions of social groups (Crandall & Stangor, 2005; Stangor, Sechrist, & Jost, 2001).

Stereotypes focus on attributes that distinguish members of a group from people who fit into alternative categories. Stereotypical attributes are not absolutely necessary for category membership (Allport, 1954/1979). For instance, possessing both an X and a Y chromosome constitutes the only necessary attribute for being classified as male. Stereotypes of men, however, contain characteristics that are associated with, but are not necessary for, maleness. For example, having facial hair is strongly associated with being male but is not a defining characteristic of the category (i.e., a man who grows no facial hair still fits into the category of male).

Therefore, even when people endorse a particular stereotype, they recognize that their stereotypes represent probabilistic associations. Someone who claims that "men are more competitive than women" generally does not mean that "all men are more competitive than all women" (i.e., that the least competitive man in the world exceeds the competitiveness of the most competitive woman). In reality, group differences between men and women on specific psychological traits pale in comparison to the variability of individual differences within each sex category (e.g., between different women; Hyde, 2005; see Chapter 1, especially Figure 1.1, which illustrates the high degree of overlap for most traits that show gender differences). Given people's daily exposure to a variety of individuals of both sexes, only the dullest and most rigid person could maintain simplistic stereotypes of "all women" and "all men."

The probabilistic nature of stereotypes suggests considerable flexibility in how people apply them. Ironically, however, it also makes stereotypes remarkably resistant to disconfirmation. Because people expect "exceptions to the rule" to occur, they do not easily abandon their stereotypes unless those exceptions become so frequent that they shake the foundations of the stereotyped belief. A person who stereotypes men as more competitive than women is unlikely to revise this belief because of an encounter with a few exceedingly competitive women (we review, in detail, how people handle such exceptions later in this chapter).

Gender Categorization Is Primary

Categorization is a necessary first step for stereotypes to develop. For example, the ability to distinguish among nationalities, ethnicities, and religions is what allows stereotypes about different groups to emerge. Classification is aided by physical differences between groups (e.g., skin color, facial features, and height) or other noticeable features (e.g., clothing and language). Someone who failed to distinguish among Christians, Muslims, and Jews could not have beliefs about which attributes are associated with each group. Similarly, if people did not categorize others as male or female, gender stereotypes would not exist. However, because people learn very early in life to classify others as male and female (see Chapter 3), gender categorization becomes a quick, automatic process. Try *not* categorizing the next stranger you meet as male or female; we suspect that you will find it impossible to be truly "gender blind." The importance of gender categorization in daily social interaction is revealed in those rare cases in which someone's sex category is ambiguous. When we encounter such an individual, the question "Is that a he or a she?" swamps all other considerations, and the uncertainty of the answer creates significant discomfort for most perceivers.

Research using the "who said what" method, a paradigm that reveals who perceivers tend to lump together, shows the importance of gender as a way of categorizing others (Taylor, Fiske, Etcoff, & Ruderman, 1978). Imagine watching a conversation among a diverse group of people and later being tested on "who said what?" You are more likely to confuse people whom you spontaneously (perhaps unconsciously) categorized together. Thus, if you categorized by gender, you might misattribute a statement made by Anna to Wendy but not to Paul. This paradigm suggests the primacy of gender categorization. For instance, when targets vary by race (Black and White) as well as by sex, within-sex errors occur significantly more frequently than within-race errors, showing that people spontaneously make greater use of sex than race when categorizing others (Stangor, Lynch, Duan, & Glass, 1992). The same thing occurs outside the laboratory. Both recall and diary methodologies reveal that, in daily life, people of the same sex get mistaken for each other more frequently than people of similar age, race, height, build, or occupational role (A. P. Fiske, Haslam, & Fiske, 1991).

Of course, perceivers *could* categorize others based on necessary or defining features without making any further stereotypical inferences. For instance, one could imagine a person who classifies others as male or female, but stops there, making no further assumptions based on gender. Our minds, however, do not work this way. Rather, people categorize others into groups precisely because it allows them to make assumptions about what others are like, simplifying an otherwise overly complex social world.

Imagine treating each new individual you meet without making any assumptions based on the various categories into which you normally put them. Consider how disruptive it would be if, as a lawyer, you walked into the courtroom on the first day of a trial and failed to classify others based on the categories of judge and lawyer but instead treated the judge as just another participant in a casual social setting. If your greeting was informal ("Hey there, how's it going?"), no matter how friendly the judge, she or he would probably not respond well to your failure to categorize and to act on the normal distinction between judge and attorney in the courtroom context.

This example illustrates some important points. Social categories tend to be associated with different social roles and functions. The judge and the lawyer have different roles in the courtroom, and for the trial to proceed smoothly everyone must understand and agree on these categories and the roles they imply. Daily life typically relies on categorization and the various assumptions (stereotypes and scripted roles) that social categories entail. Further, categories are often related to social status (e.g., the judge is supposed to have greater status in the courtroom than the lawyer).

The cultural ubiquity of gender as an important social characteristic is, like the judge–lawyer distinction, also rooted in role and status differences. These social structural differences, in turn, can explain why gender stereotypes take the form that they do as well as why people generally agree (even across various cultures) about which traits are stereotypically female versus male. However, although the categories of judge and lawyer legitimately create assumptions about, for example, who has the authority to lead the trial, gender categorization and stereotyping can create unfair treatment.

The Content and Origins of Gender Stereotypes

Gender stereotypes include a variety of attributes commonly associated with men versus women. These include physical characteristics (e.g., men as physically strong and women as delicate), preferences and interests (e.g., assuming that women like to shop and men like to watch and play sports), social roles (e.g., women as primary caregivers in the family and men as protectors and providers), and occupations (e.g., men as miners, stockbrokers, and engineers; women as nurses, elementary school teachers, and domestic workers; e.g., see Ashmore, Del Boca, & Bilder, 1995). Psychological research, however, has focused mainly on the personality traits that gender stereotypes assign to men and women.

Decades of studies show that gender stereotypes attribute traits related to agency, ambition, and power to men and traits related to nurturing, empathy, and concern for others to women (Deaux, 1995; Spence & Buckner, 2000; Twenge, 1997a). These constellations of traits have been labeled variously as an agentic, instrumental, or competence dimension (emphasizing the notion of "agency" or being active, assertive, and task oriented) for "masculine" traits and as a communal, expressive, or warmth dimension (emphasizing concern for others, the expression of feelings, and putting others' needs above one's own) for "feminine" traits.

Is the Content of Gender Stereotypes Determined by Gender Roles and Hierarchy?

As discussed in Chapter 1, social role theory proposes that the personality traits associated with the two sexes follow from the different social roles and jobs that men and women occupy as well as differences in social status associated with these roles. Another way of stating this hypothesis is that the traits associated with women ought to reflect the characteristics one would generate in response to the questions, "What does it take to be a mother?" (the traditional domestic role associated with women) and "What are the characteristics of people in low-status positions"? By contrast, the traits associated with men ought to reflect those that one would generate in response to the questions, "What does it take to be a protector and provider?" (the traditional roles associated with men) and "What are the traits of people with high status and power?"

Research confirms that simply telling people about a division of labor between imaginary groups creates similar stereotypes to those associated with men and women. One study described an alien society in which Orinthians were typically "city workers' and Ackmians were usually "child raisers" (Hoffman & Hurst, 1990). Specifically, participants read descriptions of 15 members of each group that listed each individual's social group, occupation, and personality traits (e.g., "Damorian is an Orinthian who works in the city and is individualistic, warm, and creative").

Each description included one agentic, one communal, and one gender-neutral trait (so that the individual Orinthians' and Ackmians' personalities were described as equally "masculine" and "feminine"). However, the roles associated with each group differed such that 12 of 15 Orinthians were city workers and only three were child raisers, with the reverse ratio used for the Ackmians. Despite the fact that each Ackmian and Orinthian was assigned both agentic and communal personality traits, the information about their typical roles (city worker vs. child raiser) led participants to perceive the two groups quite differently. Overall, participants rated the Orinthians (mostly city workers) as the more agentic group and the Ackmians (mostly child raisers) as the more communal group. In short, the traits associated with the roles typically performed by the group not only became associated with each group but also produced gender-like group stereotypes. This occurred even though the personality trait information about individual group members did not support these role-based stereotypes. Thus, this study suggests that stereotypes are inferred from roles and not from observation of the traits of individual members of each group.

Interestingly, people may generate precisely the same kinds of gender-like stereotypes in response to manipulations of status as they do for manipulations of roles. People tend to assume that high-status group members have more agentic or competent traits, whereas low-status group members are assumed to have communal, warm, and expressive traits. People infer that members of groups at the top of the social hierarchy must be competent and ambitious (Eagly, Wood, & Dickman, 2000; S. T. Fiske et al., 2002). By contrast, because those who have little power need to be careful to secure high-power people's good will, perceivers often assume that low-status group members are warm and expressive, although this effect disappears when the low-status group is viewed as dangerous, uncooperative, or exploitative or as agitators for social change (S. T. Fiske et al., 2002).

Using the same strategy of describing fictional groups, Conway, Pizzamiglio, and Mount (1996) manipulated groups' relative status while being careful to say that the groups had similar roles. The Bwisi and Mwangai were described as Pacific Islanders. To manipulate status, one group was said to have more elaborate clothes, a more prominent place in religious rituals, and access to special foods (note that there was no manipulation of occupational or child-rearing roles). Participants rated the higher status group as relatively more agentic and the lower status group as relatively more communal.

In sum, the gendered division of labor and gender hierarchy work hand in hand, leading people to associate agentic competence with men and communal warmth with women. By seeing how people respond to fictional groups about whom they have no prior assumptions, while separately manipulating roles and status, researchers have established that gender roles and gender hierarchy are each sufficient to create gender stereotypes. In addition, regardless of whether roles (e.g., working outside the home vs. child rearing) or status indicators are manipulated, similar stereotypes are generated. Of course, in real life roles and status tend to be intertwined, with men's roles not only demanding greater agency but being accorded greater status and women's roles not only requiring nurturance but also having lower status. Further, because gender is so strongly associated with these role and status differences, gender itself becomes a diffuse status characteristic (or cue to status) that generally lends men more authority than women (Ridgeway, 2001a, 2001b; Rudman & Kilianski, 2000).

Cross-Cultural Consistencies in Stereotype Content

Because a gendered division of labor and a gender hierarchy exist in roughly similar forms across many cultures, social role theory (Eagly et al., 2000) predicts cross-cultural consensus about which traits are associated with men and women. In other words, if women have a nurturing role and men a breadwinner role in most cultures, gender stereotypes should be cross-culturally similar rather than different. The most extensive examination of the content of gender stereotypes across cultures was conducted by J. E. Williams and Best (1990) and their collaborators, who examined gender stereotypes in 25 nations across the globe (in North and South America, Europe, Africa, and Asia).

These researchers used a list of 300 personality traits previously developed by personality researchers (not specifically to assess gender stereotypes but to create a comprehensive tool for assessing personality). Participants rated each trait on this list, known as the Adjective Check List (Gough & Heilbrun, 1980), indicating whether the trait is "more frequently associated with men than with women," "more frequently associated with women than with men," or "not differentially associated with the two sexes" (J. E. Williams & Best, 1990, p. 21).

This method has some weaknesses. First, accurately translating traits into different languages while keeping their meaning constant is difficult; even in nations that share the same language, specific traits may have different connotations in popular usage (e.g., the United States and England have been characterized as "two nations separated by a common language"). Second, the picture of gender stereotypes one obtains may differ if people generate their own list of traits as opposed to responding to one provided by the researcher. Third, the method uses a relatively simple forced-choice response format that may not yield finer distinctions about which traits are most strongly associated with each sex. Fourth, the researchers were unable to obtain a random selection of nations or random samples of participants within those nations. Nevertheless, Williams and Best's research has great value: It is unique in its scope and attention to the content of stereotypes in a diverse set of nations, yielding significant insight into cross-cultural consistencies in gender stereotypes.

Table 4.1 (adapted from J. E. Williams & Best, 1990) lists the personality traits that yield the most cross-national agreement as stereotypically female or male. Specifically, the traits in Table 4.1 were rated as strongly associated with men or with women in at least 20 of the 25 nations studied. For the most part, these traits match the content

TABLE 4.1. Gender Stereotypes across 25 Nations

Masculine traits	Feminine traits
Adventurous	Sentimental
Dominant	Submissive
Forceful	Superstitious
Independent	Affectionate
Strong	Dreamy
Aggressive	Sensitive
Autocratic	Attractive
Daring	Dependent
Enterprising	Emotional
Robust	Fearful
Stern	Soft-hearted
Active	Weak
Courageous	Sexy
Progressive	Curious
Rude	Gentle
Severe	Mild
Unemotional	Charming
Wise	Talkative

Note. Adapted from Williams and Best (1990). Copyright 1990 by Sage Publications, Inc. Adapted by permission.

of male–female stereotypes in the United States and, overall, seem to fit the expectations of social structural theories, such as ambivalent sexism theory and social role theory. Consistent with the former, men appear to be perceived as bad (e.g., aggressive, rude) but bold (competent, adventurous, active) and women as wonderful (warm, affectionate gentle) but weak (submissive, dependent, fearful). In terms of social role theory, women's wonderful traits suit them to nurturing others and their weak traits reinforce their lower status in a gender hierarchy. By contrast, men's bold traits suit them to the roles of protector and provider, suggesting they have the competence and courage required to fulfill these roles, and their bad (as well as bold) traits reinforce their power and status, characterizing them as suited to dominate and to lead when the going gets tough.

Other analyses of these data support the idea that the cross-cultural similarity between gender stereotypes stems from gender roles and gender hierarchy. J. E. Williams and Best (1990) examined the relationship of the stereotypical male and female traits generated in each nation to basic motivations taken from Murray's (1938) classic taxonomy of human needs. Some of the motives Murray described clearly represent a quest for power, status, and achievement. These include dominance (strong-willed pursuit of own goals even at the expense of others), autonomy (being independent of others), aggression (a competitive orientation toward others), exhibition (a desire for social recognition of one's achievements), and achievement (being hardworking and goal oriented). Other basic human motives reflect a desire to nurture, please, and get along with others more than to obtain or exercise personal power. These include nurturance (being cooperative and sympathetic toward others), succorance (desire to avoid of confrontation with others), deference (preferring to let others be in charge), and abasement (subordinating one's own needs to those of others).

The traits that people in each nation most strongly associated with each sex were rated (by a set of well-informed American judges) on each of Murray's motivational dimensions. Stereotypically masculine traits consistently related to power and achievement motives, whereas stereotypically feminine traits were related to nurturing, relationships, and power-avoidant motives. In all of the nations, the stereotypical male traits were higher on all of the power- and achievement-related motives than were stereotypical female traits. Similarly, in all nations, stereotypically female traits were higher on all of the motives related to being nurturing and avoiding power in comparison to stereotypically male traits.

Evaluative Aspects of Gender Stereotypes: Liking versus Respect

Go back and consider the traits you listed, in response to the request at the beginning of this chapter, as stereotypically male versus female. You may want to compare them with the traits that are cross-culturally stereotyped as masculine and feminine in Table 4.1 to see whether the traits you listed express similar themes of agency and communality. Additionally, separately consider each set of traits you generated (for men and for women). How favorable and likable are these traits? If you are similar to most American research participants, the traits you associated with women are more positive (on the whole) than the traits you associated with men (Eagly & Mladinic, 1989, 1993).

Initially, the finding, at least in the United States, of greater favorability in attitudes toward and stereotypes of women compared with men (Eagly & Mladinic, 1989) was a bit of a shock to researchers because it contradicted a truism that relatively disadvantaged or low-status groups are viewed less positively than advantaged or dominant groups (Allport, 1954/1979; Jost & Banaji, 1994; Jost et al., 2001). Negative stereotypes have long been assumed to reinforce lower status groups' disadvantage; for example, stereotypes of a group's incompetence make it less likely that employers will hire a member of that group. As noted in Chapter 2, objective indicators of status and power across the globe show a relative disadvantage for women compared with men, yet women tend to be better liked than men.

If you look again at Table 4.1, you will see that many of the traits listed on both sides are desirable, but the desirable traits associated with each sex correspond to quite different dimensions. People's evaluations of others typically occur on two dimensions, with one dimension representing traits related to an individual's power, ability, and status and the other concerning likeability, agreeableness, and nurturance toward others. Whether this distinction is labeled as competence versus warmth (Fiske et al., 2002) or agency versus communion (Abele & Wojciszke, 2007), there is increasing evidence and consensus among researchers that these represent the fundamental dimensions by which people are perceived (accounting for more than 80% of the variance in people's impressions of others; Wojciszke, Bazinska, & Jaworski, 1998). Across cultures, favorable stereotypical male traits typically reflect agentic competence and favorable stereotypical female traits reflect communal warmth.

Agentic competence breeds respect, whereas communal warmth fosters liking (Wojciszke, 2005). We *respect* others who have the traits enabling them to achieve positions of power and influence, the skills and competencies to get what they want, and the drive to achieve. Such people have traits, motives, and skills oriented toward fulfilling their own goals. By contrast, we *like* others who are helpful, are sensitive to others' needs, and empathize with others' concerns. Such people are oriented more toward fulfilling others' goals rather than focusing on their own ambitions.

Although people often respect and like the same individual, these two types of evaluation can be independent, and this is especially true when considering group perception (S. T. Fiske et al., 2002). Consider your attitude toward a tough but highly capable leader in your life, who demanded your compliance with his or her agenda (such as a tough coach or challenging teacher). You may not always have liked (or may even have intensely disliked) this person, but he or she commanded your respect. By contrast, you no doubt have known somebody who is highly agreeable, sympathetic, and accommodating. Such people are easy to get along with and highly likeable, but they risk losing the respect of others, especially if their eagerness to please leads them to suppress their own opinions, goals, and needs.

Taken to the extreme, the stereotypically "masculine" type achieves respect but sacrifices being liked because personal ambitions override any concern for or accommodation to others. The positively evaluated traits of assertiveness, independence, and ambition can, if overdone, become rebelliousness, stubbornness, and arrogance. Both the positive and negative versions of these traits are "self-profitable" (Peeters, 1983) or, in popular parlance, involve "looking out for Number 1." By contrast, if taken to an extreme, the stereotypically feminine type elicits liking at the cost of being disrespected. Concern for others, empathy, and loyalty can become dependence, naïveté, weakness, and gullibility (i.e., being a self-sacrificing doormat that others constantly tread on). These stereotypical female traits are "other-profitable" (Peeters, 1983): of benefit to others but not directly beneficial to the individual who possesses them.

Thus, people view having agentic competence as more important and relevant for themselves, but generally prefer others to show communal warmth (Abele & Wojciszke, 2007). And perceptions of others' warmth typically have a greater effect on overall feelings toward others than judgments of their competence (Wojciszke, 2005). This helps to explain why women generally received more favorable evaluations than men when Americans were asked to indicate their overall attitudes (Eagly & Mladinic, 1989, 1993). Nonetheless, being respected (even if not liked) carries distinct advantages if one's overall aim is to have status and power.

Do people in nations other than the United States also have more positive stereotypes of women than men? J. E. Williams and Best (1990) attempted to answer this question by having American judges rate the favorability of each of the 300 traits that participants in other nations had rated as masculine or feminine. Averaging across 25 nations, Williams and Best found slightly more favorable stereotypes of men than of women; however, the overall difference was quite small. Further, within almost half of the individual nations studied, the feminine stereotype was more favorable than the masculine stereotype. Consistent with other research involving Americans (Eagly & Mladinic, 1993), the United States was one of the nations in which the female stereotype was rated more favorably than the male stereotype.

Recall, however, that the favorability ratings of each trait were derived from American raters' views, not from informants within each of the nations Williams and Best studied. Because American judges may have a different sense of each trait's favorability than people in other nations and some connotations may be altered by translation, these ratings need to be interpreted with considerable caution. More recent research on the favorability of gender stereotypes in seven nations used a different and, arguably, better method (Glick et al., 2004). Specifically, instead of having people respond to a predetermined adjective checklist, participants generated their own list of traits they personally associate with men and women (known as spontaneous stereotypes). Each participant then rated the favorability of the traits he or she had generated on a –3 (*extremely unfavorable*) to +3 (*extremely favorable*) scale. Having participants list the traits themselves should have more accurately captured what people habitually think of men and women. Also, because participants judged the favorability of each trait themselves, the meaning or connotation of traits could not get lost in translation. Average favorability ratings for stereotypes of men and women in each nation are reported in Figure 4.1. Although stereotypes of each gender were, on average, rated positively, stereotypes of women were more positive than stereotypes of men in every nation studied.

Thus, depending on which method is preferred, the cross-cultural research suggests that people possess about as favorable (J. E. Williams & Best, 1990) or more favorable (Glick et al., 2004) stereotypes of women than of men. Given the methodological problems with Williams and

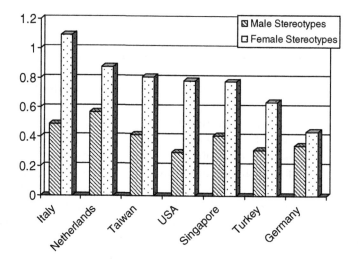

FIGURE 4.1. Favorability of male and female stereotypes across cultures. Ratings could potentially range from –3 (*extremely unfavorable*) to +3 (*extremely favorable*). Data from Glick et al. (2004).

Best's use of American judges to rate trait favorability, the latter conclusion seems more likely. In either case, it is clear that general beliefs about women do not reflect antipathy or dislike.

In sum, cross-cultural studies of gender stereotypes indicate that people across the globe associate men with agency, power, and dominance and women with nurturance, succorance, and deference. Cross-cultural variation occurs on favorability ratings of gender stereotypes, but women generally appear to fare well when it comes to liking. By contrast, stereotypes across cultures consistently suggest associations of men with power and status. In short, people like women but have greater respect for men.

The existence of so much cross-cultural agreement about the content of gender stereotypes fits with social structural theories but contradicts a purely cultural approach (see Chapter 1 for this distinction). If stereotypes were merely the products of accidental historical circumstances and culture-specific beliefs as the cultural approach supposes, greater cross-cultural variability in gender stereotypes should occur. By contrast, we have argued that the cross-cultural consistency in gender stereotypes can be explained through a social structural approach: Similarities in stereotypes occur because of cross-cultural similarities in social structure, including common gender roles (men as protectors and providers; women as nurturers) and power differences between the sexes (see Chapter 2 on the ubiquity of male dominance). Evolutionary perspectives offer another alternative: that gender stereotypes show cross-cultural consistency because they reflect biologically based, and therefore pan-cultural, differences between women and men (Buss, 2003). This explanation casts gender stereotypes as accurate reflections of the ways that men and women naturally differ. The next section reviews evidence that gender stereotypes may be more accurate than once thought. However, even if perceivers are accurate about average differences between men and women, group stereotypes still create unfair discrimination when applied to judgments about individuals. Also, stereotype accuracy about average differences between the sexes does not imply that these differences have biological origins.

Are Stereotypes Exaggerated or Accurate?

Prejudice theorists have long assumed that stereotypes may contain a kernel of truth but are greatly exaggerated and, therefore, inaccurate (Allport, 1954/1979). After all, if stereotypes serve to simplify a complex social world, they can only do so by sacrificing accuracy (i.e., by conveniently lumping diverse individuals into general categories). Consistent with this view, perceivers generally view out-groups as more homogeneous (*they* are all alike) compared with in-groups (*we* are all individuals). This tendency is known as the out-group homogeneity effect (for a review, see Ostrom & Sedikides, 1992). Further, when people form new categories, they overestimate similarities within categories and differences between them (Tajfel, 1981). In other words, categorization appears to promote the formation of exaggerated stereotypes.

With respect to gender stereotypes, research presented earlier in this chapter showed that people construct and maintain gender-like stereotypes of fictional groups of city workers versus child raisers even when information about individual group members contradicts those stereotypes (Hoffman & Hurst, 1990). Additionally, numerous studies, involving gender as well as other social groupings, show how stereotypes lead to biased (i.e., inaccurate) perceptions of individual category members (these processes, which concern the application of stereotypes, are reviewed in Chapter 5). Stereotypes, once formed, resist change and result in inaccurate perceptions of individuals who are subjected to those stereotypes.

Assessing the overall accuracy of stereotypes, however, is quite complicated (see Judd & Park, 2005, for an excellent discussion of the issues). Stereotype accuracy is usually assessed by how well people estimate average differences between groups. But this is not the only form of accuracy; how well people estimate the variability of a trait within groups is also important (Judd & Park, 2005). That is, accurate gender stereotypes would not only correctly estimate the average difference between men and women on a host of traits (e.g., nurturance, aggression) but also accurately specify how much variation exists within each sex (e.g., how much women vary on specific traits, such as nurturance or aggressiveness). A glance back at Figure 1.1 illustrates the importance of examining variability within groups, not just average differences.

To examine the accuracy of gender stereotypes, Swim (1994) asked participants to estimate average sex differences on various traits (e.g., helpfulness, math skills, verbal skills, and aggression). She then compared these estimates with those obtained by several published meta-analyses of sex differences for these same traits. This method yielded mixed support for gender stereotype accuracy across two studies in that people tended to estimate actual sex differences accurately 38% of the time, to overestimate sex differences 28% of the time, and to underestimate sex differences 34% of the time. In addition, the same stereotype (e.g., the tendency to emerge as a leader) was either overestimated or underestimated, depending on the specific sample; only one trait (happy) was rated consistently accurately (Swim, 1994). A later study that also used this method found that, across five samples, participants' stereotypes correlated reasonably well with research on sex differences (median rs = .36–.47; Hall & Carter, 1999). However, both studies also noted considerable variation in individuals' accuracy. For example, people who endorsed cultural stereotypes, scored high on social dominance orientation, evinced a rigid cognitive style, or showed less interpersonal sensitivity reported exaggerated stereotypes (Hall & Carter, 1999).

Overall, when it comes to estimating average sex differences, people do not appear consistently to overestimate, as earlier prejudice researchers assumed. But whether stereotypes are accurate remains unclear. Recall, however, that even if people could accurately estimate average differences between the sexes, they may still be inaccurate in another way: by overestimating similarities within each group (Judd & Park, 2005). Unfortunately, variability estimates have not been a focus of research on the accuracy of gender stereotypes. As noted in Chapter 1, research on sex differences reveals that, for most attributes, the variation within each sex (e.g., among individual women) is much greater than average differences between the sexes (Hyde, 2005).

Being perceptually attuned to average differences while ignoring the considerable variation within groups easily leads to unfair discrimination when group stereotypes are applied to individuals (Eagly & Diekman, 2005). For example, even if women on average were less assertive than men, it is not fair to automatically assume that an individual woman is less assertive than an individual man and to deny her a job based on this assumption. Unfortunately, when people interact, they typically interpret ambiguous information about others as being consistent with stereotyped expectations (e.g., Darley & Gross, 1983) and also actively elicit behavior that confirms those expectations (Snyder, 1984). To make matters worse, people have implicit (or automatic) gender stereotypes that can leak into judgments and behaviors without people's awareness (e.g., Banaji & Hardin, 1996; Banaji, Hardin, & Rothman, 1993; Banaji & Greenwald, 1995). All of these processes, reviewed in more detail in Chapters 5 and 6, can have a snowball effect, perpetuating unfair gender discrimination.

Additionally, sex differences in behavior, whether accurately perceived or not, do not imply biological origins for those differences. The social structural perspective predicts that differences in men's and women's roles and status produce and sustain sex differences in behavior. Gender stereotypes thus gain accuracy because people are pressured and trained to behave in role-consistent and stereotype-consistent ways (see Chapters 6 and 7). Indeed, people readily and flexibly adapt to the roles they are asked to play and their status within those roles. One of social psychology's most famous studies showed that the behavior of normal college students randomly assigned as "guards" and "prisoners" in a simulated prison quickly exhibited extremely different kinds of behavior, determined by their relative roles and power, not some "essence" of their being (Haney, Banks, & Zimbardo, 1973). The students assigned the powerful role of guard acted with forcefulness, assertion, and (for some) callousness, in keeping with their conceptions of the role and their situational power. Other students assigned to be prisoners showed (after an initial phase of rebellion) deference, anxiety, and fearfulness, traits consistent with and elicited by a subordinate and powerless role.

When social categories are confounded with underlying biological categories (as they are in the case of gender), people too readily leap to essentialistic inferences. For instance, when Hoffman and Hurst

(1990) told participants that their fictional groups of city workers and child raisers were biologically different—not just members of the same species with different social roles—participants formed more extreme stereotypes about the groups. Thus, people readily infer that gender differences are produced by biology rather than situational factors, such as differing roles and status, even though research shows that social roles and power strongly influence behavior.

In sum, although the question of stereotype accuracy remains a vexing issue for researchers, keep in mind that (1) even "accurate" stereotypes about average group differences can lead to unfair discrimination against individual members of groups, (2) discriminatory processes, such as assigning men and women to different social roles, can themselves create stereotype accuracy (i.e., stereotypes may become accurate because of the pervasiveness of discrimination) and, therefore, (3) evidence of stereotype accuracy is not evidence for biological differences between men and women. Although current research suggests that gender stereotypes contain more than a kernel of truth about average differences in men's and women's behavior, abundant evidence also shows that gender stereotypes of agency and communality are rooted in social structural causes and lead to inaccurate perceptions and unfair treatment of individual men and women.

Levels of Categorization: Stereotypes and Subtypes

We have noted that overall stereotypes of women and men represent beliefs about average differences between the sexes. But how do stereotypes accommodate the high degree of within-sex variability in the traits and behaviors individual men and women exhibit? One answer is that people regularly place women and men into more specific gender subtypes (e.g., career woman, jock, homemaker, family man). Given the breadth of the roles men and women occupy, as well as the frequent daily interaction people have with members of both sexes, gender subtyping may be inevitable. Ironically, however, rather than replacing or diminishing general stereotypes of men and women, subtyping helps to maintain them, in part, by "fencing off" exceptions to the overall stereotypic rules.

Overall stereotypes of groups persist partly because people admit exceptions to the stereotype to preserve the general stereotypic rule. Such flexibility allows perceivers to maintain their stereotypes when individual category members obviously violate categorical expectations (Allport, 1954/1979). For example, perceivers do not abandon the general belief that "Norwegians like to ski" after meeting one Norwegian who hates skiing. But what happens when exceptions to the rule are much more frequent, as happens in the case of gender, which splits humans into two broad categories? When the exceptions build, people must either revise their overall stereotype or use the exceptions to create subcategories. Perceivers generally prefer the latter option. Most perceivers do not discard the stereotype of women as gentle and kind when they repeatedly encounter women who do not act in accordance with this expectation (see Green, Ashmore, & Manzi, 2005). Instead, these women are placed into a subcategory, such as "she-devil" or "bitch." Similarly, perceivers do not give up their stereotypes of men as aggressive and bold because of some experiences with timid men; rather, the exceptions are placed into subtypes such as "nerd" or "wimp."

The frequency with which people run into exceptions to overall gender categories is not the only reason for gender subtyping. The elaboration, encapsulation, and evaluation (E^3) model of subtyping (Green et al., 2005) proposes several processes that drive the formation of subtypes. "Elaboration" refers to the need to go beyond broad categories to develop more specific and socially useful categories that can guide everyday interaction. "Encapsulation" refers to the process (already discussed) of creating subtypes to "encapsulate" (or contain) people who deviate from stereotyped expectations. "Evaluation" refers to the fact that subtypes (like general stereotypes) involve evaluative judgments, such as whether perceivers view subtypes favorably or unfavorably.

Elaboration recognizes that gender stereotypes are not limited to personality traits (the focus of most gender stereotyping research) but also encompass social roles, occupations, and physical appearance (Ashmore et al., 1995; Deaux & Lewis, 1984). For instance, thus far we have emphasized that women and men have different social roles, but each sex has more than one kind of traditional role. Consider the variety of heavily male-dominated occupations, ranging from all facets of the military to business management positions (e.g., president, CEO) to professionals (e.g., engineers, lawyers) to blue-collar workers (e.g., miners, construction workers). All of these occupations fit the category of masculine (at least in terms of sex ratios of who holds these jobs) and represent conventionally acceptable ways to enact a male role. But these jobs differ on a number of dimensions, such as social class, power, the masculine personality traits they emphasize, and their degree of physicality. Or consider the traditional female social roles of mother, nurse, teacher, fashion model, and sex object. Each is feminine but emphasizes different aspects of femininity. Thinking of mothers leads to a focus on stereotypically feminine nurturance, whereas thinking of fashion models leads to a focus on physical appearance and sexuality, representing different ways of enacting femininity.

In other words, as Green et al. (2005) point out, not only do subtypes encapsulate frequent exceptions to the general stereotype, but they also elaborate on distinctly different ways in which people can act in a stereotype-consistent manner. Subtypes such as "hottie" (sex object) and grandmother (nurturing role) both represent conventional feminine types but clearly emphasize dissimilar aspects of the overall stereotype of women. These subtypes also elaborate on the various ways in which gender intersects with other demographic characteristics, such as age, race, ethnicity, and social class. Subtypes, therefore, provide a more differentiated and rich guide to social interaction. For example, they recognize that one should not behave in the same way toward a "hottie" at a bar as one would toward a friend's grandmother at a tea party.

Unlike the elaboration and encapsulation processes, the evaluative component of subtyping does not drive the formation of subtypes. Rather, it concerns how people feel about the different types. We deal at length with this issue in the next chapter, which addresses the prescriptive function of stereotypes (how stereotypes represent norms and ideals about men's and women's behavior and traits).

Structure of Subtypes

Gender subtypes have been researched since the 1980s (Deaux, Winton, Crowley, & Lewis, 1985; Noseworthy & Lott, 1984), both in Europe (e.g., Six & Eckes, 1991; Eckes, 2002) and North America (e.g., Green et al., 2005; Carpenter & Trentham, 1998). This research has generated a bewildering array of types. One review (Green et al., 2005) found well over 200 gender subtype labels from prior studies (and one study by Carpenter & Trentham, 2001, listed 414 types!). Researchers have tried to reduce this complexity to more manageable proportions by lumping similar types together.

One way to simplify involves statistical analyses that indicate how perceivers organize or group subtypes, revealing which types are essentially the same (e.g., "nerd" and "geek" may function as interchangeable labels). In cluster analysis, participants sort the various types into piles or groups, known as "clusters." People sort psychologically similar types into the same pile (e.g., princess and cheerleader into one, grandmothers and aunts into another). Knowing how often people put certain subtypes into the same piles allows for computations of the "psychological distance" between subtypes. This process reveals clusters of psychologically related subtypes.

What do such analyses show? First, even without instructions to sort by gender, people tend to create gender-specific piles (Green et al., 2005; but see Carpenter & Trentham, 2001, for a dissenting view). Consistent with the E^3 model, these include clusters representing elaborations that are consistent with different ways of enacting a traditional gender role. For female types, separate clusters differentiate nurturing family roles (a cluster including types such as wife, mother, grandmother, and homemaker as well as the more general term "woman") from romantically attractive women (a cluster including types such as girlfriend, princess, cheerleader, and sweetheart). Similarly, separate clusters of male subtypes distinguish between male work roles (a cluster including types ranging from policeman to doctor) and romantically attractive men (a cluster including types such as boyfriend, stud, and ladies' man; Green et al., 2005).

As predicted by the E^3 model, other groupings of subtypes encapsulate deviations from traditional roles. For female types, these clusters include the most negatively evaluated subtypes, both those that violate prescriptions for feminine niceness (bitch, witch) as well as those that violate norms of feminine sexuality, whether through homosexuality (lesbian, dyke) or promiscuity (slut, whore). "Deviant" and socially rejected male types included those that violate prescriptions of male strength (wimp, wuss), violate prescriptions of heterosexuality (fag, homo), or violate prescriptions of male competence (slob, redneck).

Another cluster in Green et al.'s (2005) research included female types defined by work, both the career-woman type and jobs that women often occupy (e.g., waitress, nurse). Interestingly, people generated fewer clusters based on careers for female than for male types. Although Green et al.'s cluster analysis did not show similar effects, in past studies of gender subtypes career women have usually been closely grouped with feminists and other nontraditional types of women (e.g., Six & Eckes, 1991). Women's influx into the paid workforce represents the most dramatic change in women's roles over the past half century; in the next chapter, we consider how this social change may have altered women's self-conceptions as well as current and future gender stereotypes.

Comparing Subtypes and General Stereotypes

In addition to revealing more specific categories that people use in everyday interaction, research on subtypes has helped to complement and expand other research on gender stereotyping, which has focused almost exclusively on the personality traits associated with men and women. Gender subtyping research has shown that there are multiple ways to enact gender roles and has also highlighted how negatively people evaluate "gender deviance"; even the terms used to label deviant types often constitute highly derogatory epithets (e.g., "woos" for men, "bitch" for women). These results confirm that subtypes do not replace more general stereotypes of men and women but rather elaborate upon them.

In other words, many of the subtypes represent specific variations on more general stereotypical themes, although these variations may emphasize one aspect of the stereotype (e.g., women's nurturance in one case, their romantic attractiveness in another). Traditional male and female subtypes are associated with stereotype-consistent personality traits (i.e., the traits typically associated with each gender; Eckes, 2002; Green et al., 2005). Nevertheless, the clusters representing traditional female subtypes, whether depicted as nurturing (homemaker, typical woman, and secretary) or sexy (chick, babe, and cheerleader), receive higher ratings on warmth than on competence. Clusters representative of traditional male types (e.g., typical man, manager, and career man) receive higher ratings on competence than on warmth (Eckes, 2002).

At the same time, subtyping research expands on the almost exclusive focus on personality traits in broader gender-stereotyping research. The personality trait approach to gender stereotypes has highlighted important themes related to gender roles (e.g., women having traits suiting them to be nurturers) and power (e.g., men having traits suiting them to lead). But focusing on personality traits only indirectly implicates roles, whereas subtyping research shows how roles and occupations become directly integrated into the content of gender subtypes. Many subtypes (e.g., mother, nurse, blue collar) directly specify a role or a job associated with one gender. In fact, role and occupation distinctions account for a large number of gender subtypes (almost 40% according to Carpenter & Trentham, 1998).

Additionally, research on gender subtypes has drawn attention to how sexuality and romance influence gender stereotypes. Whereas gender role and status differences suggest gendered personality traits, sexual attraction relates more to appearance (e.g., tall, handsome, physically strong men; petite, delicately featured women). Complementing this book's focus on the role of heterosexuality in gender relations, subtyping research reveals that sexuality is closely bound to conceptions of men and women. Many subtypes of men and women are defined by sexual orientation (e.g., homosexual), promiscuity versus faithfulness (e.g., whore and stud vs. girlfriend and family man), and sexually desirable versus undesirable physical attributes (e.g., beautiful, sexy, ugly), highlighting how heterosexual interdependence shapes gender stereotypes.

Overall, gender subtyping complements rather than contradicts more general gender stereotypes. In part, the subtypes represent more specific variations on the themes defined by the broader stereotypes, elaborating on the specific ways in which men can be masculine and women can be feminine. Subtypes also help to preserve more general stereotypes of men and women by conveniently fencing off, or encapsulating, people who deviate from gendered expectations by grouping them into recognizable subtypes. This method of dealing with exceptions that might otherwise challenge broader stereotypes of men and women makes overall stereotypes more resistant to change. This is not to say, however, that broader stereotypes of men and women completely resist changes in gender roles. We consider this topic in the next chapter.

Chapter Summary

This chapter focused on the content and origins of cultural stereotypes about men and women. For the most part, research on gender stereotypes has focused on personality traits, particularly the underlying dimensions of agentic competence (associated with men) and communal warmth (associated with women). Experimental research that has manipulated the roles and status assigned to fictional groups confirms social structural predictions that typical gender roles (caretaker vs. breadwinner) and status differences between the sexes are each sufficient to create gender-like stereotypes.

Gender stereotypes not only are socially shared within a society but show impressive consistency across cultures. This poses difficulties for purely cultural explanations of the origins of stereotypes. However, because of the ubiquity of gender differences in power and roles, these cross-cultural findings are consistent with social structural explanations and do not necessarily imply biologically based differences in traits.

The evaluative connotations of gender stereotypes also show cross-cultural regularities, with men viewed as "bad but bold" and women as "wonderful but weak." Women's stereotypically nurturing traits create subjectively favorable attitudes toward women, who (as a group) are liked about as much or even more than men. By contrast, stereotypes of men suggest activity and potency, traits that lead to greater respect for men than for women.

Gender subtyping research shows that gender stereotypes specify more than personality trait differences, with subgroups of men and women organized on the basis of roles and occupations, sexual styles and appearances, and demographic characteristics (e.g., social class). Subtyping both elaborates on different ways in which men and women can enact traditional gender roles but also encapsulates those who deviate from gendered expectations. Fencing off gender deviants renders overall gender stereotypes resistant to change. Finally, because gender stereotypes reflect social realities—differences in roles and power to which men and women adapt—they may contain more than a kernel of truth. Nevertheless, as the next chapter reveals, gender stereotypes set up expectations that bias perceptions and treatment of individuals, often without perceivers' awareness. Further, stereotypes are not simply beliefs about what men and women are like but ideals that dictate how men and women ought to differ.

CHAPTER 5

Descriptive and
Prescriptive Stereotyping

Consider the following two examples of stereotypes: (1) Norwegians like to ski and (2) men are courageous. Both set up expectancies about the likely behavior of individual members of these categories. But what might happen in each case if an individual violated the stereotype of the group? In the first case, imagine that you meet a Norwegian exchange student and, as you get to know her, the subject of skiing comes up. She mentions that she never learned to ski (indeed has never even put on a pair of skis or visited a slope) and cannot see why people like this activity so much. You might express surprise that, as a Norwegian, she not only never learned to ski but has no interest in it. But, even particularly avid ski fanatics would probably not express anger toward her or actively condemn her as "not being a good Norwegian." This indicates that the stereotype was purely descriptive, an expectation that, if disconfirmed, only generates surprise, but not moral outrage, anger, or rejection toward people who violate the stereotype.

By contrast, consider a man who fails to exhibit courage. Imagine walking down the street and noticing a couple (boyfriend and girlfriend) strolling ahead of you. Suddenly a large, viciously barking dog that had been lurking in a yard rushes the couple. The boyfriend reacts by cowering behind his girlfriend, grabbing her, and sticking her between himself and the dog like a human shield. How might you (or the girlfriend, or most onlookers) react? Such behavior would probably generate not just surprise but condemnation, contempt, social rejection, and comments such as, "What is wrong with you?" for the man's failure to live up to the stereotype of masculine courage. But if the female member of the couple used her boyfriend as a shield, would onlookers or the boyfriend condemn her lack of courage? Probably not.

The reactions in these examples reveal two different functions of stereotypes when perceiving individuals: (1) a descriptive function in which stereotypes represent expectancies about what category members are typically like and (2) a prescriptive function in which stereotypes specify what category members ideally ought to be like. Stereotypes are always descriptive, but only some stereotypes are prescriptive.

Chapter 4 outlined the content and structure of gender stereotypes. The current chapter explores how stereotypes are applied, influencing perceptions and evaluations of individuals in daily social life. More specifically, we cover (1) how descriptive gender stereotypes skew perceptions of individuals, (2) how descriptive expectations become automatic, affecting perceivers' reactions without conscious awareness, (3) how and why gender stereotypes become prescriptive, and (4) whether broad social changes in gender roles over the past few decades have diminished gender stereotyping.

Descriptive and Prescriptive Functions of Stereotypes

Early stereotyping researchers realized that stereotypes can serve two basic functions (see Allport, 1954/1979). Cognitive simplification refers to using stereotypes because they make it easier to perceive and deal with others by lumping them into groups. For example, by classifying another person as a waiter, one knows the appropriate way to interact (e.g., by placing an order). The other function, known as rationalization, refers to how stereotypes enable perceivers to justify their own and their group's beliefs about and conduct toward others. Early prejudice theorists viewed this latter function in terms of rationalizing one's own faults or psychological conflicts, such as the person who hates homosexuals because he has doubts about his own sexual identity. Later theorists, however, have emphasized how stereotypes serve as socially shared rationalizations that legitimize the long-standing social practices and status hierarchies that define their society, labeled "system justification" (Jost & Banaji, 1994). Whereas the descriptive function of stereotypes serves the need for cognitive simplification, the prescriptive aspect of stereotypes helps to fulfill people's needs for system justification. Table 5.1 summarizes these terms and their relationships.

Descriptive stereotypes promote cognitive simplification by saving considerable mental effort when perceiving other people. Stereotypes free up cognitive resources so that perceivers can devote mental effort to other demands, such as paying attention to how they are presenting themselves to others. In fact, giving people category information about strangers enables them to better attend to and remember other tasks and enhances memory for stereotype-consistent information about those strangers (Macrae, Milne, & Bodenhausen, 1994). In Allport's words, rapidly categorizing other people (and basing conduct toward them on this categorization) makes "our adjustment to life speedy, smooth, and consistent" (1954/1979, p. 21). By contrast, when others do not match the stereotype of their category, perceivers need to spend more time and attention figuring them out (Plaks, Stroessner, Dweck, & Sherman, 2001). Although perceivers may dislike spending extra effort on others who violate stereotypical expectations, this alone is unlikely to cause anger toward gender "deviants."

Stereotypes become prescriptive, however, when used to justify or legitimize a social system. A central theme of this book is that conceptions of gender help to maintain and justify a gendered social structure (i.e., a gendered division of labor and gender hierarchy). Societies have a strong stake in perpetuating their practices to avoid social

TABLE 5.1 Descriptive and Prescriptive Stereotyping

Descriptive stereotypes

- Defined as beliefs about what category members are typically like
- Serve a cognitive simplification function: Placing people into categories minimizes cognitive effort in person perception and simplifies social life by generating expectancies about how to interact with different types of people
- Violations of descriptive stereotypes generate surprise but not anger or punishment
- All stereotypes are descriptive

Prescriptive stereotypes

- Defined as beliefs about what category members ideally ought to be like
- Serve a system justification function: Prescriptive stereotypes justify or rationalize a social system in which people traditionally occupy different role and status positions because of social category memberships
- Violations of prescriptive stereotypes generate anger and social punishment as well as surprise
- Only some stereotypes are prescriptive (in addition to being descriptive)

disruption or change. Further, people want to believe that their society is just (Lerner, 1980), in part because the alternative of believing that one's society lacks fundamental fairness or treats people arbitrarily and unjustly is deeply disturbing and suggests a lack of control over one's own outcomes (Jost & Banaji, 1994). Both of these motives—to maintain the status quo and to believe in the fairness of one's society—lead people toward system-justifying beliefs.

To the extent that stereotypes derive from and help to maintain well-established social arrangements woven into the fabric of society, they take on a prescriptive quality, providing ideological support for the belief that the current social structure is morally correct (see Allport, 1954/1979; Jost & Banaji, 1994). In the case of gender, stereotypes map out rules for how men and women ought to be because these rules function to maintain and to justify traditional gender roles and power differences. For instance, the vicious dog example illustrates how gender stereotypes reflect and reinforce the male protector role.

Both the descriptive and prescriptive functions of stereotypes have important implications for how perceivers view and treat individual men and women. The descriptive aspect of stereotypes creates assumptions or expectations that initiate stereotype-confirming biases, such as interpreting ambiguous information about another person as stereotype consistent. The prescriptive function of stereotypes pressures people to exhibit stereotype-consistent behavior through social rewards and punishments and, therefore, motivates individuals to conform to gender norms. We consider each of these aspects of gender stereotypes—descriptive and prescriptive—in turn.

The Descriptive Aspect of Gender Stereotypes

People use descriptive stereotypes to predict individual men's and women's character and behavior, creating expectations that act as cognitive shortcuts. These expectations help to guide people's actions toward others, especially strangers. To the extent that stereotypes are mere expectancies, waiting to be confirmed or disconfirmed through actual interaction, they may be temporarily held hypotheses that perceivers abandon when the evidence contradicts the stereotype (see Fiske & Neuberg, 1990). For instance, you might expect (based on gender) that Natalia would be more nurturing than Nate, but if personal experience consistently proves this false (e.g., Nate is solicitous and Natalia is dismissive), you are unlikely to persist in applying the same stereotypes to these individuals.

Early experimental studies of reactions to stereotype-disconfirming information quickly showed that this is true. For example, when a student was described as responding forcefully to being hassled on the street, interrupting another student to break into a class discussion, and breaking into a conversation at a party, it did not matter whether the student was named Paul or Nancy (Locksley, Borgida, Brekke, & Hepburn, 1980). In the Nancy condition, participants rated the target as highly assertive, showing no difference from participants in the Paul condition.

A number of caveats must be noted here, all of which we expand on later. First, subsequent research suggests that people may not see individuals as exceptions to the stereotype quite so readily as the Nancy–Paul experiment implied. In real life, perception is determined by what perceivers attend to, how they interpret observed behavior (rather than written descriptions such as those used in the Nancy–Paul study), and how perceivers influence targets with whom they interact. All of these processes pull in the direction of leading perceivers to think that their stereotypes have been confirmed (see S. T. Fiske, 1998, 2005, for reviews). Second, even when perceivers view someone's behavior as stereotype inconsistent, they may attempt to explain away the unexpected behavior to preserve their stereotype (Kunda & Oleson, 1995; Yzerbyt & Corneille, 2005). These processes are reviewed in detail in Chapter 6. Third, the Nancy–Paul experiment failed to assess another important question: Did people like assertive Nancy less than assertive Paul? This issue is addressed later when we consider the prescriptive aspects of gender stereotypes (and in Chapters 6 and 7, which discuss backlash toward people who violate gender norms).

Finally, because gender stereotypes are learned so early in life, they can exert subtle, insidious effects on perceptions of others. We discuss these processes in the following section, which explores how gender stereotypes create implicit associations that occur rapidly and automatically, biasing perceptions of others without our intention or awareness.

Stereotypes Create Automatic Associations

We demonstrated in the prior chapter that even people who do not endorse descriptive gender stereotypes remain aware of their contents. Like other forms of knowledge, stereotypes are part of each individual's "cultural heritage" (Devine, 1989). Moreover, they are learned very early in life, before people have the cognitive maturity to reject them. As a result, people automatically associate men with agentic traits and women with communal traits even when they disavow these stereotypes (Rudman & Glick, 2001; Rudman & Goodwin, 2004). Similarly, men are automatically linked with career and high-status roles more so than women, who are linked with family and low-status roles (Nosek, Banaji, & Greenwald, 2002a; Rudman & Kilianski, 2000). These stereotypic associations, in turn, can affect perceptions of others without intent or the conscious realization that they have done so. Because gender stereotypes are so well learned, people not only quickly categorize others according to gender but also make rapid, automatic, and involuntary stereotypical judgments (Banaji & Hardin, 1996; Greenwald & Banaji, 1995; Rudman, Greenwald, & McGhee, 2001).

Implicit stereotypes and attitudes are routinized, automatic associations between concepts, such as between social categories (e.g., men) and personality traits (e.g., assertiveness). Although it had long been assumed that well-learned stereotypes lead perceivers to make automatic category-based assumptions, researchers have only recently developed tools to assess these processes. A variety of new techniques measure implicit associations by relying on reaction time—people's responses in milliseconds—to gain insight into the way people automatically think. Such implicit measures (Fazio & Olson, 2003) have the distinct advantage of avoiding people's tendency to censor or control politically incorrect responses. Moreover, even if people want to tell the truth, they can only report what they think they believe, which relies on people's ability to introspect accurately. In other words, people may not be willing or able to accurately report their stereotypes and attitudes. Implicit measures bypass the "willing and able" problem to provide information that cannot be obtained through self-report (explicit) measures.

The first demonstrations of automatic gender associations with occupations, activities, and traits were conducted by Mahzarin Banaji and her colleagues (Banaji & Hardin, 1997; Banaji & Greenwald, 1995; Blair & Banaji, 1996). They used priming measures, which take advantage of the fact that when people have strong automatic associations between two concepts, such as "bread and butter," activating or "priming" one of the concepts leads to quicker identification of the second concept. For instance, if the word "bread" flashes on a computer screen, you will recognize the word "butter" more quickly than if "bread" had not appeared. Indeed, well-learned associations become so automatic that if we say "bread" you may have difficulty not thinking "butter." Similarly, for two opposing concepts, activating one can inhibit recognition of the other concept. For example, given that most people find spiders repugnant, activating the concept "spider" may lead to less quick recognition for pleasant words, like "yummy."

How might this apply to gender? Banaji and Hardin (1996) briefly presented male and female occupations (e.g., engineer, nurse) on a computer screen. After each occupation, participants judged the gender of a pronoun that immediately and randomly followed (e.g., he, him, she, her) by pressing one computer key for "male" and another for "female." Similarly, Blair and Banaji (1996) briefly presented gender-typed occupations, traits (e.g., strong, gentle), or activities (e.g., ballet, football) and then asked respondents to judge the gender of the name that immediately followed (e.g., Amanda, John). In both studies, people made faster judgments when the gender of the target word matched the "gender" of the activity. For example, "engineer–he" and "nurse–she" elicited faster responses than "engineer–she" and "nurse–he." Similarly, "strong–John" and "gentle–Amanda" elicited faster responses than "strong–Amanda" and "gentle–John." Interestingly, people showed stronger automatic associations of gender with occupations and activities than with stereotypic traits, perhaps because traits vary more within each gender than do roles and interests (Blair & Banaji, 1996). Another possible explanation is that people more strongly associate various activities, occupations, and objects with gender because they learn these connections especially early in life (about age 2), before they even form the concept of traits (C. L. Martin et al., 2002).

The Implicit Association Test (IAT; Greenwald, McGhee, & Schwartz, 1998) is the most popular implicit method. You can take a variety of IATs (including gender-related tests) online at *www.implicit. harvard.edu*. The typical IAT instructs people to press a specific computer key as quickly as possible when they see individual words appear on the screen, but different keys are used depending on whether the word (or a pictured object) is associated with a specific category or concept. For example, participants might be asked to press the "A" key if a type of insect (e.g., spider, blowfly) appears but the "L" key (at the other side of the keyboard) if a type of flower (e.g., daisy, tulip) appears. This task is simple, but now imagine that a second task is layered onto the first one: In addition to hitting the "A" key if an insect name appears, you must hit this *same key* if a pleasant word (e.g., lovely, yummy) comes on the screen. Further, in addition to hitting the "L" key if a flower name appears, you must hit this same key if an unpleasant word appears (e.g., death, pain).

Because most people have negative associations with insects and positive associations with flowers, they find it extremely difficult to respond quickly when (as in the prior example) they must use the same key for opposing concepts (insects and pleasant words; flowers and unpleasant words). No matter how much they wish to respond more quickly, their automatic associations interfere. Now imagine the task completely switched around so that participants must hit the "A" key for both flowers and pleasant words and the "L" key for both insects and unpleasant words. People find this task much easier; their reaction time is boosted by strong associations between insects and unpleasantness and flowers and pleasantness. By looking at how quickly people respond to the various combinations of these tasks, the IAT can assess not only the content of people's implicit attitudes but the strength of these associations. (If this seems confusing, taking an IAT online will quickly clear things up as you experience it firsthand.) Implicit tests like the IAT flexibly allow researchers to use whichever types of categories or concepts they wish to study as well as a variety of on-screen stimuli (e.g., pictures as well as words).

Taking the IAT (or related types of measures) can be a disconcerting experience. One of the first uses of the test was to measure racial prejudice. The IAT has demonstrated that even highly egalitarian Whites, who strongly oppose any kind of racial prejudice, still tend to have more positive automatic associations with Whites and negative associations with Blacks (e.g., Nosek et al., 2002a). That is, even if they are not prejudiced in their explicit attitudes, most Whites exhibit implicit racial prejudices. A lifetime of being exposed to a culture in which Whites are viewed more favorably than Blacks creates automatic associations even in people who do not want to have them.

The example of implicit racial attitudes points out several important things. First, individuals' implicit and explicit attitudes often differ. Second, measures of implicit attitudes can reveal prejudices even for highly charged topics such as race that, on standard self-report measures, people are very reluctant to indicate (e.g., most people would strongly disagree with a self-report statement such as "I am prejudiced against Black people" or "I think that Blacks are inferior to Whites"). In other words, although most White Americans normally censor their responses about racial topics, they cannot do so on an IAT.

Implicit attitudes should not, however, be viewed as truer than explicit attitudes. For example, many Whites may hold truly egalitarian conscious beliefs even if they implicitly have negative racial stereotypes

(Nosek et al., 2002a). Again, learning early and often (e.g., from adults, peers, and the media) that society values some groups more than others can seep into our cognitive systems involuntarily as a form of cultural brainwashing (Devine, 1989; Rudman, 2004). Unfortunately, in daily interaction and judgments, implicit prejudices may leak out when people fail deliberately to inhibit them or may show themselves through channels of communication that most people do not consciously monitor, mainly nonverbal behaviors such as interpersonal distance, nervous eye blinking, and defensive posture (Dovidio, Kawakami, Johnson, Johnson, & Howard, 1997; Dovidio, Kawakami, & Gaertner, 2002; McConnell & Liebold, 2001).

Even minority group members often show an implicit bias against their own group, despite explicitly endorsing highly positive attitudes toward their group. These effects illustrate the insidiousness of implicit prejudice. Like members of the majority group, people in minority groups have also been exposed to a lifetime of negative stereotypes. Because those stereotypes target their own group, minority group members can also form automatic negative associations about their social category. In general, groups with higher status and power in American society (e.g., Whites, Christians, slim people, the wealthy) show a very strong implicit bias in favor of their own group. By contrast, members of minorities (e.g., Blacks, Jews, Asians, overweight people, the poor) show, on average, a much weaker implicit in-group bias or even a bias in favor of the higher status out-group (Nosek et al., 2002a; Rudman, Feinberg, & Fairchild, 2002).

Implicit Gender Attitudes and Stereotypes

What has IAT research shown about automatic or implicit gender attitudes and stereotypes? We first consider the overall favorability of implicit attitudes toward the two sexes. We have consistently sounded the theme that gender prejudice differs from other prejudices because, even though women have less social status than men, male–female interdependence and women's traditional nurturing roles lead to positive views of women (Eagly & Mladinic, 1993). Recall that explicit attitudinal measures confirm generally more positive views of women than of men; also, explicit stereotypes of women are (overall) just as or more favorable than stereotypes of men (see Chapter 4, especially Figure 4.1). Does this reflect mere political correctness (e.g., treating women with kid gloves so that one cannot be accused of sexism), or does favoritism toward women hold true for implicit attitudes?

The findings for implicit gender attitudes are strikingly different than those that occur for other social distinctions, such as race, ethnicity, or class. As already noted, IATs based on these other kinds of groups consistently show strong in-group biases among members of high-status groups and either weak in-group biases or even out-group favoratism biases for members of low-status groups. Gender-attitude IATs show precisely the opposite: On average, men display a very weak in-group bias or neutral implicit gender attitudes, whereas women show an extremely strong in-group bias (i.e., have much more positive associations with women than with men; Rudman & Goodwin, 2004). It is not surprising that many men show some degree of implicit in-group bias: People like to think well of groups to which they belong (Tajfel, 1981), but this bias is quite weak among men (or even reversed) because of their positive implicit attitudes toward women.

What leads to relatively more favorable implicit attitudes toward women? In a series of studies, Rudman and Goodwin (2004) found that, for both male and female participants, positive implicit attitudes toward women relate to having more favorable attitudes toward mothers compared with fathers, being raised primarily by one's mother (as opposed to father), and implicit associations of men (compared with women) with greater threat (e.g., as violent and dangerous). Thus, women's role as caregivers partly accounts for positive implicit feelings about women as a group. By contrast, men's perceived dangerousness, which stems, in part, from their physical and social power, creates less positive implicit attitudes toward men. Additionally, male participants' degree of heterosexual experience predicted their implicit attitudes toward women, suggesting that sexual gratification can foster positive associations about women, a topic we examine in more detail in Chapter 10.

Implicit gender stereotypes show important consistencies with explicit beliefs. Specifically, they echo the content of explicit stereotype measures, associating women with warmth and men with agentic competence (Rudman, Greenwald, & McGhee, 2001; Rudman & Kilianski, 2000). Consistent with the proposed social structural origins of these stereotypes, people also implicitly associate women with family and men with careers (Nosek et al., 2002a). Research on implicit gender attitudes also dovetails with the idea that intimate interdependence between the sexes and women's traditional caregiving role lead to a positive glow toward women, whereas male dominance creates less overall positive feelings about men. Both sexes associate women with warmth of family; by contrast, people strongly associate men, presumably because of their greater power and aggressiveness, with violence and threat. The end result is less positive implicit attitudes toward men than toward women.

Women's and men's implicit stereotypes, however, do not always parallel each other. Recall from Chapter 3 that children exhibit strong in-group favoritism in their explicit gender stereotypes ("If it's good, it's us; if it's bad, it's them"), whereas adults do not. When researchers directly contrast desirable and undesirable traits using gender stereotype IATs, childlike in-group favoritism shows itself again (Rudman, Greenwald, & McGhee, 2001). For example, if warm is contrasted with cold, both men and women associate "cold" with the other sex (i.e., men show women–cold and men–warm associations, whereas women show female–warm and male–cold associations). Likewise, if power is directly compared with weakness, only men show stereotypical gender associations (male–powerful and female–weak); women associate power with male and female equally. By contrast, when researchers use only positive traits that differ on male–female stereotypicality (e.g., power vs. warmth instead of power vs. weakness), both men and women show robust stereotypic associations (Rudman, Greenwald, & McGhee, 2001). Similarly, no gender differences emerge on IATs that contrast career versus family, individualistic versus communal, or math versus arts; Nosek et al., 2002a; Nosek, Banaji, & Greenwald, 2002b; Rudman & Glick, 2001). When researchers control for the automatic tendency to link self with positive traits (and others with negative traits), the stereotypic associations come through loud and clear.

Gender IATs that directly contrast positive and negative traits show how people's associations of desirable traits with themselves extend to their gender in-group. In other words, an implicit self-positivity bias carries over to one's in-group (Greenwald et al., 2002). Using IATs in which all of the traits (both masculine and feminine) are equally favorable removes this bias and reveals implicit stereotypes more clearly. Given the normal "my group is good" bias, it is particularly remarkable that men's overall "good–bad" evaluative associations with each sex show weak in-group bias or even neutrality (Rudman & Goodwin, 2004). However, as noted, even men associate male gender with violence and female gender with safety, which helps to explain their weaker in-group bias on the gender-attitude IAT.

In short, implicit measures suggest that women are liked by both sexes. But recall that liking does not equal respect. Are men more implicitly (as well as explicitly) respected than women? One subtle indicator is the greater tendency for parents to name children, even if female, after their father rather than their mother (Jost, Pelham, & Carvallo, 2002).

You are more likely to meet a girl named Briana, Stephanie, Roberta, or Paula (all "female" names derived from male names) than a boy named Lindo, Kareno, or (other than in a Johnny Cash song) Sue.

In addition, implicit memory measures reveal that people are more prone to falsely attribute fame (a form of status) to male names to which they have previously been exposed than to female names to which they have similarly been exposed (Banaji & Greenwald, 1995). Moreover, both men and women automatically associate men with power (Rudman, Greenwald, & McGhee, 2001) and with positions of authority and status, whereas women are more readily associated with lower status support positions (Rudman & Kilianski, 2000). Finally, when people are simply asked to "think of a person," they are much more likely to conjure a man than a woman, suggesting that the prototype for a *person* is male (Stroessner, 1992).

In sum, implicit and explicit gender stereotypes show an impressive consistency in how they characterize men and women. (Note, however, that any specific individual's implicit and explicit attitudes may differ.) Greater liking for women relative to men occurs on both implicit and explicit measures because people associate women with motherhood, family, and warm traits. But men garner more respect than women in that people more strongly associate men with careers, status, power, and agentic traits. Implicit (like explicit) gender stereotypes reveal a powerful social consensus in perceptions of men and women, viewing men as "bad but bold" and women as "wonderful but weak."

Just how important are implicit attitudes? A meta-analysis of research on the relationship between stereotyping and discriminatory behavior revealed that implicit, compared with explicit, stereotypes and prejudices better predict behavior toward members of stereotyped categories (Greenwald, Poehlman, Uhlmann, & Banaji, in press). Further, implicit attitudes can affect behavior even when people hold relatively unprejudiced explicit attitudes (e.g., Dovidio et al., 2002). For instance, women tend to reject explicit sexist beliefs (e.g., Swim et al., 1995) but often exhibit implicit gender stereotypes as strongly as men do (e.g., Banaji & Greenwald, 1995; Banaji & Hardin, 1996; Nosek et al., 2002a, 2002b; Rudman, Greenwald, & McGhee, 2001; Rudman & Glick, 2001).

The insidious effect of automatic gender stereotyping is well illustrated by a puzzler you may have heard before. A father and son get into a terrible car accident in which the father is killed. The son is brought to the emergency room, where the surgeon exclaims, "I can't operate on him, that's my son!" Who is the surgeon? (If you have not heard this before, think about your answer before continuing.)

On hearing this for the first time, people often become confused. Having automatically assumed that the surgeon is a man, they arrive at solutions such as "The surgeon [or the deceased man] is the stepfather." Even though the surgeon's gender was never specified, people tend automatically to picture a man and subsequently have trouble realizing that the surgeon is the boy's mother. Interestingly, this "riddle" was first circulated in feminist circles in the 1970s to illustrate how even feminist activists tend to make automatic (and discriminatory) gender-based assumptions. In Chapter 7, we show how these automatic assumptions can lead to hiring discrimination against women for positions of authority.

Implicit stereotyping has garnered quite a bit of attention because it illustrates how overlearned, routinized associations can undermine even the best of intentions not to discriminate by influencing judgments without perceivers' awareness (Greenwald & Banaji, 1995). But gender stereotyping and discrimination are not always automatic. Many people explicitly and openly endorse traditional beliefs about how men and women ought to be. Although popular attitudes about gender have changed a great deal in the past 40 years, both in response to the feminist movement and women's influx into the paid workforce, people still widely endorse the ideas that not only are men and women psychologically different but that they *ought* to be different. These beliefs, in turn, create intentional and deliberate gender discrimination.

The Prescriptive Aspect of Gender Stereotypes

Recall that gender stereotypes not only set up expectancies about how men and women are likely to behave but also provide a set of social rules, or prescriptions, about what men and women ideally ought to be like. Some have argued that gender stereotypes are more prescriptive than other group stereotypes, such as racial or ethnic stereotypes (Fiske & Stevens, 1993). For instance, although one can easily imagine others telling a woman that she "ought to be more nurturing" or a man that he ought to be "more assertive," it seems unlikely that most people would tell a Black acquaintance that he or she ought to "get more rhythm" (although such direct comparisons have yet to be studied). What can be said with certainty, however, is that gender stereotypes are highly prescriptive (as research reviewed later will illustrate; see also Chapters 6 and 7).

Fiske and Stevens (1993) speculated that gender stereotypes are prescriptive for several reasons. First, gender prescriptions develop from a wealth of experience with men and women, typically much more so than with other groups; greater experience may give people a more developed sense of how men and women "should" behave and foster certainty in their beliefs. Second, people learn to categorize by gender extremely early in life, much earlier than for other categories (e.g., race). As noted in Chapter 3, children distinguish between boys and girls by age 2; by contrast, racial categories do not emerge until about age 5 (Thompson, 1975). As children develop a gender identity, they seek to create clear gender boundaries through rules about how members of each sex should behave (see Chapter 3). Third, gender is a more salient category than other group memberships, as evidenced by people's tendency to make within-sex confusions more readily than within-race confusions in recalling "who said what" (Stangor et al., 1992; S. E. Taylor et al., 1978; see Chapter 4).

But not all aspects of gender stereotypes are prescriptive. For instance, despite the stereotypical expectation that women like to shop, a woman's lack of interest in shopping probably will not lead others to ostracize her, certainly not to the same degree as they would reject the cowardly boyfriend described in the example that opened this chapter. The social structural perspective offers a particularly powerful explanation for the prescriptiveness of gender stereotypes: that they justify existing social arrangements (i.e., serve a system justification function, Jost & Banaji, 1994). More particularly, social role theory (Eagly et al., 2000) suggests that gender stereotypes become prescriptive because they help to maintain existing gender roles and gender hierarchy. To ensure that people gravitate to the roles and level of status considered appropriate for their gender, boys and men must be trained to act as leaders, protectors, and providers, whereas girls and women must be socialized to assume their traditional roles as wives and mothers. The pressure to enact these roles may be especially strong the more deeply woven they are into the fabric of society. Thus, we argue that a fourth, and perhaps most powerful, circumstance that causes stereotypes to become prescriptive is when social categories are linked to interdependent, status-differentiated roles. This kind of interdependence is also typically accompanied by frequent, but role-guided, social contact that reinforces prescriptions on a daily basis (see Ridgeway, 2001a, 2001b).

Contrasting older and contemporary stereotypes of African Americans suggests how status and role differentiation invest stereotypes with prescriptive qualities. If you have seen American movies made before the 1960s, you may have noticed highly prescriptive stereotyping of Black characters as deferent, happy to be of service, and even (if you have seen *Gone with the Wind*) apparently content to be slaves "helping" the plantation owners. The loyal and servile Uncle Tom character represented a prescriptive ideal Whites imposed in the days when both the economy and the maintenance of White privilege relied on forcing African Americans into slavery and, later, restricted occupational roles (e.g., low-status service jobs such as domestics or custodians). To keep this system running, Whites (as the dominant group) encouraged prescriptive ideals for Blacks that matched the roles they depended on Blacks to play. After slavery ended and, later, civil rights activism resulted in African Americans no longer being restricted to specific occupations or roles, racial stereotypes changed. Whites no longer depended on Blacks in the manner that, for example, plantation owners once did, nor did most Whites interact as frequently with Blacks, making it more difficult to enforce prescriptions (see Jackman, 1994). The result was that stereotypes about Blacks lost their prescriptive quality.

By contrast, many occupations remain almost exclusively female or male and gender role differentiation is still prevalent in heterosexual relationships, with men dependent on women for primary domestic and child-care responsibilities (see Chapter 8). Gender role and status distinctions create prescriptions, and intimate contact makes it easier to enforce these prescriptions on a daily basis. As long as men depend on women to perform specific roles, stereotypes of women are likely to remain prescriptive. But what about prescriptive stereotypes about men? Dominant groups have incentive to target prescriptions not only toward members of subordinate groups but toward their own group as well. Prescriptions that men should be strong, bold, and assertive reinforce men's higher status gender role just as much as prescriptions that women should be nice, nurturing, and modest.

These ideas about when and why stereotypes become prescriptive have not been systematically tested (suggesting a research opportunity for an ambitious reader). But the relationship among roles, status, and descriptive stereotypes has been well established (Conway et al., 1996; Hoffman & Hurst, 1990; see Chapter 4). Moreover, as discussed next, the specific traits that are most prescribed for women and men are consistent with the hypothesis that interdependent gender roles and status differences are implicated in prescriptive ideals about men and women.

Prescriptions (and Proscriptions) for Women and Men

The social structural approach suggests that the strongest gender prescriptions should involve traits that reflect and reinforce traditional role and power differences. In an extensive examination of contemporary prescriptions for men and women, Prentice and Carranza (2002) asked Princeton University students to consider a series of 100 traits (identified as gender-stereotypical in past research). In alternative versions of the questionnaire, participants responded to different questions about the traits. In one version, participants were asked, "How desirable is it in American society for a man to possess each of these characteristics?" In another version "woman" substituted for "man," and in a third version "person" was used. This enabled the researchers to determine, for example, which traits people view as especially desirable for men more in comparison to women and "people in general," revealing prescriptions for each sex.

Table 5.2 presents results from Prentice and Carranza's study. What are the strongest prescriptions, or "oughts," for today's women? Women

TABLE 5.2. Intensified and Relaxed Gender Prescriptions

Intensified prescriptions for women	Relaxed prescriptions for women (or who women "do not have to be")
Warm and kind	Intelligent
Interest in children	Mature
Loyal	High self-esteem
Sensitive	Common sense
Friendly	Sense of humor
Clean	Concern for future
Attentive to appearance	Principled
Patient	Efficient
Polite	Rational
Cheerful	Strong personality

Intensified prescriptions for men (or who men "must be")	Relaxed prescriptions for men (or who men "do not have to be")
Business sense	Happy
Athletic	Friendly
Leadership ability	Helpful
Self-reliant	Clean
Dependable	Warm and kind
Ambitious	Enthusiastic
High self-esteem	Optimistic
Assertive	Cheerful
Decisive	Cooperative
Strong personality	Interest in children

Note. Adapted from Prentice and Carranza (2002). Copyright 2002 by Blackwell Publishing. Adapted by permission.

are prescribed to be warm, kind, interested in children, loyal, and sensitive, traits that suit them to their prescribed roles as doting mothers and loyal wives. What are the strongest prescriptions for men? That they have business sense, athleticism, leadership ability, and self-reliance, in other words the traits that suit them for traditional male roles as provider (e.g., leadership qualities) and protector (e.g., physical prowess).

As Prentice and Carranza (2002) note, both sets of gender prescriptions (for men and for women) reflect traits generally rated as socially desirable. Thus, it should be perfectly fine and good for men to be warm, kind, and interested in children or for women to have business sense, athletic ability, and leadership skills. At the same time, some of these socially desirable traits are intensified prescriptions, traits that are especially stipulated as important for one sex to exhibit because they suit either men or women to fulfilling their gender roles.

The positivity of these prescriptions makes them less objectionable: After all, what is wrong with women showing warmth? By contrast, prescriptions for women "to act dumb" would not have the same social support. At the same time, this positive spin on what women and men are supposed to be alleviates social pressure for stereotypical prescriptions to change. In fact, research suggests that gender prescriptions have remained the same for more than 30 years; the 20 traits people deemed most desirable for women and men in the 1970s (Bem, 1974) are similar to current gender prescriptions (Auster & Ohm, 2000; Harris, 1994; Holt & Ellis, 1998).

Further, as Prentice and Carranza point out, the positive intensified prescriptions do not stand alone but are accompanied by relaxed prescriptions for each sex (see Table 5.2). Relaxed proscriptions are generally desirable traits but are not as strongly prescribed for one sex or the other (i.e., members of that sex are not pressured to live up to these standards). For women, the top relaxed prescriptions are intelligence, maturity, self-esteem, and common sense. The traits that men are not as strongly pressured to exhibit include being happy, friendly, helpful, warm, and kind. In short, societal gender ideals state that women must exhibit warmth and an interest in kids but not necessarily intelligence, maturity, or common sense. By contrast, men must have occupational acumen, leadership skills, and physical prowess but not necessarily helpfulness or warmth toward others. Thus, although women are not prescribed to act dumb, neither are they as strongly pressured as men to exhibit competence.

As Table 5.3 shows, proscriptions, the negative traits that are undesirable for each sex, are equally important. Prentice and Carranza define

TABLE 5.3 Intensified and Relaxed Gender Proscriptions

Intensified proscriptions for women (or who women "must not be")	Relaxed proscriptions for women (or who women "are allowed to be")
Rebellious	Yielding
Stubborn	Emotional
Controlling	Impressionable
Cynical	Child-like
Promiscuous	Shy
Arrogant	Naïve
	Superstitious
	Weak
	Melodramatic
	Gullible

Intensified proscriptions for men (or who men "must not be")	Relaxed proscriptions for men (or who men "are allowed to be")
Emotional	Rebellious
Approval seeking	Solemn
Impressionable	Controlling
Yielding	Stubborn
Superstitious	Promiscuous
Child-like	Self-righteous
Shy	Jealous
Moody	Arrogant
Melodramatic	
Naïve	

Note. Adapted from Prentice and Carranza (2002). Copyright 2002 by Blackwell Publishing. Adapted by permission.

intensified proscriptions as traits considered to be particularly disapproved for one sex and relaxed proscriptions as traits that, although undesirable, are still more permissible for one sex than the other. In other words, which undesirable traits do people particularly strongly punish versus tolerate when exhibited by women versus men? As seen in Table 5.3, the intensified proscriptions for women suggest that people have the least tolerance for women who enact masculine, power-grabbing traits such as rebelliousness, stubbornness, or dominance. By contrast, being yielding, emotional, impressionable, child-like, and naïve are relaxed proscriptions for women, traits that, although not exactly desirable, are tolerated. For men, people least tolerate emotionality, approval seeking, impressionability, and readiness to yield to others. By contrast, men are not as penalized for being rebellious, solemn, controlling, or stubborn.

What does this all add up to? It suggests that men accrue social rewards for displaying traits related to competence, power, and status and are not too severely punished if this spills over into acting in a callous, rebellious, or dominant manner. Men can expect social disapproval for any display of weakness (e.g., boys don't cry or use their girlfriends as human shields) or being too open to the influence of others. By contrast, women can expect social rewards for exhibiting traits such as warmth and domesticity and little disapproval if they are yielding, child-like, or naïve. Women, however, garner disapproval for exerting dominance or control over others, consistent with the adage that "an aggressive man is assertive; an aggressive woman is a bitch."

Research on gender subtypes reinforces the picture of prescriptive gender stereotypes discussed previously. Chapter 4 reviewed how exceptions to gender stereotypes become grouped into subtypes. Subtypes that violate prescriptive stereotypes receive very negative evaluative reactions and derogatory labels. For instance, women who do not nurture are "bitches" and men who lack strength are "wimps." Subtypes that are consistent with conventional gender roles (e.g., for men: businessman, athlete; for women: mother, wife) instead receive positive evaluations (Green et al., 2005).

Established gender prescriptions and proscriptions match up well to ambivalent sexism theory (see Chapter 2). Prescriptive gender stereotypes suggest that women receive social rewards (benevolent sexism) if they embrace a nurturing, supportive role and punishment (hostile sexism) if they challenge male power. For men, prescriptive gender stereotypes suggest social rewards (benevolence toward men) for traits related to being protectors and providers and a limited form of punishment (hostility toward men) if this shades into more heavy-handed displays of dominance.

Gender prescriptions represent an explicit and intentional form of sexism that leads people to react more negatively to gender deviance. Various theories (e.g., social dominance theory; Sidanius & Pratto, 1999) predict that because men gain the most material benefits by maintaining the status quo, they should hold more highly prescriptive gender attitudes than women do. In fact, as a group, men invariably score higher on measures of overtly sexist attitudes that endorse traditional gender roles (e.g., Glick et al., 2004, Swim et al., 1995). In turn, those men who most strongly express traditional attitudes have more negative reactions toward people who violate gendered prescriptions (e.g., Glick et al., 1997).

Nonetheless, gender prescriptions can also become so well learned that they automatically influence behavior, even among people who explicitly reject sexist attitudes. For example, women, who often reject traditional beliefs about women's roles, are just as likely as men to show automatic negative reactions to female authority figures (Rudman & Kilianski, 2000) and to express dislike for "women who act like men" (e.g., by self-promoting [Rudman, 1998], or exhibiting a competitive, ambitious style [Rudman & Glick, 1999]; see Chapter 7).

Prescriptions about Sexuality

As noted in Chapter 4, investigations of gender subtypes reveal that sexuality and appearance attributes are key components of gender stereotyping. These dimensions reveal additional prescriptions for both sexes: to be heterosexual and to enact sexuality in "gender-appropriate" ways (e.g., if female, to not be promiscuous; see Table 5.3).

People generally treat homosexuality as a particularly strong violation of gender prescriptions and associate it with a host of other violations of how men and women are supposed to be. Cluster analyses reveal that most people group the subtype lesbian (itself negatively evaluated) with a cluster that includes derogatory subtypes, such as "bitch," that suggest of violations of feminine niceness (Green et al., 2005). In general, both male and female homosexuals are stereotyped as having physical attributes, role and occupation interests, and personality traits associated with the other sex (e.g., Kite & Deaux, 1987; Madon, 1997). In other words, gay men are stereotyped as physically effeminate (e.g., slight and physically weak), as interested in "feminine" roles and occupations (e.g., careers in fashion or nursing), and as possessing stereotypically feminine personality traits (e.g., nurturing, sensitive, emotional). By contrast, lesbian women are viewed as having more masculine physical traits (e.g., strong or athletic), "masculine" role and occupation interests (e.g., athletics and blue-collar careers), and stereotypically masculine personalities (e.g., competitive, forceful, independent).

Perhaps the prescription to be heterosexual is so strong that people subject homosexual men and women to an extreme form of encapsulation as "gender deviants" who contradict gender stereotypes in every way, "fencing off" homosexuals both mentally and socially. Some homosexual men and women attempt to resist such stereotyping. For instance, many homosexual men endorse antieffeminacy (devaluing feminine traits) and, like most heterosexual men, may purposefully display masculinity (Taywaditep, 2001). As a result, people recognize the macho homosexual male as a separate subtype. Because the masculine homosexual male type violates fewer gender prescriptions (only those of sexual orientation, not those of personality, role and occupation interests or physical characteristics), people evaluate the macho gay male subtype more favorably than the effeminate gay male subtype (Clausell & Fiske, 2005). We explore attitudes toward homosexual men in more detail in Chapters 7 and 11.

Gender "rules" (prescriptions and proscriptions) have profound implications for social interactions. They galvanize stereotyping effects by lending them a kind of moral authority. But even when stereotypes lack a prescriptive quality, they can still cause perceptual and behavioral confirmation biases that lead people to perceive and treat men and women differently. When strong prescriptions are added to the mix, so too are strong social rewards for stereotype-consistent behavior and punishments for gender deviance (Rudman & Fairchild, 2004). For example, in Chapter 7, we explore how women's as well as men's reactions to female leaders reflect the rules that, above all, women must be nice and not exert obvious forms of dominance over others. As you might imagine, exercising a leadership role while simultaneously fulfilling this gender prescription is not an easy task.

Are Gender Stereotypes Changing?

Are shared stereotypes of men and women stable over time or subject to significant change? Given that the systematic study of gender stereotypes, using a consistent set of measures, began in the 1970s, comparative historical data are quite limited. However, comparisons (from U.S. data) from the 1970s through the present day hold great theoretical interest given that this time period captures a widespread shift in women's roles, from the typical adult woman being exclusively a homemaker to a massive influx of women into the paid workforce. From a social structural (e.g., social role theory) perspective, this change in women's roles ought to have led to a corresponding change in stereotypes about women. By contrast, the relative lack of change in men's roles ought to promote more stability in stereotypes of men.

More specifically, social role theory suggests that occupational roles have considerable power to overcome the more generalized gender roles that affect women's and men's behavior (Eagly et al., 2000). Job requirements push men and women to act in conformity to the occupational role, even if this is inconsistent with their typical gender role (e.g., if managers are expected to be highly agentic, female managers will tend to adopt agentic traits). Recall that people generally view work outside the home as requiring stereotypically masculine (agentic) traits. Social role theory suggests that as more and more women moved out of the home and into the workforce, social stereotypes ought to have changed, leading people to ascribe more agency to women and thereby reducing the stereotypical gender gap on this dimension. Similarly, women's self-concepts ought to have changed, becoming increasingly agentic as they adapted to their new occupational roles. By contrast, because women still act as the primary homemakers and child rearers (even if they also work outside the home), no change would be expected on stereotypically feminine expressive or communal traits, either in stereotypes or self-concepts. Similarly, because men's roles have not experienced dramatic changes, stereotypes about and the self-concepts of men would be expected to show relative stability from the 1970s to the present day.

With respect to individuals' self-concepts, the changes predicted by social role theory seem to have occurred. Based on personality tests, American women's self-perceived assertiveness and dominance, which are both important aspects of agency, rose from the 1970s to the 1990s (Twenge, 2001). Because personality tests predate stereotyping research, relevant data extend back even further. In her meta-analysis, Twenge (2001) found that American women's self-ratings on agentic traits rose and fell in concert with major social role changes in roles. Women's self-perceived agency rose during the World War II years, when women moved into the paid workforce to replace men who went off to war, then decreased in the postwar years, when most women moved back to exclusively serving the wife and homemaker role; and then rose again from the 1970s onward as women moved into the paid workforce in ever higher numbers. In comparison, men's self-perceptions on agentic traits remained constant over these many decades.

However, general stereotypes of women have not mirrored changes in women's self-concepts. Comparing the responses of students at the same university in the 1970s and the 1990s, the decades that saw the greatest shift in terms of adult women working outside the home, Spence and Buckner (2000) found an increase in women's self-reported agency (just as Twenge's data showed). However, these changes were not evident in general stereotypes about women (i.e., the traits people perceive as generally more characteristic of women). In other words, as individuals, women perceived themselves as more agentic, but both women and men still perceived "women in general" to be less agentic than men.

Why would gender stereotypes of women as less agentic persist even as women increasingly saw themselves as agentic? First, recall that as more and more women become "exceptions" to the stereotype, subtypes (e.g., the career woman) develop to account for those exceptions, allowing the more general stereotype to remain intact. Thus, the prototype of woman (i.e., the stereotypical woman) remains the same even though more and more women fit into subtypes that do not match the typical woman category. The subtyping process allows people to accommodate social change without altering their overall gender stereotypes.

Second, the tendency to think of gender in essentialistic terms may increase people's cognitive resistance to changing their gender stereotypes. To the extent that people view gender-typed personality traits as part of a fundamental essence of femininity and masculinity, they are unlikely to modify their stereotypic beliefs. Essentialism may motivate people to dismiss women's agentic behavior as situationally determined (e.g., as how women act at work), not as a reflection their true personalities or essential characteristics.

Finally, not all occupations are alike and the jobs many women hold are themselves stereotyped as feminine. Even as most women in America have moved into the paid workforce, occupations have remained highly sex segregated. Female-dominated occupations are typically associated with "feminine" or communal traits rather than agency (Glick, Wilk, & Perreault, 1995). Many female-dominated jobs represent (poorly) paid versions of women's traditional roles. For example, day-care workers, whose role is child rearing, are predominantly female. Not surprisingly, the day-care worker job is stereotyped in a traditionally feminine manner (as caring, nurturing, empathetic) because this matches the occupational role, reinforcing rather than challenging traditional stereotypes (Glick et al., 1995). Think of the most highly female dominated jobs (e.g., nursing, teaching children, secretarial work); most are stereotyped as requiring feminine traits and as not requiring a particularly high degree of agency. As long as occupations remain segregated by gender, social role theory predicts limited change in gender stereotypes.

Of course, women have increasingly moved into many traditionally male occupations. For instance, many midlevel managers in the United States are now women (see Chapter 8). Here too, however, subtle examples of sex segregation reinforce traditional gender roles and stereotypes. As managers, women are overrepresented in stereotypically feminine human resources departments, and men still dominate more stereotypically masculine technical and sales management roles. However, the more that women take on leadership roles in business and government, which inevitably require agency, the more stereotypes about women are likely to change.

Historical data do not support the notion that gender stereotypes have fundamentally changed; however, research on dynamic stereotypes suggests that Americans embrace a narrative of change in which women are becoming increasingly more agentic over time. Diekman and Eagly (2000) asked people to characterize women and men of the past (in 1950), of the present, and of the future (in 2050). People's perceptions of change were consistent with social role theory: They perceived women as more agentic today than in 1950 and expected increasing agency among women in the future (with differences between women and men on agency predicted to almost completely melt away). To a lesser extent, people also assumed that women are becoming less communal in their personalities over time. By contrast, men were viewed as having more stable agentic traits, although possibly taking on a bit more communal personality traits in the future. Along with these projected changes in female agency, people also perceive women as becoming more powerful, especially within relationships and, to a lesser extent, politically and economically (Diekman, Goodfriend, & Goodwin, 2004).

Expectations for change are important because if current and future stereotypes respond to new social conditions, they create a sense that further social change is possible without a hostile backlash. Changes in stereotypes may lead people to view additional change as tolerable or inevitable, perhaps even as desirable, reducing resistance to change. However, people's perceptions that women are changing does not necessarily indicate approval for those changes. Are people content with the idea of women becoming more agentic? Perhaps they believe that women are changing but are unhappy about it because the changes violate prescriptive stereotypes about how women *should* be. Recent work suggests that people not only expect women to become increasingly agentic but also envision social acceptance for this change (Diekman & Goodfriend, 2006). In other words, people seem to anticipate accommodation more than resistance to changes in women's roles and personalities.

A considerable amount of research on backlash toward women who enact agency, reviewed in detail in Chapter 7, suggests, however, that to expect little resistance to changes in female agency may be too rosy a view. Although people may believe in the abstract that agentic women are celebrated rather than rejected, when faced with real women behaving in agentic ways, people do not seem to react as positively. This disapproving reaction may occur because women who behave agentically are also viewed as not being sufficiently communal, a trait that remains a strong prescription for women. Thus, although people may evaluate female agency positively, they nevertheless may punish individual women whose agentic behavior suggests insufficient feminine niceness (e.g., Rudman, 1998; Rudman & Glick, 1999).

Overall, social role theory fosters optimism about the possibilities for social change, especially if sex segregation in the job market continues to break down. As more women move into work roles once dominated by men, women ought to be viewed as equally capable and agentic. Further, as women earn their own incomes, gender hierarchy decreases, undermining traditional status and power distinctions between the sexes. Thus, structural changes in roles, propelled in part by economic conditions (e.g., the need for two incomes to support a family) and technological changes (e.g., machines, such as forklifts, that make physical differences in strength immaterial), have considerable power to alter gender relations and gender stereotypes.

At present, the evidence for dynamic stereotypes is mixed. Historical comparisons from the 1970s to the present suggest that women have become increasingly agentic in their self-concepts, even though gender stereotypes show little evidence of change. Nonetheless, Americans currently appear to embrace a historical narrative in which they believe that women have become more agentic and expect this trend to continue in the future. Other aspects of gender stereotypes, however, show minimal changes over time and little expectation for future change. People believe that men, consistent with stability in their social roles, have not changed much in the past 50 years and will not change radically in the future. Further, when it comes to the central traits viewed as defining femininity, both descriptive and prescriptive stereotypes that women are and ought to be more communal than men remain strong and appear likely to continue into the future.

Chapter Summary

Stereotypes set up not only descriptive expectations about how people believe men and women differ but also prescriptive norms about how each sex should behave. These descriptive and prescriptive functions are crucial for understanding how gender stereotypes influence perceptions of and interactions with members of each sex, especially when people's behavior deviates from gender stereotypes. The descriptive aspect of gender stereotypes reduces perceivers' cognitive effort by allowing them to quickly and efficiently classify other people. Because gender stereotypes are learned so early in life and used so often, they become automatic, implicit associations that influence perceptions of and behavior toward others without perceivers' awareness. Like a bad habit, gender stereotypes are hard to shake and even highly egalitarian people tend automatically to use them. This has pervasive effects. For instance, people automatically accord women less status than men. In turn, this can lead people to respond less positively to female leaders (see Chapter 7).

The prescriptive element of gender stereotypes reflects people's desire to justify and maintain a highly gendered social structure in which men and women have different roles and different degrees of status and power. Stereotypes justify gender roles as natural, desirable, and morally correct. Thus, stereotypes are not merely automatic associations, but they have an ideological purpose, helping to ensure the continuation of traditional gender roles and hierarchy. Although increasing gender equality in American society should lessen gender prescriptions over time, people today still demand that women exhibit greater warmth than men and that men show greater agency than women. Overall, gender stereotypes have thus far shown remarkable resistance to social changes (primarily in women's roles), perhaps because subtyping accommodates those changes. However, Americans do generally believe that women have become more agentic over time and will continue to do so, reflecting women's increased participation in the paid workforce. In comparison, the relative constancy of men's roles over time is mirrored by people's general belief that men's traits have not changed as much as women's. From a social structural perspective, future changes in gender stereotypes will depend in large measure on whether the job market continues to be highly sex segregated and whether women achieve greater representation in the most powerful, high-status positions in society.

CHAPTER 6

Self-Sustaining Prophecies

Imagine that you are asked to perform a task in which you must learn how to interweave strands of material in a specific pattern. How much would you enjoy this task? How self-conscious would you feel about doing it? Would you mind if others watched while you performed it? Now imagine that the very same task is described in one of two different ways: as a form of "hair braiding" used by hairstylists to achieve a fashionable look or as a form of "rope braiding" used by sailors and construction workers to achieve a rope of superior strength. Would the framing of this task make a difference in how you would feel about performing it? Young adult men asked to perform this behavior while being videotaped reported much more discomfort when the task was described as "hairstyling" than when it was described as "rope reinforcing" (Bosson, Prewitt-Freilino, & Taylor, 2005), suggesting that the same skill can be a point of pride or shame, depending on whether it is described as masculine or feminine. You can easily imagine how other skills might evoke similar reactions; for example, twirling a stick might make men feel more proud if it is framed as a martial arts skill versus baton twirling. Similarly, women might feel happier learning the same pattern of knee bends if they are described as ballet positions versus warm-up exercises for football players. As these examples show, the behavior itself is not as important as whether it is framed as suitable for one's gender.

In this chapter, we review the myriad ways that gender stereotypes cause people to construct a social reality that supports them. We focus on several processes that add up to a self-sustaining prophecy for stereotypes that allows them to perpetually regenerate in the culture at large. These are outlined in Figure 6.1. First, people self-stereotype, using stereotypical expectancies as a compass to guide their own interests and activities in ways that reinforce gender beliefs. In essence, people voluntarily conform to gender norms because it often "feels right" to do so. Second, stereotypic expectancies about others can cause them to be seemingly confirmed, either because perceivers misread other's actions as stereotype consistent or because they elicit behavior from others that "proves" the stereotype is true. Third, external demands to uphold gender prescriptions cause people to involuntarily conform to them to avoid social punishment. As a result, men and women behave in ways that validate the perceived legitimacy of gender prescriptions as "rules" for behavior and reinforce the notion that deviations ought to be punished. Finally, these processes gain added strength because gender stereotypes are so well established and accepted that many people feel they have permission to use them freely, without guilt or compunction, in a way that is no longer true of stereotypes about other groups

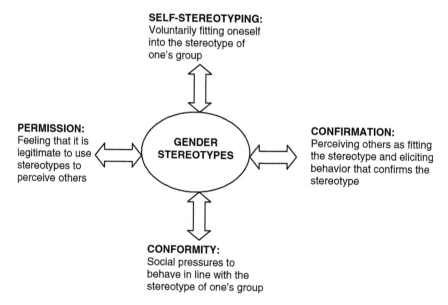

FIGURE 6.1. Processes that perpetuate gender stereotypes.

(e.g., racial stereotypes in the United States). Thus, one of the most important ways that gender stereotypes are perpetuated is through their largely uncontested and invisible nature.

Stereotypes Are Perpetuated through Self-Stereotyping

Because gender identity is likely the most prominent and significant identity that people have (see Chapter 3), it should not be surprising that men and women strive to fit into their own-gendered "culture" in order to embody the traits, interests, and occupations deemed appropriate. Self-stereotyping for the sake of gender identity involves willingness to adhere to a set of gendered rules when making decisions about your life's course and to forfeit genuine interests if they collide with these rules. An important way in which this is manifested is self-selection bias (Ickes, Snyder, & Garcia, 1997), which refers to how people choose the situations, roles, and occupations they pursue. These choices strongly affect the talents individuals develop and exhibit, the social influences to which they are exposed, and the degree of social status and power they can obtain.

Educational and occupational choices are two well-documented domains in which self-selection has been shown to be strongly influenced by gender stereotypes. These choices are of special importance from a social structural perspective because they have the power to reinforce or to challenge the gendered division of labor and status hierarchy. For example, if women generally choose not to pursue traditionally masculine high-status work roles because they are "gender inappropriate," conceptions of these roles as masculine are perpetuated.

On the one hand, in many industrialized nations, great strides have been made in recent decades toward opening up opportunity for women to have the career of their choice. On the other hand, academic majors and occupations still remain highly sex segregated. For example, secretaries and dental hygienists are largely female, whereas executives and dentists are largely male. If you had the power to match the number of women to the number of men in occupations, you would have to switch the careers of approximately 65% of the women to do so (Reskin & Padovic, 1994; Tomaskovic-Devey, 1995). The sex-based segregation of the job market fosters sex-typed images of occupations that, in turn, promote continued occupational sex segregation (Cejka & Eagly, 1999; Eagly & Steffen, 1984)). As a result, male-dominated occupations are those in which masculine attributes are thought to be necessary for success, whereas female-dominated occupations are those in which feminine attributes are deemed important (Glick, 1991). Importantly, occupations requiring masculine attributes are higher in status and yield the highest earnings (Cejka & Eagly, 1999; Glick, Wilk, & Perreault, 1995).

Gender Differences in Math and Science Skills

Prominent among high-status masculine occupations are jobs that require math and science skills. Unfortunately, even as our information society relies increasingly on technological and quantitative talents, the number of women pursuing college degrees and careers in math and science is declining, thereby widening the extant gender gap (Panteli, Stack, & Ramsey, 2001). In part, this gap stems from self-selection effects that date back to adolescence. For example, students who take high school math and science courses tend to pursue a science-related career, and men are more likely to take these courses than women (Eccles, 1984). Beginning in elementary school, both boys and girls stereotype math as a masculine domain (Wigfield et al., 1997). People tend to gravitate toward classes, majors, and careers that they believe they are likely to be talented in, and self-perceptions of academic abilities are influenced by adolescents' own gender stereotypes as well as their mothers' gender stereotypes (Jacobs & Eccles, 1992). Thus, even if a girl does not self-stereotype and enjoys and has talent in math and science, her mother may nonetheless convince her to put her time and energies into something more "gender appropriate."

It is important to note that girls (and their parents) have less confidence in their math ability even during early adolescence, when girls either outperform boys (as indicated by grades and scores on standardized tests; Eccles, 1984) or perform similarly (Hyde, Fennema, & Lamon, 1990). Thus, the *belief* that math is a masculine skill predates the reality, strongly suggesting that gender stereotypes create the reality (rather than the reverse). It is not until high school that gender differences favoring males become apparent (Fan, Chen, & Matsumoto, 1997), creating a disparity that continues as students reach the college level and career-entry stage (Lefevre, Kulak, & Heymans, 1992). In concert, the pattern implicates sex stereotypes as a deciding factor regarding the talents that adolescents believe they possess, choose to pursue, and, subsequently, excel at. As a result, the stereotype that men are better at math is sustained by the choices that women and men make, and these choices ultimately bolster the accuracy of the stereotype as women drop out and men pursue mathematics in differing numbers.

Gender Differences in Status Seeking

Beyond careers in math and science, women also show less interest than men in pursuing occupations that confer the highest economic and social rewards (Konrad, Ritchie, Lieb, & Corrigall, 2000; Pratto, Stallworth, Sidanius, & Siers, 1997). For example, compared with men, women are less interested in becoming politicians, bankers, corporate lawyers, and CEOs and more interested in becoming teachers, social workers, and public defense lawyers (Pratto et al., 1997; Rudman & Heppen, 2003). The sex-typed nature of these careers undoubtedly helps to explain this self-selection bias; because prestigious positions remain strongly male dominated, it is more normative for men to occupy them (Cejka & Eagly, 1999). According to social role theory (Eagly, 1987; Eagly et al., 2000), gender socialization processes cause men and women to internalize different expectations for their behavior, including the expectation that men should be status seekers, whereas women should be nurturing. These gender differences both stem from, and perpetuate, status differences for men and women, with men more likely to be leaders and women their supporters, in domains that range from the athletic field to the workplace.

Consistent with the influence of social roles and stereotypes on desired occupational attributes, a meta-analysis found that men more often than women value earnings, power, and leadership, whereas women more often than men value interpersonal relationships and helping others (Konrad et al., 2000). Even female physicians at a prestigious medical school value professional recognition and leadership less than male physicians and place more emphasis on relationships with their patients and students (Buckley, Sanders, Shih, Kallar, & Hampton, 2000).

The gender gap in values reflects ideological differences that promote men's higher standing in the social hierarchy. Pratto et al. (1997) showed that men are drawn to hierarchy-enhancing occupations that perpetuate existing status hierarchies by, for example, protecting the wealth of the privileged class. In contrast, women are more likely to be drawn to hierarchy-attenuating occupations that help the disenfranchised. Because these types of occupations also differ in terms of access to resources (e.g., stock options, salary, social contacts), ideological differences between the sexes help to explain men's greater interest in and ability to acquire economic and social power.

Thus, despite legislative policies (e.g., affirmative action) and sociocultural changes that have encouraged women to move into the labor force and compete with men, women remain underrepresented in high-status occupations in part through self-selection. Whether women's choices stem from internalized gender norms and expectancies or reflect differences in values and ideology, the outcome is that women continue to have less financial, political, and social power compared with men. Consequently, the stereotype that men have more status in society is perpetuated.

In sum, self-stereotyping and the resulting self-selection of men and women into different roles are important reasons why gender stereotypes and gender hierarchy are perpetuated. But this is only one piece of a complex puzzle. In the following section, we review how, in daily social interaction, perceivers' gendered expectations create social realities that seemingly confirm the accuracy of gender stereotypes.

Stereotypes Are Perpetuated
through Social Interactions and Confirmation

As we explained in Chapter 5, gender stereotypes are both *descriptive* (setting up expectations about how men and women are likely to behave) and *prescriptive* (dictating norms about how men and women *ought* to behave). Both aspects of stereotypes can lead to stereotype-confirmation processes. *Perceptual* confirmation occurs when people perceive others in ways that make them seem stereotype consistent, and *behavioral* confirmation occurs when perceivers behave in ways that actually elicit stereotype-consistent behavior from others (Geis, 1993; Merton, 1948; Rosenthal & Jacobson, 1968; Rosenthal & Rubin, 1978; Snyder, 1984; Snyder & Haugen, 1994; Snyder & Swann, 1978). Not only do these processes reinforce gender stereotypes by making them appear to be correct, but they also create a reality that lends them accuracy.

How Stereotypes as Expectancies Bias Perceptions and Behavior

Perceptual and behavioral confirmation processes happen because stereotypes act as expectancies about others, and expectancies bias our social interactions in numerous ways (for reviews, see S. T. Fiske, 1998; Kunda & Spencer, 2003; S. C. Wheeler & Petty, 2001). Stereotypes act as working models (Bartlett, 1932) or heuristics (Bodenhausen, 1993; Chaiken, Liberman, & Eagly, 1989) that determine what perceivers expect during social interactions. Expectancies are particularly intriguing because of their power to perpetuate themselves even when they are wrong. Next, we discuss the roles of biased inferences, attention to information, and behavioral confirmation in preserving stereotypes. These self-sustaining processes illustrate how stereotypes can be reinforced even when they are not accurate.

Biased Inferences

Imagine hearing that Judy, a homemaker, "hit someone." How aggressive is she? Was this "hit" a light slap or a serious punch? People given this scenario tend to dismiss the incident as not being very aggressive because they imagine Judy spanking a child. When given the same information about Joe, a construction worker, perceivers are more likely to conclude that the "hit" was a punch and a significant instance of aggression (Kunda & Sherman-Williams, 1993). Similarly, if you are told that a young man got in a car accident, you might infer that he was driving too fast, whereas you might assume that an old man was distracted. These examples illustrate how stereotypes bias the interpretation of information about individuals as a result of their group memberships. Because information is often ambiguous or unclear or can be construed in multiple ways, people use their stereotypes as an inferential guide. Whether or not these inferences are correct, the beliefs behind them remain intact.

Biased Attention to Information

When an individual's behavior seems ambiguous or mixed, stereotyped expectancies lead perceivers to focus on the information that confirms the stereotype while ignoring or reinterpreting the information that contradicts it (Darley & Gross, 1983; Hoffman & Hurst, 1990). As a result, it is often easy for perceivers to believe that an individual's behavior is consistent with stereotyped expectations, even if that person's behavior provides just as much "proof against" as "proof for" this conclusion. For example, when people watched the same slide show depicting a woman described as either a waitress or a librarian, they inferred behaviors that were consistent with their stereotyped expectations (Cohen, 1981). Seen drinking something alongside a man, she was more likely to be viewed as having a *beer* with her *boyfriend* in the waitress condition but having *wine* with her *husband* in the librarian condition. Further, people recalled stereotype-consistent behaviors better than stereotype-inconsistent behaviors (e.g., bowling in the waitress condition but reading a book in the librarian condition). Although bowling and reading a book were always part of the slide show, people remembered behaviors that matched the stereotype label more than behaviors that were mismatched.

Interestingly, when perceivers evaluate someone who can be categorized on the basis of their gender or ethnicity (e.g., an Asian female), their perceptions can be altered depending on the salience of the gender or ethnic category. For example, after reviewing the college application of a female Asian American, evaluators whose attention was drawn to her gender recalled that she had a lower math SAT score compared with evaluators for whom her ethnicity was made salient (Pittinsky, Shih, & Ambady, 2000). Because her actual SAT score did not differ across conditions, evaluators' memories were influenced by stereotypical assumptions that women have poor quantitative skills, whereas Asians have strong quantitative skills.

Eliciting Stereotype-Consistent Information

Perceivers are not mere passive recipients of information; they can also direct social interactions in ways that fulfill their beliefs (Darley, Fleming, Hilton, & Swann, 1988). For example, a professor might be more likely to ask a student of Asian ethnicity how many hours she or he studied over the weekend than whether the student had attended a party. The question is designed to elicit information that confirms the stereotype that Asian students tend to be studious (Lin, Kwan, Cheung, & Fiske, 2005). One of the first questions women are asked when they meet someone new is "Do you have any kids?," which often elicits information that confirms the stereotype that women are nurturing. By contrast, men are typically asked, "What do you do for a living?," which promotes the stereotype that men are the chief providers. If women were commonly asked to describe their occupations and men to discuss their children, information that could disconfirm existing stereotypes would be elicited. Instead, gendered expectations often lead individuals to shape social experiences in a way that perpetuates their preexisting beliefs.

Behavioral Confirmation

The processes just described suggest how perceivers can walk away from interactions with their stereotypes not only intact but reinforced, even when they could have been counteracted. This effect is known as perceptual confirmation. More powerfully, stereotypes guide perceivers' behavior during interactions in ways that cause others to conform to stereotypes (Snyder, 1981). As a result, the stereotype becomes a "proven" fact. A classic example by Snyder, Tanke, and Berscheid (1977) serves to illustrate. Male students, provided only with a picture, interviewed female students over the telephone. Half of the men were randomly given a photo of an attractive woman, the other half were given a photo of a plain woman. The conversation was unscripted and tape-recorded on two different channels. Independent analyses of the women's tape recordings showed that attractive women were warmer and friendlier than plain women during the interaction. The men's erroneous beliefs led them to confirm their stereotype that attractive women are desirable; because they behaved warmly toward them they elicited friendliness from the women, resulting in a self-fulfilling prophecy (Merton, 1948). Similarly, when male interviewers were led to believe that female job applicants were attracted to them, the women showed flirtatious behavior during the interview (without realizing it; Ridge & Reber, 2002). Of course, women are also prone to inducing behavioral confirmation. For example, when women are led to believe that a man is sexist, they can elicit negative behaviors from him that confirm their false belief (Pinel, 2002). Thus, perceivers' actions can lead others to fulfill a prophecy by behaving as expected.

Skrypnek and Snyder (1982) showed how behavioral confirmation applies to the workplace. Men were given the task of negotiating a labor division for a collaborative project with an unseen partner, whom they were told was either female (as they all were) or male. Because the men assigned sex-typed tasks to their partner, they elicited either masculine or feminine behavior that seemingly "confirmed" the partner's "gender" (although they were all female). Similarly, female employees are often assigned tasks that draw out their interpersonal skills (e.g., human resource management), whereas male employees are assigned tasks that elicit leadership skills (e.g., production management; Frankforter, 1996). If the tasks were switched, the women would appear to be productive leaders and the men would appear to be interpersonally skilled.

Finally, because gender stereotypes are so highly prescriptive, they act as normative expectancies about how men and women ought to be.

This fact energizes behavioral confirmation processes because targets expect (and receive) social rewards for confirming stereotypes. As a result, perceivers do not even need to be present to elicit behavioral confirmation. In one study, female job applicants were told that a male evaluator for an upcoming interview either had traditional or nontraditional beliefs about women. When they returned for the interview, women who believed their interviewer was a chauvinist dressed more femininely, wore more jewelry and make-up, and behaved more femininely (e.g., downplayed their ambitions) during the interview compared with women who believed he was nontraditional (von Baeyer, Sherk, & Zanna, 1981).

In addition, Zanna and Pack (1975) found that women who believed that an attractive, as opposed to an unattractive, man would see their responses described themselves in a manner that conformed to female stereotypes and performed more poorly on a purported intelligence test. Thus, women displayed more stereotypical behaviors when they wanted to impress a man who either had power over them or who they found to be desirable. These examples show how the merely anticipated expectations of others can shape subsequent behavior.

Finally, when people are simply motivated to get along with others (i.e., have affiliation motives), they are more likely to conform to gender stereotypes. For example, Sinclair and her colleagues found that people rated themselves higher on gender-stereotypic traits when they had high, as opposed to low, affiliation motives (S. Sinclair, Huntsinger, Skorinko, & Hardin, 2005). The need to be liked triggers gender conformity because individuals presume that they will be rewarded with social approval if they perform their gender.

Stereotypes Are Perpetuated through Conformity Pressures

Throughout this volume, we emphasize the prescriptive nature of gender stereotypes; that is, that sex-linked stereotypes dictate how men and women should behave. As noted in Chapter 1, when beliefs are prescriptive, they act as injunctive norms (Cialdini & Trost, 1998). Injunctive norms prescribe the value of social behaviors (what ought to be), whereas descriptive norms merely inform us as to how others typically act. As a result, violating injunctive norms generally results in stronger and more emotional reactions compared with violating descriptive norms, as in the example of different reactions to a Norwegian who does not ski (a violation of a descriptive stereotype) versus a man who fails to show courage when his girlfriend is threatened (a violation of a prescriptive stereotype) illustrated in Chapter 5. Thus, a unique outcome of violating a prescriptive stereotype is that violators are punished. This fact greatly increases the pressure for people to confirm gender stereotypes and to avoid the suggestion of gender deviance at all costs.

The need to avoid gender deviance can lead men and women to not even try to correct their faulty performance on a task when they believe their mistakes are gender driven. For example, Prentice and Miller (2006) asked Princeton University undergraduates to estimate the number of dots briefly presented to them on slides. (Pretesting ensured that dot estimation was not considered a gendered skill.) They then gave the students false feedback; some were told they had overestimated the number of dots, whereas others were told they had underestimated them. The type of error feedback provided was unimportant; what mattered was the type of social comparison information given. The critical group was told that their dot estimation score differed from a cross-sex participant's score, whereas the control group was told their performance was similar to that of a same-sex participant. Note that feedback concerned the performance of a single woman or man. Nonetheless, the critical group assumed the task would yield robust gender differences, and they did not even try to correct for their dot estimation bias on subsequent trials. By comparison, the control group did not endorse dot estimation as gender typed, and they attempted to improve their faulty performance when afforded the opportunity to do so.

If people fail to correct their performance on a novel (and arbitrary) gendered ability, as Prentice and Miller's (2006) findings show, it is not hard to imagine how gender conformity might prevent men and women from attempting to cross gender boundaries in areas traditionally linked to gender. For example, it can help to explain why girls tend to avoid math and why they (and their parents) lack confidence in their aptitude, as described earlier in this chapter. Similarly, boys tend to avoid activities that girls seem designed for (e.g., dance and figure skating). As the example at the beginning of this chapter shows, men were distressed by the simple act of braiding when it was described as "hairstyling" as opposed to "rope reinforcement."

A similar study goes even further by providing a vivid example of how gender conformity can curb people's talents and motivation to perform well (Sharps, Price, & Williams, 1994). Mental rotation is a skill that men typically perform better than women (for a review, see Valian, 1999). However, when researchers described a mental rotation task as predictive of success in interior design, women actually performed better than men. Men outscored women only when the task ostensibly predicted success in aviation engineering. Similar to the dot estimation task, people were motivated not to do well when success put them at risk for gender deviance. Because men typically outscore women on mental rotation, the reversed effect in the feminine condition testifies to the power of gender conformity to release the motivational brakes (for women) and to apply them (for men). It also signals the extent to which people inhibit themselves to avoid crossing gender bounds.

Penalties for Cross-Sex Behaviors Perpetuate Stereotypes

Chapter 3 illustrated how children police gender boundaries (e.g., through taunts in the schoolyard), but they learn how to do so from adults. Parents and teachers alike judge cross-sex behavior harshly, and this is particularly true for boys (Cahill & Adams, 1997; C. L. Martin, 1990; Sandnabba & Ahlberg, 1999). The result is that more boys than girls are diagnosed with gender identity disorders, and the threshold for recommending clinical assessment is lower for boys (Zucker, Bradley, & Sanikhani, 1997). These are severe reactions that can result in long-term emotional dysfunction (Isay, 1999), but adults are willing to take that risk because of the fear that cross-sex behavior signals latent homosexuality (Kite & Deaux, 1987; Pleak, 1999). Because masculinity and femininity are psychological opposites, when boys want to play with dolls or girls want to play with trucks they are viewed as having the essence of the other gender, which leads to the fear that they will be attracted to their own sex. This fear may pertain more to boys, given that girls can be tomboys without raising serious doubts about their sexuality (Thorne, 1993; see also Chapter 7).

Nonetheless, both genders risk social rejection when they engage in cross-sex behaviors. Indeed, while developmental psychologists show that boys are especially constrained to gender prescriptions, social psychologists (who study adults) have emphasized the ways that they handicap women. The key to this apparent contradiction is that gender prescriptions demand that boys act aggressively, whereas girls are pressured not to "step on others' toes," a prescription that is more costly to them later in life, when they attempt to climb the career ladder. In other words, gender prescriptions help to preserve a hierarchy in which men are particularly encouraged to gain status and power and women are discouraged from this pursuit. We reserve a thorough treatment of how gender stereotypes create obstacles to achieving success in cross-sex domains for Chapter 7. Here, we focus on how cross-sex behavior leads to strong social pressures through ostracism and punishment of gender deviants. Given that girls and boys are socialized from birth to behave in feminine and masculine ways, and that they suffer "jeer pressure" when they deviate from gendered scripts (see Chapter 3), it is not surprising that most women and men are conditioned to think, feel, and act so differently as to appear to warrant the common expression "the opposite sex."

The Penalty of Social Rejection

Rewards for conformity and rejection for deviance play a powerful role in the self-sustaining prophecy of gender stereotypes. Although enforced conformity has some evolutionary advantages for complex social animals (e.g., it smoothes group functioning and minimizes conflict), the cost to individuals can be high. Indeed, one way of understanding the power of injunctive norms is to observe what happens when people *do not* conform.

A classic study by Schachter (1951) suggests that punishment of deviants is severe. Schachter recruited groups of student social workers whose task was to read and discuss the case of "Johnny Rocco," a budding juvenile delinquent. In deciding on a course of action, the majority in each group voted for a mix of support and discipline. But Schachter planted a deviant who wanted stiff punishment for Johnny. The groups' responses to the deviant were consistent. At first, they paid him the most attention, trying to persuade him to conform. When it was clear they would not succeed, they ignored him completely, cutting him off. Later, they voted to have him ousted from the group. When told they were blocked from that recourse, they assigned him menial tasks so that he eventually would remove himself from the group. The remarkable consistency across groups demonstrates that people are well versed in how to treat deviants. As a result, it is not surprising that people are susceptible to capitulating to peer pressure: The social consequences of deviance are harsh, as viewers of *Survivor* and similar television programs (where the ultimate punishment is to be voted out of the group) can attest.

As Schachter (1951) demonstrated, deviants risk being ostracized. Ostracism activates the same region of the brain that is activated when suffering physical pain and cognitive conflict or discrepancy (the dorsal anterior cingulate cortex; Eisenberger, Lieberman, & Williams, 2003). Ostracism damages people's sense of belonging and thus their self-esteem (Leary & Baumeister, 2000; K. D. Williams, 2007). If you have ever suffered ostracism yourself, you likely remember the sadness and anger you felt; being ostracized increases both (Leary, Kowalski, Smith, & Phillips, 2003; Leary, Twenge, & Quinlivan, 2006; K. D. Williams et al., 2002).

Ostracized individuals employ many countermeasures to reinstate themselves as worthy members of a group, including conforming to an incorrect majority's opinion (K. D. Williams, Bernieri, Faulkner, Grahe, & Gada-Jain, 2000). However, people do not need to actually suffer rejection to experience conformity pressures; the mere threat of becoming a social outcast will suffice. For example, a female colleague asked a male friend, "If you had the chance to be the other sex for a day, would you take it?" Before he could answer, she added that "Most women say yes, but most men say no." He blushed and confessed he was going to say "yes"—after all, he knew what it was like to be a man; what was it like to be a woman?—but now he felt pressured to say "no." The simple information that "most X would do Y" compels people to follow suit when gender is at stake. Classic social psychological research shows that individuals will withhold or change their dissenting opinions for fear of social reprisals (Asch, 1952, 1955; Deutsch & Gerard, 1955; Janis, 1982; Kelley, 1952; Noelle-Neumann, 1993), with potentially tragic consequences. For example, social pressure on NASA engineers to agree to launch despite their grave concerns led to the disintegration of the space shuttle *Challenger* (Esser & Lindoerfer, 1989). The fear of ostracism is sufficiently powerful that people will go against their better judgment to avoid it.

The Threat of Backlash and Cultural Stereotype Maintenance

Having established people's awareness of punishment for norm violation and how it leads to conformity pressures broadly, we turn specifically to social reprisals for gender deviance. Rudman (1998) termed these reprisals *backlash effects* because they undermine women's progress by eliciting gender conformity, which perpetuates sex stereotypes that advantage men (e.g., by endowing them with higher status). If people fear backlash for gender nonconformity, their subsequent actions are likely to bolster and perpetuate cultural stereotypes. But even though backlash effects tend to reinforce male status, they can be particularly harsh toward individual men, who are punished for showing any "feminine" weaknesses that undermine male status (Berdahl, 2007a). Men have a lifetime of experience observing their peers being teased or ostracized for effeminate behavior, creating strong normative pressures toward highly masculine self-presentations (Pleck, 1981; Pleck, Sonenstein, & Ku, 1993; Thompson & Pleck, 1986). Similarly, women may pretend to be hyperfeminine to placate men with traditional gender beliefs (von Baeyer et al., 1981; Zanna & Pack, 1975). Thus, it seems likely that fear of backlash is a significant force vis-à-vis keeping men "manly" and women "feminine."

Figure 6.2 outlines the role that fear of backlash plays in cultural stereotype maintenance. Cultural stereotypes provide the standard against which actors judge their own behavior; if they violate gendered expectancies, they may fear backlash. In that event, they are likely to engage in recovery strategies to avoid backlash and reinstate themselves as worthy group members. These strategies may include closeting gender-deviant behavior, lying about it, and doubling up on efforts to conform to gender norms. These behaviors prevent deviant actors from standing out as atypical role models; as a result, sex stereotypes are allowed to persist, unchallenged. In this way, recovery strategies replenish cultural stereotypes, as the feedback loop indicates. Finally, given that the threat of rejection injures belonging and self-esteem (Leary & Baumeister, 2000), if recovery strategies are designed to bolster these, we would expect

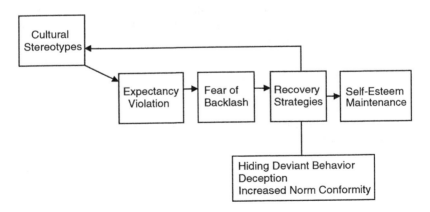

FIGURE 6.2. A model of the role of actors' fear of backlash in cultural stereotype maintenance. Adapted from Rudman and Fairchild (2004). Copyright 2004 by the American Psychological Association. Adapted by permission.

greater self-esteem on the part of threatened deviants who engage in them compared with those who do not.

Testing the Model Using Gender Deviance

Rudman and Fairchild (2004) tested the model shown in Figure 6.2 by giving undergraduate men and women false feedback on gender knowledge tests. The masculine knowledge test included 30 items about cars and motorcycles, sports, finance, weapons, and physical violence (e.g., the best way to punch an opponent). The feminine knowledge test included 30 items about beauty, fashion, cooking, and dating etiquette. The tests purported to assess knowledge that "society expects college-aged men [women] to possess." In reality, they were designed to assess fairly obscure knowledge so that participants would believe the false feedback (i.e., be unable to ascertain their true score). For example, the masculine test required identifying the first people to use flamethrowers in battle (Turks or Greeks), whereas the feminine test required identifying the first company to invent hair coloring (L'Oreal or Clairol). Table 6.1 shows sample test items.

Fear of Backlash

Participants believed the tests were being developed for an upcoming project; in reality, they were used to manipulate deviance. In the deviant condition, people were told they scored high on the cross-sex test. In the normative condition, they were told they scored high on the same-sex test. The measures were computerized, and the software program (after calculating their score) announced they had qualified for the winner's lottery to be held at the end of the study. Although you might find it remarkable that deviants found the feedback credible, people are highly skilled at making sense of their reality. For example, a male deviant remarked that he had probably learned a lot about fashion over the summer, having spent it with his sister in Hollywood. A female deviant attributed her high score to the fact that she had three brothers who were sports fans. Nonetheless, when participants were asked how they would feel if their success was publicized (e.g., on a Web site advertising the project), deviants expressed more fear of backlash than their normative counterparts. In particular, deviants expressed concern that their friends would tease them, that others would view them as odd, and that they would be disliked.

TABLE 6.1 Sample Items for Gender Knowledge Tests

Female Knowledge Test

1. You wear Manolo Blahniks on your (head vs. feet).
2. The company first to develop hair coloring was (Clairol vs. L'Oreal).
3. Children typically start to teethe when they are (over vs. under) 1 year old?
4. Children should not be given which medication? (ibuprofen vs. aspirin)
5. Leftovers can be safely kept at room temperature for up to (4 hours vs. 2 hours).
6. A roux is best described as a (sauce vs. cake).
7. Compared to men, women need more (iron vs. zinc).
8. Exercises that improve a woman's sex life are called? (Kegel vs. Pilates)
9. According to *The Rules*, if you are in a long distance relationship, how many times should a man visit you before you visit him? (3 times vs. 1 time)
10. According to *The Fabulous Girl's Guide*, if you've spent the night with a bad lover, in the morning you should (politely ask him to leave vs. feed him breakfast).
11. What was the first Web site devoted to women? (Glamnet.com vs. Ivillage.com)

Male Knowledge Test

1. A dime is what kind of play in football? (defensive vs. offensive)
2. The name of the Carolina NHL team is (Thrashers vs. Hurricanes).
3. To help an engine produce more power, you should (inject the fuel vs. reduce displacement).
4. In nature, the best analogy for a spark plug is (solar fire vs. lightning).
5. Soldiers in World War II often used what type of guns? (Gatling vs. Tommy)
6. The first people to use primitive flamethrowers in battle were (Greeks vs. Turks).
7. The material used between bathroom tiles is called (spackling vs. grout).
8. If you need to replace the tank ball in a toilet, ask for a (flapper vs. ball cock).
9. Hugh Hefner first published *Playboy* magazine in (1963 vs. 1953).
10. After shooting a deer, bear, elk, or turkey, you must attach a (kill tag vs. ID tag).
11. When punching someone, you should aim your fist (a foot beyond target vs. directly at target).

Note. Items were used in Rudman and Fairchild (2004, Experiment 3).

Recovery Strategies

To provide deviants with means to avoid backlash, the computer program asked participants if they would be willing to publicize their scores on the Web site advertising the project. If so, would they be willing to provide their name and a digital photo, to be taken by the experimenter? Following their response, they reported their interest in occupations and sports that were stereotypically masculine (e.g., military officer, professional athlete, boxing, football), feminine (e.g., fashion model, social worker, softball, gymnastics) or gender neutral (e.g., novelist, film actor, tennis, volleyball). Consistent with Figure 6.2, deviants who feared backlash were less willing to publicize their success on the Web site and showed a stronger interest in gendered activities compared with deviants who did not fear backlash (and with normatives, whose fear of backlash was uniformly low). Thus, the threat of backlash led deviants to closet their success and to increase their gender conformity to redouble their efforts to appear "normal."

Participants were also provided with the chance to enter the winner's lottery (for a $100 cash prize). However, they had to tell the experimenter whether or not they had qualified for the test (i.e., what their scores were). The experimenter then gave them a ticket to (privately) place in a box clearly marked "Male Knowledge Test Winner" or "Female Knowledge Test Winner." All participants acknowledged they had qualified, but deviants who feared backlash were more likely to lie to the experimenter about which test they had succeeded in compared with deviants who did not fear backlash and with normatives. They were also more likely to place their lottery ticket in the wrong box. Thus, whether the behavior was public or private, deviants engaged in deception to protect themselves when they felt threatened by backlash. In sum, deviants were more likely than normatives to engage in recovery strategies by hiding their success, deceiving the experimenter, and conforming to gender norms, but particularly if they feared social rejection.

Cultural Stereotype Preservation

People who disconfirm stereotypes are precisely those best able to challenge, and thereby weaken, cultural stereotypes (e.g., Brewer, 1988; Fiske & Neuberg, 1990; Kunda & Thagard, 1996). Thus, counterstereotypical actors should play a pivotal role in stereotype reduction. However, in line with Figure 6.2, actors who feared backlash hid their deviance and conformed to stereotypes to avoid social rejection. As a result, the people most able to challenge stereotypes are least likely to do so when the threat of backlash is prominent. The end result is stereotype preservation in the culture at large.

Are deviants aware that their actions promote stereotypes? To find out, Rudman and Fairchild (2004) asked participants to estimate the stereotypes of future visitors to the Web site publicizing the winners' scores. Results were as expected, with gender deviants who hid their success estimating that future visitors to the Web site would show stronger stereotypes compared with deviants who did not hide. These results support the model's assumption that people who hide their counterstereotypical behavior contribute to a social reality in which gendered beliefs are allowed to persist, unchallenged.

Self-Esteem Maintenance

The model shown in Figure 6.2 also assumes that deviants engage in recovery strategies to maintain their self-esteem. However, Rudman and Fairchild (2004) did not find support for this assumption. Instead, deviants who feared backlash reported decreased self-esteem whether or not they hid their success or conformed to gender norms. Thus, the path from recovery to self-esteem is suspect. Instead, a negative path leading directly from fear of backlash to self-esteem maintenance may be in order. Indeed, these findings are a testament to the power of the threat of ostracism to reduce self-esteem (Leary & Baumeister, 2000; K. D. Williams, 2007). As a result, it appears that fear of backlash and strategies to avoid it have negative consequences for actors (reducing self-esteem) as well as for society (maintaining cultural stereotypes).

In sum, cultural stereotypes can create expectancy violations for actors who succeed in atypical domains. People who fear backlash for counterstereotypical success are likely to hide their cross-sex behavior, use deception, and increase their gender conformity as a means of avoiding ostracism. These actions sustain cultural stereotypes by depriving perceivers of the opportunity to have their stereotypes challenged. Instead of witnessing an atypical role model, perceivers may be led to believe that the person is a typical group member. In this way, fear of backlash reinforces stereotypes in the culture at large.

Fear of Deviance and Overperforming Masculinity

A number of other studies have also manipulated gender deviance by giving men false feedback on personality tests to lead them to believe they have feminine or masculine personalities. For example, men who were told they were feminine responded by showing more support for violence, including the war on Iraq, compared with men who were told they were masculine (Willer, 2005). Similarly, in pilot research, Rudman and Fairchild found that male deviants were more interested in violent computer games (e.g., "War Lords") as lottery prizes compared with normative counterparts. Additional research found that men led to believe they were gender deviant endorsed domestic violence more so than normative men; they also threw harder punches, as measured by an electronic sensor attached to a punching bag (Vandello, Bosson, Cohen, Burnaford, & Wasti, 2007). These results suggest that violence is a powerful means by which men separate themselves from women, and that fear of being feminine promotes male aggression (see Chapter 11). Just as football coaches and sergeants exhort their players and troops to "show no mercy" and "hit the enemy hard" to prove they are not "ladies" and "pussies," an individual may resort to aggression to prove to himself he is a man.

In support of this view, research has shown that when men fear that others will view them as gender deviants, they respond by rejecting women who pose a threat to male dominance. For example, Maass, Cadinu, Guarnieri, and Grasselli (2003) tested whether men whose masculinity was questioned would attempt to restore their gender identity by harassing a feminist. Harassment consisted of the opportunity to send the woman pornographic photos over networked computers. Results supported their predictions: Men who were told they scored "feminine" on a personality test sent more (and more offensive) pornographic photos to the feminist compared with men who believed they had scored "masculine" on the test. In additional research, men were more likely to harass a woman by asking her sexist questions during a job interview if their gender identity had been threatened beforehand (Pryor, Hesson-McInnis, Hitlan, Olson, & Hahn, 2001). In this case, the woman had performed well on a masculine knowledge test, making her particularly likely to be harassed because, like feminists, she challenged the legitimacy of male superiority (Dall'Ara & Maass, 2000; see also Berdahl, 2007b).

Homosexual men are another group that threatens the legitimacy of male superiority. This is particularly true if they are effeminate, because they violate gender prescriptions more so (and more visibly) than macho gay men do. Thus, prejudice toward feminine gays might be exacerbated when men's gender identity is threatened. To test this hypothesis, men were asked to perform a personality test on computers that ostensibly measured their reaction time as well as their responses to heighten the credibility that the test measured their true personality (Glick, Gangl, Gibb, Klumpner, & Weinberg, 2007). Again, the researchers gave false feedback regarding how masculine or feminine the men were. Following this, they provided descriptions of two types of homosexual men: masculine gay men (described as athletic and logical thinkers) and feminine gay men (described as neat, talkative, and emotional). As predicted, compared with normative counterparts, male gender deviants showed more negative attitudes toward the feminine, but not the masculine, gay man. These results show that the threat of gender deviance leads people to become stronger enforcers of gender prescriptions in how they treat other people, completing the cycle in which prescriptions lead, ironically, to reinforced prescriptions (Rudman & Fairchild, 2004).

Taken together, a picture emerges of a vicious cycle in which cultural stereotypes define appropriate behavior for men and women, who then respond to deviations by fearing backlash. In turn, this causes them to behave defensively in a manner that perpetuates cultural stereotypes. Along with hiding, deception, and increased norm conformity, we can add male gender deviants' interest in aggression and willingness to harass those who threaten male supremacy as behaviors that strengthen gender prescriptions. Next, we emphasize a final way in which gender stereotypes and prejudice are perpetuated: by their relative imperviousness to political correctness norms and general invisibility.

Stereotypes Are Perpetuated through Cultural Permission

In Chapter 5, we noted that even if you do not personally subscribe to them, gender stereotypes are so prevalent that you are undoubtedly aware of their content and may make automatic gender-biased assumptions (i.e., have implicit stereotypes). But it is not necessarily the case that merely possessing these stereotypical associations results in applying them toward others. People who are genuinely motivated to be egalitarian can work to inhibit their own use of stereotypes or attempt to correct for these stereotypes when they recognize their influence.

However, the motivation to avoid using stereotypes is, like stereotypes themselves, dependent on the attitudes or norms of the wider culture. In the United States, for example, there has been a dramatic change in the acceptability of using racial stereotypes. The civil rights movement successfully created normative pressures to be egalitarian, replacing traditional, hierarchical norms that once justified differential treatment of African Americans (Allport, 1954/1979). As a result, American respondents often refuse to answer questions about their attitudes toward minorities or express that they have absolutely no prejudice toward them (e.g., Judd, Park, Ryan, Brauer & Kraus, 1995; McConahay, 1986; Spence, 1993). For example, when Whites are asked to report their attitudes separately toward Blacks and Whites, the difference between these two scores is typically zero; in other words, the modal response is "no preference" (Greenwald et al., 1998; Nosek et al., 2002a).

There has been considerable debate concerning whether such changes in social norms reflect true changes in people's attitudes or political correctness. That is, are people truly more egalitarian or just less willing to show their prejudices for fear of being rebuked? Implicit measures of stereotyping and prejudice (e.g., the Implicit Association Test [IAT], introduced in Chapter 5) have been used to help to resolve this question. These measures show that many socially disapproved prejudices have, in part, simply gone "underground." For example, in contrast to the modal response of "no preference" using self-reports, the vast majority (80%) of Whites show an automatic preference for Whites over Blacks on the IAT (Nosek et al., 2002a, 2002b). Likewise, people report low levels of prejudice toward Jews, the elderly, and poor people that are belied by strong automatic biases against these groups (Nosek et al., 2002a; Rudman et al., 2002; Rudman, Greenwald, Mellott, & Schwartz, 1999).

However, although some people may report they are unprejudiced on questionnaires because of political correctness norms, others are genuinely internally motivated to be egalitarian (Plant & Devine, 1998). They report feelings of guilt and anxiety when they slip up and their behavior does not match their egalitarian values (for a review, see Monteith & Voils, 2001). In particular, Monteith and her colleagues have devised a paradigm that asks people whether they should exhibit egalitarianism (e.g., by welcoming a gay couple into their neighborhood) and whether they would follow suit. For those who show a discrepancy between how they should and would react, the result is typically feelings of guilt and anxiety (i.e., compunction) and more inhibition of prejudice on subsequent measures (e.g., rating jokes about homosexuals as offensive and not funny; Monteith, 1993; Monteith, Deneen, & Tooman, 1996).

In sum, some people use political correctness norms to calibrate their behavior and are especially sensitive to indicators of how others might react to the use of stereotypes or expressions of prejudice. In contrast, those who have internalized egalitarian norms police themselves because of a genuine desire to avoid using stereotypes or being prejudiced. Note, however, that in describing the research on these motivations, we have mainly reported on studies of racial and ethnic prejudices. Why? Because gender prejudice in many of its forms remains socially acceptable and even invisible in its application, as we discuss next.

The Normative Nature of Gender Prejudice

Is there social disapproval, compunction, and guilt when it comes to expressing gender prejudice or using gender stereotypes (as is increasingly the case with other prejudices)? Although people typically feel guilty when their prejudices toward Blacks, gays, or other minorities are revealed (e.g., Monteith et al., 1996; Monteith & Voils, 2001; Fazio & Hilden, 2001), they feel less compunction about sexism. Using the same "should–would" paradigm described previously, participants reported feeling more amusement than guilt or discomfort when their sexism was exposed (Czopp & Monteith, 2003).

Another sign that sexism is not treated as a serious moral flaw comes from research on attitudes toward feminists. Although feminists deserve the lion's share of credit for advancing women's rights, college-age adults do not identify with feminists (e.g., Buschman & Lenart, 1996; R. Williams & Wittig, 1997), and attitudes toward them are surprisingly negative (Haddock & Zanna, 1994; Renzetti, 1987; Rudman & Fairchild, 2007). Feminist stereotypes are also unflattering, in that feminists tend to be viewed as competent but cold (S. T. Fiske et al., 2002). Moreover, they are stigmatized as unattractive, sexually unappealing, and likely to be lesbians (Goldberg, Gottesdiener, & Abramson, 1975; Rudman & Fairchild, 2007; Swim, Ferguson, & Hyers, 1999; Unger, Hilderbrand, & Madar, 1982). Imagine if most African Americans began to disdain Rosa Parks, Martin Luther King, Jr., and other civil rights workers; one imagines this would generate newspaper headlines and considerable alarm.

Such differences, however, are in keeping with historical differences in the treatment of prejudice toward women, in contrast with other groups. For instance, seminal texts on prejudice (e.g., Allport 1954/1979) did not even acknowledge sexism, a term that was not coined until the 1970s, likely because it was not identified as a problem. Even though many features of male–female relations matched internationally recognized tenets of prejudice (including inequality in access to employment, public office, and property ownership), sexism was ignored until the Women's Movement drew attention to this side of relations between the sexes (Rudman, 2005). The notion that there was "a problem" in how women were treated was not widespread, even in the mid-1960s. When Title VII of the Civil Rights Act of 1964 was passed, lawmakers added "sex" as a protected class to the categories of race, color, religion, and national origin in order to scuttle the bill

(Kessler-Harris, 2002), firmly believing that their colleagues would not vote for a bill that made differential treatment of women a crime. This strategy, despite its ineffectiveness, reflects a stronger cultural proscription against prejudice toward minorities as opposed to women, toward whom discrimination is often couched as benevolent protection.

This suggests that sexism and its concomitants (gender stereotypes, norms, and prescriptions) are so normative that people, even early prejudice researchers, did not recognize them as a form of prejudice. One reason for this is that historically and cross-culturally men have been socially dominant compared with women. It is difficult for fish to see the water they swim in. Another reason is that prejudice toward women often takes the form of benevolent paternalism (see Chapter 2). As we note in Chapter 4, stereotypes that women are "wonderful" but "weak" bolster favorable attitudes toward women but at the cost of undermining respect toward them. Women themselves may not recognize sexism but instead may view male dominance as part of the natural order, at least until they have had their "consciousness raised." The reason they need to have, in feminist parlance, a "click experience" (i.e., one in which they suddenly grasp gender inequality) is because gender prejudice is so normative as to be invisible.

A final reason why gender prejudice is more acceptable concerns the fact that the central prescriptions for men (competence) and women (warmth) involve positive traits, which can mask their ability to reinforce gender inequities. It is difficult for people to view the prescription that women should be nicer than men as prejudice, given that niceness is a valued trait. It does not imply that women should not work outside the home or that women are stupid, but instead sets up a mandate that women should care for others and eschew the self-serving attributes that characterize men in general and leaders in particular (e.g., assertiveness, decisiveness, ambition, and competitiveness). As we describe in Chapter 7, this leads to a "lack of fit" between perceptions of female gender and leadership that is costly to gender parity. Nonetheless, because the traits that are valued in women are positive (albeit indicative of their traditional roles as low-status caregivers), both genders may be relatively unaware of their ability to undermine the status of women as a group (Rudman, 2005).

This is not to deny that there have been significant changes in gender-related attitudes. For instance, the notion that women are likely to work outside the home and that they ought to receive equal pay for equal work is accepted as a matter of course in American society in a way that simply was not the case decades ago (see Chapter 8). On the other hand, gender stereotypes remain alive and well, and their use is not subjected to the same sort of social disapproval that has become attached to expressions of racial and ethnic prejudice.

Chapter Summary

We have described the self-sustaining prophecy of stereotypes by discussing how people use stereotypes as a compass pointing them in gender-conforming directions, which promotes the accuracy of gender beliefs. Moreover, expectancy effects and behavioral confirmation processes lead perceivers to falsely detect that stereotypes are accurate and seduce actors into confirming perceivers' beliefs. Further, actors who fear backlash reinforce stereotypes by behaving defensively. In particular, men appear to be extremely reactive to anything that questions their masculinity, so much so that some may resort to aggression and harassment to reinstate their gender identity. Finally, the relative acceptance and invisibility of gender prejudice (compared with other types) means that people are less likely to confront gender biases in themselves and others.

All of these processes likely depend on gender essentialism, defined in Chapter 1 as the belief that men and women are natural "opposites." If people believe in male and female essences, then nonconformity with gendered expectations signals a potentially deep flaw. If you are not "really" a man or a woman, your whole gender identity is threatened. People's concerns about being a good member of their gender group and their fears about not having the "right" gender characteristics lead them to police their own and others' behavior. In turn, this reinforces the general consensus of how men and women are and how they ought to be. Moreover, if gender stereotypes are believed to be based on innate differences between women and men, then people will not see much reason to challenge or change them. The upshot is that the stereotypes may come to possess more than a kernel of truth, as men and women alike strive to uphold them. In this way, stereotypic expectancies and prescriptions act as self-sustaining prophecies on a cultural scale. When both internal and external forces pressure men and women to act in disparate ways, the perceived accuracy of gender stereotypes is bolstered, despite the general similarity between men and women on most psychological traits.

CHAPTER 7

Obstacles to Gender Nonconformity

When the Baltimore Symphony hired Marin Alsop, she became the first female conductor of a major American orchestra. She experienced tremendous resistance from the musicians, who complained she was interpersonally "insensitive" and a musical "lightweight." In an interview, Ms. Alsop confessed that her initial reaction to all the criticism was to run ("Who needs this?"), but she persevered and is now widely accepted (Wakin, 2005). One key to her success has been a tempering of any tendency to appear pompous, along with teaching herself to be more assertive at the podium (e.g., to not apologize by looking away when she asks the brass section for more volume). She also avoids gestures like raising a pinky when holding the baton that would make a man appear to be sensitive but can make a woman look frilly. Thinking through the gender issues surrounding conducting has helped her to overcome enormous challenges to become a respected leader of the orchestra.

In Chapter 6, we described how men and women self-select themselves into sex-typed interests and activities and shy away from any suggestion of gender deviance to protect their gender identity and avoid backlash. Increasingly, however, substantial numbers of women, like Marin Alsop, not only have withstood social pressures against pursuing cross-sex talents and skills but have achieved success and acceptance by male and female peers. Such individuals can be thought of as gender vanguards, who puncture stereotypes in a widening variety of fields as they pursue self-fulfillment.

The potential impact of individuals who challenge gender stereotypes cannot be underestimated. According to impression formation theories, the best way to thwart descriptive stereotypes of any kind is to behave in a counterstereotypical manner (e.g., Brewer, 1988; S. T. Fiske & Neuberg, 1990; Kunda & Thagard, 1996), and this is as true on a cultural level as it is on an interpersonal level (Rudman & Fairchild, 2004). For example, if men flooded the ranks of nurses and nannies, the stereotype that they were less nurturing than women would disappear. However, the tendency to subtype token vanguards (isolated "exceptions to the rule") and to derogate them for violating gender prescriptions (e.g., to subtype a powerful woman as an "iron maiden" or a boy who likes to dance as a "sissy") prevents group-based stereotypes from being eradicated (see Chapter 4). Therefore, it is only when a critical mass of such vanguards emerges that stereotypes and the pressures against pursuing counterstereotypical interests are likely to dissipate.

It is important to recognize that stereotypes have undergone significant change in response to pioneering vanguards in the past. Consider the following examples: Women were once thought to be too "irrational" to be worth educating or allowed to vote, African Americans were believed to be physically incapable of athletic prowess (and thus were not allowed to participate in professional sports), and Irish immigrants to America were ghettoized because they were thought to be drunken, slovenly, and promiscuous. The sheer number of disconfirming examples eventually rendered these stereotypes obsolete. Nonetheless, some gender stereotypes may be harder to change than others. In particular, prescriptive gender stereotypes that are associated with a strong structure of roles (e.g., women as caregivers, men as protectors) are especially well established and accepted as legitimate. Thus, we might expect some challenges for (both male and female) gender vanguards.

In this chapter, we expand on the self-sustaining prophecy of gender stereotypes by considering obstacles to counterstereotypical success. First, we consider how cultural stereotypes can affect vanguards from "the inside out" by causing them to perform poorly in counterstereotypical pursuits. Second, we show how they affect vanguards from "the outside in" when perceivers communicate their disapproval of atypical women and men. In tandem with Chapter 6, our aim is to elaborate on the means by which gender prescriptions exert influence on people and prevent them from reaching their full potential while nourishing stereotypes in the process. At the same time, we note how individuals can negotiate these pressures and succeed despite the social pressures stereotypes create.

Stereotype Threat Challenges Counterstereotypical Success

As noted in Chapter 6, occupations that require math and science skills remain strongly sex typed, and the number of women pursuing college degrees and careers in math and science is declining (Nosek et al., 2002b; Panteli et al., 2001). The gender gap in math performance that appears in high school and college (Fan et al., 1997; Lefevre et al., 1992) can be explained, in part, by cultural beliefs that men are "naturally" better at math than women. This belief can create added anxiety that threatens women's ability to perform well on mathematics tests (Dar-Nimrod & Heine, 2006). According to stereotype threat theory (Steele, 1997, 1998; Steele, Spencer, & Aronson, 2002), people underachieve on academic tests when they fear confirming a negative stereotype about their group (e.g., that they are less intelligent or gifted in math than members of other groups). Specifically, "the existence of such a stereotype means that anything one does or any of one's features that conform to it make the stereotype more plausible as a self-characterization in the eyes of others, and perhaps even in one's own eyes" (Steele & Aronson, 1995, p. 797).

Consistent with the theory, many investigations have found that women's math performance suffers relative to men's, particularly when the stereotype is salient, such as when the test administrator mentions that men tend to perform better than women on the test. In contrast, women in control groups (for whom the stereotype is defused) often perform just as well as men (Shih, Pittinsky, & Ambady, 1999; Spencer, Steele, & Quinn, 1999; J. L. Smith & White, 2002; Walsh, Hickey, & Duffy, 1999). For example, Spencer et al. (1999, Study 2) gave male and female participants practice sections of the quantitative Graduate Record Exam and found that men outscored women but only when participants were told in advance that the test typically shows gender differences. When they were told that the test did not show gender differences, women performed as well as men. Researchers have found similar stereotype threat effects simply by asking women to indicate their gender before taking a math exam, a common administration practice

(Shih et al., 1999). Thus, it is relatively easy to make the gender–math stereotype salient for female test takers.

Although you might suspect that women who excel at math would be immune to stereotype threat, Steele (1997) argued that susceptibility to stereotype threat increases when domain identification is high; if a test is not relevant to your identity, it won't matter to your self-esteem how well you performed. It follows, then, that women interested in math should be especially vulnerable to stereotype threat. In fact, researchers have demonstrated stereotype threat effects for women who are high in math ability (e.g. Schmader, 2002; Spencer et al., 1999). As a result, women who strive to succeed in math may have to fight the anxiety and distraction that comes from stereotype threat when they most need and want to perform well.

Although the majority of studies documenting stereotype threat have focused on minority groups, high-status groups have also shown susceptibility to its influence. For example, men who were told that a test involving decoding nonverbal cues measured social sensitivity scored lower than women, whereas no gender differences appeared when the test was described as assessing information processing (Koenig & Eagly, 2005). Similarly, White men scored low on a math test when they were told that Asians typically did better (Aronson et al., 1999) and poorly on an athletic test when told that Blacks typically did better (Stone, Lynch, Sjomeling, & Darley, 1999).

Although research on stereotype threat has been mainly concerned with demonstrating its effects, attention has been paid to how the threat might be ameliorated. For example, women showed markedly better performance on a math test when they were exposed to a socio-cultural explanation for why men outperform them in math compared with when they were exposed to a genetic explanation (Dar-Nimrod & Heine, 2006). Thus, learning that gender differences are not necessarily innate can buffer women from stereotype threat. In addition, other types of stereotype threat have proven to be tractable. In one study, women who were primed with low-status female stereotypes (through television ads) were subsequently reluctant to volunteer for a leadership position (Davies, Spencer, & Steele, 2005). However, when the leadership role was framed in terms that appeal to women's strengths (e.g., as a problem solver), the effect of stereotype threat on their interest in leadership was eliminated (Davies et al., 2005). These findings are promising signs that stereotype threat effects are malleable and need not impede women's aspirations and performance in masculine-typed domains.

Backlash Effects: Punishing Gender Vanguards

Even if people manage to avoid stereotype threat on their way to becoming gender vanguards, they face another significant obstacle: other people. From childhood on, violating gender prescriptions results in strong reprisals, or backlash effects, from parents, teachers, and peers alike (see Chapters 3 and 6). The first experimental demonstrations that perceivers punish gender deviance in adults were conducted in the 1970s (Bartol & Butterfield, 1976; Cherry & Deaux, 1978; Costrich, Feinstein, Kidder, Marecek, & Pascale, 1975; Derlega & Chaiken, 1976). In a series of studies, Costrich et al. (1975) found that women who took on leadership roles or who communicated assertively (i.e., stood up for themselves) were rated as unpopular and likely to be psychologically disturbed. Men who did not show these behaviors (i.e., who were communal and passive) suffered the same consequences. Similarly, a man who self-disclosed his problems to a stranger and a woman who chose not to were viewed as more neurotic than a stoic man and a self-disclosing woman (Derlega & Chaiken, 1976). In studies of gender-role reversals, when a woman was described as being at the top of her medical school class or a man as being at the top of his nursing school class, both were expected to suffer serious social reprisals (Cherry & Deaux, 1978; Yoder & Schleicher, 1996).

For those aspects of gender stereotypes that are highly prescriptive (e.g., that women must be nice and men must be strong and independent), deviations from the norm can elicit hostile reactions. Although both genders risk backlash when they violate gender prescriptions, backlash toward agentic women (compared with communal men) has particularly serious consequences for gender equality because it impedes women from reaching the highest echelons of power. Next, we describe an impression management dilemma that challenges women's economic advancement. Specifically, we consider (1) the need for women to disconfirm female stereotypes in order to be perceived as competent leaders and (2) how negative reactions toward ambitious and capable women present a difficult hurdle for women in performance settings. The picture that emerges represents a catch-22 for women, such that they may be penalized if they disconfirm feminine stereotypes but overlooked for leadership roles if they do not. Later in the chapter, we address backlash toward men who go against prescriptive norms of masculinity. This form of backlash can be even more brutal, including violence against gay men (see Chapter 11) and harassment of "weak" men (see Chapter 8). But because exhibiting masculine personality traits is necessary for advancement in most high-status careers, penalties for female stereotype disconfirmation tend to reinforce men's status. Thus, backlash against both sexes, whether toward powerful women or weak men, consistently serves to reinforce overall male dominance and the stereotypes that support it.

Backlash toward Agentic Women

As seen in the example of Marin Alsop, women who strive to succeed in male-dominated roles face a dilemma. The first step to being hired is to be seen as a good match for the position. However, the attributes that characterize masculine roles, such as executives and managers (e.g., competitive, assertive, and decisive), are stereotypically male qualities, resulting in a perceived "lack of fit" between female gender and leadership (Cejka & Eagly, 1999; Eagly & Karau, 2002; Glick et al., 1995; Heilman, 1983, 2001). Therefore, when women compete against men (e.g., for employment and promotions), it may be necessary for them to disconfirm female stereotypes or risk losing to male rivals who will be deemed better qualified (e.g., Glick, Zion, & Nelson, 1988).

In fact, women are often advised to act "more like men" in order to break the glass ceiling (Wiley & Eskilson, 1985). For example, women have been exhorted to lower the pitch of their voices in order to fit the masculine prototype of leadership (Karpf, 2006; Tannen, 1994), and industry consultants routinely advise women to alter their clothing, body language, and presentation style. Why? Because unless she presents herself as an atypical woman, a female candidate for a masculine-typed occupation is likely to be judged as less suitable than a man (Glick et al., 1988; see also Dodge, Gilroy, & Fenzel, 1995; Heilman, Block, & Martell, 1995). Women must show that they are exceptions to descriptive stereotypes that they are less agentic, because such stereotypes make them seem less suited for powerful roles (Eagly & Karau, 2002). However, disconfirming female stereotypes is necessary but not sufficient to clear the hurdle, because when women present themselves as self-confident, assertive, and competitive to be viewed as qualified for leadership roles, they risk backlash for having violated prescriptive stereotypes of feminine niceness. In short, women must navigate between avoiding being assimilated into the descriptive female stereotype (i.e., as not agentic) while not exhibiting so much agency that they violate prescriptive stereotypes that women "must be" communal. The failure to "soften" female agency results in backlash.

Specifically, agentic women are rated as highly competent and capable of leadership, but they are also viewed as socially deficient and unlikable by both male and female perceivers (Heilman, Wallen, Fuchs,

& Tamkins, 2004; Rudman, 1998; Rudman & Glick, 1999, 2001). For example, evaluators rated a woman described as a successful manager identically to male counterparts on competence measures, but they also viewed her as more hostile (e.g., more quarrelsome, bitter, selfish, and devious) than successful male managers (Heilman et al., 1995). This type of bias is evident in the epithets often applied to powerful women, such as "dragon lady," "battle-ax," and "iron maiden" (Kanter, 1977; Tannen, 1994). For example, when Margaret Thatcher was Britain's prime minister, journalists referred to her as "Attila the Hen" and "Her Malignancy." Similarly, when Hillary Rodham Clinton began to exert power within her husband's administration, the cover of *Spy* magazine went so far as to depict her with her skirt blowning up, à la Marilyn Monroe, but in this case revealing a large penis. Attacks on powerful women often target their sexual attractiveness while casting them as destroyers of male virility (e.g., "iron maiden," "ice queen," "ball breaker," and "castrating bitch"). Such epithets signal the extent to which powerful women violate gender prescriptions for women to yield to men economically, politically, and sexually. Because people's notions of power and gender are so intertwined as to be inseparable, powerful women incite discomfort and derision. When people behave out of role, they are punished (Goffman, 1959).

Why do some people view successful female leaders as incongruous and disturbing? In addition to failing to conform to prescriptive stereotypes of femininity, powerful women embody a status incongruity or clash between the power of their role and their sex. Sociologists distinguish between status based on achievement (earning your way to the top) and ascribed status based on personal characteristics (e.g., sex, race, and age; Berger, Webster, Ridgeway, & Rosenholtz, 1986). Women are automatically allocated lower status than men (Rudman & Kilianski, 2000), so much so that when they enter an occupation, the perceived status of the occupation can drop significantly (Nieva & Gutek, 1981; Touhey, 1974). Thus, a powerful woman may make people uncomfortable because of the discordance between her ascribed status as a woman and her achieved status as a leader (Lips, 1991). This incongruity jeopardizes preexisting rules for gender roles, forcing people to do more mental work to reconcile the perceived contradiction.

Additionally, men may see powerful women (compared with men) as more of a threat to their own status. For example, when Harvard University undergraduate men believed that a future interaction would place them in a subordinate role with a female supervisor, they showed less pro-female implicit attitudes compared with men who believed they would play the role of supervisor (Richeson & Ambady, 2001). That is, the mere thought of being subservient to a woman was sufficient to downgrade the positive attitudes that men typically have for women, as illustrated by the "women are wonderful" effect (Eagly & Mladinic, 1989; Rudman & Goodwin, 2004; see Chapters 4 and 5). Indeed, role congruity theory suggests the effect is better described as "the women are wonderful when" effect: when they are not in charge. That is, women are wonderful provided they are communal and adhere to traditional female roles. However, because women also subscribe to prescriptive gender stereotypes, backlash against agentic women is not only exhibited by men (e.g., Rudman, 1998), as we discuss later in the chapter.

Backlash for female agency places women in a double bind. If they act competently and aggressively, they risk negative reactions for being insufficiently feminine. But if they are modest and communal, they risk being viewed as incapable of leadership. As S. T. Fiske and Stevens (1993) note, "Both of these scenarios could result in sexual discrimination. In one case, discrimination would result from not behaving like a woman should, and, in the other case, from behaving too much like a woman" (p. 181). In other words, more so than men, ambitious women may have to choose between being respected but not liked (by displaying agentic qualities) or being liked but not respected (by displaying communal qualities). As reviewed next, evidence of backlash effects exists at every stage of employment, from hiring and salary negotiations to promotion and leadership evaluations.

Hiring

If you have been interviewed for a job, you no doubt tried to project a confident image to your would-be employer by highlighting your past accomplishments and emphasizing your skills. Self-promotion during job interviews is important for both genders, but it matters especially for women, who must present themselves as highly confident and capable in order to counter negative female stereotypes. However, although self-promotion is necessary for high competence ratings, it decreases women's likeability ratings and, consequently, their likelihood of being hired (Rudman, 1998; Rudman & Glick 1999, 2001). In contrast, self-promoting men are viewed as highly competent, likable, and hirable, suggesting that only women face social pressures to be modest (Daubman, Heatherington, & Ahn, 1992; Gould & Slone, 1982; Heatherington et al., 1993). Similarly, Buttner and McEnally (1996) found that women who used a direct and assertive strategy when applying for a job were less likely to be recommended for it than men who used the same strategy. Thus, agentic women (but not men) may pay a price for behaviors that are necessary to embark on a successful career.

Salary Negotiations

Once hired, the risk of backlash for agency can put women at a serious financial disadvantage. Although assertiveness is necessary for success in the business world, it is viewed negatively in women (Costrich et al., 1975; Crawford, 1988; Powers & Zuroff, 1988), even when it involves self-defense (Branscombe, Crosby, & Weir, 1993). This constraint on women's behavior can have serious economic effects during salary negotiations (Janoff-Bulman & Wade, 1996). For example, even when controlling for other factors that may influence salary negotiations, female MBAs routinely accept lower salary offers than male MBAs (Bowles, Babcock, & McGinn, 2005; Gerhart & Rynes, 1991; Stevens, Bavetta, & Gist, 1993), especially when the appropriate salary range is unclear (Bowles et al., 2005). In a study of professional school graduates, men were eight times more likely than women (57% vs. 7%, respectively) to negotiate their initial salary offers, resulting in a considerable income gap (Babcock & Laschever, 2003). However, when women are asked to negotiate starting salaries for a peer, they are just as aggressive as men (Amanatullah, 2007), suggesting that women are responding to fears of backlash when they negotiate for themselves.

Some evidence showing differential treatment of male and female negotiators indicates that this fear is warranted. Bowles, Babcock, and Lai (2007) found that male managers were more inclined to work with "nice" women who accepted their compensation offers compared with women who attempted to negotiate for more money. In contrast, negotiating for a higher salary had no effect on evaluators' willingness to work with male candidates. These findings suggest that women "do not ask" for higher pay, more responsibility, or greater recognition (Babcock & Laschever, 2003) because they (correctly) fear negative reactions from others.

Promotion

Whereas women may encounter a "glass ceiling" that bars them from organizational power, men are more likely to ride a "glass escalator" that accelerates them into management positions (Maume, 1999; C. L. Williams, 1992). For example, Ann Hopkins was a highly successful accountant who brought in more clients and generated more income than many of her male colleagues. Nonetheless, she was denied promotion to partnership in her firm (whereas men less qualified were ushered in the door) for being too masculine. Her evaluators suggested she needed a course in charm school, where she might learn to speak and dress more femininely, even though masculine qualities were necessary for her job (S. T. Fiske, Bersoff, Borgida, Deaux, & Heilman, 1991). In other words, violating feminine niceness prescriptions can result in poor performance evaluations and adversely affect promotion considerations (Heilman, 2001; Lyness & Judiesch, 1999). In a series of experiments, agentic women vying for the role of vice president of an airline were viewed as interpersonally hostile (e.g., abrasive, pushy, and manipulative). As a result, they were not recommended for the higher paying, prestigious position (Heilman et al., 2004). Were these women "hostile"? No, the inference came solely from the information that they had succeeded in their past position.

Computer simulation studies have shown that even small amounts of backlash can have cumulative effects on female representation in high-power positions. For example, one study assuming equal gender representation at entry level found that even when only 1% of hundreds of decisions were due to gender bias, the people promoted to the highest levels of the organization were largely (65%) men (Martell, Lane, & Emrich, 1996). Thus, even trivial disadvantages can accumulate to have substantial long-term effects.

Leadership Evaluations

Once a woman navigates the double standard for agency to obtain a high-powered job, she may continue to pay a price for stereotype disconfirmation, even though it may be required for career success (Eagly, Makhijani, & Klonsky, 1992; McIlwee & Robinson, 1992). Gender prescriptions require women to be nice; when their leadership behavior deviates from this rule, their evaluations suffer. For example, business students evaluated female managers who led in a stereotypically feminine style positively, but those who led in a stereotypically masculine style were rated more negatively then male counterparts (Bartol & Butterfield, 1976). Meta-analytic studies of leadership evaluations and effectiveness reveal only small advantages for male leaders; however, when women led in a stereotypically masculine style, this gender difference was exacerbated (Eagly et al., 1992). Further, female leaders are also evaluated more negatively than male leaders when they exhibit anger (Brescoll & Uhlmann, in press), use intimidation strategies (Bolino & Turnley, 2003), deliver discipline (Atwater, Carey, & Waldman, 2001; Brett, Atwater, & Waldman, 2005), or criticize subordinates (Sinclair & Kunda, 2000). These findings are consistent with considerable research demonstrating that women have less latitude in their communication style compared with men (Carli, 1990, 2001; Carli, LaFleur, & Loeber, 1995; Tannen, 1990) because of feminine prescriptions to be "nice."

Ironically, social pressures may have led women to adopt a more communal leadership style that is more effective than the autocratic style often associated with male leaders. A meta-analysis of studies, conducted in the United States and abroad, showed that female leaders tended to mentor and empower subordinates more so than men, whereas male leaders were more likely to be absent, passive, or uninvolved (Eagly, Johannesen-Schmidt, & van Engen, 2003). Not surprisingly, a democratic leadership style is associated with greater employee satisfaction and morale, whether adopted by a woman or a man (Judge & Piccolo, 2004). Perhaps for this reason, corporations have begun to recognize the value of an inclusive, participatory approach to leadership (Offermann & Gowing, 1990; Peters, 1988; Rosener, 1990). The trend toward "feminization" of management, with corporations increasingly valuing interpersonal skills, would seem to be a positive development for women. By softening the traits required of managerial positions, the lack of fit between female stereotypes and requisite job characteristics is weakened.

However, although women's leadership style appears to confer an advantage, there is an important caveat. The addition of feminine qualities to managerial job qualifications usually occurs in lower and mid-level management positions, for which skills such as fostering cooperation and motivating subordinates are deemed important, in addition to agency and competence. However, in top executive positions (Martell, Parker, Emrich, & Crawford, 1998) and in high-powered arenas such as politics (Huddy & Terkildsen, 1993) and the military (Boyce & Herd, 2003), the emphasis is more squarely on agentic qualities, such as ruthlessness, competitiveness, and decisiveness. Thus, the perceived incongruity between female traits and leadership qualities still hinders women's ability to ascend to the highest ranks of power. As a result, women are most effective as leaders in gender-balanced organizations; when occupations are masculine or when subordinates are mainly men, male leaders are rated as more effective than female leaders (Eagly, Karau, & Makhijani, 1995).

Undermining Female Authority

Once women have attained leadership roles, backlash from coworkers can have negative effects on their work experiences. In a study of California hospitals, Heim (1990) observed that female nurses were reluctant to follow the orders of female doctors, thereby undermining the doctors' authority. In a laboratory test, women who succeeded in a masculine domain were more likely to be sabotaged by their peers compared with comparable men or women who had succeeded in a feminine domain (Rudman & Fairchild, 2004).

Female authority may be especially resisted when there are few women occupying leadership roles in an organization. For example, Ely (1994) found that female subordinates in male-dominated law firms had surprisingly negative attitudes toward the female partners in the firm. They criticized the female partners for acting like men, rated them as having unpleasant personalities, and viewed their authority as illegitimate, despite giving them high competence ratings. However, when women comprised at least 15% of the firm's partners, these effects disappeared. Thus, the more women leaders there are in an organization, the greater their acceptance, a fact that underscores the importance of female vanguards.

Emotional and Implicit Reactions to Agentic Women

Research has also demonstrated negative responses to agentic women using less controlled indicators, including evaluators' emotional responses (Butler & Geis, 1990; Koch, 2005) and implicit attitudes (e.g., Rudman & Kilianski, 2000). For example, Carranza (2004) found that female evaluators frowned in response to self-promoting women, whereas male evaluators smiled at them derisively. Being frowned upon or laughed at reflects severe disapproval, which is likely to hinder women's ability and willingness to act assertively. Nonverbal reactions toward female leaders have also been investigated, including facial display and body language. In both laboratory studies (Butler & Geis, 1990) and replications in the field (Koch, 2005), results indicated that negative emotions were displayed more frequently in response to female leaders than to male leaders.

In addition to negative emotional reactions, female leaders may elicit unfavorable implicit attitudes (Carpenter & Banaji, 1998; Richeson & Ambady, 2001). For example, Rudman and Kilianski (2000) found more negative implicit attitudes toward female than male authority figures (e.g., doctors and professors), particularly on the part of respondents who automatically associated male gender with high-status roles (e.g., leader, boss) and female gender with low-status roles (e.g., subordinate, helper). These results suggest that deeply ingrained beliefs about status hierarchies can contribute to spontaneously negative reactions to female leaders.

Finally, implicit stereotypes that automatically link men to agentic traits (e.g., individualistic, assertive, competitive) and women to communal traits (e.g., modest, caring, nice) play a role in backlash effects (Rudman & Glick, 2001). People who possessed these automatic stereotypes were particularly likely to rate agentic female managerial applicants as unlikable and, therefore, as unqualified for a management position. Thus, implicit stereotypes help to explain why strong, self-confident women are disliked and why, for women, being liked is more important than being perceived as competent when they compete for managerial jobs (Phelan, Moss-Racusin, & Rudman, 2007).

In sum, violating prescriptive stereotypes can negatively impact women's ability to obtain employment, fair compensation, career promotions, and positive performance evaluations. Moreover, women who succeed in masculine occupations risk troubled relationships with coworkers that undermine their authority. As a result, it is not surprising that more women than men perceive their work environments to be socially exclusive and difficult to navigate (Catalyst, 2001; J. Martin & Meyerson, 1988; Mor Barak, Cherin, & Berkman, 1998; Pfeffer, 1989). Next, we consider factors that are known to diminish backlash and then delve more deeply into its underlying causes.

Moderators of Backlash

Although research has provided clear evidence that agentic women suffer negative consequences, studies have also suggested ways to overcome backlash. Women who temper their agentic qualities with displays of communal warmth can convey their competence with a much lower risk of backlash (e.g., Carli, 2001; Carli et al., 1995). For instance, when assertive, self-confident women also professed to be "cooperative team players" during a job interview, they were viewed as both competent and likable (Rudman & Glick, 2001). Similarly, when successful female managers were also described as communal, they were rated as far more likeable than successful female managers for whom no communal information was provided (Heilman & Okimoto, 2007). As noted, people evaluate both female and male leaders favorably when they use a "people-oriented," inclusive style (Eagly et al., 1992). Thus, display-ing both agentic and communal qualities may be effective for alleviat-ing backlash. Having to manage a style that is both authoritative and nice—to direct while not being directive—presents an additional burden for female leaders. Because men do not suffer penalties for assertive behavior, they have more freedom to lead without having to temper their authority with careful displays of niceness. Nonetheless, many van-guards, including Marin Alsop, manage to find the right mixture of toughness and femininity that allows them to succeed as leaders, even in male-dominated arenas.

Another moderator of backlash effects concerns the nature of the management role. When a manager position was described as requiring solely masculine traits (e.g., competitiveness and decisiveness), agentic female applicants were liked less than agentic male applicants, but they were equally likely to be hired (Rudman & Glick, 1999). By contrast, when the management role additionally required feminine traits (e.g., being a good listener), agentic women suffered hiring discrimination (Rudman & Glick, 1999). As a result, it is particularly important for women to soften their agency with displays of niceness when the man-agement role requires feminine interpersonal skills as well as agency (Rudman & Glick, 2001). Ironically, the inclusion of feminine warmth as a requirement for the job gives raters psychological "permission" to discriminate against agentic women because such women come across as "too cold."

Are there gender differences in backlash effects? For the most part, the research discussed in this chapter shows that men and women equally punish counterstereotypical targets (see also Rudman & Phelan, in press). However, there are exceptions. First, compared with men, women are less likely to judge assertive female speech harshly (Carli, 1990, 2001; Carli et al., 1995). Thus, women who use powerful com-munication styles are more effective with female than with male audi-ence members. However, in this research, women spoke powerfully and persuasively about topics other than themselves. By contrast, backlash research using a hiring paradigm requires women to speak directly and assertively about their own qualifications, experience, skills, and suc-cess. These behaviors may still be viewed as taboo, even among female perceivers, despite their necessity for overriding negative female stereo-types concerning competence. In support of this speculation, immodest female confederates (who boasted about their academic prowess) were evaluated as competent but socially unattractive by female participants (Powers & Zuroff, 1988). Nonetheless, men can show much stronger backlash effects than women, such as when they engage in harassment as a means of resisting women's entrée into masculine occupations (see Chapter 8). They are also more likely than women to rate female leaders negatively (Eagly et al., 1992; Rudman & Kilianski, 2000).

Second, there are some situations in which women react more negatively than men to female agency. In one study, perceivers were asked to evaluate male and female job candidates for promotion to manager. When the occupation was masculine, women were more likely than men to show gender bias, including rating the female candidate as less qualified and less likely to be promoted, compared with the male applicant (Garcia-Retamero & López-Zafra, 2006; see also Biernat & Fuegen, 2001). In another study, men who believed their own success depended on their partners' competence were gender fair when asked to choose between an agentic woman and an agentic man; in contrast, women uniformly chose the agentic man (Rudman, 1998; Experiment 3). That is, when men stood to benefit from a confident and competent woman, backlash disappeared. That this benefit did not reduce women's tendency toward backlash is consistent with field research showing that female subordinates can be hard on female superiors (Ely, 1994; Heim, 1990).

Overall, the majority of backlash studies indicate that both genders respond similarly to power displays from women. The absence of sex differences is consistent with the notion that backlash stems from prescriptive gender stereotypes, and men and women score similarly on these measures (e.g., Prentice & Carranza, 2002). Similarly, as noted, implicit gender stereotypes predict backlash (Rudman & Glick, 2001), and sex differences rarely appear on these measures (e.g., Greenwald et al., 2002; Nosek et al., 2002a; Rudman & Kilianski, 2000).

Consequences of Backlash
for Cultural Stereotype Maintenance

Figure 7.1 shows the full model developed by Rudman and Fairchild (2004) to illustrate the role of backlash in cultural stereotype maintenance. In Chapter 6, we presented the bottom row, which outlines how actors' fear of backlash can preserve cultural beliefs. The top row outlines the role of perceivers, a role that is particularly important because a lifetime of witnessing and experiencing social reprisals for gender deviance is what spurs atypical actors to avoid backlash at all costs.

Several things are important to note about the top row of Figure 7.1. First, cultural stereotypes provide the standard against which perceivers judge actors' behaviors; if actors violate gendered expectancies, they are perceived to be deviant. Second, backlash is more likely to occur when people believe it is justifiable. For example, research using a hiring paradigm may justify backlash because it grants evaluators legitimate power over applicants' outcomes (i.e., the power of authority; French & Raven, 1959). As a result, perceivers may believe that discriminating against deviants is within their rights. Backlash may also be justified by emotional processes, including threat, anger, and a desire for revenge (Rudman & Fairchild, 2004). Chapter 6 described several laboratory studies showing that men whose gender identity was threatened reacted angrily to a feminist (Maass et al., 2003), a woman who succeeded on a masculine test (Pryor et al., 2001), and effeminate gay men (Glick et al., 2007). In each case, men led to believe they were "feminine" (but not men assured they were "masculine") abused others who were themselves atypical of their gender, suggesting that gender identity threat was necessary to justify men's backlash.

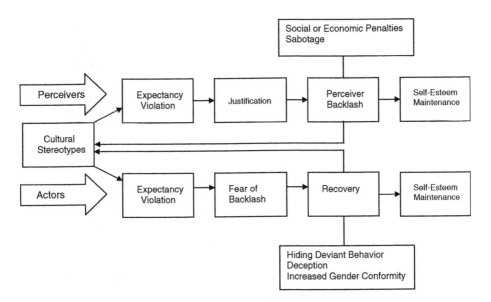

FIGURE 7.1. A model of the role of backlash in cultural stereotype maintenance. From Rudman and Fairchild (2004). Copyright 2004 by the American Psychological Association. Reprinted by permission.

In addition, Figure 7.1 suggests that when perceivers engage in justifiable backlash, their self-esteem is likely to increase. Rudman and Fairchild (2004) tested this hypothesis using the sabotage paradigm described earlier (in which people who lost a contest were allowed to undermine the victor's future success). In two experiments, participants' self-esteem was assessed immediately following sabotage. In each case, people who had sabotaged gender deviants showed increased self-esteem, whereas people who sabotaged gender normatives showed diminished self-esteem (suggesting guilt for having done so). Thus, sabotaging deviants may be self-reinforcing because it is viewed as justifiable and has psychological benefits for perceivers, even though it is costly for both targets and society.

The cost to society concerns the feedback loop from perceiver backlash to cultural stereotypes shown in Figure 7.1. That is, backlash hinders atypical women and men so that there are fewer visible vanguards that challenge cultural stereotypes and fewer role models for others who might also like to do so. In this way, backlash helps to preserve gender stereotypes by keeping atypical men and women out of the spotlight. Just as actors who fear punishment for deviance are likely to hide their actions (see Chapter 6), perceivers render counterstereotypical actors less visible by throwing up obstacles to their success. As a result, stereotypes are allowed to thrive in the culture at large. Because cultural stereotypes are the reason why atypical individuals are perceived as deviants, the result is a vicious cycle. As Figure 7.1 illustrates, perceivers and actors alike contribute to this cycle in ways that hinge on backlash. Until there is more social acceptance of stereotype-disconfirming behaviors, gender stereotypes are likely to remain strong.

Backlash toward Atypical Men

Because of its consequences for the preservation of gender inequality, we have focused on negative reactions to agentic women. However, counterstereotypical men also risk backlash effects. For example, compared with agentic men, communal male applicants are rated as less competent and hireable for managerial roles (Rudman, 1998; Rudman & Glick, 1999, 2001). Backlash effects for both men and women implicate prescriptive stereotypes as their root cause. Communal men are rated as highly likable but, because they violate prescriptions for male agency, are rated as particularly incompetent. By contrast, agentic women are rated as highly competent but, because they violate prescriptions for feminine niceness, are viewed as particularly unlikable. Each gender "takes a hit" on the dimension that is valued most for their sex (agency for men, warmth for women; see Chapter 4) when they break prescriptive rules. Not being agentic and not being liked can each be sufficient to disqualify individual men and women from leadership roles.

Thus, the overall consequences of backlash can be similar for male as well as female gender vanguards: exclusion and rejection. For example, research described earlier in this chapter showed that both men and women who violated gender stereotypes were likely to be viewed as unpopular and psychologically disturbed (Cherry & Deaux, 1978; Costrich et al., 1975; Derlega & Chaiken, 1976). In addition, men who showed proficiency in a feminine domain (knowledge of children's developmental skills) risked being sabotaged by their peers and thus prevented from earning financial rewards, just as women skilled in a masculine domain (knowledge of football) were sabotaged (Rudman & Fairchild, 2004).

However, it is often the case that men who venture into "women's work" are richly rewarded. Although fewer than 20% of elementary teachers, librarians, and nurses in the United States are male, they are disproportionately represented in administrative jobs at the top of their field (C. L. Williams, 1995). Moreover, although the ballet is strongly associated with women, 86% of the artistic directors of American ballet companies are male (La Rocco, 2007). Because men are generally accorded greater status than women, they dominate leadership roles even when they are tokens (Crocker & McGraw, 1984) or in traditionally feminine professions (C. L. Williams, 1992). Consider also that the people touted as "geniuses" in such feminine domains as cooking, dance, fashion design, and hairstyling tend to be men. Thus, backlash toward vanguards in cross-sex occupations may asymmetrically apply to women more than men. Nonetheless, there are instances in which men suffer more backlash than women for gender deviance. As noted in Chapter 6, developmental research shows harsher penalties for boys who exhibit cross-sex behaviors compared with girls, likely because "sissy" boys are viewed as latent homosexuals. We discuss this phenomenon next.

Implicit Inversion Theory
and the Stigma of Homosexuality

A gender prescription that casts a shadow over both sexes, but particularly strongly targets men, is the stigma associated with homosexuality. A chief component of gender identity is heterosexuality, the only normative sexual category in American culture (Herek, 1989). Homosexuals are often viewed as deviants by virtue of their same-sex sexuality, but they are also viewed as more generally cross-typed in a way that underscores essentialist beliefs about gender (i.e., that male and female are mutually exclusive categories; see Chapter 5).

The predominant view of same-sex sexuality is that it stems from inverted gender differences. This view evolved from the work of early sexologists and was adopted by prominent thinkers, including Freud (1905/2000). H. Ellis and Symonds (1897) used the term "congenital gender invert" to define a homosexual as a person who possesses characteristics of the other sex. Public opinion and contemporary theories of homosexuality remain rooted in implicit inversion theory, the belief that there are essential gender differences, which have somehow become inverted (Bailey & Pillard, 1991; LeVay, 1993, 1996). As a result, people rate the characteristics of gay men as being more like the stereotypical characteristics of women rather than of heterosexual men and the characteristics of lesbians as closer to men than to heterosexual women (Kite & Deaux, 1987). In this view, a homosexual is born with the "essence" of the other gender and will, therefore, behave in gender-deviant ways from birth on. As noted in Chapter 6, children (especially boys) who show interest in cross-sex toys, clothes, activities, and friends risk being viewed by adults and peers alike as incipient homosexuals. Gender identity and sexual identity are thought to be inseparable, so that even though sexual identity develops much later, any trend toward femininity in boys is seen as cause for alarm regarding their subsequent sexual orientation.

If these popular implicit inversion beliefs were correct, gender nonconformity in childhood ought to predict later same-sex sexuality. However, the research evidence is mixed. Some gay men show interest in cross-sex friends, toys, and activities from an early age (Bailey & Zucker, 1995) and a correspondingly low interest in masculine activities, especially those involving physical aggression (Blanchard, McConkey, Roper, & Steiner, 1983). And some lesbians show gender-discordant interests in childhood (Baily & Zucker, 1995). But it is also the case that many gay men and lesbians have gender-conforming childhoods and continue to express masculinity and femininity in adulthood (Grossman, 2002; Phillips & Over, 1992; Savin-Williams & Cohen, 2004). This makes sense because gender identity is a critical identity established in earliest childhood, long before sexual identity develops. Moreover, many gay men deliberately display more masculine behaviors to avoid the extreme negative social reactions (mostly from other men) that target overtly effeminate men (Taywaditep, 2001). Nonetheless, many people still believe that homosexuals are gender inverted.

As a result, individuals may be faced with the stigma of being mislabeled as a homosexual when they show interest in cross-sex domains. For example, men reported great distress when they were videotaped performing a braiding task labeled as "hairstyling," unless they were allowed to declare their heterosexuality beforehand (Bosson, Prewitt-Freilino, & Taylor, 2005). The fear of being misclassified as a lesbian also discomforts women, particularly female athletes whose participation in sports leads others to stereotype them as lesbians (Blinde & Taub, 1992; Bosson et al., 2005). However, the stigma of homosexuality is particularly troubling for men who cross gender bounds. For example, men are more easily threatened by a gender-deviance manipulation than are women (Bosson et al., 2005; Rudman & Fairchild, 2004), and it is difficult to inoculate men against this threat (Bosson, Taylor, & Prewitt-Freilino, 2006). Moreover, consider the relatively greater latitude for heterosexual women to display same-sex physical affection (e.g., greeting each other with a kiss) compared with the lack of latitude that exists for such displays among heterosexual men. Similarly, women are allowed to "cross-dress" (e.g., wear pants and suits), whereas men are rebuked if they wear feminine clothes.

In part, people's low tolerance for anything that even hints at male homosexuality reflects how the ascribed status associated with being male is tied to heterosexuality. Homosexual men are not endowed with the generally higher status of their gender; on the contrary, they are vilified and victimized (Franklin & Herek, 2003; Herek, 1989; Ronner, 2005). One reason homosexual men drop in status is because they are viewed as feminine and women, as a class, have relatively low prestige. Further, "black sheep"—members of a group who, by deviating from group norms, threaten the whole group's sense of status or identity—can be especially vilified (Marques & Yzerbyt, 1988). As a result, male gender vanguards face a triple threat: to their status, to their sexuality, and to their gender identity. By contrast, women may feel proud of masculine attributes because they boost their cultural status (Rudman & Fairchild, 2004).

Finally, there is evidence that women's sexuality is more contextual and fluid compared with men's (e.g., more women than men report being bisexual, and more lesbians than gay men report having had heterosexual sex), likely because for men there is less latitude for experimentation (Baumeister, 2000). Thus, it appears to be more difficult to pin women to heterosexuality, and it is less central to their gender identity. As noted, women more often than men wear clothes associated with the other sex and demonstrate same-sex displays of physical affection, signs that the behavioral standards are more lax for women in this respect. As a result, female, compared with male, gender vanguards are not as likely to face (or feel threatened by) the stigma of homosexuality to the same degree. Instead, they have to catapult the double hurdle of prejudice toward women as less agentic and prejudice toward agentic women as unfeminine and unattractive.

The picture as a whole suggests that both men and women are constrained by gender prescriptions but that obstacles to breaking free are different. Men are especially constrained to exhibit heterosexual masculinity and not to show any weakness, whereas women have greater freedom to "act like men" to a certain degree, but only if they simultaneously pull their punches and assure others of their fundamental niceness and communality. In the end, the costs to men come more in the effort it takes to always "tough it out" without seeking help, whereas the costs to women are that gender prescriptions make it difficult for them to achieve status and power.

Chapter Summary

Just as stereotypes in the past have been overthrown by disconfirming examples, gender vanguards are important for thwarting prescriptive sex stereotypes. In this chapter, we highlighted two obstacles to becoming a gender vanguard and suggested that they need not be an impenetrable blockade. First, stereotype threat, the fear of confirming a negative stereotype, can reduce people's ability to perform well in cross-sex domains, resulting in performances that perpetuate the stereotype. Because high-status domains are stereotypically masculine, stereotype threat can impede women when they most need to perform well, such as by creating anxiety and uncertainty in math testing and leadership situations. However, stereotype threat need not encumber women as gender vanguards; it can be eliminated when (1) attention is not drawn to gender differences on a task or exam, (2) sociocultural explanations are offered for gender differences (to reduce perceptions that they are innate and unavoidable), and (3) performance is framed in ways that emphasize women's strengths.

Second, gender vanguards who perform well risk backlash from others, who may penalize them for deviating from gender prescriptions. Backlash particularly hinders agentic women from competing on an equal footing for prestigious, male-dominated occupations. Fortunately, there is evidence that women can overcome backlash by managing a blend of both agency and communality, and research on leadership style suggests that doing so results in being a more effective leader. Although men tend to be promoted to leadership roles even in female-typed professions, backlash can have negative consequences for men who are too "modest" or "nice." The need to chronically manage an impression of masculine competencies psychologically restricts men as much as its complementary pressures affect women, robbing each of their free choice to engage in those activities and professions that best match their individual interests and capacities.

Finally, men and women who violate gender prescriptions may suffer backlash effects that stem from different reasons. Men may be more likely to risk the stigma of homosexuality than women, whereas women risk being viewed as cold and unlikable. When men "act like women" their status falls and their gender and sexual identity are questioned, whereas when women "act like men" their status rises but their femininity and social attractiveness are questioned. Although obstacles to overcoming prescriptions differ for men and women, they similarly reinforce stereotypes by encouraging people to toe the gender line. Further, backlash against both sexes acts to reinforce gender inequality by rewarding niceness and deference for women but agency and assertion for men.

CHAPTER 8

Sexism in the Workplace

Meet the Jetsons, the family of the future, as imagined by cartoonists in the 1960s. George flies to work in his bubble car while Jane whips up instant meals from a tiny pill using a nuclear energy oven. Even though the Jetsons live in a biomorphic building with a robot for a maid, in terms of gender relations, they might as well be the Flintstones. Dad works and worries about money while mom either stays at home or shops. Even Rosie, the robot maid, is a gender stereotype: She has a matronly shape, wears a frilly apron, is understanding, and cries easily. Although the show's creators were highly imaginative when it came to the technological gadgets that, if invented, promised to transform daily life, they could not envision the real change that families underwent. In fact, it seems they had things exactly backward. Flying cars and house-keeping robots have not materialized, but there has been a dramatic shift in gender relations. The legislative and sociocultural changes that led to women doubling their presence in the workforce since the 1950s (Diekman & Eagly, 2000) are nothing short of a revolution. Women and men today inhabit a social world that George and Jane Jetson would not recognize.

Does this mean that sexism is over and done with? In this chapter, we show that, although women have taken enormous strides toward gen-der equity at work, traditional gender ideologies and assumptions (i.e., sex-typed stereotypes, roles, and status beliefs) linger. Thus, although sex discrimination in the workplace has diminished, it has not disappeared. This chapter reviews the (often subtle) factors that make women's working lives harder to navigate than men's, especially when they seek to be leaders in male-dominated occupations. Yet it is important to bear in mind just how much things have changed. Since 1962, when "The Jetsons" premiered, women not only have flooded into the paid workforce in unprecedented numbers but also have made significant inroads into previously all-male occupations. Despite continuing obstacles, there is ample reason to believe that progress toward full gender equality will continue to unfold.

Gender Equality: The Glass Half Full

Figure 8.1 shows that the proportion of American women in the workforce nearly doubled from 1950 to 2005. Women now make up almost half of the U.S. workforce, and 36% of managers are female (U.S. Bureau of Labor Statistics, 2006). Economic pressures have increased the need for families to have dual incomes; these have combined with egalitarian norms to radically alter attitudes toward working women. The days when working outside the home was considered odd for middle- and upper-class women are long gone (Spence, 1999). Moreover, legislative changes now prohibit sex discrimination and render workplace behaviors that have disparate impact on women (e.g., sexual harassment) legally actionable. As a result, women's ability to capitalize on their advances is stronger than at any other time in history. In recent

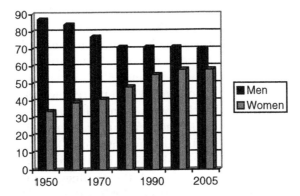

FIGURE 8.1. Percentage of women and men participating in the U.S. civilian labor force from 1950 to 2005. Data from U.S. Census Bureau (2005).

years, women have begun to shatter the glass ceiling and gain entry into the upper levels of organizational power (Stroh, Langlands, & Simpson, 2004). In short, women today have rights and opportunities that their foremothers could only dream about.

Nonetheless, there are sobering indicators that gender inequities stubbornly persist (for reviews, see Eagly & Carli, 2007; Ely & Meyerson, 2000; Lips, 2003, Valian, 1999). At the top levels in Fortune 500 companies, women make up only 2.6% of CEOs (Mero, 2007) and 16% of non-CEO corporate officers (Catalyst, 2006). If a wider variety of organizations are considered (e.g., charitable foundations and social service agencies), women hold 23% of top executive positions (U.S. Bureau of Labor Statistics, 2007). Within politics, 15% of congressional representatives, 14% of senators, and 16% of state governors are women (White House Project, 2006). Moreover, even women with advanced professional degrees earn 66% of what men with comparable educations earn (U.S. Census Bureau, 2007b), and the wage gap widens over career spans (Olson & Frieze, 1987). After tracking the advancement of more than 30,000 managers, Lyness and Judiesch (1999) found that the wage gap increases in higher level positions, with women in upper levels of management receiving fewer promotions and salary increases than comparable men. Even among the most highly paid executives and lawyers, men earn considerably more than women (Bertrand & Hallock, 2001; Wood, Corcoran, & Courant, 1993). Moreover, men in female-dominated professions (e.g., elementary school teachers and nurses) are typically paid more than women (C. L. Williams, 1995). Thus, although a considerable portion of the gender wage gap reflects differing career choices (with women being more likely than men to choose to work for nonprofit organizations or in fields that offer lower salaries), direct salary discrimination continues to occur.

The gender wage gap is complex, and economic studies yield different estimates of its size and persistence. Some studies find that the wage gap has shrunk to between 5% and 15% in recent decades (Sailer, Yau, & Rehula, 2002; see Jackson, 2006, for a review), whereas others suggest scant evidence that the gap is narrowing (Lips, 2003). Between the 1970s and 1990s, women made substantial progress in closing the gap, but this trend has stagnated in recent years (Blau & Kahn, 2007; Catalyst, 2006). The U.S. General Accounting Office (2001) found that in 7 of the 10 industries investigated, the earnings gap between men and women actually widened between 1995 and 2000. Thus, it is difficult to state definitively the extent of women's progress toward pay equity. Despite these ambiguities, there is consensus that occupations remain highly sex segregated, with men prominent in occupations that confer the most economic and social power (Catalyst, 2006; Cejka & Eagly, 1999; Glick et al., 1995; Jackson, 2006; Pratto et al., 1997).

More generally, when evaluating progress toward gender equality at work, it is easy to justify either optimism or pessimism depending on which indicators one chooses to focus on. Looking at the trajectory from the days when employment outside the home was virtually prohibited for women and they possessed almost no political or economic rights to today's circumstances, there is cause for optimism that progress will only continue apace. As some authors note, the glass ceiling has been shattered so frequently that it may be time for this particular metaphor to be abandoned, and although relatively low numbers of women occupy positions of high authority and power, this should be compared with the number of women (virtually zero) who had such positions in the past (Eagly & Carli, 2007; Jackson, 1998). When shifting our perspective instead to the distance that women need to span in order to achieve complete equality and toward recent indicators that progress may be stalling (or occurring at a lesser rate), there is cause for concern. Although much has changed, an imagined ideal society in which men and women share equal power and status remains unrealized. However, given that men as well as women have increasingly adopted gender equality as a goal to strive toward and the legislative changes that now protect women's rights, it is likely that advances for women will continue, although perhaps more slowly (Jackson, 2006). Next, we consider why gender discrimination remains a potent problem in the workplace, while also highlighting signs of progress and promise for women.

Sex Stereotypes and Status Beliefs Influence Evaluations

In Chapter 7, we stressed that women need to disconfirm stereotypes regarding men's greater agency, initiative, and ambition in order to be hired for leadership positions and, subsequently, advance their careers. We describe evidence for this assertion from controlled investigations that use the same stimulus materials (e.g., identical résumés and scripts for job interviews) and vary only the applicants' sex. This is called the "Goldberg paradigm," named for the researcher who initially showed that people evaluated the same written essay more favorably if it was (supposedly) written by a man rather than a woman (Goldberg, 1968).

Similarly, the identical résumé receives higher marks when a man's name appears at the top as opposed to a woman's (Fidell, 1975). In a meta-analysis of more than 100 Goldberg-inspired studies, Swim, Borgida, Maruyama, and Myers (1989) found that the effect of gender on evaluations was generally small, although men had a somewhat larger advantage in studies using résumés for job applications (as opposed to essays) and when the job was sex typed as masculine (compared with feminine or neutral).

Subsequent work using the Goldberg paradigm has continued to find sex discrimination for male-dominated jobs, with male applicants favored over female applicants despite equal qualifications (for reviews, see Deaux & LaFrance, 1998; Eagly & Karau, 2002; S. T. Fiske, 1998). As a result, women continue to be underrepresented in managerial and high-status professions (e.g., Reskin & Ross, 1995). Moreover, even when women are hired they continue to suffer economic discrimination (i.e., to receive less money for the same position; Babcock & Laschever, 2003; Reskin & Padovic, 2002; Roos & Gatta, 1999). Next, we present possible reasons for the Goldberg effect that underscore how sex-based stereotypes and status differences influence women's evaluations in the workplace.

Undervaluing Women's Skills and Contributions

One reason why a woman's identical qualifications are discounted relative to a man's concerns the different attributions people make for why a woman or man has been successful. Specifically, women's successes on stereotypically masculine tasks are often construed as being due to luck or extreme effort, whereas men's successes are more often attributed to natural talent or skill (Deaux & Emswiller, 1974; Swim & Sanna, 1996). Because luck and effort are unreliable, transitory causes of performance (whereas talent and skill are a sure bet), women are disadvantaged even when their achievements match men's point for point. This situation worsens when women and men work in teams, a frequent occurrence in the workplace. Especially in masculine domains, women's contributions are devalued relative to men's because women are presumed to be less competent, less influential, and less likely to have played a leadership role (Heilman & Haynes, 2005). In mixed-group settings, women often experience their lower status as a particular kind of "invisibility." When a woman says something, it is often ignored; however, when a man says the same thing, it is carefully attended to and discussed (Haslett, Geis, & Carter, 1992).

Another reason why identical qualifications do not add up to gender equality is captured by the feminist adage that "for a woman to be good, she has to be twice as a good as a man." In other words, women have to outperform men in order to be viewed as their equal (Foschi, 2000). For example, when perceivers watched a videotape of applicants for a managerial job (either male or female) who presented themselves as having communal traits, they rated the man's competence higher than the woman's, even though the applicants used the same script and were trained to behave similarly (Rudman, 1998; Rudman & Glick, 1999). Because men's ascribed status is higher than women's, and because status and perceived competence are robustly related (S. T. Fiske et al., 2002), the male applicant earns points for competence simply by virtue of his sex (Ridgeway, 2001a).

In addition, as a general rule, perceivers require more compelling information to disconfirm than to confirm stereotypic expectations (Biernat & Ma, 2005). In masculine domains, a mediocre man may be presumed to be competent, whereas a woman has to thwart beliefs about female incompetence by performing exceptionally well (Eagly & Karau, 2002; Glick et al., 1988). This problem, termed "overperformance demands" (Parker & Griffin, 2002), particularly afflicts women in male-dominated occupations, where the fit between a woman's gender and her job makes her particularly suspect as an employee (Johnson, 1991; Goldenhar, Swanson, Hurrell, Ruder, & Deddens, 1998). Women subjected to this burden feel they must chronically prove themselves and agree to every demand made on the job, lest they be judged unworthy (Parker & Griffin, 2002).

Shifting Standards

Another way that women are handicapped by stereotypes concerns the difference between people's subjective and objective ratings of their accomplishments. For example, a woman who wins the U.S. Open tennis championship might be lauded as extraordinary, even more so than a man accomplishing the same thing. However, when you look at the objective value of her performance (in terms of prize money earned, amount of newspaper coverage, and product endorsement offers), the numbers overwhelmingly favor the male champion. The subjective rating reveals a shifting standards effect, whereby the woman is viewed as excellent "for a woman" (Biernat, 2003). To illustrate, people might say a woman is tall (on a 7-point scale ranging from *short* to *tall*) but still estimate her actual height to be shorter than most men (Manis, Biernat, &

Nelson, 1991). The subjective measure uses other women as a reference point; the objective measure takes men into account. Similarly, a woman in the workplace may receive higher competence ratings than a man and still be undervalued because her intelligence is being compared to a lower standard than his (Biernat & Kobrynowicz, 1997). Ironically, this situation can make it more likely for a woman to be short-listed for a job but less likely than a man to be hired for the same job (Biernat & Fuegen, 2001). Thus, high evaluations and performance ratings do not necessarily translate to equitable rewards.

Shifting hiring criteria is another means of discrimination that can disadvantage both women and men. When jobs are male dominated, evaluators may shift the job criteria to give men an advantage over women. For example, when candidates for a police chief job were described as a "streetwise" man and an educated woman, evaluators rated being streetwise as more important than having a formal education. However, when the choice was between an educated man and a streetwise woman, education received more weight than being streetwise (Uhlmann & Cohen, 2005). The opposite effect occurred for candidates applying for a women's studies professorship. In this case, the hiring criteria shifted from being more of an academic to an activist, depending on the female candidate's strengths (and the male candidate's weaknesses). Thus, in each case, people shifted the hiring criteria to favor the gender-typical applicant's strengths, no matter what they were. This is likely because evaluators felt that a police chief "ought to be a man," whereas a women's studies professor "ought to be a woman" and adjusted accordingly. Because this type of discrimination is linked to the sex typing of the job, it acts to preserve gender segregation in the workforce. In so doing, it ultimately favors men as a group over women because the most high-paying and high-status jobs are male dominated.

Gender Roles in the Workplace

Social role theorists posit that because gender stereotypes stem from traditional labor divisions (men as providers, women as caregivers), gender becomes a diffuse role, a set of role expectations that people generalize across a variety of social situations (Eagly et al., 2000). When gender roles leak into the workplace, the result is termed "sex-role spillover" (Gutek, 1985). For example, women may be more likely than men to be expected to plan social events at work in addition to fulfilling their job description.

Consistent with sex-role spillover, greater demands for student support are placed on female than on male professors (Basow, Phelan, & Capotosto, 2006; Bennett, 1982), and female supervisors are expected to be more nurturing and supportive than male supervisors (Gutek & Morasch, 1982). These expectations add appreciably to women's workload and undermine their authority by reinforcing sex-linked norms for behavior and status differences. There is evidence that helping behaviors are more required of women than of men in organizations simply because they are an expected part of being female but benefit them less because such efforts by women are taken for granted when it comes time for promotion (Allen & Rush, 2001; Heilman & Chen, 2005; Kidder & Parks, 2001). In a survey of employees from a variety of work settings, Allen (2006) found that men who engaged in nonrequired helping ("organizational citizenship") reported receiving more promotions; this relationship was much weaker for female employees. In concert, these findings indicate that helping behaviors are less optional for women, who are expected to engage in more service-oriented activities, for which they will be less likely to be noticed and rewarded than men.

Even when a woman is promoted to supervisory roles, her career trajectory is likely to differ from male counterparts in ways that reflect sex-role spillover (Jacobs, 1992; Lyness & Thompson, 1997). Although women now occupy more corporate management roles than ever before, they tend to obtain human resource positions that involve people skills rather than more valued positions, such as overseeing finances or operations (Frankforter, 1996). Women's prescriptive role as caregivers funnels them into lower status management positions as opposed to the core business positions that are associated with the highest economic and social rewards.

Sex-role spillover and related forms of discrimination can also affect women's job satisfaction and career longevity. In a study of senior executives, Lyness and Thompson (1997) found that women were less satisfied with their positions than similarly placed men; the authors suggest that subtle forms of bias were responsible for this disaffection. In a study of Fortune 500 companies, more women than men left their management positions over a 2-year period (Stroh, Brett, & Reilly, 1996). The reasons women gave for leaving did not involve family issues; instead, women were dissatisfied with their role in the company. Because the type of work female managers are expected to perform often involves stress from interpersonal conflict (e.g., when managing personnel) and emotional labor (e.g., having to be a support system as well as a professional), researchers have pointed to emotional labor as a factor in female management turnover (Guy & Newman, 2004; Pugliesi, 1999). The overall picture suggests that, to some extent, female supervisors are consigned to a women's world of management, which underutilizes their talents, overloads their interpersonal duties, and rewards them less economically.

Nonetheless, women are increasingly moving into executive suites despite these impediments, and researchers have identified ways of accomplishing this feat. There are at least two paths, both of which undermine the credibility gap by which women are perceived to be less legitimate leaders than men (Cabrera & Thomas-Hunt, 2007). First, women can breach the gap through irrefutable displays of expertise and ability (Pugh & Wahrman, 1983; Steinpreis, Anders, & Ritzke, 1999). If a woman has already succeeded as an executive, there is no question that she will be an effective leader. Second, and more promisingly, women can gain legitimacy by association if they are sponsored by a high-status third party, such as existing executives or board members (e.g., Ibarra, 1997; Yoder, 2001; Yoder, Schleicher, & McDonald, 1998). In other words, cultivating powerful social networks can bypass the credibility gap and usher women into executive roles.

However, even when women reach the top executive level, sex-role spillover may help determine the status of the company they are appointed to lead. Using archival data from FTSE 100 companies in Great Britian, Ryan and Haslam (2005) found that women were more likely than men to be hired as CEOs when organizations were in financial crisis (e.g., when the company's stock had consistently fallen in the months before appointment). In contrast, men were more likely than women to step into leadership roles when companies were economically robust. Because this phenomenon places female leaders at increased risk for failure and criticism, the authors termed it the "glass cliff."

What causes the glass cliff has not been determined, but one possibility is that women are hired to manage organizational units in crisis because these positions require communal traits such as fostering morale and teamwork. In essence, board members may be hiring a nurse to administer therapy to an ailing company. Given female prescriptions to be nurturing, it is not surprising that women tend to be more mentoring and empowering in their leadership style compared with men (Eagly et al., 2003). As noted in Chapter 7, women's more inclusive leadership style tends to result in higher employee morale and job satisfaction. Although these are important outcomes, more pertinent to the glass cliff phenomenon is whether female leadership has a positive effect on an organization's bottom line. The answer may be yes. A comprehensive review of studies examining the relationship between leadership gender and economic performance revealed that companies fare better financially to the extent that women are included as business leaders (i.e., as corporate officers and board members; Eagly & Carli, 2007). For example, Fortune 500 companies with the highest percentages of female executives experienced a 34% higher return to shareholders than those with the lowest percentages of female executives (Catalyst, 2004). Although these data are correlational, they suggest that hiring a female CEO when a company is floundering may reflect a sound business decision.

Another, less optimistic, explanation for the glass cliff is that a woman's leadership reputation may be more readily gambled away than a man's. This points to a form of discrimination that assumes women have other alternatives than to work for a living, namely to get married and be provided for by men. If it can be applied to the glass cliff phenomenon, a woman's failed bid for leadership may be viewed as less tragic than a man's precisely because women have the fallback position of being financially protected within the traditional confines of marriage. Even today, it is not unusual for women to be told that they earn less than male counterparts because "he has to provide for a family," as though only men bear this responsibility (J. C. Williams, 2000).

Benevolent Sexism and Paternalism at Work

The belief that men should protect and provide for women is a tenet of benevolent sexism (Glick & Fiske, 1996; see Chapter 2). Recall that benevolent sexism is a paternalistic form of prejudice that is likely to be accepted by both sexes because it ascribes positive traits to women (e.g., niceness and morality) that endow them with a halo rather than the hostility that corresponds to readily detected sexism. As a result, paternalism may seep into the workplace without anyone thinking twice about its pernicious effects. For example, male supervisors may offer more praise for a female, as opposed to a male, subordinate's accomplishments. On the surface, being praised is positive (what woman would complain?); but praise is patronizing when it substitutes for tangible rewards (e.g., promotion or pay raises) that are more likely to be allocated to men (Vescio et al., 2005). Thus, a woman's boss might praise her to the skies while shortchanging her monetarily or failing to promote her. Moreover, the expectation that women will not perform as well as men can lead to soft forms of bigotry (e.g., overhelping, taking over, or limiting responsibilities) that perpetuate the stereotype that women are weak. For example, female police officers are differentially deployed in stereotypic ways that block them from dangerous assignments, double them up on patrols, and exclude them from specialist duties that are necessary for career advancement (Parker & Griffin, 2002).

Paternalism flourishes because it ostensibly protects women, but it is also tied to the fact that men and women are uniquely intimate and interdependent in heterosexual romantic relationships and domestic life (Glick & Fiske, 1996). The fact that women have traditionally gained social and economic status through their sex appeal (e.g., marriage to men) has repercussions for women in performance settings. If few women occupy leadership roles in an organization, those who succeed may be viewed as having done so illegitimately (i.e., by "sleeping their way to the top"; Ely, 1994). Token female authority figures have to contend with suspicions regarding how they got there, ranging from promiscuity to being called an "affirmative action baby" (Heilman & Blader, 2001).

As a result, a woman's physical attractiveness can be a double-edged sword at work. On the one hand, physically attractive workers of both sexes tend to make more money (Frieze, Olson, & Russell, 1991). On the other hand, although physical attractiveness advantages male applicants for managerial roles, sometimes "beauty is beastly" for their female counterparts (Heilman & Stopek, 1985). This is especially true if women emphasize their sex appeal by, for example, wearing a short skirt. Emphasizing sexiness did not harm evaluations of a woman when she was said to work in a traditionally feminine support role (receptionist) but led to hostility and perceptions of lower competence if she was said to be a manager (Glick, Larsen, Johnson, & Branstiter, 2005). Society strongly urges women to be physically attractive—media messages promote it and women's attention to their looks suggests it is one of the attributes women are most valued for—but it emphasizes their gender in a way that underscores their fitness for mating rather than for powerful professions.

Not surprisingly, women's sex appeal can result in biased evaluations by male supervisors. Men primed to think of women as sex objects (compared with nonprimed men) evaluated female job applicants as friendlier and more hirable for an entry-level position, but, importantly, they also saw them as less competent, suggesting that while they might be valued as eye candy around the office, they would not be seen as suitable for promotion (Rudman & Borgida, 1995). Romantic expectations can also cloud men's judgment of female coworkers, to the point at which an attractive woman's poor performance may be overrated or overlooked (Goodwin, Fiske, Rosen, & Rosenthal, 2002). Although the benefits of physical attractiveness for working women might appear to be advantageous, they are sharply limited and accompanied by a devaluation of their competence and an increase in sexual objectification. Moreover, attractive women's advantage in the workplace is evident only for low-status, not high-status, occupations (Glick et al., 2005; Heilman & Stopek, 1985). Thus, power based on sex appeal has limited effectiveness for women, underscoring its dubious benefits.

Finally, benevolent sexism perpetuates gender inequality by affording women the alternative of marriage and raising a family over pursuing a career. In a study of premedical students (Fiorentine, 1988), the attrition rate was much lower for men (36%) compared with women (57%). A closer look at the data showed that attrition was equally unlikely among male and female students who were doing well (e.g., getting good grades in their demanding courses). It was only among students with lower grades that the sex difference in attrition appeared. The same poor performance led men to persevere whereas women dropped out, likely because they felt they could fall back on plans to marry and raise a family. Because gender prescriptions place greater value on women's success in relationships than on their success at work (see Chapter 5), it is easier for a woman to forfeit high professional ambitions, to opt out of medical school in favor of domestic or low-status alternatives (e.g., becoming a nurse instead of a doctor). Compared with men, they are less at risk for disapproval and might even be socially rewarded for sacrificing their ambitions on the altar of the family hearth.

In sum, the road to advancement within organizations is more difficult for women (Ragins & Sundstrom, 1989), requiring resourceful female vanguards. Nonetheless, many women have managed to overcome these obstacles to realize their ambitions, thereby paving the way for those who would follow; and the more that women occupy powerful roles, the easier it becomes (Eagly & Carli, 2007; Ely, 1994). This is particularly important given that more women than ever before are invested in their careers, including mothers of young children. It is increasingly common for women with children to remain in the workforce, at which point the balance between professional and home obligations becomes critical (Biernat & Wortman, 1991). Even gender researchers who are optimistic about women's progress concede that the burden of work-family conflicts is still largely placed on women (Jackson, 1998, 2006). Next, we consider this obstacle to women's professional advancement.

Home and Workplace: Women's Gender-Role Conflict

After years of learning gender roles and expectations, children grow up, typically get married, and assume adult gender roles as if they had been programmed from birth to do so (they were; see Chapter 3). Despite the dramatic shift in women's work roles, a corresponding shift in men's domestic roles has not occurred. Survey data suggest that, in households with working wives, husbands continue to do little housework (less than one third; Blair & Lichter, 1991; Lennon & Rosenfield, 1994). An economist might suggest that in a fair exchange of labor, the person earning the most money ought to do less housework. However, even when working wives earn a salary equal to their husbands, they continue to do the lion's share of the domestic work (Blair & Lichter, 1991). This phenomenon has been termed the "second shift" (Hochschild, 1989) to underscore the burden carried by working wives. Not surprisingly, this burden is exacerbated when career women become mothers (Perkins & DeMeis, 1996). In a study of working mothers employed primarily in corporations or academia and whose professional responsibilities and commitment were equal to their husbands, both spouses agreed that the woman carried out most of the child care tasks except for one: playing with children (Biernat & Wortman, 1991). Nonetheless, wives gave their husbands high marks for being a good parent and reported feeling guilt for not being a better parent. Ironically, shifting standards benefit men on the home front: Because men are stereotypically held to a lower parenting standard (not expected to do as much), they get more credit for the parenting contributions that they do make.

Hochschild (1989) argued that the costs of the second shift are punitive psychologically for women and that they are fed up with it. This viewpoint has been challenged by researchers complaining that Hochschild used obsolete data (from 1965) while ignoring evidence showing that wives benefit psychologically from outside employment (Barnett & Baruch, 1987; Pleck, 1992) and dual-career families are happier and healthier than single-earner families (Crosby, 1991; Harriett & Rivers, 1996). Despite evidence that women's careers benefit both themselves and their families, media attention to Hochschild's (1989) analysis has shaped public opinion and continues to reverberate in books and articles that question whether women can handle their double roles. In a controversial article, Belkin (2003) reported that women who graduated from Ivy League colleges were defaulting on their careers to lead more traditional lives as wives and mothers. The *New York Times* deemed an article suggesting that Ivy League women were focused on motherhood more than their careers worthy of front-page news (Story, 2005), but such reports are flawed because they are based on selected anecdotes rather than systematic research.

Similar examples in the media are not hard to find. The now infamous *Newsweek* cover story, "The Marriage Crunch" (Salholz, 1986), ominously warned that a woman over the age of 35 had only a 5% chance of getting married. Twenty years later, *Newsweek* published a retraction ("Rethinking 'The Marriage Crunch'") when it was discovered that the actual probability was 40% (McGinn, 2006). An online *Forbes* editorial, "Don't Marry a Career Woman" (Noer, 2006), misused social science data to caution men that a career woman is less likely to be a happy, faithful wife. Pundits warn that women's careers are costly for their children (e.g., Hewitt, 2002; Graglia, 1998; Skow, 1989; Sommers, 2000), whereas the most comprehensive longitudinal study of child development conducted in the United States shows they are not (National Institute of Child Health and Human Development, 2005; see also Crosby, 1991). Thus, an unjustifiable fuss is being made about women needing to eschew their work to return to the hearth and home.

If the idea that women were opting out of the workplace in favor of domesticity were true, it ought to be supported by scientific data. But, in fact, women's representation in the workplace has shown no signs of abating (Eagly & Carli, 2007; Jackson, 2006). On the contrary, women have increasingly occupied management positions over the last decade, and among dual-income married couples, the percentage of women who earn more than their husbands rose from 15% in 1981 to 25% in 2005 (U.S. Census Bureau, 2007a). Moreover, as shown in Figure 8.2, surveys comparing women's responses to the question, "What is your ideal working situation?" in 1997 and 2007 reveal that the no-work option remains extremely unpopular (about 20% in both time periods). Because both surveys were limited to women with children younger than 18 years, proponents of opting out might expect more respondents in 2007 to prefer being a stay-at-home mother, but this is not the case. What is the case is that there is a tendency for more mothers of minor children to prefer part-time (as opposed to full-time) work in 2007 compared with 10 years earlier.

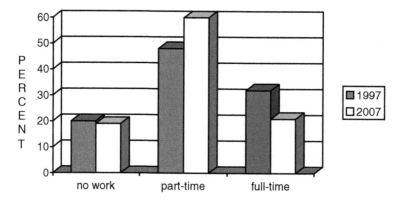

FIGURE 8.2. Percentage of women with children under 18 responding to "What is your ideal working situation?" in 1997 (*N* = 457) and 2007 (*N* = 414). Data retrieved from "Fewer Mothers Prefer Full-Time Work," by Pew Research Center, July 12, 2007, *pewresearch.org/pubs/536/working-women*.

Injustice Is Invisible at Home

Although considerable evidence appears to refute the psychological costs of the second shift to women, you might still expect them to complain about it, yet they typically do not. In study after study, couples report that they do not see inequities in domestic labor as unjust (e.g., Biernat & Wortman, 1991; Lennon & Rosenfield, 1994; Major, 1993; Sanchez, 1994; for a review, see Grote, Naylor, & Clark, 2002). In fact, women do not judge the second shift to be unfair until they are doing about 75% of the workload; even 66% is viewed as fair (Lennon & Rosenfield, 1994). Thus, even though it is no longer the case that professions are a "man's world" but "a women's work is in the home," the dramatic shift in work roles for women has not changed their domestic load appreciably. Instead, women are expected to do both a man's job and a woman's job—in essence to be both George and Jane Jetson—and they do it without complaint.

The paradox of couples viewing domestic inequities as fair may be partly understood in terms of entitlement, meaning the expectation that one should receive something valuable (Major, 1993). Because gender prescriptions dictate that women should do the bulk of the family work, wives may feel less deserving of their husband's help with housework and child care, and husbands may feel more entitled to their spouse's domestic work, leading to an asymmetric division of labor that is perceived as legitimate. Another possibility is that justice notions may be more readily applied to the office than at home, where work is more typically viewed as a labor of love. In fact, some evidence suggests that women enjoy family work, so they do not view it as a scourge, whereas most men have yet to acquire a taste for it (Grote et al., 2002). Nonetheless, it is hard to believe that women are enthusiastic about housework, and this explanation does not account for why women are also often blind to inequities in the workplace, as described next.

Injustice Is Invisible at Work

If justice issues pertain more to the workplace, women ought to be sensitized to sex discrimination in that setting. However, another paradox that researchers have uncovered is the tendency for women to acknowledge that sexism harms women as a group but not themselves. Even when women are equal in terms of job prestige, education, training, and experience yet still earn 60% of what their male counterparts earn, they do not view themselves as deprived (although they readily admit that women as a group are disadvantaged; Crosby, 1982). This phenomenon, termed "denial of personal discrimination" (Crosby, 1984), is a puzzle and one that is not restricted to women; other disadvantaged group members claim they have not personally experienced discrimination, although they admit it hinders their group (Clayton & Crosby, 1992; Crosby, Cordova, & Jaskar, 1993). It appears, then, that targets of prejudice view themselves as isolated exceptions to a general rule. Because denial of personal discrimination is widespread and it is logically impossible for every group member to be an exception to a rule, psychological explanations have been offered for this paradox.

Women's lower sense of entitlement may again provide a key to unlocking this puzzle. When tennis champion Monica Seles publicly argued that women should earn the same prize money that men earn, her colleague Steffi Graf responded by saying, "We make enough, we don't need more" and Mary Jo Fernandez added, "I'm happy with what I have; I don't think we should be greedy" (Valian, 1999, p. 161). When demands for equality are viewed as greed, it is a sign that perceived entitlement is low. It is difficult to imagine the reverse situation, with men downplaying or dismissing an economic advantage that women might have over them. In fact, laboratory experiments have repeatedly shown that when given the opportunity to determine their compensation, women reward themselves with less money than men do even when they performed as well, suggesting that men have a stronger sense of entitlement (for a review, see Major, 1987).

Social comparisons may also play a role in denying personal discrimination. If women compare themselves with other women, they may feel that their salary is justified. But when they are given specific information regarding gender-based pay inequities, they see the injustice (Major, 1987). In addition, although clearly speculative, it seems likely that women deny discrimination because to do otherwise is to risk a loss of morale and self-esteem that would encumber them in their careers. Nobody wants to approach their job with the sense of helplessness and bitterness that prejudice awareness entails. This helps to explain why even women with PhDs in science, who are trained to be objective and critical thinkers, report that they are not personally discriminated against, even though they believe that women scientists generally are (Cole & Singer, 1991). Indeed, this explanation might apply even more so to inequities on the home front. Wives may be especially averse to viewing their husbands as unjust and likely seek to avoid rancor in their marriages.

The Maternal Wall

Although we have suggested that work–family conflicts are more media fabricated than real, there is a genuine collision between women's family and career roles that can result in job discrimination for pregnant women and working mothers, a phenomenon known as the maternal wall (Crosby, Williams, & Biernat, 2004). In this case, there is evidence that work–family conflict indeed distresses women; not because they are fed up with it but because supervisors and colleagues perceive them to be putting in less time as a result of family responsibilities (Frone, Russell, & Cooper, 1992; Vinokur, Pierce, & Buck, 1999). Thus, work–family conflict may have more to do with attitudes toward working mothers than women's own sense of being overburdened.

Although the maternal role is highly prescriptive for women, pregnant women and working mothers are at risk for experiencing prejudice based on both benevolent and hostile sexism. On the one hand, paternalistic assumptions about women's physical limitations and proper place as homemakers and mothers can foster patronizing discrimination. For example, pregnant women often receive unsought help and are addressed by diminutive endearments, such as "honey" (Walton et al., 1988). On the other hand, many people look askance at pregnant career women because of a perceived conflict between fulfilling home and workplace responsibilities (Crosby et al., 2004). As a result, pregnant female job candidates can suffer both patronizing and hostile discrimination. For example, women who wore a pregnancy prosthesis while posing as a customer were patronized (e.g., smiled at and called "honey"), but when they applied for a job they received more hostility (e.g., scowling and rudeness) compared with the same women who did not wear the prosthesis (Hebl, King, Glick, Singletary, & Kazama, 2007).

Once the child is born and the mother returns to the workplace, prejudice is likely to continue (Cuddy et al., 2004). In general, working mothers make 60% of the earnings of working fathers (Crosby et al., 2004). This discrepancy is at least partly due to employers having stereotypical assumptions about working mothers' priorities and ability to perform well on the job (even when their performance evaluations are glowing). This type of prejudice, termed "family responsibilities discrimination," has now been identified and combated in legal proceedings (J. C. Williams, 2000). For example, an attorney who worked for an insurance company was consistently promoted while she was childless, but after she had two children her promotions ceased because her employers assumed she would not be interested in or capable of handling added responsibilities (*Trezza v. The Hartford*, cited in J. C. Williams, 2000). Paternalism rewards women for conforming to caregiving roles but can yield to hostility when they also occupy roles that confer high status. Because the concepts of career and family are still strongly and automatically associated with male and female gender, respectively (Nosek et al., 2002a), working mothers may elicit hostility based on prescriptive roles ("You really ought to be home with your kids"). However, because the maternal wall is beginning to be recognized by the courts as an actionable form of sex discrimination, this type of prejudice is beginning to receive the attention it deserves as an obstacle to gender fairness (Press, 2007). As we discuss next, sexual harassment was similarly long overlooked as a form of sex discrimination but has now become a focus of concern in the corporate world.

Sexual Harassment in the Workplace

In 1991, Anita Hill challenged Clarence Thomas's ability to serve as a Supreme Court justice by accusing him of sexual harassment when she worked as his assistant in the U.S. Department of Education. Among her complaints was that he bragged about his pornography collection and made a joke regarding a pubic hair in a can of Coke. The televised Hill–Thomas congressional hearings were gripping to watch, and, while ultimately resolved in his favor, they provided a "national teach-in" on sexual harassment, a blatant form of discrimination that afflicts women far more than men. When the first author tried to explain their import to her grandmother, who had worked in retail for many years, she sighed and said, "Oh honey, we just called it life!"

The grandmother's response is noteworthy for at least two reasons. First, it underscores the pervasiveness of "life," or rather men's tendency to sexualize their relationships with women, even at work. Second, it shows how far women have come since her generation. Sexual harassment has been ruled as a form of sex discrimination under Title VII of the Civil Rights Act of 1964 and Title IX of the Educational Amendments of 1972. Under federal mandate, most colleges and universities have formal sexual harassment policies and grievance procedures, and many businesses and organizations have followed suit. As a result, women are legally protected from a chronic form of discrimination, and this protection is widely recognized. Suing your employer is not the ideal mechanism of social change, and lawsuits can put women at risk for many reasons. They are costly in terms of money, time, and stress, and they can damage a woman's career by labeling her a troublemaking whistle-blower. But the fact that the option even exists marks a historic achievement for women's rights.

Components and Causes of Sexual Harassment

Sexual harassment has received prolific research attention, as investigators have attempted to define its victims (mostly women) and perpetrators (almost always men) and to illuminate its components, causes, and consequences (Wiener & Gutek, 1999; Gutek & Done, 2001; Pryor, Geidd, & Williams, 1995; Stockdale, Visio, & Batra, 1999). A useful taxonomy divides sexual harassment into three main types: sexual coercion, unwanted sexual attention, and gender harassment (Fitzgerald, Gelfand, & Drasgow, 1995). Sexual coercion (aka *quid pro quo* sexual harassment) is when the perpetrator assigns outcomes that are contingent on sexual compliance. For example, a supervisor may coerce a female employee into having sex in order to keep her job or to obtain a promotion, or a professor may offer a student a better grade in exchange for sexual favors. This is the type of sexual harassment most likely to be labeled as such by both women and men, but it is relatively rare in that only 5% to 10% of women report having experienced it (Fitzgerald et al., 1995, who also provide the following percentages). Unwanted sexual attention is more common (20–25%), and involves treating a woman as a sex object by talking to her suggestively, leering at her, sending her lewd e-mails, or grabbing her inappropriately. *Gender harassment* is by far the most prevalent type (50%) and involves degrading women as a group by telling sexist jokes and posting pictures of women as sex objects. A professor who refers to the women in his class as either "frizzies" or "fuzzies" depending on their hairstyle, a coworker who uses a pornographic screen saver, and a foreman at a plant calling himself the "Mayor of Pussyville" because he has women working for him are examples of gender harassment, the legal term for which is "hostile work environment."

Like other forms of sex discrimination, sexual harassment can take both patronizing and hostile forms, which can be characterized as reflecting approach and rejection motivations, respectively (S. T. Fiske & Glick, 1995; Stockdale et al., 1999). In the patronizing case, the harasser's motives may primarily be sexual, perhaps coupled with a desire for a dating relationship. His behavior becomes harassing when the woman's refusals to cooperate fall on deaf ears. The perpetrator in this case is treating the woman as if she were incapable of knowing her own feelings, and he persists in the belief that she is weak and gullible, so he attempts to persuade her to change her mind. This type of harassment can be classified as unwanted sexual attention, and it is not restricted to the workplace (see Chapter 10).

Hostile harassment is more likely to reflect motives to exclude and demean women in an attempt to drive them out of male-dominated jobs (Gutek, 1985; Gutek & Done, 2001). Because it has serious implications for equal opportunity, we discuss it in detail next. Hostile harassment sometimes also targets men who do not live up to prescriptions for masculinity in terms of appearance and physical strength, behaviors (e.g., "toughing out" difficulties without complaint), or traits such as assertiveness (Berdahl, 2007a; Stockdale et al., 1999). Thus, hostile harassment of "weak" men, who are castigated for being "girly men," functions similarly to hostile harassment of women, by reinforcing the masculinity of the job or workplace (Franke, 1997; Maass et al., 2003). Punishing gender deviants effectively rebukes men and discourages women from pursuing masculine domains (Berdahl, 2007b; Rudman & Fairchild, 2004; see Chapter 7).

Hostile Work Environments

Because hostile work environments are particularly likely in settings that are male dominated, their main purpose may be to reinforce the masculine identity of the workplace (Berdahl, 2007b; Franke, 1997). In essence, a hostile (meaning sexualized) workplace posts a sign for women reading "Boy's Club—Keep Out." In Chapter 6 we described how individual men retaliate when their gender identity is threatened (e.g., by sending a woman graphic e-mails; Maass et al., 2003). Similarly, men may collectively retaliate when female interlopers penetrate their club, threatening their exclusively masculine culture.

For example, the first class action sexual harassment suit filed in the United States was based on the prejudiced treatment of female miners in northern Minnesota (Bingham & Gansler, 2002). For more than 20 years, the mining company did nothing to stop the daily abuse the female miners experienced (e.g., incessant propositioning, sexual insults, pornographic graffiti, groping, and stalking). That a foreman at a Minnesota brewery called himself the "Mayor of Pussyville" came to light in a suit filed charging that female brewery plant workers were repeatedly harassed and endangered during their jobs (e.g., their tools and equipment were tampered with; *Huffman v. Pepsi-Cola Bottling Co.,* 1994). Women in the police force and the military are also frequent targets of sexual harassment (Parker & Griffin, 2002; Pryor, 1995). When Shannon Faulkner successfully sued Virginia Military Institute (VMI) for having accepted her on merit but then refusing to admit her based on her sex, VMI was forced to allow women though its gates. In retaliation, the first class of female cadets was subjected to chronic harassment, and VMI male cadets openly wore "Better Dead Than Co-Ed" T-shirts (Allen, 1996; Nossiter, 1997).

These examples may suggest that sexual harassment is primarily a case of "the blue collar blues" for women. However, when women began to work on Wall Street in the 1980s, the men in many financial firms retaliated with sexual antagonism, resulting in several lawsuits and mass media attention. Perhaps the most publicized case involved the infamous "boom boom room" at Smith Barney, where lap dancing and various forms of vulgar behavior were celebrated, but it was hardly an isolated instance (Antilla, 2002). More generally, sexual harassment can occur in any setting in which women and men work together, including universities, banks, retail outlets, and factories, as the litany of legal cases shows (Conte, 1990).

Nonetheless, particular types of workplaces are more likely to foster sexual harassment than others. Research on sexual harassment has emphasized the importance of the workplace environment—its norms, structure, and culture—which can encourage or inhibit harassment by those who are prone to engage in such behavior (Gutek, 1985; Pryor et al., 1995). The presence of sexualized images of women (e.g., nude calendars, graphic magazines, and Internet pornography shared via e-mail) primes men to view women as sexual objects. Once primed, men are more likely to engage in sexualized behaviors, such as standing too close to or touching female coworkers (McKenzie-Mohr & Zanna, 1990). Research has shown that it is surprisingly easy to prime men in this way; simply showing them regular TV commercials that portray women as scantily clad and lusted after increases men's likelihood of treating a woman as a sex object during a job interview (Rudman & Borgida, 1995). Therefore, workplace environments in which such images are frequently seen are likely to show an increased incidence of sexual harassment.

Power differences between men and women also intensify the problem. In organizations in which men generally hold positions of greater status and power, women are at greater risk of sexual harassment. For better or worse, power makes individuals more likely to act on their impulses (Galinsky, Gruenfeld, & Magee, 2003). For some men, having power over a woman is automatically linked to viewing women in a sexual manner (Bargh & Raymond, 1995), and when men are given the power to decide whether a women gets hired, men who are prone to sexually harass are more likely engage in this behavior (Rudman & Borgida, 1995). Therefore, the fact that men tend to monopolize the most powerful positions in most organizations puts women at greater risk for harassment.

Leaders have a significant amount of influence over organizational norms, which can suppress harassment or permit it. Women are less likely to report sexual harassment if they perceive that management tolerates it (Pryor, LaVite, & Stolle, 1993). Similarly, workplaces in which the norms of behavior do not stress professionalism foster sexual harassment (Pryor et al., 1995). Lack of professionalism includes a general tolerance for disrespectful treatment of others, frequent use of obscenities, and expectations for employees to perform tasks not formally required by the job. Such informal atmospheres can encourage sex-role spillover and the sexualization of the workplace. Consistent with the general co-appearance of hostile and patronizing forms of discrimination, in workplaces where women report that they receive generally disrespectful treatment, 67% also had received sexual comments intended to be complimentary compared with 38% for women who reported never having been treated disrespectfully at work (Gutek, 1985). Overall, the combination of a male-dominated workplace, in terms of numbers and power, with an informal work environment that permits or encourages sex-role spillover puts women at much higher risk of harassment.

Consequences of Sexual Harassment

If sexual harassment were simply a fact of life, something women get used to or learn to cope with well, it would not present the serious obstacle to gender equity that it does. However, researchers have uncovered a wealth of evidence suggesting that women are negatively affected in numerous ways. Not surprisingly, their job satisfaction plummets, which leads to attrition (Bingham & Gansler, 2002; Fitzgerald, Hulin, & Drasgow, 1995; Parker & Griffith, 2002; Schneider, Swan, & Fitzgerald, 1997). Depression and anxiety resulting from psychological distress are among the best documented outcomes of sexual harassment (Fitzgerald, Drasgow, Hulin, Gelfand, & Magley, 1997; Schneider et al., 1997; Magley, Hulin, Fitzgerald, & DeNardo, 1999; Glomb et al., 1997). Even when harassment is relatively infrequent and takes a milder form, the psychological consequences are severe. Women who experience low, moderate, and high levels of sexual harassment show more negative psychological outcomes than women who experience no sexual harassment (Schneider et al., 1997). Moreover, women who do not interpret their experiences as sexual harassment (e.g., who reported behaviors that are legally classified as harassment but did not label them as such) suffer the same psychological distress as women who acknowledge that they have been harassed (Magley et al., 1999; Schneider et al., 1997). Thus, whether mild or severe, labeled or unlabeled, sexual harassment harms women psychologically.

The chronic stress that accompanies harassment also endangers women's physical health (Fitzgerald, Hulin, et al., 1995). The female miners who filed the first class action hostile environment lawsuit paid a high price for remaining in their jobs, including physical and psychological disability (Bingham & Gansler, 2002). Some of the miners' stress came from the fact that they litigated against the mining company, which engendered hostility from supervisors, coworkers, and their union; it also subjected them to a lengthy legal process that included invasive interrogation on the part of defense lawyers (Bingham & Gansler, 2002). Although they ultimately won their case, as did many of the women on Wall Street (Antilla, 2002), the emotional, psychological, and physical costs of waging even successful lawsuits can be tremendous.

Nonetheless, the collective impact of successful sex discrimination suits cannot be overstated. Media attention exposes the problem of sexual harassment and educates women about their civil rights. It also educates employers about their responsibilities. When organizations allow women to be sexually antagonized or discriminated against in other ways and they lose in court, they take corrective action. For example, when the Central Intelligence Agency was threatened with a class action suit charging differential deployment of women, unfair promotion practices, and a laissez-faire attitude toward harassment, the administration took steps to ensure equal opportunity to avoid the lawsuit (Weiner, 1994). As K. D. Williams (2002) notes, "Legal liability has a remarkable ability to focus the mind. Sexual harassment has been around a long time; employers got serious about it only once they faced legal liability. The threat of liability, rather than the damages awarded in individual lawsuits, is what leads to social change" (p. 101).

Legal action in response to discrimination is not always necessary; women can effectively band together to advance their cause, as the saga of Lawrence Summers illustrates. In 2005, Summers, then Harvard University's president, suggested that one reason women in science lag behind men might be innate gender differences. This touched off a highly publicized maelstrom from female faculty that, combined with efforts to inform Summers about the factors that hinder women's progress, led him to reverse his position and pledge $50 million dollars toward improving Harvard University's climate for women, including expanded academic grants and child care (Bombardieri, 2005; Dillon, 2005; Sacchetti, 2006). The outcry over Summers's remarks led to other positive developments for female scientists, including national media attention on how to foster women's progress in science (e.g., Rimer, 2005) and the election of a record-breaking number of women to the highly prestigious National Academies of Sciences (Dean, 2005). Thus, collective action is an important means by which women can combat sex discrimination in the workplace.

Chapter Summary

We sought to juxtapose the remarkable advances that women have made in the workplace with the obstacles they continue to face. Some obstacles are internal, such as women's lack of entitlement and denial of personal disadvantage, but many are external (i.e., driven by other people's prejudices). Both types of processes, however, stem from the same underlying source: buying in to legitimizing gender ideologies. As a result of the revolution in women's professional roles, it is no longer axiomatic in popular opinion that men are superior to women in intelligence and aptitude, but subtler beliefs (e.g., that women are less ambitious and ought to be more concerned with home and children than men) still hinder women's workplace advancement.

Sexism, then, is hardly obsolete, although it has shape shifted in some ways. Old-fashioned sexism is alive in the form of biased evaluations of women's skills, products, and performance in the workplace, biases that are propped up by sex-typed attributions of their success (luck vs. skill) and shifting standards. It is also alive in the form of sex-role spillover effects, which import gender norms into performance settings. Because women have traditionally gained power indirectly (by attracting men), they are at risk for being viewed as better suited for mating than for professional purposes. This can cast suspicion on the legitimacy of token female authority figures and lead to appearance-based hiring effects for low-status jobs.

New-fashioned sexism can also be linked to sex-role spillover effects. Because of women's traditional role as caregivers, they are perceived to have "people skills." Consequently, although women have made gains in middle-management roles, they are more likely to be consigned to human resources than production work. Although media make much ado about the conflict between women's domestic and professional roles, the facts are more consistent with viewing women's careers as beneficial for their families rather than detrimental. Because more women today choose to work when they are pregnant or the mothers of small children, the maternal wall is now recognized as a new legal frontier focused on family responsibilities discrimination. Similarly, sexual harassment at work is a long-standing problem, but it has been acknowledged as a gauntlet that (mostly) women have to run, and public awareness of sexual harassment and its illegality has been heightened. The good news is that life for working women today does not need to be as unjust as it was in their grandmothers' day.

Finally, benevolent sexism is as old as corsets, but it has only been recently named and recognized as a form of sexism rather than merely "complimentary" to women. Unmasked as paternalism, we can begin to see how it leads to soft forms of bigotry that reward women with "praise, not pay"; curtails their responsibilities, and undermines their ability to anneal themselves for the exigencies of leadership. It also provides women with opting-out alternatives (marriage and motherhood) that men do not readily have.

Nonetheless, far from opting out of the workplace, women continue to choose to balance family and career rather than abdicate their ability to shape public spheres. The advances they have made in the past were achieved without the benefit of the legal protections in place today and when attitudes were far more blatantly sexist. Despite substantial hurdles, women have taken their place next to men in the workplace and are beginning to flex their muscle as powerful business and political leaders. As a result, although no one can guarantee that future progress will be smooth or linear, there is considerable cause for optimism that sexism in the workplace will continue to diminish over time.

CHAPTER 9

Love and Romance

After 3 years of intense courtship, Ken has proposed to Marcy and, happily, she has accepted. While they have many wedding details to work out, and no doubt the occasion will be as momentous for Ken as for Marcy, it is clear from conversations with them that it is really Marcy's "day." She knows where she wants the ceremony to take place, what the wedding party will wear, which flowers to order, and what kind of music and food will be on hand. In fact, she has even picked out the ring Ken will buy for her. Other than assisting with the guest list, Ken has taken a back seat in planning the event, claiming he merely wants to be "told what to do." If this does not strike you as the typical way that most nuptials unfold, then imagine the reverse, with Ken designing the wedding and Marcy mostly acquiescing to his ideas.

In this chapter, we examine how male dominance and heterosexual interdependence intersect within heterosexual romantic relationships. We consider the many virtues and benefits of romantic love, underscoring its importance and centrality for human happiness. At the same time, we consider the subtle ways in which traditional ideologies about heterosexual romance can also unwittingly preserve male dominance. Throughout, we distinguish between romantic love itself and traditional romantic ideologies, which represent prescriptive cultural beliefs about how love should be enacted.

Readers should understand from the outset that our aim is not to diminish or deride heterosexual romantic love; indeed, we will review its many demonstrated rewards. Nor is our aim to substitute our own ideological prescriptions about how people should act in relationships for traditional notions of romance. Rather, we seek to inform readers about how traditional gender ideologies have become incorporated into cultural views of romance in ways that they may not have reflected upon. Like cultural stereotypes that are so well learned that they automatically influence our perception and behavior, cultural ideologies about romance are so prevalent that they create scripts people may enact without thinking twice. In short, this chapter is oriented toward helping readers to "think twice" about traditional notions of romance so that they can make their own decisions.

Romantic love refers to the intense attachments formed between people who are in love, including feelings of wanting to merge with another person, sexual attraction, and the desire to protect the other's welfare. In addition to its emotional properties, falling in love may be a basic drive that is as important as sex, thirst, and hunger (Aron, Fisher, Mashek, Strong, Li, & Brown, 2005). As scores of poems, songs, and novels attest, there are few things in life more rewarding.

By contrast, traditional romantic ideologies refer to prescriptive cultural scripts that dictate how love should unfold and be enacted. These scripts are highly gendered because they distinguish how members of each sex "should" demonstrate love, specifying differing "love roles" for men and women. Traditional romantic ideologies have so deeply influenced our cultural views of romantic love that many people are not free to simply and wholeheartedly experience love, but instead feel constrained to enact love in specific, highly gendered ways.

By constraining people's choices, traditional romantic ideologies can diminish the quality of heterosexual romantic relationships. Further, there is growing evidence that they also represent an obstacle to attaining complete equality between the sexes. In particular, we argue that gendered romantic ideologies are an important linchpin for benevolent sexism because they emphasize love as the defining feature of women's lives and as conflicting with, rather than complementing and supplementing, women's independence and autonomy. In essence, traditional romantic ideologies encourage the "fairer sex" to limit their personal ambitions in exchange for the love and protection of men. This proposition is consistent with social structural theories of gender relations that emphasize the subtle ways that women may be co-opted into supporting male dominance (Glick & Fiske, 1999; Jackman, 1994; Ridgeway, 2001b).

In addition, we underscore the consequences of traditional romantic scripts for men, who may experience conflict between cultural notions of masculinity and their natural desire to express feelings of love and nurturance toward their romantic partners. Like women, men may also feel forced to live up to unrealistic cultural ideals about their romantic role. If this chapter has a provocative aim, it is this: to help readers consider whether the benefits of romantic love can be retained and perhaps even enhanced for partners of both sexes once they are freed from the constraining, traditional cultural notions of how a man should love a woman and a woman should love a man.

The Benefits of Romantic Love

Romantic love itself is wonderful and life affirming. It is easy to see why falling in love is viewed as a panacea for people's ills, and there is considerable evidence to support the many cultural references to love as a mood-altering drug. Subjectively, people report feelings of high energy and euphoria, accompanied by impressions of transcendence, such as feelings of "walking on air" (Hatfield & Rapson, 1993; Hendrick & Hendrick, 1992). Love can be so powerful that it may be difficult to concentrate on anything other than blissful thoughts of the loved one. Moreover, people in love report more positive attitudes toward the world in general, viewing reality through rose-colored glasses (Hendrick & Hendrick, 1988).

Objectively, men and women alike experience passionate love as a neurological and hormonal high. People in love show activity in neural substrates that are positively linked to elation and negatively linked to depression (Bartels & Zeki, 2000). When falling in love, men and women automatically coordinate their testosterone levels (with men showing lower and women higher levels) to accommodate mutual sexual desire (Marazziti & Canale, 2004). Studies of pair bonding in monogamous prairie voles suggest that the hormones oxytocin and vasopressin are also part of the "cocktail" of romantic love that prepares people for mating (Winslow & Insel, 2004); both of these hormones are produced by the street drug Ecstasy, known for its hypersocial, euphoric effects (Wolff et al., 2006). When couples who have recently fallen in love view pictures of their partner, it activates the motivation and reward systems in the brain, suggesting that passion is a drive whose fulfillment is as rewarding as sating an addict's need for cocaine (Aron et al., 2005). In other words, falling in love may be a drive as primal as hunger or thirst. Finally, the notion that people are "out of their minds" when they fall in love suggests a strong connection between sexual pleasure and ecstasy (derived from Greek roots meaning "to stand outside of oneself, or outside of one's mind"; Baumeister, 1989, p. 100), and sexual passion has long been described as ecstatic. Taken together, the findings are tantalizing in their suggestion that love acts like a euphoric drug on the human body.

When people fall in love, they long to merge with their beloved, to cease being two separate selves. There is evidence that their desire is cognitively manifested; newlyweds automatically identify with the traits that describe their partners but not themselves, suggesting that love blurs the boundaries between two people (Aron, Paris, & Aron, 1995). For example, imagine that your partner is athletic (but you are not), whereas you are musical (but your partner is not). On reaction time tests, you might quickly and mistakenly recognize the athletic trait as belonging to yourself, and your partner might similarly adopt the musical trait.

People also show a strong tendency to endow their romantic partners with highly favorable, often idealized, attributes, a practice that appears to benefit the health of close relationships (Murray, Holmes, & Griffin, 1996; Murray & Holmes, 1997). That is, couples who idealize their partners tend to have less conflict and more stable relationships than those who view their partners as flawed, mortal beings. Ironically, oft-heard marital advice to "be realistic" about the virtues and vices of our partners may act to undermine, rather than benefit, our romantic relationships.

By any measure, satisfactory intimate relationships powerfully enhance the psychological and physiological well-being of both sexes (Berscheid & Reis, 1998). Thus, romantic love and its sexual expression are among the most sought after and intense experiences two people can share. However, when wrapped in traditional romantic ideologies that exalt women for their beauty and selfless "purity" (e.g., their devotion to others), love becomes culturally fused with benevolent sexism and may encourage women to accept less independence and autonomy in exchange for men's romantic adoration and love. Such traditional notions can also constrain men, who may feel that they need to live up to romanticized ideals, like the "knight in shining armor," in order to attract a female partner. In the following section, we review the historical and cultural development of traditional notions of romance.

The Cultural Evolution of Love
as the Basis for Marriage

To understand traditional ideologies of romance, it is crucial to consider their cultural evolution. Not that long ago, people did not marry for love, even in individualistic cultures. In fact, the concept of passionate love as a basis for marriage is only about 200 years old (Coontz, 2005; Westermack, 1903). Before then, men and women married to secure alliances, to increase their families' property and wealth, and to ensure that sufficient progeny would be around to inherit the gains. If a wife did not produce children (or had only female children), this "failure" was deemed grounds for divorce. Before the Industrial Revolution, living conditions were sufficiently bleak that marriage was based on enhancing one's chances of survival rather than the desire for self-fulfillment that now leads people to emphasize appearance, personality, and mutual attraction (Hafner, 1993). Nonetheless, pragmatic marriages remain common in many parts of the world where the typical union is arranged through the couple's relatives; often, bride and groom do not see each other until shortly before they are wed (Kottak, 2004). The success of these marriages is often a source of puzzlement to Westerners. However, when people do not expect much emotional or sexual fulfillment from marriage, they are not greatly disappointed by its absence (Hafner, 1993; McNulty & Karney, 2004). Moreover, arranged marriages can lead to increased love and passion over time as the couple's mutual appreciation unfolds (Brehm, 1998; Gupta & Singh, 1982).

The expectation of emotional rewards from marriage was a luxury made possible by the rising standard of living during the Industrial Age. Even so, women, as the more biologically and socially vulnerable sex, were encouraged to be more pragmatic than men when choosing a mate (Maushart, 2001). Today, many Westerners would consider a pragmatic match (e.g., based on financial security) to be hopelessly crass, a sign of the advances that women have made in securing their economic independence but also of the value placed on emotional gratification when people marry for the sake of love. Ideally, the couple "falls madly in love," and this propels them to legalize their union.

Medieval to Modern Notions of Romance

Although love-based marriages are a recent historical phenomenon, the idea of romance began much earlier. Historians have pegged its beginnings to 12th-century France, in the court of Eleanor of Aquitaine

(Heer, 1962). Inspired by the feudal system and adopted at first in the spirit of play, this new form of gender relations involved knights courting ladies of higher birth, with women playing the role of lord and men the role of servant. To win a lady's esteem and affection, knights carried out various wishes for them, which ranged from simple services to acts of bravery and heroism. In return, knights sought tokens of affection, such as a kiss or a perfumed handkerchief, and would kneel to receive them, a ritual that survives today in men's practice of kneeling before a woman to propose marriage. In other words, romance as an ideology began between men and women of different status, with women having the upper hand. Thus, we can trace the origins of men putting the women they love "on a pedestal" to the medieval origins of romance. Elevating women to a "higher status" in matters of the heart began because of the genuine disparity in social class between ladies and knights in medieval France. Today, however, it informs heterosexual relations across the social strata (De Rougemont, 1956), and the notion of the "pedestal" of love may restrict women as much as it elevates them in men's affections. Further, although such romantic ideologies were once confined to industrialized nations, they are now embedded across a wide spectrum of cultures in an increasingly interconnected world (Hatfield & Rapson, 2006).

In their current manifestation, traditional romance narratives endow women with the trappings of superior status in a superficial and placating way. While women are "courted" by men, the qualities for which they are sought after, such as youth, beauty, and sexual modesty, are actually low in status (and short in shelf-life) compared with the qualities for which male partners are valued (e.g., power and wealth). Moreover, they accentuate prescriptive stereotypes that men are active initiators, whereas women are passive, emotional responders. From their intensive study of college students, Holland and Skinner (1987) describe the typical course of conventional notions of romance as having more than a hint of these stereotypes. After a man and a woman discover their mutual attraction:

> The man learns and appreciates the woman's qualities and uniqueness as a person. Sensitive to her desires, he shows his attraction by treating her well: for example, he pays attention to her, he buys things for her, takes her places she likes, and shows that he appreciates her special qualities. She in turn shows her admiration and care for him and allows the relationship to become more intimate. The relationship provides intimacy—both emotional and physical. It also provides prestige by demonstrating that

the woman is attractive—she has attracted a man... If the woman is more attractive than the man, he can compensate by treating her especially well. The man's treatment of the woman is a sign of (his assessment of) her attractiveness relative to his. If the woman's attractiveness is the lesser of the two, she compensates by lowering her expectations for good treatment. The woman's expectations of the man are a sign of (her assessment of) his attractiveness relative to hers. (Holland & Skinner, 1987, pp. 89–90, 101–102)

According to this gendered script, the man is stereotypically active ("buying her things" and "taking her places") while the woman passively "admires" him. Moreover, the script itself is not particularly intimate or loving in that it treats both partners as commodities in a sexual market-place, specifying (1) a set of gender-based exchanges (the man appreci-ates her by expending resources, the woman cares for him and consents to sex), and (2) a means of compensating for unequal attractiveness (his less favorable treatment of her, her lowered expectations of him). These exchanges are also viewed as a means of providing both partners with a source of social prestige; she has captured a man's attentions, and he has (ideally) captured an attractive woman.

One of the hallmarks of a culturally defined schema or ideology is that, although actual relationships are not destined to follow the model, "experience is anticipated, interpreted, and evaluated in light of it" (Holland & Eisenhart, 1990, p. 94). For example, women who cut their romantic teeth on *Gone with the Wind* might expect their mate to sweep them off their feet and carry them up a staircase to the bedroom. When reality does not match the model, it may be brought into sync with men-tal tricks. In one study, researchers had women read a story describing a whirlwind romance; the women claimed it was very much like their own love story even though their own experience (reported weeks earlier) shared very little in common with it (Averill, 1985).

In sum, traditional romantic ideologies have been translated from the royal courts of France to the present in ways that help us to trace the roots of modern practices, including men's "courting" of women and holding them in high esteem for traits such as modesty and depen-dence. Also the idea that men grant women's wishes through deeds and services in exchange for affection has survived, with the added reward of sexual favors. Our conventional notions of romance began as a game played by knights and their ladies, who had greater social and economic status than their courtly suitors. Ironically, today these traditional ideas may help to maintain women's lower cultural status. Women may be worshipped as "the fairer sex" and placed on a pedestal by men who seek to capture their devotion and love, but, as we describe later, this exchange is not conducive to gender equality.

Romance and Ambivalent Sexism

Recall that placing women on a pedestal is an aspect of benevolent sexism, and benevolent sexism harms gender equality because it envisions women as a "protected class" (with men, knights or not, doing the protecting). Benevolent sexism exalts women on dimensions (e.g., unselfishness and purity) that maintain their low status as a group by upholding feminine ideals that, if lived up to, undermine women's power and influence in public life. Women's traditional purviews are love, family, relationships, and tending to others, which endow them with a duty to be selfless (e.g., willing to sacrifice personal ambitions to help the family as a whole). Highly gendered romantic ideologies encourage women to exchange men's protection for their autonomy: their right to be men's equals on the dimensions that society values most, such as achievement, recognition, money, and power.

It was not as though women had better options than to accept this traditional exchange. At the time that the ideology of romance blossomed in France, prevailing views of women were based on a hostile sexism reinforced by religious justifications (Painter, 1940). Medieval Christianity was explicit about women's inferiority to men. Steeped in a religion that blamed Eve, the first woman, for people's fall from grace, impugned women as "unclean," and sometimes burned them at the stake as heretic witches, a benevolent view of their sex must have seemed like a miracle to medieval women. In this context, romantic ideologies that worshipped women were an important counterbalance to hostile sexism.

Moreover, even today conventional scripts about romance serve some positive functions. They offer a ritualized set of "rules" that enable the sexes to overcome a highly segregated childhood, marked by avoidance of the other gender (see Chapter 3). Further, by encouraging benevolence, romantic scripts may counter male tendencies to compete, dominate, and aggress, making them kinder, gentler partners. Thus, men's benevolence toward women is not solely designed to perpetuate the status quo but also reflects a genuine desire to share a long and happy life with a devoted partner.

However, the same positive features of traditional romantic ideologies described previously can easily devolve into justifications for inequality. For instance, traditional romantic ideology suggesting that it takes "the love of a good woman" to "civilize" a man can easily become a rationalization for traditional roles. For example, in an attempt to appeal to female voters, President Reagan once jovially stated that "If it wasn't for women, us men would still be walking around in skin suits carrying clubs." Although he meant this as a compliment, his audience—representatives of the International Federation of Business and Professional Women—did not see it that way. As one Republican woman commented, "To me he seemed to be saying that the only reason we're here is to create families" (Isaacson, 1983).

Such views of women as the fairer sex who need men as their protectors once justified excluding women from dangerous, demanding, or stressful occupations (e.g., firefighters, pilots, police work) "for their own good." While employment discrimination based on sex is now illegal, benevolently justified or protective restrictions may still occur in romantic relationships, where the notion of men as protectors remains prevalent. This kind of protectiveness may have mixed motives: It may simply be loving but could also be based on sexist assumptions that women cannot take care of themselves, or it might even be manipulative (a strategy of control). Thus, a male partner's protectiveness can create interpretational ambiguity for female partners. For example, imagine a husband who assumes control of the family finances because it would be "too demanding and stressful" for his wife. Is he being benevolent or sexist or both (i.e., thinking he is being nice, but making sexist assumptions), or is he simply using protectiveness as an excuse? Given the long history of paternalism in gender relations, the wife may be uncertain about her husband's motives. (A similar situation in close relationships would be a father who imposes greater restrictions on his daughter than his son.)

Determining how to react to a male partner's protective restrictions may be especially difficult in romantic relationships because partners are rightly expected to care for each other, with the male partner traditionally enacting a protective role. Not only are men socialized to be protective toward female partners, but some women (those who endorse benevolent sexism) may expect or even demand male protectiveness, even at the cost of restrictions on their freedom.

A pair of studies conducted in Spain (Moya, Glick, Expósito, de Lemus, & Hart, 2007) examined how women deal with the tricky issue of a male partner's protective restriction of their behavior. In one study, female psychology majors were told that they were eligible to participate in a counseling internship involving clinical work with men who had been convicted of domestic abuse or sexual assault. The women were informed of this opportunity during a session attended by their steady male romantic partners, ostensibly to make sure that the internship would not "cause problems" for their relationship. The male partners, sequestered in another room, were recruited as experimental confederates to write a note strongly opposing participation in the internship, claiming "I would convince her not to do it." The notes were scripted, but in the boyfriends' own handwriting. Depending on random assignment, the boyfriend simply opposed the girlfriend's participation or added a benevolent justification ("I would be very concerned for her safety").

How did women react when given the note from their boyfriends? When a benevolent justification was provided, most women reacted positively. However, when the boyfriend gave no justification, women's reactions depended on their own endorsement of benevolent sexism: Those with high scores reacted positively and did not view their boyfriends as "discriminating against me as a woman," but those with low scores reacted less positively and suspected that the boyfriend was being at least somewhat sexist.

In a second study, Moya et al. (2007) used a similar scenario but added another benevolent justification. Spanish law students imagined being offered a legal internship working with male criminals incarcerated for violent crimes but who claim to have been falsely convicted. They also imagined their romantic partner strongly opposing the internship, again with no explanation or with a benevolent justification. This time, however, female law students were exposed to one of two benevolent justifications: (1) their male partner saying "I am concerned that it would not be safe *for you*" or (2) "I am concerned that it would not be safe *for a woman*" [italics added]. Women who endorsed benevolent sexism reacted positively in all three conditions, regardless of whether a justification was provided or the benevolence was personalized ("... for you") or generic ("... for a woman"). However, for women who reject benevolent sexism, the justification mattered a great deal. As before, they did not react positively to a restriction without an explanation but did react positively to a personalized benevolent justification. Interestingly, the simple change from "for you" to "for a woman" had a big impact on these women's reactions. Although they accepted a personalized benevolent justification and saw it as nondiscriminatory, they viewed the generic justification (which invoked their gender category) much less positively and rated is as discriminatory. In subsequent debriefings, women were made aware that their boyfriends' statements were not genuine, and the authors made sure no harm was done to their relationships as a result of their participation in the study.

In sum, women who endorse benevolent sexism appear to accept that their male partners are acting "for their own good" when imposing a protective restriction, even when the partner does not explicitly say so. By contrast, women who reject benevolent sexism pay close attention to their male partner's explanations, accepting at face value the justification that "I am concerned for your safety." But when a benevolent justification explicitly referred to their perceived vulnerability "as a woman," they suspected that they were facing discrimination.

Is there anything inherently wrong with a boyfriend having concern for a girlfriend's safety? Of course not, and she should be concerned with his safety as well. The problem, however, is that protective paternalism has long been used, either intentionally or unintentionally, to restrict women's freedom and independence. In romantic relationships, both women and men may have a tough time deciding where the line between justified concern and protective paternalism should be drawn. In specific cases, whether a male partner's protective actions are only benevolent, benevolently sexist, or even deliberately manipulative may depend on the eye of the beholder.

As the previous experiments suggest, people differ as to whether they want their relationships to be characterized by traditional roles (e.g., the man as the protector). These differences may depend on how they were socialized (e.g., whether parents encouraged their sons to be chivalrous "knights" and daughters to be "princesses"). At the same time, as the next section describes, all of us were exposed early and often to traditional romantic ideals. Women, in particular, are socialized from a very young age to believe that their bodies, emotions, and psychology make them especially designed for romance, that it is the essence of being female.

Romantic Socialization: Scripts Even a Child Can Follow

Take a guess: Who is the author who appears in the *Guinness World Book of Records* as having published the most books? Is it Philip Roth? John Irving? Stephen King? As prolific as these authors are, they do not even come close to Dame Barbara Cartland, who published more than 700 books before she died in 2000 (at the age of 98). Her books sport titles such as *The Wings of Love, The Drums of Love, The River of Love,* and

Love in the Clouds. Now guess who primarily reads her books: men or women? That one was easy.

Romantic socialization starts early for girls and is included in the pervasive cultural modeling of gender roles. Children are continually exposed to models of gender-linked behavior in storybooks, video games, and films and on television (see Bussey & Bandura, 1999, for a review). By age 4, girls prefer romantic fairy tales, whereas boys prefer adventure tales (Collins-Standley, Gan, Yu, & Zillman, 1996). The currently popular marketing of "princess culture" to young girls (e.g., by Disney and Club Libby Lu) is projected to be the largest girls' franchise in marketing history (Orenstein, 2006). By early adolescence, magazines for girls heavily promote attractiveness and dating as constant themes (Pierce, 1990), themes that continue in women's magazines such as *Cosmopolitan* and *Glamour.* Thus, women are encouraged to view their worth in terms of their ability to attract the other sex from an early age (K. A. Martin, Luke, & Verduzco-Baker, 2007).

A content analysis of the romantic fiction popular with women showed that men were depicted as desirable mates if they had material resources and were aggressive and bold, whereas women were depicted as desirable mates if they were beautiful, friendly, and timid (Whissell, 1996). Content analyses of television ads also yield a heavy reliance on gender stereotypes (Furnham & Mak, 1999; Lovdal, 1989), and women exposed to gender-typed media in laboratory studies show less interest in personal achievement compared with women exposed to neutral media (Davies, Spencer, Quinn, & Gerhardstein, 2002; Davies et al., 2005; Geis, Brown, Jennings, & Porter, 1984). In short, it does not appear that the Women's Movement has made much of an impact on the cultural diet offered to girls and women when it comes to romantic fantasies. In the next section, we outline the ways that gender stereotyping influences the development of romantic attachments in young women and men.

Adolescence and Romance

In Chapter 3, we described how children, absent the strong heterosexual impulses that motivate the majority of adolescents and adults to seek out members of the other sex, are free to ignore or even denigrate their gender out-group. The onset of puberty dramatically changes this situation as heterosexual adolescents become intensely interested in forming romantic attachments with members of the other sex. Not all is transformed, however. Gender differences in interaction styles, which have been well practiced and honed in same-sex interactions through-out childhood, remain. The general themes of greater male assertive-ness and female accommodation continue, laying the groundwork for male dominance in adulthood.

Adolescence is a notoriously awkward time of life for many reasons, but the difficulty in negotiating romantic relations and a sexual (not just a gender) identity are chief among them. Adolescence is also a time of rapid and significant physical changes (many of them connected to sexual maturation) that increase both boys' and girls' self-consciousness about appearance, social acceptance, and self-identity. Some authors have contended that adolescence is particularly difficult for girls (e.g., Gilligan, 1982), whereas others have focused on the problems that boys experience negotiating the transition to adulthood (Pollack, 1998). Considering the stumbling blocks both sexes face, such as the greater prevalence of eating disorders among girls (Feingold & Mazella, 1998) or the behavioral problems and poor achievement that are more likely to be seen in boys (Hoff-Summers, 2000; Pollack, 1998), it seems safe to say that adolescence is troublesome for members of both sexes. To some extent, girls and boys face similar problems; however, already established differences in male and female behaviors and cultural expectations spe-cific to each sex also create differences in the nature and consequences of the challenges boys and girls face.

Attracting Members of the Other Sex and Physical Appearance

A central challenge for both sexes is how to attract romantic partners. In both adolescents and adults, physical attractiveness is an extremely important determinant of romantic attraction for heterosexuals (Spre-cher, 1989). This is also true for homosexual men (Sergios & Cody, 1986) but not necessarily for homosexual women (Deaux & Hanna, 1984). One of the most painful adolescent ironies is that the increased importance of physical appearance (in order to be sexually attractive) coincides with rapid physical changes, some of which, like facial acne, can diminish attractiveness.

Although adult males traditionally have been able to overcome def-icits in looks by amassing wealth or power (Sprecher, 1989), less physi-cally attractive adolescent males typically do not have such resources to boost their romantic eligibility. One advantage boys have compared with girls, however, is that the effects of puberty on the male body are more in line with the male cultural ideal (Rosenblum & Lewis, 1999). Boys experience an increase in muscle mass and a growth spurt that brings them closer to the desired physical appearance for men. An increase in physical strength and height can also translate into increased interpersonal power and influence. These changes are so important that boys who do not "keep up" with their peers are at risk for taking anabolic steroids (Lenahan, 2003). By contrast, in cultures that value an unrealistically thin body ideal for women, the physical changes girls experience are more problematic. Girls' percentage of body fat increases during puberty. This physical change, combined with a cultural value on a more wispy (or, increasingly, a well-toned) feminine form, seems like a potent recipe for eating disorders, such as anorexia and bulimia, which girls experience at a much higher rate than boys (Feingold & Mazella, 1998).

Girls also have to contend with physical changes related to reproduction. Menarche (the onset of menstruation) marks an abrupt and dramatic transition in a girls' life. Menstruation can be a positive experience, but it is also stigmatized (Roberts, Goldenberg, Power, & Pyszczynski, 2002) and can, therefore, increase adolescent self-consciousness. The fact that the menstrual cycle can affect mood feeds exaggerated stereotypes that adolescent girls and women are too emotional and irrational. In terms of antisocial behavior, however, the reality is that boys and men are more likely to lash out in aggressive, irrational behavior (Pollack, 1998). Stereotypes about women's emotionality, reinforced by the idea that women are uncontrollably moody as a result of hormones, provide a convenient excuse for some men to disregard women's concerns, whether in interpersonal relationships or the workplace. For instance, a boyfriend might blame a fight on his girlfriend "PMSing," and men might dismiss the notion of female world leaders on the presumption that women become irrational on a monthly basis.

In short, the importance of physical appearance to attracting romantic partners combined with the physical changes of adolescence affects both sexes. Boys and girls alike experience increased self-consciousness and concern with their physical appearance. The physical changes of adolescence, however, may act to increase boys' interpersonal power as they become larger and more muscled. In comparison, girls change in ways that bear a problematic relationship to contemporary physical ideals for their sex. Nonetheless, both sexes are pressured to embody the unrealistic, cultural ideals of their gender, which can create anxiety and disrupt well-being (see Chapter 10).

Heterosexual Romance, Interdependence, and Power

After a childhood spent avoiding the other gender and developing different social norms in peer relations, adolescent heterosexual relations are bound to be at least somewhat difficult to negotiate. Cultural scripts of romance, such as the norms about how a date is expected to proceed, provide normative guides to cross-sex interaction. In some cultures, scripts that rigidly proscribe sexual contact may be strongly enforced by adults, who select appropriate marital partners based more on an alliance of families than individual preference (Kottak, 2004). However, in Western nations, adolescent sexuality has become more a matter of individual freedom, subject to limited parental oversight (Giordano, 2003; Manning, Longmore, & Giordano, 2005). Nonetheless, cultural norms or scripts that inform adolescent expectations about how to interact with potential romantic partners remain strong. Further, the contents of such scripts are still consistent with relatively traditional gender norms and reinforce gender differences in interaction styles (Holland & Eisenhart, 1990; Rose & Frieze, 1989, 1993).

For example, although formal dating is less common among contemporary adolescents than used to be the case, dating scripts still suggest that the male partner takes a more active role than the female partner (Holland & Skinner, 1987; Rose & Frieze, 1989, 1993). The boy is supposed to initiate the date, pick the girl up, pay her way, and deliver her home safely. Boys are also expected to initiate sexual contact. In short, the cultural ideal is consistent with the gender schema that boys ought to be active and assertive and that the adult male assumes the role of protector and provider. Male chivalry is considered to be an integral part of romance.

Girls, however, are expected to act in line with a more passive, feminine gender schema. Cultural scripts advise girls about how they are expected to accommodate boys in order to attract them. This advice can be summed up as "play up to his ego, introduce topics that you know he knows something about or likes to talk about, don't confront him openly or be too assertive, laugh at his jokes, and admire his accomplishments" (Maccoby, 1998, p. 196). After having spent their childhood short-circuiting male dominance by avoiding boys, adolescent girls are expected to allow boys to "take charge" in order to promote romance. Traditional romantic ideologies suggest that girls and women ought not to exert direct influence over male romantic partners. The female partner is expected to exert influence using more subtle and indirect strategies (such as getting him to be so devoted that he wants to please her).

Power dynamics within adolescent romantic relationships are complex. On the one hand, boys' generally more assertive interpersonal style increases the likelihood that they can exert direct influence within the relationship (Carli, 2001). For instance, whereas boys are more likely to state a preference or an opinion in a confident and assertive manner, girls are more likely to qualify what they say (e.g., "I don't know, but ... ") or to turn a statement of preference into a question (e.g., "Maybe it would be fun to go to the movies?"). These differences are most evident in heterosexual, rather than same-sex, interactions, suggesting that girls are following the traditional cultural script to be less assertive toward male partners (Carli, 1990).

On the other hand, boys (as well as girls) are eager to please partners to whom they are attracted, lending the less interested partner a greater degree of power over the one who most fervently wants to begin or maintain the relationship (this is known as the "principle of least interest"; Waller & Hill, 1951). Differences in male and female sexuality can affect this balance of power. On average, adolescent boys and men tend to think about sex and to be motivated to engage in it more frequently than adolescent girls and women (for a review, see Baumeister, Catanese, & Vohs, 2001). This difference may be due to both biological factors (the evolutionary advantages of male promiscuity) and cultural reasons (a sexual double standard that encourages male conquests and derogates female promiscuity as being slutty). Women's traditional role as gatekeepers to sex (deciding when and "how far to go") can be a source of power within heterosexual romantic relationships. In essence, sex is often treated as a female resource that is exchanged in return for other desired "goods," such as male attention (Baumeister & Vohs, 2004). Traditional cultural scripts of romance reinforce this idea. For instance, the central message of *The Rules* (Fein & Schneider, 1995), the female dating guidebook mentioned in Chapter 2, is that women ought to be "mysterious" and "play hard to get" in order to pique male interest and to give them power within heterosexual relationships.

For male adolescents, the combination of a persistent sex drive with a more assertive, aggressive style of interaction can spill over into sexual coercion. The prototypical rape scenario, in which a stranger forcibly assaults a woman, is relatively rare compared with sexual coercion by acquaintances, friends, boyfriends, and husbands (Hickman & Muehlenhard, 1997; see Chapter 11). Sometimes this can simply be a matter of misinterpretation. Both adolescent boys and men are prone to incorrectly interpreting female friendliness as sexual invitation (Abbey, 1991). Further, cultural scripts about sexual interaction, such as the notion that girls and women ought to "play hard to get," encourage boys and men to interpret "no" as a token form of resistance (i.e., to think that "'no' doesn't really mean 'no'"). This, in turn, makes men more likely to engage in sexual aggression (see Chapter 11).

In sum, adolescent relationships present both sexes with the challenge of devising satisfying ways to interact with members of the other sex after a childhood spent apart. For heterosexual adolescents, sex segregation begins to break down as they attempt to become romantically intimate. In heterosexual relationships, a new set of power dynamics evolves, but it remains shaped by traditional gender schemas and scripts that specify how romance is "supposed to" unfold. The relatively more assertive interpersonal styles that boys have practiced throughout childhood among their same-sex peers lend them more direct power in heterosexual relationships. Cultural scripts and ideals of heterosexual romance also reinforce the idea that girls ought to accommodate by flattering the male ego and letting the boy be more "in charge" in the relationship. As a result, an interest in heterosexual romance may be an initial step in the transition to greater male power in adulthood. This is not to say that power flows in only one direction: The traditional female role as sexual gatekeeper can lend girls, especially those who are considered to be most desirable, considerable interpersonal power, although often this power is indirectly exercised and can be counteracted by male sexual coercion.

The Glass Slipper Effect

By the time women reach college age, they have been duly "educated in romance" (Holland & Eisenhart, 1990). Even today, women are chronically subjected to the notion that their primary goal in life should be to attract a mate and raise a family rather than seek economic rewards and prestige directly. Advice from books on dating (*The Rules*), magazines like *Cosmopolitan*, and radio pundits like Laura Schlessinger ("Dr. Laura") proclaims that "feminism is dead" and what a woman really ought to do is learn how to catch and keep a man. At the same time, women in college are strongly motivated, often with family support, to also be achievement oriented, independent, and focused on careers. These competing beliefs can create intrapsychic conflicts for women.

If you ask a roomful of young women, "How many of you are waiting for Prince Charming?" few hands are likely to be raised. Yet women may still be influenced by a lifetime of exposure to romantic fairy tales, pretend play in girlhood centered on traditional roles (girlfriend, bride, princess, and mother), and the social emphasis on attracting boys during adolescence (K. A. Martin et al., 2007). These well-learned cultural scripts of romance, repeatedly practiced in girls' lives, may translate into a later power and resource disadvantage. If women implicitly believe that a man will provide for them, they may become less ambitious for themselves. Childhood romantic fantasies may become so deeply embedded that they unconsciously affect adult women's aspirations.

To test this hypothesis, Rudman and Heppen (2003) used the Implicit Association Test (IAT; Greenwald et al., 2002), which measures beliefs and attitudes that people may not be aware of and does so in a manner that cannot be easily controlled. As expected, women were reluctant to report associating male romantic partners with chivalry; nonetheless, they demonstrated this association on the IAT. That is, they were more likely to associate their romantic partners with fairy tale words (e.g., Prince Charming, White Knight, protector, hero, magic, castle) than with similarly favorable reality-based words (e.g., kind, patient, intelligent, witty), a sign that they possessed implicit romantic fantasies. In addition, the more women possessed implicit romantic fantasies, the less interest they showed in obtaining direct power for themselves. Specifically, compared with women who scored low on the romantic fantasy IAT, women who scored high aspired to lower income careers and showed less interest in prestigious occupations (e.g., being CEOs, corporate lawyers, and politicians). They also showed less interest in further education (e.g., a graduate or professional degree) and were less willing to volunteer for a leadership role in an upcoming experiment.

We caution readers that Rudman and Heppen's (2003) research is based on correlations and, therefore, does not show that implicit romantic beliefs have a causal influence on women's aspirations. Nonetheless, they termed their results the "glass slipper" effect because women who implicitly idealized men as romantic heroes who will rescue and provide for them were less interested in pursuing their own fortunes. As a result, women who have absorbed gendered romantic scripts may hobble their own ambitions and aspirations, putting their faith in romance. Although traditional romantic ideologies are subjectively pro-female, they are also benevolently sexist. The glass slipper effect suggests that women may be co-opted by romance in ways that lead them to cede power, status, and resources to men, presumably as a result of the implicit belief that these will "trickle down" once Prince Charming rides in, thereby reinforcing gender inequality.

What about men? Rudman and Heppen (2003) found that men did not implicitly associate their romantic partners with fairy tale fantasies (e.g., Cinderella, Sleeping Beauty, princess, and maiden), but they did associate them with sexual fantasies (e.g., Venus, sex goddess, and sex kitten). However, men's implicit fantasies were not related to their anticipated income, interest in high-status occupations, or willingness to be a group leader. Thus, the research suggests that only women may have to fight implicit romantic beliefs in themselves before they can step out of their "glass slippers" and rise through the glass ceiling. Because implicit beliefs are likely to be nonconscious, they may act as hidden barrier to women's ability to capitalize on their hard-won advances and opportunities. However, awareness of socialization processes that can foster implicit romantic fantasies may help women to counteract them when they ponder decisions that affect their future.

The Costs of Romantic Ideologies for Men

The prior discussion might suggest that men are not particularly affected by romantic ideologies. As noted earlier, boys' fantasy play is focused on adventure without romance. As adolescents and adults, men tend to eschew romance novels and make fun of "chick flicks." Yet men experience intense feelings of passionate love, and they have also absorbed cultural scripts of romance. For example, cross-cultural research suggests that men and women share more similarities than differences in their attitudes toward romantic love (Sprecher et al., 1994), and they experience love with the same intensity (Hatfield & Rapson, 1996). Even teenage boys have been found to be unexpectedly emotional when they fall in love (Giordano, Longmore, & Manning, 2006). For example, they report feeling disoriented and unable to speak in the presence of their girlfriends; they also report having less sexual power in the relationship than do teenage girls. These results so contradicted the stereotype of teenage boys being more interested in "hooking up" than having committed relationships that they received considerable media attention (Grossman, 2006).

In fact, men may be even more romantic than women. Men tend to fall in love more often and faster than women, and it is harder for them to end a premarital relationship (Baumeister & Bratslavsky, 1999; Dion & Dion, 1985; Hendrick & Hendrick, 1995; Hill, Rubin, & Peplau 1979; Peplau & Gordon, 1985). They also tend to believe in love at first sight and that love can overcome all obstacles more so than women (Spaulding, 1970). Compared with women, men tend to score higher on explicit measures of traditional romantic beliefs (Rudman & Heppen, 2003; Sprecher & Metts, 1989). Moreover, men are just as likely as women to idealize their partners, viewing them as especially attractive, intelligent, and kind (Murray et al., 1996). Thus, rose-colored glasses are worn by both sexes when they fall in love (Hendrick & Hendrick, 1988).

Like women, men experience a conflict between romantic ideologies and their quest for independence, but in a different way. Whereas it is socially expected for women to "put love above all," men are expected not to fall too deeply in love, a state that suggests weakness and dependence rather than masculine autonomy. As a result, strong feelings of love and attachment may cause men to question their gender identity. For example, teenage boys report feeling "like a little girl in a relationship" (Grossman, 2006, p. 41) and worry that it is "effeminate [for a guy] to fall in love so hard it's like the whole world has been turned around" (Dion & Dion, 1985, cited in Myers, 2005, p. 450). Similarly, adult men report strong feelings of tenderness, devotion, and love toward their partners with the caveat that "they are not like other men," even though they are (Hite, 2006, p. 121). Because men deny their feelings to other men, they are unaware of their gender's emotional similarities. As a result, the stereotype that romantic love is primarily a female emotion can be a cause of distress and shame for men when they fall in love.

Indeed, there is some evidence that men in relationships can be more emotionally vulnerable than women. When couples are instructed to talk about serious conflict or breaking up, their physiological responses reveal that men's heart rate and blood pressure increase more so than women's (Gottman, 1993). This suggests that thoughts of ending the relationship are especially physically taxing and aversive for men. One reason why men may feel more turmoil over breakups concerns the fact that they are socialized not to disclose their emotions to their male friends, whereas women can find comfort and support from their female friends (Douvan & Adelson, 1966; Sharabany, Gershoni, & Hofman, 1981). In contrast to women's socialized need for intimacy, men are socialized against intimacy. In fact, wives and girlfriends often serve as the one socially acceptable outlet for men's self-disclosure. As a result, men in romantic relationships are more likely to have put all of their emotional eggs in one basket. Therefore, the loss of a girlfriend or wife comes at a great emotional cost for men. Consistent with this view, most married men report that their wives are their best friends, whereas women are more likely to have a same-sex friend serve this role (Hite, 2006). In addition, both men and women report having more meaningful interactions with women, as opposed to men, and the amount of time they spend with women is negatively related to loneliness (Wheeler, Reis, & Nezlek, 1983).

The dark side of this asymmetry is that men can have a difficult time disengaging from romantic relationships. Although films such as *Fatal Attraction*, *The Crush*, and *Swimfan* have popularized the idea that women are psychologically unstable when men reject them, the reality is that rejected men do most of the stalking (Davis, Coker, & Sanderson, 2002; Haugaard & Seri, 2003). Stalking consists of repeated physical following or unwanted communication (e.g., by letter, e-mail, or other means). It typically coincides with incessant rumination about the target and feelings of depression, anger, or jealousy (Dennison & Stewart, 2006). Because stalking and physical abuse are highly correlated (Melton, 2007), and stalking can cause victims serious mental and physical health problems (Amar, 2006; Davis et al., 2002), it represents a serious crime. Yet it was not until 1990 that stalking was classified as such in the United States, and the justice system is not always responsive to stalking victims (Logan, Walker, Jordan, & Leukefeld, 2006).

Men are also more prone to physically harming intimate partners, often in reaction to female rejection (e.g., breaking up or sexual infidelity; see Chapter 11). For 20% of female victims of nonfatal violence, offenders were intimates such as husbands or boyfriends compared with 3% of male victims who were harmed by wives or girlfriends; the percentages for murder victims (i.e., people murdered by their partners) are 33% for women and 4% for men (Rennison, 2003). An insidious way that traditional romantic ideologies support these behaviors is by labeling them as crimes of passion. Crimes of passion are acts of abuse, especially assault or murder, against a spouse or other loved one attributed to a sudden strong impulse, such as a jealous rage or heartbreak, as opposed to a premeditated crime. Although the term is not officially recognized in law, it is sometimes used by defense lawyers because a crime is viewed more sympathetically by jurors when it is a crime of passion. Ironically, people hurt the ones they love with more impunity than total strangers, even though the former constitutes a gross betrayal of trust in addition to a heinous crime.

Why would abusive behavior be viewed as less immoral when the perpetrator is in love? People's external attributions for crimes conducted in the throes of passion (e.g., as less calculated and controllable) are partly to blame. The ancient Greeks used the term *theia mania* (or madness from the gods) to describe the sudden overthrow of reason associated with falling in love, and the connection between love and madness has survived to present times. As the Spanish proverb states, "Love without madness is not truly love." Sexual arousal can cause people to "throw caution to the wind" and behave in morally questionable ways (Ariely & Lowenstein, 2006). At its extreme, passionate love can cause people to sacrifice everything that society deems important: their family, their career, their dignity, and even rationality itself (E. N. Aron & Aron, 1997). Indeed, people in love have been known to exhibit symptoms that appear under the clinical diagnostic headings of mania, depression, and obsessive–compulsive disorder (Tallis, 2005). If men are thought to be literally out of their minds when they stalk or abuse the women they love, then they cannot be held responsible for their actions. This provides insight into why domestic violence was long thought to be a private matter and not a serious crime (Lemon, 2001). Chapter 11 reviews relationship violence, committed by women as well as by men, in greater detail. As women's status relative to men has risen, so too has gender parity in relationship aggression.

In sum, it is not just women who are constrained by traditional ideologies of romance and mixed messages in contemporary culture. Men are socialized to be bold and assertive but are also expected to restrain these traits in heterosexual romantic relationships, treating their partners with chivalrous politeness and solicitous protection. They are simultaneously pressured to not be overtly dependent on their partners or "too emotional." Thus, traditional romantic ideologies can make negotiating romantic relationships difficult for men, especially in a contemporary culture where their female partners are increasingly independent so that the old "rules" seem not to apply. The next section specifically considers the perceived conflict between traditional romantic ideologies and the quest for gender equality. This is popularly mistaken as an inherent conflict between feminism and romance.

Feminism and Romantic Relationships

Popular stereotypes of feminists, such as media portrayals of feminists as lesbians who resent men (Bell & Klein, 1996; Misciagno, 1997), characterize them as radical man-haters. There are at least two reasons why this has happened. First, feminist thinkers pointed out how traditional gender roles within heterosexual romantic relationships foster gender inequality long before social scientists conducted the research we have reviewed in this chapter. For example, Simone de Beauvoir (1952) argued that traditional marital relationships functioned to imprison women (see also Firestone, 1970; Hite, 1987; Millett, 1970). It is easy to caricature such criticisms of traditional romantic roles as being a complete rejection of heterosexual romantic relationships and as generally hostile toward men. (This is one reason why we have been so careful to distinguish heterosexual romantic love itself from traditional ideologies about romance.) The mistaken perception that feminists generally reject both heterosexual relationships and dislike men feeds a popular stereotype that feminists are "man-hating lesbians."

Second, the outspokenness of feminist activists violates traditional prescriptions that women should be nice, polite, and modest. As Chapters 6 and 7 showed, female assertiveness elicits hostile backlash. More particularly, feminists are often viewed as wanting women to "have control over men" rather than seeking equality between the sexes. This notion is a frequent theme of items on contemporary measures of sexist hostility toward women (e.g., Glick & Fiske's, 1996, Hostile Sexism scale). Many people seem to view feminists as both angry (toward men) and as "gender deviants" (Unger & Crawford, 1996). Many women, as well as men, endorse negative feminist stereotypes (e.g., that they are unattractive lesbians; Swim et al., 1999; Unger et al., 1982; Williams & Wittig, 1997).

Negative cultural stereotypes of feminism have led many women to avoid identifying themselves as feminists (e.g., Buschman & Lenart, 1996; Williams & Wittig, 1997). In her interviews with women of various ages, Sigel (1996) found (understandably) mixed attitudes toward feminism; although women appreciated the benefits derived from the Women's Movement, they worried it had gone too far and undermined relations with men. This suggests that popular negative portrayals of feminists (e.g., as "feminazis") have tainted people's conceptions of feminism's goals. A belief that feminism is incompatible with heterosexual romantic relationships (and not just with traditional ideologies of romance) may be particularly damaging to people's willingness to identify as feminists. The next section reviews research that examines the sources of these popular beliefs about feminism as well as whether these beliefs have any merit. Importantly, this research suggests that, far from detracting from heterosexual romantic relationships, feminist beliefs (especially when endorsed by male partners) actually enhance their health, stability, and well-being.

Feminism and Romance Are Popularly Perceived to Be Incompatible

Given unflattering feminist stereotypes, it seemed likely that feminism might be viewed as incompatible with romance, and, if so, this may help to account for feminism's current lack of popularity. In other words, people may shy away from feminism because they mistakenly perceive it to be a roadblock to emotional or sexual happiness in heterosexual romantic relationships.

To test this hypothesis, Rudman and Fairchild (2007) examined the relationship between feminist orientations (i.e., feminist identity and attitudes toward feminists) and beliefs that feminism provokes heterosexual relationship conflict. As expected, women and men alike scored low on feminist orientations if they perceived feminism to be troublesome for romance. For example, people who endorsed beliefs that "feminism can cause women to resent men," "feminism can add stress to relationships with men," and "most men would not want to date a feminist" were less likely to identify with feminists, to report positive attitudes toward them, and to endorse women's civil rights (e.g., support the Equal Rights Amendment). In an additional study, Rudman and Fairchild asked people to judge photos of plain and pretty women. Consistent with the unattractive feminist stereotype, plain women were rated as more likely to be feminists than pretty women (see also Goldberg et al., 1975; Unger et al., 1982). However, the unattractive feminist stereotype was wholly explained by beliefs that plain women are low on sex appeal or likely lesbians, suggesting that people believe that "unsexy" women (i.e., women who cannot rely on men to provide for them) instead turn to feminism. These unfavorable beliefs can lead young adults to view feminism as antithetical to romance and a hindrance to their own relationships.

But Is Feminism Actually Good for Relationships?

Many people may perceive a conflict between feminism and romance, but are these beliefs accurate? Rudman and Phelan (2007) conducted both a laboratory survey (with college students) and an online survey (with older adults) to investigate whether feminist women, or men with feminist partners, experience troubled relationships. As a measure of feminism, responses to the statement "I am a feminist" were combined with how warmly people felt toward feminists and career women. Comparable items (e.g., "My partner is a feminist" and partner's attitudes toward feminists and career women) were combined to assess perceptions of the partner's feminism.

Looking only at heterosexuals who reported currently being in a relationship, both studies showed that women paired with feminist men reported better relationship health (greater relationship quality, stability, and sexual satisfaction) than women who were paired with nonfeminist men. Thus, irrespective of a woman's own feminism, a feminist male partner may be beneficial for romantic relationships. In addition, for the older adults, men paired with feminist (as opposed to nonfeminist) women reported greater relationship stability and sexual satisfaction. Thus, men may benefit from, as opposed to being troubled by, feminist female partners.

Does women's feminism hurt relationships? The straightforward answer is no. There were no direct correlations between women's feminism and relationship health indicators in either survey. However, female feminists were more likely to select feminist men as their partners, and because male partners' feminism predicted healthy relationships for women, it appears that women's feminism is also good for intimate unions.

Finally, Rudman and Phelan (2007) were able to test whether feminist stereotypes are accurate by combining the samples from both of their studies. If feminist stereotypes are accurate, then feminist women should be more likely to report themselves as being single, lesbian, or sexually unattractive compared with nonfeminist women (cf. Goldberg et al., 1975; Rudman & Fairchild, 2007; Swim et al., 1999; Unger et al., 1982). The findings showed no support for these hypotheses. In fact, feminist women were more likely to be in a heterosexual romantic relationship than nonfeminist women.

In sum, people perceive feminism and romance to be incompatible, but the evidence suggests that these beliefs are inaccurate. On the contrary, men report greater relationship stability and sexual satisfaction when their female partners are feminists. Further, women paired with male feminists report particularly happy and stable relationships, irrespective of their own feminism. In addition, because feminist women are likely to select feminist men as their partners, women's feminism indirectly benefits their relationships. Thus, contrary to popular beliefs, feminism may actually be beneficial rather than detrimental to relationships for both women and men.

Finally, although we can only speculate, it is worth considering why feminists, alone among civil rights pioneers, have been subjected to unflattering media portrayals and inaccurate stereotypes that cast them as unattractive lesbians. Because stereotypes of feminists demonize them on sexual dimensions, these views are similar to attacks directed at women who challenge male dominance by being successful and powerful. Recall from Chapter 7 that the media often portray such women as frigid, "castrating bitches" and thus unsuitable sexual partners. The similarity of these attacks to feminist "lesbian baiting" is that they may make women anxious that if they are overly ambitious, assertive, or independent, men will not love them. Whenever women challenge patriarchy, they risk derogation of their sexuality, which implies that they will wind up lonely spinsters if they do not toe the line. The result is that women may understandably curb their personal ambitions or refrain from embracing their collective power if they believe that the alternative puts their relationships and emotional lives at risk.

Chapter Summary

In this chapter, we confronted the intersection of male dominance and heterosexual independence through the lens of traditional ideologies of how romance is "supposed" to be enacted that perpetuate prescriptions for male assertiveness and female passivity. From adolescence to adulthood, romantic socialization may promote patriarchy by encouraging men to take the initiative and women to acquiesce, with the exception of sexual gatekeeping. Cultural romantic scripts are rooted in a historical past in which knights courted ladies, and they flourished during a medieval period when there was a strong need for benevolence to counter overtly hostile sexism. In the modern world, the trappings of traditional romance ostensibly place women in high esteem, but this ideology values women more for their selfless devotion to others than for their ability to succeed in public spheres. Men also suffer from cultural romantic scripts, not least because traditional notions of romance undermine men's ability to directly express their intense feelings of love and devotion without fear of being judged as "unmanly." In addition, the cultural scripts that dictate having more shallow male friendships may make men overly reliant on female partners for emotional sustenance and, in some cases, leave them vulnerable to behaving badly if their partners reject or abandon them.

The tendency for young adult women to implicitly associate male partners with chivalry and heroism suggests that romantic socialization may condition women to rely on men for protection and provision rather than to seek power directly. Further, women are just as likely as men to eschew feminism when they believe it will undermine romance, a charge that is contradicted by evidence that feminist beliefs may be beneficial to maintaining a healthy and satisfying heterosexual romantic relationship. The fact that both genders eschew feminism when it is perceived as incompatible with love is understandable; however, the perception is not only unwarranted, but may undermine women's ability to capitalize on collective power to advance gender equality.

Heterosexual men and women rely on each other to fulfill basic needs (e.g., for love, sexual gratification, and reproduction). As we have stressed, romantic love is one of the most rewarding experiences two people can share. However, a childhood steeped in antipathy toward the other sex does not prepare people particularly well for intimate adult partnerships. Traditional cultural scripts of romance may enable women and men to overcome childhood hostility by idealizing one another as loving caregivers or heroic protectors. However, to the extent that these ideals reflect restrictive cultural views that prescribe men to be bold, assertive, and unemotional and women to be passive and modest and to wait for their prince to rescue them, gender equality is not well served. Traditional gender-typed "love roles" limit people's ability to express their full human capacities, and diminish their ability to form more perfect unions. Fortunately, heterosexual romantic love can flourish without a reliance on traditional romantic ideologies that restrict the emotional and professional lives of either partner.

CHAPTER 10

Sex

If you must leave me, at least allow me to kiss your lips before you
go." His silky voice had an undercurrent of lust which warned Iona
of the danger in which she stood. Impulsively, she attempted to push
past the man who barred her way, and instantly found herself clasped
in his arms. She was so slight and slender that he seemed to enfold
her, his hands having a surprising strength, and the folds of his velvet
cloak swirled around her so that she felt overpowered. As she threw
back her head the dying light revealed the whiteness of her skin, the
surprising color of her eyes and the delicate features which had been
half-hidden by the darkness of her fur-trimmed cloak. His smile broad-
ened as he leaned over her eagerly. He had not been mistaken: here
was loveliness.

—Barbara Cartland (*The Little Pretender*)

The romantic scripts we examined in the last chapter are sometimes coy
about the details of sex but are clear that men and women are supposed
to have very different roles when it comes to the physical consummation
of romantic longings. This chapter focuses on heterosexual sex and the
ways in which cultural romantic scripts shape popular conceptions of
how men and women are supposed to behave in the bedroom. Consistent with the general theme of this book, we concentrate on how these
traditional scripts emphasize a dominant sexual role for men and a

more passive one for women. Gendered sexual scripts echo the greater dominance culturally ascribed to men, infiltrating into people's most intimate lives. But they can also reduce both men's and women's autonomy and satisfaction, in this case by prescribing how they "should" act as heterosexual beings.

We have consistently stressed that sexual intimacy and marriage are features that make gender relations unique (compared with relations between other social groups). No other groups are expected to transition from indifference or even hostility (in childhood) to physical attraction (by adolescence) to sexual intimacy and love (by early adulthood) in the course of their development. Because of these dramatic changes, the transition is not always smooth, as is evident in the common expression that there is a "war between the sexes." One of the most complicated fronts in this "war" stems from the collision between sexual intimacy and sexism. As we describe in this chapter, male dominance and heterosexual interdependence form a combustible mix that fosters ambivalent attitudes about sexual behavior and the other gender.

Traditionally, men and women have been pressured to express their sexuality in very different ways, with men being driven by lust and women more interested in commitment. This perspective relies on stereotypical views of both genders that particularly demean men but also deny women a vital and healthy interest in sex. Today, increased gender equality and the sexual revolution have altered this landscape so that people have more freedom to make choices about their relationships, independent of gender roles. Nonetheless, prescriptive stereotypes and roles maintain a strong hold on gender relations, and misconceptions about sex and sexuality lead to myths that perpetuate the gendered status quo while detracting from healthy heterosexual unions. As in the prior chapter, this chapter shows how traditional ideologies about heterosexual relationships act as constricting "rules" that not only reinforce gender inequality but may often act to reduce both partners' relationship satisfaction. Whereas the last chapter focused on heterosexual romantic love more generally, this chapter focuses more particularly on sexual attraction and sexual behavior.

Sex and Power

For most of their lives, people are wary of being strongly influenced or manipulated by others. Viewing such attempts as attacks on their independence, they vigorously defend against them (Brehm & Brehm,

1981). The exception to this rule is when we have been seduced by another to fall passionately in love. Note that popular terms such as "to fall in love" or to be "lovesick" connote a drop in status, as though we have been brought to our knees. In other words, sexual longing is often viewed as an Achilles' heel (i.e., a fatal weakness that leads to one's downfall). Sexual attraction is an extremely potent means by which we can be influenced, but it also allows us to exert influence over others. The power of sex appeal as a seductive tool to influence others is inarguably important to people, as evident by a multibillion dollar advertising industry that chronically exploits sex appeal. Next, we describe how traditional cultural scripts of romance shape the use of sexual power, with a focus on how men and women are taught to enact sexual desire and the cognitive and behavioral effects that result from the intimate links among gender, sex, and power.

Sexual Scripts of Romance and Power

As the opening passage illustrates, heterosexual erotic scripts commonly emphasize male initiative and female submission (Belsey, 1994; Impett & Peplau, 2003). The man is expected to initiate sexual activity and the woman to demur for as long as possible until she swoons in response. The emphasis is on his strength and aggressiveness and her delicacy (i.e., weakness). She is a beautiful object to be possessed by his lustful power.

Given their cultural prominence, we might expect that gender-typed erotic scripts function to enhance people's sexual pleasure. However, research suggests that people who try to "perform gender" (i.e., to embody gender ideals) in the bedroom actually experience diminished sexual satisfaction (Sanchez, Crocker, & Boike, 2005). This is a particularly surprising finding for men, who are popularly thought to have their sexual pleasure enhanced by hypermasculinity, such as "being in charge" (Rudman & Fairchild, 2007). However, men as well as women experience reduced sexual autonomy when they feel forced to behave in accord with gender roles during physical intimacy. The feeling that one is "not free" to act naturally, in accord with the impulses of the moment, inhibits the ability to experience the "letting go" that provides sexual release (Sanchez et al., 2005). Being compelled to take the dominant, initiating role may also be stressful for men because it introduces pressure to demonstrate their sexual prowess and competence (i.e., creates "performance pressure"). Thus, playing the dominant role in the bedroom may undermine, rather than enhance, men's physical pleasure.

In addition, the popular idea that women achieve sexual satisfaction by eroticizing their submissive role (MacKinnon, 1987) has been challenged. In the romantic view, women are aroused when a "real man" takes charge, only experiencing true sexual pleasure when they relinquish control (e.g., the swooning submission of the typical female character in a romance novel). However, in actuality, women who behave submissively in the bedroom experience reduced sexual autonomy and, as a result, more difficulty becoming sexually aroused (Sanchez et al., 2005; Sanchez, Kiefer, & Ybarra, 2006; see also Impett & Tolman, 2006). Nonetheless, because women are socialized to believe that their role in the bedroom is passive and supportive, they automatically link sexual words (e.g., sex, naked, climax, and caress) with submissive words (e.g., submit, comply, slave, and yield), whereas men show no such pattern (Sanchez et al., 2006). Instead, men who automatically associate women with sex also tend to connect women and weakness, suggesting that men also possess associations between female gender and sexual submissiveness (Leibold & McConnell, 2004).

Sexual submissiveness not only reduces women's sexual pleasure but can also decrease their physical safety and health. For example, women are taught to treat sex as a service or favor that they render to men and to strategically submit to a male partner's sexual needs even when they are not ready or interested (Wertheimer, 2003). One result is that women often fail to report date or acquaintance rape because they tend to blame themselves for men's sexual aggression and to feel humiliated (Finkelson & Oswalt, 1995). Date rape is also exacerbated when men buy into sexual scripts concerning women's token resistance (saying "no" when they really mean "yes"; Osman, 2003). Further, because they emphasize spontaneity and surrendering to passion, erotic scripts curtail women's ability to protect themselves when they have consensual sex. For instance, women who read romance novels were less likely to report that their partners use a condom (Diekman, McDonald, & Gardner, 2000) and even women who describe themselves as feminists are reluctant to insist that their partners wear them (Bay-Cheng & Zucker, 2007; Gavey & McPhillips, 1999).

Similarly, traditional sexual scripts can jeopardize men's safety. For example, men who endorse masculine ideologies are more likely to engage in unprotected sex (Noar & Morokoff, 2002), and the pressure to be hypermasculine (i.e., tough, competitive, and aggressive) has been linked to both promiscuity and sexual anxiety (Philaretou & Allen, 2003). While adolescent men who enact masculinity through physical aggression or athletic prowess are likely to begin dating early (Epstein,

1996; Swain, 2000), aggression and athleticism are also predictive of binge drinking and driving while intoxicated (Sabo, Miller, Melnick, Farrell, & Barnes, 2002). The pressure to "be a man" encourages men, particularly young men, to exhibit their masculinity through high-risk behaviors such as dangerous driving, physical violence, and promiscuous sexuality (Barker, 2005).

Sex and Violence

In Chapter 11, we take up the topic of male sexual aggression as a significant underpinning of patriarchy. Here, we concentrate on the cognitive effects of socializing men to be sexually dominant and women to be submissive. Unfortunately, sex and violence are so often linguistically paired that both genders automatically mentally connect them; however, only men (not women) who are primed with sexual words (e.g., bed, sheet, and wet) subsequently show aggressive behavior (Mussweiler & Förster, 2000). This is likely because men are often portrayed as sexual aggressors, whereas women are more likely to be portrayed as sexual victims. In other words, the link between sex and violence has different connotations for men and women.

It is important to note that most men do not automatically link sex to dominance and coercion (Sanchez et al., 2006). However, men who are sexual aggressors (e.g., who engage in sexual harassment) show a different pattern. First, they automatically associate power with sex (Bargh, Raymond, Pryor, & Strack, 1995), suggesting that these men find power to be sexually arousing (according to Henry Kissinger, "Power is the ultimate aphrodisiac.") Second, men with a history of sexual aggression automatically associate hostility with women (Leibold & McConnell, 2004). When these men played a game against a powerful woman, they were more physically aggressive toward her than they were toward a powerful male opponent (Leibold & McConnell, 2002). Thus, for some men, their perceptions of and relationships with women are adversarial, and sex is a domain used to enhance their power.

The fact that some men strive to dominate women sexually has implications for women's attitudes toward men as a whole as well as toward sex. Women who automatically associate men with threat-related words (e.g., violent, danger, hazardous) also show a strong preference for women over men, using the Implicit Association Test (IAT; Rudman & Goodwin, 2004). Thus, some men's aggressive style of exercising power over women may undermine gender relations by reinforcing perceptions of men as insensitive (at best) or victimizers (at worst). Sexual aggression undermines trust between women and men and, therefore, harms heterosexual relations.

Additionally, gender differences in attitudes toward sex may add to this conflict. There is considerable evidence that, compared with men, women report less favorable attitudes toward sex, less interest in it, and less likelihood of fantasizing about it (for reviews, see Baumeister et al., 2001; Oliver & Hyde, 1993). However, because of cultural double standards for male and female sexuality, self-reports are not particularly trustworthy; in particular, women might fear being labeled promiscuous if they admit to liking sex. To avoid this problem, Rudman and Goodwin (2004) administered to participants a sexual attitude IAT that used pictures of couples engaged in sexual versus playful activities, a procedure that controlled for physical touching and romance. Results revealed that men's implicit attitudes were strongly pro-sex, whereas women's attitudes were neutral (i.e., they did not show either a pro- or anti-sex bias). Additional research has confirmed this gender difference using other versions of the sexual attitude IAT (Geer & Robertson, 2005). Because responses on the IAT are not consciously controlled, the difference in men's versus women's liking for sex appears to be genuine. This is not to suggest that women are innately less interested in sex, because the IAT discrepancies may well reflect the socialization of sexual double standards. Also, we stress that women's attitudes were not anti-sex but rather less pro-sex in comparison to men's.

Finally, in Rudman and Goodwin's (2004) research, women who implicitly liked men also implicitly liked sex, suggesting the importance of sex-related attitudes for gender relations. Recall, however, that women who associated men with threat and violence also showed implicit dislike of men. Because women's liking for men and heterosexual sex are linked, male aggression can, by extension, reduce women's liking for sex. What about men's attitudes? Presumably, men who implicitly like sex should also like women (mirroring the findings for women), but this was true only for men who had a history of sexual gratification. By contrast, men who implicitly liked sex but were sexually frustrated showed negative attitudes toward women. Thus, men's interest in heterosexual sex promotes positive attitudes toward women only for men who are not sexually deprived. The pattern of results for both genders suggests that when traditional cultural scripts play out in the realm of sexual behavior, men's aggressive use of power (e.g., by being sexually demanding or coercive) and women's passive use of power (e.g., through sexual withholding or teasing) diminish liking for the other sex, negatively affecting gender relations. Thus, on the sexual front, the "war between the sexes" is based, in part, on the traditional ways in which men and women attempt to exert power over each other, to their mutual detriment.

Gender, Sexuality, and Status

Because of sexual anatomy, receptive sex is equated with being female. Although this need not imply a more passive role during sex, the notion that "receptive = submissive" is deeply embedded in traditional notions about sex. A strong sign that gender, sexuality, and status are intertwined is illustrated by the use of sexual euphemisms (e.g., "getting screwed") for being robbed or duped. The person "getting screwed" is, metaphorically speaking, being equated with the female role during sex. This gendered metaphor for weakness or being abused by others is so pervasive that it is maintained even in all-male environments. For instance, male convicts construct a gendered hierarchy in prison even though women are absent (Sabo, Kupers, & London, 2001; Slater, 2006). At the top of the prison food chain are macho men who are willing and able to fight; at the bottom are those who are too weak to fight off sexual abuse by other men: They are labeled as "women" and "bitches." More generally, the common use of "ladies" and "pussies" as a pejorative in masculine organizations (e.g., by football coaches and drill sergeants) equates weakness with being female.

Exploited male prisoners experience threats that are more commonly experienced by women: being sexually objectified and at risk of being raped (Valian, 1999). The fear of being victimized "like a woman" helps to explain why the U.S. military refuses to open its doors to avowed homosexuals. Men in the military (and elsewhere) fear becoming the object of gay men's sexual attention (Kimmel, 1995). However, the reality is that heterosexual (not homosexual) men are more likely to sexually abuse other men, particularly in all-male institutions, such as prison, as a means of asserting power (Herek, 1993).

This is a dark view of gender relations that underscores the connection among gender, sexuality, and power in a way that is both pejorative toward women and used to punish men who are viewed as not manly enough (Berdahl, 2007a). The ubiquity of such hostile characterizations of the feminine sexual role has led some commentators to suggest that all heterosexual intercourse is a form of sexual assault (Dworkin, 1987). We reject this extreme view. As a human activity, sexual intercourse has the potential to be highly fulfilling for both partners, but the cultural derogation of women's receptive role corrupts what could otherwise be mutually pleasurable by coloring it with hostile sexism and contempt.

Seducing Men to Avoid Violence

Throughout human history, women have been disadvantaged by their relatively smaller size and strength as well as a lower social status. In the past, sex differences in social status were often so extreme that women were treated as little more than men's property. To avoid oppression and scorn, women learned to seduce men, countering men's power by taking advantage of men's dependence on women for sexual pleasure (Greene, 2003). Such seduction did not free women from patriarchy, but it tempered the brutality with which they had been treated and gave rise to the idealization of beauty and romance as female domains. Sexually attractive women could counter men's physical and economic power, using sexual seduction like kryptonite, to manipulate men to do their bidding. But to do so, women had to be thoroughly educated. Writing in 2 BC, the Roman poet Ovid offered his advice in *The Art of Love*:

> Rare, however, is the face without a fault. Hide these blemishes with care, and so far as may be, conceal the defects of your figure. If you are short, sit down, lest when standing you should be thought to be sitting; if you are a dwarf, lie stretched at full length on your couch, and so that none may see how short you are, throw something over your feet to hide them. If you are thin, wear dresses of thick material and have a mantle hanging loosely about your shoulders. If you are sallow, put on a little rouge; if you are swarthy, see what the fish of Pharos will do for you... If your fingers are stumpy and your nails unsightly, don't gesticulate when you are talking. Don't open your mouth too wide; let the dimples on either side be small, and let the extremity of the lips cover the upper part of the teeth. Don't laugh too often and too loud. Let there be something feminine and gentle in your laughter, something agreeable to the ear. You should leave uncovered the top of your shoulder and the upper part of your left arm. That is especially becoming to women who have white skin. At the mere sight of it, I should be mad to cover all I could touch with kisses.

Ovid went on to describe in great detail how women should talk, walk, dress, and express their emotions, encouraging them to pout and, if necessary, to cry to enhance their appeal to (and influence over) men. The overall message was that every movement should be artificial and rehearsed; spontaneity and "being natural" would incite disdain. Ovid was adamant that women must disguise and hide the process by which seduction takes place; with the exception of hair brushing, all grooming should be done out of sight. It is remarkable how much the spirit, if not the letter, of his advice is echoed by contemporary magazines and books designed to teach women how to "capture" a mate (e.g., *The Rules*). Nonetheless, seducing men sexually began as an effort to curb hostile sexism, to protect women from male oppression. Although seduction can turn the tide in women's favor, as described in the next section, it also manipulative and, therefore, fosters ambivalence on the part of men about their own sexual needs and toward women's bodies.

Ambivalence toward Sex and Women's Bodies

Women's success at manipulating men through sex makes men understandably ambivalent about seduction. On the one hand, men celebrate women's sexual allure and are enthusiastic about women who have it; on the other hand, they disparage women who use sex to gain power (e.g.,"temptresses") or purely to manipulate (e.g., "teases"; Landau et al., 2006). Thus, men's eagerness for sex is tempered by their anxiety that women's sexual power will undermine their virility and leave them subservient to women. From the lessons of Sampson and Delilah to the myths of modern-day athletes told to avoid sex before the big game, men are taught to associate ejaculation with the loss of masculine vitality (Lederer, 1968) and to view women's sexual influence as poisonous and debilitating (Spiro, 1997). At the same time, men adore and worship women, and they are unabashed about their desire for sex. As a result, women are both exalted and punished for their sexuality, resulting in the pedestal–gutter dichotomy (Tavris & Wade, 1984). Women who sexually gratify men within the confines of monogamous relationships may be treated well by male partners, whereas women who flaunt their sexuality, use it manipulatively, or demand payment for it are stigmatized.

What is deeply problematic for women is that there is no bright line between being cherished and blemished, and there are costs no matter which way they fall. To elicit benevolent sexism, women must learn to curb their natural instincts (e.g., not to actively seek sex even when they want it) and wrap their sexual desires in the guise of worshipful love and romance. The alternative is met with condemnation. Women who are perceived as wanting sex (e.g., by initiating it or by wearing sexy clothes) are belittled as "sluts" and more likely to be sexually victimized (Aubrey,

2004; Pollard, 1992). Moreover, people who endorse benevolent sexism are less likely to sympathize with the victim of an acquaintance rape if she has behaved "improperly" (e.g., by inviting a man to her apartment or initiating kissing; Abrams, Viki, Masser, & Bohner, 2003).

The overarching issue is that women are exhorted to be sexy (to attract men), but they do not have the same social permission as men do to be actively sexual. To be sure, times have changed and the double standard has lessened in many countries, including the United States. Nonetheless, attitudes about female sexuality remain ambivalent at best (Crawford & Popp, 2003; Marks & Fraley, 2005). Despite the sexual revolution and the contemporary "hook up" culture (i.e., sex without commitment), women are reluctant to tell men what they want sexually for fear of appearing to be overly demanding and scaring them away (Kamen, 2002). Moreover, evidence suggests that "hooking up" is not privately endorsed by either gender (Lambert, Kahn, & Apple, 2003). Among adolescents who are socially pressured to engage in it, "friends with benefits" mostly involves girls providing oral sex to boys without reciprocity (Manning et al., 2005). The reason is that girls (more than boys) report that they feel ashamed of their bodies. As described next, women are more conflicted about their bodies than men, in large part because of the mixed cultural messages they receive about their sexuality.

Beauty Is a Beast

Physical attractiveness is important for both sexes, but it is particularly emphasized for women as a requisite for attracting a mate. Women the world over are pushed toward impossibly high standards of beauty and receive strong cultural messages that their bodies are unacceptable as they are, thus promoting a variety of body-altering practices (Jackman, 1999, 2001). Barbie, the perennial role model for girls, is proportioned so that that her figure is unattainable; the probability of having her figure is only 1 in 100,000 (Norton, Olds, Olive, & Dank, 1996). By adolescence, girls are at much higher risk than boys of developing eating disorders, such as bulimia and anorexia (Feingold & Mazella, 1998). As they mature, women become susceptible to demands that they alter their bodies in numerous ways, including undergoing breast implantation and other cosmetic procedures (e.g., Botox injections, surgery) that have the side effect of decreasing the body's sensitivity and expressiveness (Jeffreys, 2005).

From corsets (which led to actual displacement of women's internal organs) to push-up bras, women have historically altered their bodies to appeal to men. An extreme example is foot binding. Not outlawed until the 1930s, foot binding was practiced in China for about 1,000 years on upper-class women to achieve a look considered by men to be erotically pleasing. Binding began at about age 6 and the feet were so deformed (bend your hand so that your knuckles are about an inch from your palm to get an idea of just how deformed) that women could not walk on their own, needing assistance to hobble (Jackson, 1990). Although high-heels are much less dangerous than foot binding, they can deform women's feet and cause significant back problems. It is difficult to imagine men voluntarily choosing to wear any article of clothing that is equally painful, much less deforming. By contrast, many women are willing to endure considerable discomfort or outright pain (e.g., body waxing and cosmetic surgery) as they strive to embody cultural ideals of beauty and femininity. Women are also eager to mask the naturalness of their facial features and expressions with cosmetics. Their widespread use reflects women repackaging themselves for male consumption (Wolf, 1991), a motive that harks back at least to Ovid's time. Breast enlargement surgery is another example.

Why are women encouraged to reshape themselves so extensively to be sexually attractive? That is, why are feminine standards of beauty so unnatural that, to meet them, women have to undergo pain and suffering? One answer is suggested by terror management theory, which argues that people need to distance themselves from the human body to allay fears associated with mortality (Goldenberg et al., 2001). After all, it is the body that expires, and mortality is a fact of life for humans and animals alike. To reduce death anxiety, humans have erected strong defenses, including exalting characteristics that distinguish them from animals. Because women's reproductive capabilities (e.g., menstruation, pregnancy, and lactation) are particularly salient reminders of our animal natures (and, therefore, death), they elicit fear and disgust (Grabe, Routledge, Cook, Andersen, & Arndt, 2005; Landau et al., 2006). To be acceptable to men, women must cleanse themselves of these reminders by any means possible (e.g., hair removal, hiding menstruation). In other words, because women are "closer to nature," their bodies need to be sanitized to remove the stain of creaturehood because creaturehood is a strong reminder of death (Goldenberg, Pyszczynski, Greenberg, & Solomon, 2000; Haidt, McCauley, & Rozin, 1994; Landau et al., 2006).

Because dealing with the problem of mortality is one of the central tasks of religion, many religions also stress the need for women to "purify" themselves. In the Judeo-Christian tradition, women have been deemed the "unclean" sex (requiring special purifying rituals, especially after menstruation) and the first woman is blamed for mankind's fall from grace into sexuality and, as a result, mortality (see Chapter 11). Even today, women remain strongly associated with cleanliness (Kipnis, 2006; Prentice & Carranza, 2002). To avoid the stigma of uncleanness, women are pressured to be sexually modest and "pure"; indeed, ascribing sexual purity to women is a feature of benevolent sexism, which is particularly strong in traditionally religious cultures (Glick et al., 2000). Some cultures use extreme measures to ensure sexual purity for women. In many African and Arabic nations, young girls undergo painful genital mutilation to guarantee a lack of sexual feeling and to better ensure virginity before marriage (Jackman, 2001; Mernissi, 1987).

As a result of women's association with bodily processes (e.g., sexual reproduction), cultural attitudes toward their bodies are ambivalent. On the one hand, women are often displayed seductively wearing few, if any, clothes to appeal to men's desire for sex (Lin, 1998). On the other hand, women are exhorted to be sexually modest in their clothing and demeanor (i.e., to avoid the appearance of sexual eagerness) to uphold female prescriptions for purity. In Islamic cultures, women's bodies may be completely covered (e.g., by a burqa) to keep them from sexually tempting men. Thus, the message about women's bodies is not only ambivalent but insulting to men because it implies that they are unable to control themselves. The solution to ambivalence toward women's bodies has been to simultaneously idealize and stigmatize them, which is harmful for women, as we discuss next.

Self-Objectification

Impossibly high standards for female beauty can cause women to become deeply dissatisfied with their bodies. Compared with men, they develop a more negative body image, like their bodies less, and suffer more body shame (Feingold & Mazella, 1998; McKinley & Hyde, 1996; Muth & Cash, 1997). During puberty, women are more likely than men to report feeling betrayed by their bodies and feeling that their bodies have become separate from themselves (E. Martin, 1987). Dissociating one's self from one's body is a form of self-objectification. More specifically, self-objectification theory argues that women internalize cultural messages that their bodies are objects to be consumed by men; as a result, their bodies become objects in their own minds (Fredrickson & Roberts, 1997).

By chronically portraying women as sex objects, the media play a significant role in self-objectification (McKinley, 2002). For example, women who read beauty magazines internalize extreme cultural standards of thinness and are more likely to be ashamed of their bodies (Morry & Staska, 2001); television ads that portray women as sex objects have similar effects (Lavine, Sweeney, & Wagner, 1999). Strict cultural standards for beauty cause women to self-objectify, and failure to meet those standards creates body shame, which promotes eating disorders (e.g., Noll & Frederickson, 1998; McKinley & Hyde, 1996). A meta-analysis of controlled experiments found that, in the majority (84%) of studies, viewing idealized female images caused an increase in women's body shame (Groesz, Levine & Murnen, 2002).

Beyond media exposure, other common life experiences can evoke self-objectification. For example, women asked to try on a swimsuit (in private) reported more self-objectification and body shame compared with women asked to try on a sweater (Fredrickson, Roberts, Noll, Quinn, & Twenge, 1998). Women who tried on a swimsuit also performed poorly on a subsequent math test (Fredrickson et al., 1998) and ruminated about their bodies even after re-dressing (Quinn, Kallen, & Christie, 2006). No comparable effects occurred for men. These findings suggest that self-objectification disrupts women's lives not only by making them feel bad about themselves but by robbing them of cognitive resources, including the ability to concentrate on important tasks.

In addition to body shame, self-objectification has been linked to other negative psychological outcomes, including depression and anxiety (Muehlenkamp & Saris-Baglama, 2002; Harrison & Frederickson, 2003; Tiggemann & Kuring, 2004). Women suffer from depression at much higher rates than men, and self-objectification helps to explain why (Fredrickson & Roberts, 1997). Moreover, self-objectification has been tied to sexual dysfunction. Masters and Johnson (1979) argued that viewing the self as a sex object impedes women's sexual functioning by distracting them from their own pleasure, and research supports this view. First, women primed with self-objectifying words reported more negative emotions toward and less interest in sex compared with women primed with body-affirming words (Roberts & Gettman, 2004). Second, women who self-objectify also show sexually avoidant behaviors (Faith & Schare, 1993). Thus, self-objectification may impede women's sexual health in addition to having negative emotional and cognitive consequences (Fredrickson & Roberts, 1997).

Men's behavior toward women also exacerbates self-objectification. The male sexual gaze is discomforting to physically maturing girls as they begin to notice that men often evaluate women in terms of their breasts (Young, 1992). Women are also subject to stranger harassment (Gardner, 1995), defined as behaviors such as "wolf-whistles, leers, winks, grabs, pinches, catcalls, and [sexual] remarks" (Bowman, 1993, p. 523). In a survey of college students, 33% of women reported experiencing these events at least twice a month, and stranger harassment was positively correlated with self-objectification (Fairchild & Rudman, in press). Women also suffer frequent reminders of objectification in the form of obscene phone calls, indecent exposure, and being followed in a frightening manner. In a national sample of Canadian women, 85% of respondents reported experiencing these forms of unwanted sexual attention, and those who did so expressed fears of using public transportation, walking alone at night, and being home alone at night (MacMillan, Nierobisz, & Welsh, 2000). Thus, stranger harassment can limit women's independence by restricting their movements. Sometimes stranger harassment is so severe that extreme measures need to be taken. In an effort to protect women from being groped on the subway, Japan and Brazil have designated separate subway cars for women during rush hour ("Japan tries women-only train," 2005; Sussman, 2006).

Unfortunately, objectifying images of girls and women are increasingly prevalent in media-saturated cultures (American Psychological Association, Task Force on the Sexualization of Girls, 2007). But men might be persuaded to try to avoid objectifying women if they recognized how it harms them as well. For example, men exposed to female models showed decreased satisfaction with their own bodies (which they perceived to be too scrawny and thin; Lavine et al., 1999). Presumably, highly attractive women caused men to feel self-conscious and not sufficiently masculine or attractive to obtain them. Moreover, men exposed to *Playboy* centerfold models reported reduced sexual attraction toward their wives (Kenrick, Gutierres, & Goldberg, 1989). Men's relationships with women are also harmed because, as noted, women who self-objectify show decreased interest in and satisfaction from sex (Faith & Schare, 1993; Roberts & Gettman, 2004; Sanchez et al., 2006). Because healthy sex lives promote happy unions (e.g., Laumann et al., 2006), the negative physical and psychological effects of objectifying women harm men by undermining their intimate relationships.

Menstruation

When cultures idealize and objectify women, women are obligated to conceal their bodies' physical functions, including menstruation. Most women spend a quarter of their adult lives menstruating (Unger & Crawford, 1996), but it continues to be a source of stigma (Kowalski & Chapple, 2000). In the past, menstruating women were viewed as witches, capable of poisoning food and dulling knives (Lips, 1988; Snow & Johnson, 1978). Even today, they are viewed by some subcultures as "unclean" and not allowed contact with others (Siegel, 1986). Menstruation can elicit disgust (T. A. Roberts, 2004); for example, when college students were asked to put a clean, newly unwrapped tampon in their mouths, less than one third complied (Rozin, Haidt, McCauley, Dunlop, & Ashmore, 1999). As a result, mothers, peers, and advertisements for menstrual products advise women to keep their menstruation a secret, lest the stigma demote their social status (Brumberg, 1997; Coutts & Berg, 1993). In fact, people who suspected that a female confederate was menstruating (because a tampon dropped out of her purse) reported not liking her and showed avoidance behaviors (T. A. Roberts et al., 2002). Further, women who were misinformed that a male experimenter knew they were menstruating believed he would be prejudiced against them, and they were unwilling to even try to make a positive impression (Kowalski & Chapple, 2000).

As a result of taboos about menstruation, men are poorly informed and tend to misattribute female moods to premenstrual syndrome (PMS); they also believe that menstruation has a debilitating effect on women's lives, whereas women find it merely bothersome (Brooks-Gunn & Ruble, 1986). Because of the stigma surrounding women's bodies, it is not surprising that men have misconceptions about them. In the next section, we discuss common misconceptions that men and women have about their own bodies.

Sex, Lies, and Bodies

Both women and men live their lives embodied, and the difference between actual and idealized bodies can cause anxiety and sexual problems. Although we have emphasized women's body esteem, men also internalize (masculine) cultural ideals for their bodies. For example, men who read fitness magazines are more likely to suffer from lower body esteem and disordered eating (Morry & Staska, 2001). Of course, men in general are not immune to the desire for a more appealing body. As you might judge from the number of advertisements offering solutions, men are particularly self-conscious about body odor, balding, and penis size (Schooler & Ward, 2006). Moreover, men are at risk of taking anabolic steroids, not being content merely to engage in bodybuilding exercise, to enhance their muscularity (especially athletes and adolescent boys; Lenahan, 2003).

The Myth That Size Matters

A serious misconception men have about their bodies is that penis size is related to their masculinity and to female sexual satisfaction. For example, men on average tend to underestimate their penis size, and the smaller the estimation, the more they worry that they might be homosexual (Lee, 1996). Cultural scripts that require men to be "big and strong" may translate to needlessly anxious desires for a larger reproductive organ, despite the fact that there is no evidence linking size to sexual orientation, virility, or women's satisfaction.

In an Internet survey of 52,000 heterosexual men and women, 45% of men desired a larger penis, whereas more than 85% of women expressed satisfaction with their partner's size (Lever, Frederick, & Peplau, 2006). In addition, more than 70% of women report that penis size is not important to their sexual satisfaction (Francken, van de Wiel, van Driel, & Weijmar Schultz, 2002). Undermining the possibility that women misreported their true desires, researchers found that women's sexual arousal (measured physiologically) was not dependent on the size of men's penises depicted in erotic materials (Fisher, Branscombe, & Lemery, 1983). Nonetheless, a survey of physicians reporting on the sexual beliefs of their patients found that men have exaggerated beliefs about the importance of penis size for sexual performance and that men feel unmanly if they experience occasional erection problems (Pietropinto, 1986). Thus, the myth that "size matters" may undermine men's sexual satisfaction and their gender identity.

The Myth of Female Sexual Inadequacy

Cultural erotic scripts that assign women low sexual agency (i.e., passive submission) are also troublesome for heterosexual relationships. Women are expected to be overcome with passion during intercourse, the *sine qua non* of human sexual behaviors. However, the vast majority of women (> 70%) do not experience orgasm as a result of intercourse (Gupta & Lynn, 1972; Hite, 2003). Nature placed the primary source of men's pleasure in their penis (the point of contact during intercourse) while locating it at a distance from women's vagina (in the clitoris, located above the vagina). This arrangement, dubbed the "vagina–clitoris fiasco" (Kipnis, 2006, p. 46), ensures that orgasm from vaginal penetration alone is abnormal for women. As a result, there are large gender differences in motives for engaging in sexual intercourse, with men emphasizing orgasm and women stressing emotional intimacy (Carroll, Volk, & Hyde, 1985). Nonetheless, the cultural portrayal of intercourse (e.g., in movies and pornography) misleadingly shows women enjoying sexual climax from intercourse as much as men do, which can cause the majority of women to believe there is something wrong with them if they do not achieve orgasm through intercourse alone.

The idea that women are "missing something" (i.e., are inadequate) is a thread that runs through many cultural beliefs about the experience of being female (Kipnis, 2006). Freud famously termed it "penis envy," but there is no empirical evidence to support his view. It seems more likely that women feel inadequate sexually because they expect their bodies to perform commensurately with men's during intercourse. When they do not, women may feel forced to fake orgasms to please their partners, to pretend that they are as biologically responsive to intercourse as their mates (Hite, 2003). Not surprisingly, this can lead to resentment toward men, not only for the implicit pressure to fake orgasms (so that men can feel they performed well) but also for the gender gap in sexual pleasure (Kamen, 2002; Lavie-Ajayi, 2005).

Freud linked penis envy to the fact that men's sexual organs are visible, whereas women's are largely hidden. The idea that women are "defective men" because their genitalia are "invisible" harks back to Aristotle and has influenced Western biomedical theory ever since (Maines, 1999; Walton, Fineman, & Walton, 1996). However, as described previously, it appears that men (not women) suffer from penis envy (i.e., desire for a larger one). Moreover, in terms of sheer real estate, women may have the advantage. The actual geography of women's nerve endings devoted to pleasure and tissue that is engorged during arousal spans an area that is at least as large as, if not larger, than the nerve endings and tissue devoted to men's pleasure (Sherfey, 1973). Thus, like the tip of an iceberg, "the clitoris itself is only the visible portion of a vast anatomical array of sexually responsive tissue" (Hite, 2006, p. 69). In other words, women are not biologically shortchanged when it comes to sexual pleasure. However, they are more likely to require sexual acts that do not involve intercourse (e.g., oral or manual stimulation) to experience orgasm. Because of the cultural primacy of intercourse as the sexual act and misconceptions regarding women's bodies, women are not likely to be as sexually satisfied as are men.

In fact, it has been estimated that 43% of women between the ages of 18 and 55 years suffer from sexual dysfunction (Laumann, Paik, & Rosen, 1999). Lack of interest in sex is the most common problem for women, with about 33% reporting they regularly did not want sex (compared with 14% of men). Because sexual dysfunction is strongly associated with relationship satisfaction and quality of life for both sexes, it is a serious public health problem. However, the medical community has been more responsive to men's needs. For example, only 20% of men suffer from erectile dysfunction, yet men have readily been offered pharmaceutical solutions (e.g., Viagra, Cialis, and Levitran), whereas drugs that have shown promise for alleviating women's dysfunction (e.g., Intrinsa) have been banned by the Food and Drug Administration, causing some female scientists to criticize the double standard and to point out that women are being treated paternalistically by the scientific establishment (Enserink, 2005). This is not to imply that pharmaceutical solutions are women's best option; in fact, there is some evidence that education can improve women's sexual pleasure (Davis, Blank, Lin, & Bonillas, 1996; Van Wyk, 1982; Wilcox & Hager, 1980). However, the double standard vis-à-vis medical attention suggests that men's sexuality is treated with more respect than women's, perhaps because of the underlying ambivalence about female sexuality.

Sex and Marriage

Once upon a time, there was a young maiden whose life was toil and drudgery until magic transformed her long enough to capture the heart of a prince before she disappeared, forced to return to her life of woe. Enchanted by her beauty, the prince scoured the kingdom until at last he found and rescued her by making her his bride. Whether the story is *Cinderella, Sleeping Beauty, The Princess Bride, Pretty Woman,* or their many cousins, the themes are similar in that women wield power through their beauty while men do so through their status.

Desirable Mating Characteristics

Are the fairy tales themes true? At first blush, they appear to be credible. Research investigating mate preferences in 37 cultures shows that men are more likely than women to report wanting a physically attractive mate, whereas women are more likely to desire a mate with material resources (Buss, 1989). However, in their reanalysis of these findings, Eagly and Wood (1999) provide a caveat by considering the degree of gender equality within each culture. Although men continued to prefer physically attractive mates irrespective of their culture's degree of gender equality, women's preference for mates high in material resources was strongest in cultures where women were low in status. Thus, when women are empowered, they are less constrained to seek male partners who can provide financial security.

Nonetheless, although many women no longer expect or desire to be completely provided for by their husbands, they may still strive to "marry up" whenever possible, to literally wed someone taller, older, better educated, and wealthier. Anthropologists term this "hypergamy" and link it to women's evolutionary need to seek mates who will be good providers and protectors for their children (Fisher, 1992). Analyses of responses to personal ads suggest that women respond to men on the basis of income and education, whereas men respond to women on the basis of attractiveness; moreover, age is negatively related to men's interest in women but positively related to women's interest in men (Baize & Schroeder, 1995; Smith, Waldorf, & Trembath, 1990). The idea that pretty, young women want to mate with older, wealthy men is culturally accepted even in nations where gender equality is reasonably high. For example, it is much more common for older men to wed young women (often termed "trophy wives") than for older women to marry young men. Hypergamy may be an obstacle to gender equality in marital relations because it guarantees that wives start out "behind the eight ball in the game of marital power politics" and will be unlikely to ever catch up (Maushart, 2001, p. 77). Commenting on the power disadvantage that traditional marital roles confer to wives, Bernard (1972) noted, "Take a young woman who has been trained for feminine dependencies, who wants to 'look up' to the man she marries. Put her at a disadvantage in the labor market. Then marry her to a man who has [an] advantage over her in age, income, and education ... then expect an egalitarian marriage?" (p. 146).

However, there is also considerable evidence to support the matching hypothesis (also called "homogamy"), which posits that people prefer mates who are similar to themselves, at least within cultures that are relatively gender fair. In American samples, when men and women consider the traits they want in a long-term partner, they prefer people who are similar in attractiveness, education, and socioeconomic status (Berscheid, Dion, Walster, & Walster, 1971; Berscheid & Walster, 1978; Blackwell & Lichter, 2004; Feingold, 1988). Because similarity breeds not only attraction (Byrne, 1971) but also mutual respect and understanding, one might expect more egalitarian nations to foster happier marital relations. That is exactly what researchers investigating 29 cultures found (Laumann et al., 2006; see also Gorner, 2006). Couples from nations high on gender equality reported greater sexual satisfaction (e.g., Canada, Spain, and Sweden; the United States ranked in fifth place) compared with nations low on gender equality (e.g., China, Thailand, and Japan). Thus, the more equal the society, the greater is the sexual satisfaction in marriage for both women and men.

Trends in Modern Marriage

Although the United States is still a "marriage culture," with most people getting married at some point in their lives, they are entering marriage at a slower pace and with different expectations compared with previous generations (Bianchi & Casper, 2002; Coontz, 2005; Zernike, 2007). Since the 1960s, many Americans have chosen to cohabitate before marriage; they are also marrying later in life so that, on average, Americans now spend half their adult lives outside of marriage (Bianchi & Casper, 2002; Bumpass & Sweet, 1989; Coontz, 2005; S. Roberts, 2006). As described in Chapter 9, people today are unique in their ability to pursue marriage out of desire rather than reproductive necessity. Moreover, for the first time in the history of civilization, they are able to avoid reproduction with nearly 100% efficiency through the use of birth control. As a result, people now form unions in which children are optional. A 2000 poll showed that 13 million American couples have chosen to be child-free, the largest number in U.S. history (Belkin, 2000). Thus, for many couples, marriage may no longer be primarily about raising a family but about emotional and sexual intimacy.

Despite the many benefits of love-based marriages, divorce rates have skyrocketed in industrialized nations. On average, women initiate divorce at higher rates than men (Amato & Previti, 2003; Heaton & Blake, 1999; Montenegro, 2004), suggesting that women's increased economic independence plays a role in their freedom to divorce. However, the reasons why women divorce may have more to do with their need for marital equality and emotional fulfillment, which, for many, may still not be sufficiently gratified in modern marriages, which helps to explain why women express more dissatisfaction with marriage than do men (Baumeister & Bratslavsky, 1999; Duncombe & Marsden, 1993; Hite, 1987, 1991; Langford, 1999). Next, we focus on inequality, novelty, and gender differences in relationship socialization as factors that trouble modern marriages and, in turn, have an impact on sexual satisfaction within marriage.

Inequality

Although marriage has undergone more changes in the past three decades than it has in the past 300 years, it remains an institution that favors men more than women (Coontz, 2005; Maushart, 2001). After marriage, women are still expected to adopt their husband's surnames, and children (regardless of their sex) are more often named after their fathers than their mothers (Jost et al., 2002; Twenge, 1997b). In addition, even in dual-income marriages, wives are still obligated to perform most of the domestic labor (e.g., housework and child care; see Chapter 8), so much so that professional women often joke that what they really need is a "wife." Not surprisingly, inequities in domestic labor predict initiating divorce for women (Frisco & Williams, 2003). Further, men are often still in charge of making the major decisions, including where the couple will live and determining how money will be spent (Peplau & Gordon, 1985; Vora, 2007).

How important is gender equality for relationship success? A review of the couples therapy literature concluded that gender-stereotyped roles are harmful for relationship stability and satisfaction (Johnson, 2003). In contrast, equal sharing of power has been found to contribute to marital success for both women and men (Deutsch, 1999; Steil, 1997). A longitudinal study found that 81% of marriages failed when men were unwilling to share power with their wives (Gottman & Silver, 1999). A strong foundation of equality helps couples to successfully balance work and family (Haddock, Zimmerman, Ziemba, & Current, 2001) and enhances intimacy and well-being for both partners, qualities that are essential for sexual happiness (Coltrane, 1996; Steil, 1997). Egalitarianism is clearly important for marital stability. Yet most couples fall into unequal relationship patterns without their conscious intent (Knudson-Martin & Mahoney, 1996, 1998; Zvonkovic, Greaves, Schmeige, & Hall, 1996). As a result, inequality remains a challenge in modern marriages. In their interviews with married couples with children, Knudson-Martin and Mahoney (2005) found that marital equality is enhanced by challenging male entitlement, the invisible power that men accrue through their ascribed status. Women typically instigated this challenge, but once the men in their study were made aware of their gender entitlement, they consciously worked to equalize power in their marriage, including sharing financial decisions and domestic labor. As a result, marital and sexual satisfaction improved.

Novelty

Another challenge for married couples is lack of novelty, which can lead to boredom in the bedroom. After about 4 years, sexual passion has typically declined (Brehm, 1998; Gupta & Singh, 1982; Rose, 2002). When a relationship begins, there is the tension and thrill of not knowing exactly what the other person feels or whether the relationship will last. Passion is enhanced by the thrill of flying without a net. By contrast, marriage is grounded and comforting, but the surprises may be few. There is a reason why novels and films emphasize the barriers and mishaps involved with seduction, ending with "and they lived happily ever after" rather than focusing on the subsequent relationship. Tension and uncertainty are stimulating, even if not well suited for a lifetime of domestic comfort.

Lasting love thrives on a couple's interconnectedness, so much so that the number of activities shared may be more important for marital satisfaction than emotional intensity (Berscheid, Snyder, & Omoto, 1989). But because people are socialized to connect sexual passion to love, they can be misled about the health of their marriage once sexual passion declines (Carlson & Hatfield, 1992). Couples interested in preserving passion are well advised to shake up their routine, invent new ways to surprise one another, and find exciting pastimes to pursue together because emotions and sexual excitement are elicited and enhanced by unexpected positive events (Berscheid, 1991). According to one theory, changes in intimacy (rather than the absolute level) spur passionate feelings (Baumeister & Bratslavsky, 1999). For new couples starting from zero, the intimacy level is readily increased. For couples with more mileage, events that encourage seeing the partner in a new light (e.g., taking up new activities, going on vacation) or physical reunions after one partner has been absent can promote passion. For some couples, making up after an argument can lead to satisfying sex, likely because of fluctuations in intimacy. Thus, there are many ways that couples can sustain sexual attraction for one another during the course of a marriage, and avoiding predictability is chief among them.

Relationship Socialization

Men and women are socialized so differently that their approaches to marriage seem to come from different "operating manuals." Men are repeatedly exhorted and culturally primed to pursue sex, as often (and with as many women) as possible. Not surprisingly, men, compared with women, report greater desire for short-term sexual relationships, prefer greater numbers of sexual partners, and require less acquaintance time with a potential partner before consenting to sex (Schmitt, Shackelford, & Buss, 2001). By contrast, women are socialized for love; fairy tales and romance novels prepare them for a future of gallant attentions and intense emotions, an unrealistic ideal that few husbands can be expected to fulfill over the long haul. As the saying goes, "Women want one man to fulfill all their desires; men want just one desire fulfilled by many women."

Both operating manuals undermine people's ability to find marital satisfaction: for men by encouraging infidelity, and for women by encouraging unrealistic expectations. Wives report that they read romance novels for emotional gratification that husbands do not provide (Radway, 1987), whereas men are predominant consumers of pornography. As described in Chapter 9, women implicitly idealize romantic partners as chivalrous and heroic, whereas men's implicit fantasies of their partners are sexualized (Rudman & Heppen, 2003). Being programmed to idealize the other sex differently may result in disparate expectations for intimate relationships that lead to disappointment.

Finally, heterosexual unions can be troubled by stereotypes that women are emotionally expressive and men are instrumental (i.e., task oriented), which can cause women to do more emotional work in relationships (Duncombe & Marsden, 1993). Although both men and women report having to work at their relationships, women are expected to accommodate men's lower interest in communicating and expressing their emotions (Burns, 2002). This is like asking women to solve relationship problems on their own. Indeed, women are more sensitive to marital problems than are men. In a national survey of divorced couples, 26% of the men said they were caught off guard by the divorce (i.e., unaware of the problems in the relationship) compared with 14% of women, and emotional abuse or neglect is a primary reason why women divorce (Montenegro, 2004).

Marital dissatisfaction can lead to infidelity, a prevalent cause of divorce (Amato & Previti, 2003). Although the vast majority of people report that monogamy is ideal for marriages, estimates of marital infidelity range from 15% to 50% for women and from 25% to 50% for men (Stone, Goetz, & Shackelford, 2005). Although men report engaging in infidelity more so than women (Wiederman, 1997), there are signs that women may be catching up (D. S. Smith, 1995). However, women are more likely to justify extramarital relationships on the basis of a need for love, whereas men tend to justify them on the basis of a need for sex (Glass & Wright, 1992). Because it is commonly thought that men more readily separate sex from love, people believe that female infidelity is more threatening to a marriage than male infidelity (Sprecher, Regan, & McKinney, 1998). But for both sexes, extramarital relationships are typically unhealthy. Although the secrecy of an affair can fan the flames of passion (Driscoll, Davis, & Lipetz, 1972; Lane & Wegner, 1999; Wegner, Lane, & Dimitri, 1994), relationship quality in affairs tends to be poor because of the lack of interdependence (Berscheid et al., 1989; Foster & Campbell, 2005; Richardson, 1988). Infidelity damages marriages by fostering a lack of trust and, as noted previously, may lead to divorce (Amato & Previti, 2003).

In sum, marriage as an institution has radically changed in the last 30 years, with higher divorce rates and more people choosing alternative lifestyles. The extent to which marriage remains unequal (e.g., men making the most important decisions while women handle domestic chores) factors into a high rate of marital dissolution, but the fact that men and women are socialized to have competing desires and expectations also looms large. Finally, long-term relationships can lack passion and novelty, which can lead to infidelity and divorce. But because interconnectedness may be more important than emotional intensity, waning sexual passions can cause couples to misread the health of their marriage. Moreover, passion can be rekindled by injecting surprise and novelty into the relationship.

Chapter Summary

Heterosexual relations are challenged by multiple factors that impede men's and women's ability to fulfill one another sexually. Because male–female relations begin in an atmosphere of childhood avoidance, men and women need cultural scripts designed to bring them together. However, heterosexual erotic scripts are fraught with stereotypes and are so narrow in scope that they encumber sexual satisfaction by inhibiting people's ability to relax and simply pursue their own and their partner's pleasure. Moreover, erotic prescriptions that men should be dominant and women submissive lead to misconceptions, including myths about male penis size and female sexual inadequacy. Because of the lack of information about female sexual pleasure, women and men may be more than literally having sex "in the dark."

The conflict between heterosexual interdependence and male dominance (i.e., sexual intimacy and sexism) helps to explain the so-called war of the sexes. As the "weaker sex," women used sexual attraction to counteract their historical treatment as men's property, in other words to "enslave their masters" through sexual seduction. Men countered by stigmatizing and objectifying women's bodies as well as demanding impossibly high standards of beauty and purity that remain in place today. The pressure for women to live up to these standards and the tendency for both sexes to view women's bodies as objects for male consumption harm women's health and well-being in multiple ways. Further, male ambivalence toward women's sexuality has resulted in dichotomizing women as either worthy of benevolence (if they faithfully serve men in monogamous relationships) or hostility (if they violate prescriptions for purity by being overtly sexual).

Gender inequality vis-à-vis sexuality is also evident in the language that is often used to equate female receptiveness with victimization, reflecting an implicit schema of heterosexual relationships in which men "use and abuse" women sexually. Although this schema reflects genuine disadvantages in women's size and strength, it also indicates their relatively low social status. As a result, "weak men" are also viewed as "pussies" and potential sexual victims. The cultural message is that women are worth less than men, and femininity is a stigma. Ironically, to the extent that women are subordinated in a society, they face more incentive to select powerful, high-status mates (e.g., who are older, wealthier, and better educated), which only reinforces gender hierarchy in the home. Moreover, women continue to be burdened with the bulk of the domestic and emotional labor involved in marital relations, additional signs of their continued lower status. Not surprisingly, women are less satisfied with sex and marriage than men, and they are more sensitive to marital problems.

Gender socialization contributes to dissatisfaction with marriage because it ensures that men and women enter into relationships with different expectations and goals. Despite the sexual revolution, women are not likely to be sexually sophisticated about their bodies and, therefore, are less likely to be sexually satisfied. Similarly, men are not well prepared for the emotional intimacy that women expect in heterosexual relationships. The result is a high divorce rate in Western cultures. Gendered scripts for sexual intimacy mislead women to expect intense emotions and men to expect lasting sexual passion that marriages have difficulty sustaining. Men are not educated sufficiently about their partners' bodies, and the likelihood of being paired with a sexually unhappy woman can lead them to seek sexual release outside the relationship. Although extramarital affairs offer excitement, they are a poor replacement for the profound trust and intimacy that two people in a committed relationship ideally share.

Fortunately, research suggests that fostering equality within heterosexual relationships can increase overall relationship health and promote sexual satisfaction for both male and female partners. Freedom from restrictive notions of sexual roles in which men initiate sexual activities while women passively submit can allow heterosexual couples to focus on mutual pleasure rather than trying to "perform" culturally prescribed sexual scripts.

CHAPTER 11

Gender and Violence

Imagine hearing that someone in your neighborhood has been murdered. Conjure up an image of the murderer and of the victim. Did you imagine a male killer? If you did, crime statistics support your assumption. Across the globe, killing is overwhelmingly perpetrated by men, who commit more than 90% of murders (excluding infanticide, the figure rises to greater than 97%; Daly & Wilson, 1990). Did you also imagine a specific victim? If not, do so now. Is the imagined victim female or male? If you envisioned a female victim, you can no longer cite crime statistics to support your guess. Men not only commit serious violence at a much higher rate than women but are also the predominant victims of fatal violence. According to the U.S. Department of Justice, men, not women, are more likely to be victims for all violent crimes except for rape and sexual assault (U.S. Bureau of Justice Statistics, 2007). In 2005, within the United States, men constituted about 80% of all murder victims, almost as high as the proportion (90%) of murderers who were men (Federal Bureau of Investigation, 2007). Figure 11.1 reports the percentage of U.S. murders in 2005 committed by male versus female perpetrators on victims of each sex. This figure confirms the popular belief that men are more violent than women but also shows what many people often overlook: that male violence most often targets other men rather than women.

We do not intend to deny the violence that men commit toward women or that women perpetrate. Indeed, the prior thought experi-

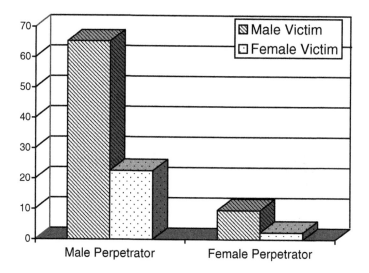

FIGURE 11.1. Percentage of murders perpetrated by men and women on male and female victims. Data from U.S. Bureau of Justice Statistics, 2007.

ment was a bit unfair. If we had specified an assault between strangers, you may have correctly envisaged male–male violence as the most likely scenario (e.g., a barroom brawl or street fight). If, instead, we had indicated that the violence occurred within an intimate relationship, assuming a male perpetrator and female victim becomes more realistic. U.S. crime statistics show that men are more likely to be murdered by nonintimates, such as acquaintances and strangers, than by either relationship partners or family members. By contrast, female victims tend to have known, even to have loved, the person who murdered them. Including only cases in which the killer's identity is known, Figure 11.2 reveals the percentage of male and female murder victims in the United States broken down by the victim's relationship with the killer: intimate partner, other family member, acquaintance, or stranger. Figure 11.2 illustrates that female victims were more commonly murdered by an intimate partner, compared with a relative, acquaintance, or stranger. For instance, the percentage of female murder victims killed by husbands or boyfriends was almost four times the percentage of women killed by a stranger. By contrast, men's risk of being murdered by a stranger was more than double that of being murdered by a wife or girlfriend. (Please note that if one included as part of the total number murders in which the identity of the perpetrator is unknown, the percentages reported in Figure 11.2 would be considerably lower because the total

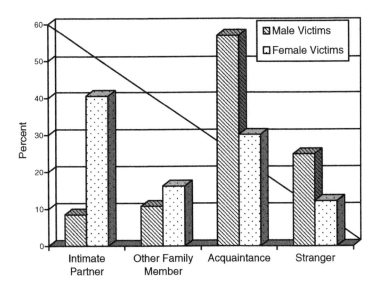

FIGURE 11.2. Relationship of murder victims to perpetrators. Data from U.S. Bureau of Justice Statistics, 2007.

number of murders is larger. For example, the number of women killed by intimates drops to 30% and the number of men killed by intimates drops to 3%, still a substantial gender difference.)

In sum, no significant analysis of violence can ignore the ways in which aggression is shaped by gender. But, as suggested previously, violence and gender interrelate in a complex and situation-dependent fashion. Outside of intimate relationships, men are many times more likely both to perpetrate and be victimized by serious violence (e.g., murder, assault). Within heterosexual romantic relationships, however, women experience considerably more danger of victimization (see Frieze, 2005, for a review). Yet even within relationships, the story is not as straightforward as the general stereotype of abusive men and victimized women suggests. In industrialized societies, where women's status has generally risen, research reveals considerably more "gender symmetry" (Straus, Gelles, & Steinmetz, 1980) in the most common forms of heterosexual relationship violence (e.g., slapping, throwing an object at one's partner). Some studies even suggest that women exhibit slightly more of such aggressive behaviors than men (see Archer, 2000, 2006, for reviews). By contrast, for the most serious forms of relationship violence (e.g., choking), which more often result in injury or death, men remain the predominant (though not exclusive) perpetrators and women the predominant victims (Frieze, 2005). In highly traditional societies, the picture is even more lopsided, with male partners initiating all forms of relationship violence much more frequently than female partners (Archer, 2006).

The relationship between gender and violence reflects our more general theme of ambivalence. Being female sometimes offers protection against violence. For instance, whereas social norms dictate that boys should be physically rough with each other, boys learn that it is wrong to "hit a girl," an act viewed as out of bounds, even cowardly. For example, when men responded to various scenarios designed to elicit anger, they reported being more likely to respond aggressively if the target who provoked them was male (Harris, 1994). Further, they expected more social approval for responding violently to a man and disapproval for responding aggressively to a woman. In general, there appears to be considerable inhibition against men being violent toward women. A meta-analysis of laboratory experiments by Archer (2007) supports Figure 11.1 by showing low levels of male-to-female physical aggression compared to the three other categories (i.e., male-to-male, female-to-female, and female-to-male), at least in the United States.

Benevolently sexist beliefs suggest that women both deserve and need men's protection from violence. Yet this ideology also suggests that men's protection depends on women's acceptance of gender prescriptions. For example, when women challenge male authority or violate ideals of feminine modesty, violence can swiftly replace protection, especially in cultures where women have little status or power. Such violence often occurs within intimate relationships because male partners have strong motivations to control their female partners' behavior. Further, in strongly male-dominated cultures, social norms support a man's "right" (or even "duty") to "control your woman."

This chapter explores the complex relationships between gender and violence. We focus on (1) within-sex violence, which usually occurs between men, and (2) between-sex violence, predominately male violence toward female relationship partners. We concentrate on male-initiated aggression because it is far more common than female-initiated aggression. Because we reviewed gender differences in the development of aggressive behavior in Chapter 3, this chapter addresses only adult violence. More specifically, the current chapter reviews both evolutionary and social structural explanations for (1) men's violence toward other men, (2) violence within heterosexual romantic relationships, and (3) explicitly sexualized violence toward women (sexual assault and rape).

Violence, Sex, and Dominance

We have noted that, across the globe, the most serious form of interpersonal violence is almost exclusively perpetrated by men (Daly & Wilson, 1988, 1990). When it comes to intergroup violence (such as organized warfare between gangs, tribes, or nations), the male link to violence is even stronger. Men dominate military organizations and even though some armed forces now include female soldiers (e.g., the U.S. Army), women are typically excluded from direct combat duty. Indeed, although interpersonal aggression probably comes more quickly to mind as an exemplar of violence, organized intergroup violence has, over the course of human history, been many times more deadly. For instance, the many millions killed in the wars and genocides of the 20th century undoubtedly dwarf the number of people murdered through interpersonal violence in the same period.

Consistent with our recurrent themes, the nature and frequency of violence (both within and between the sexes) can be understood within the context of men's greater structural power coupled with intimate interdependence between the sexes. You may recall the example that opened Chapter 2, an alien society in which the ehormbs dominated the jumeres but also depended on a narcotic-like pheromone that the jumeres secreted through their skin, having its most powerful effect when given willingly. We suggested that to secure a continuous supply of the pheromone, individual ehormbs might try to attract desirable jumeres by providing resources, leading to potentially violent competition among the ehormbs to secure status and wealth. Note that the violent competition in this scenario occurs among the ehormbs, with the desirable jumeres as prizes they may "win." As objects of desire, the jumeres would not normally be targets of ehormb violence. But when the jumeres prove difficult to control through incentives (i.e., when rewards fail to elicit compliance), ehormbs might resort to violence. For instance, a jumere who refused a powerful ehormb's advances might elicit aggression.

This example illustrates how male dominance and intimate heterosexual interdependence create differing motivations for male-perpetrated violence toward men as opposed to women. Men's quest for dominance can motivate violence between men as they compete for status and resources and, ultimately, for women. By contrast, the tendency for men to view women as "prizes" offers women some immunity or protection from this competition, so long as women remain "decorative objects" who cheerlead men from the sidelines.

But men also retain dominance in part by exerting control over women. This includes attempts to keep women out of direct competition with men for status and resources, such as by encouraging women to remain in traditional roles where they depend on men to provide for them. Thus, hostile sexism is more likely to be directed at a "career woman" and benevolent sexism at a "homemaker" (Glick et al., 1997). Further, sexual motives, such as the desire to ensure a female partner's fidelity, can increase men's motivation to exert control by threatening or committing violence. Indeed, suspected sexual infidelity is the most common reason why men murder female partners (Wlson & Daly, 1996).

In sum, men's violence toward other men probably results from direct competition, whereas the desire to exert control (especially within relationships) may more often motivate men's violence toward women. Both competition and control motives can elicit aggression. Competition can directly lead to violence as self-interested parties clash over limited resources. Within close relationships, however, aggression may emerge when other strategies for maintaining control (such as incentives) fail to work. Men's greater social status and resources can promote violence toward women because the powerful experience fewer inhibitions in how they act toward subordinates (Keltner, Gruenfeld, & Anderson, 2003). But intimate interdependence can mitigate violence toward women, which may be most likely to occur only if men fail to influence female partners through other means. We first consider male–male violence before examining violence within heterosexual relationships. In both instances, we review evolutionary as well as social structural explanations that connect gender to aggression.

Man's Violence toward Man

In Chapter 1 we noted the absence of evidence for large (or even moderate) evolution-based sex differences for most personality traits, skills, and behavior. Aggression is an exception to this general rule. Several lines of evidence point to the possibility that men are "wired" for aggression more so than women: (1) the size and consistency of differences in aggression across cultures (Daly & Wilson, 1990), (2) the emergence of sex differences in rough-and-tumble play early in childhood (Dunn & Morgan, 1987), (3) similar sex differences in aggression among humans' primate cousins (Meany et al., 1985), and (4) the fact that exposure to prenatal male hormones increases subsequent aggressive behavior

(Goy et al., 1988). At the same time, even theorists who emphasize an evolutionary explanation acknowledge that social structure and culture strongly influence men's aggression as well as that women have the capacity to aggress. We first review the evolutionary account and then turn to social structural explanations about how gender shapes violence.

The Evolution of Male–Male Violence: Is Heterosexuality the Root of All Evil?

Even a cursory examination of the Adam and Eve story suggests that the human fall from grace can be blamed on sexual lust. Eve, who "saw that the tree was good for eating and that it was lust to the eyes" (Genesis 3:6) tempted Adam with fruit (often used as a literary symbol for sexual passion). Immediately after giving into temptation, both members of the original couple become aware and ashamed of their nakedness. Further, after eating the fruit, God tells Eve "because you have done this ... your man shall be your longing, and he shall rule over you" (Genesis 3:16–17), seemingly connecting women's sexual desire for men to male domination. Adam and Eve do not engage in sex until after the fall. Sex produces the first male peers, brothers Cain and Abel, whose tragic male–male rivalry ends in murder. In other words, in the Judeo-Christian origin story, sexuality leads to patriarchy ("... he shall rule over you") and, at least indirectly, to men's violence toward each other.

Although evolutionary theory offers a competing worldview to biblical literalism, the origin story it tells also proposes a connection between sex and violence. In fact, one can argue that some evolutionary theorists view heterosexuality as the "root of all evil." Recall (from Chapter 2) the sexual selection theory of patriarchy, which suggests that women, because of their greater reproductive investment, select socially dominant men as mates because such men can provide greater resources for offspring (Trivers, 1972). Thus, men's sexual motivation (to gain sexual access to fertile women) is the engine that drives their competitive, often violent, quest for status and resources. In other words, when men violently compete over resources (e.g., land or wealth), the underlying or original motive is to attract mates. Further, evolutionary theorists posit that men try to ensure that their resources are providing for their own, and not another male's, offspring by guarding female mates, making sure that they do not have sex with other men (Daly & Wilson, 1988; Daly et al., 1982; Smuts, 1995). An evolved desire for paternity certainty is hypothesized to have made men more prone to sexual jealousy, which is a powerful source of violence toward women, a topic we explore later in this chapter.

Social dominance theorists (Sidanius & Pratto, 1999) take the evolutionary approach a step further. They suggest that men gained an evolutionary advantage by competing with other men in groups as well as individually. Thus, sexual selection motivates men not only to compete for individual dominance within their own social group but also to band together, forming male alliances aimed at eliminating the competition: men from other groups. Using male alliances to attack or control other groups has a host of potential evolutionary benefits. Even low-ranking men within a dominant group stand to gain material advantages: although their individual status may be low within their group, they gain a share of the status and spoils their group accrues by appropriating the resources of other groups (e.g., their land and possessions). Group exploitation can occur through warfare or can be institutionalized through such arrangements as colonization and slavery, allowing long-term exploitation of the other group.

Social dominance theory suggests that sexual access to women in subordinated groups is another important benefit for men in dominant groups. Men from dominant groups can more easily persuade or coerce women who have few resources and little power to have a sexual relationship. So, for example, despite laws against miscegenation (marriage across racial lines) in the old South, sex between White male slave owners and enslaved women was common (see Jackman, 1994). One prominent example is Thomas Jefferson's offspring with Sally Hemmings. As a result, many African Americans who undergo genetic testing to discover which part of Africa their ancestors came from find that they have both European and African ancestry. Male slave owners and colonialists throughout history had the "benefit" of supplementing a traditional marriage to a member of their own group with (often covert) sexual relationships with women from subordinated groups. From an evolutionary point of view, violent oppression of male competitors, combined with sexual exploitation of women in subordinated groups, maximizes men's reproductive success.

In short, the evolutionary perspective suggests that sexual selection for competitive, dominance-seeking men is the distal source of most of the world's ills. War, conquest, colonialism, and slavery all stem from male–male competition to amass resources, status, and wealth, which, in turn, allows men to attract (or to coerce) female mates. This approach yields an important insight into why men are both the predominant initiators and targets of interpersonal and intergroup violence.

Patriarchy Oppresses ... Men?

As suggested, social dominance theory offers a somewhat surprising twist. It not only suggests that heterosexuality is the underlying root of women's oppression (i.e., that men seek to dominate resources to attract women and to control women's sexuality to prevent infidelity), but that patriarchy aims just as strongly at aggressively oppressing male competitors. Social dominance theorists have labeled this the "subordinate male target hypothesis" (Sidanius & Pratto, 1999). Contradicting the notion that women in minority groups are doubly disadvantaged (as female and a minority), this hypothesis states that violent oppression primarily targets men, not women, in low-status groups. Men view men in other groups as their direct competitors. Although subordinate men may have value if controlled and exploited for their labor, they remain a threat. Any hint of rebellion or attempts to change the power structure may elicit violence toward subordinated males, helping to ensure that they remain "in their place." By contrast, female members of subordinated groups represent less of a threat and more of an "opportunity," exploitable both for their labor and as potential sexual partners.

Consistent with the subordinate male target hypothesis, many studies show more aggressive reactions to Black male than to White male targets. For example, White participants role-playing police officers who must quickly decide whether to "shoot" a suspect are quicker in deciding to shoot Black (compared with White) male suspects when they appear on a computer screen aiming a weapon (Correll, Park, Judd, & Wittenbrink, 2002; Greenwald, Oakes, & Huffman, 2003). Participants are also more likely to mistakenly "shoot" a Black (compared with a White) man carrying an object (e.g., a cell phone) that is not a weapon (Correll et al., 2002; Greenwald et al., 2003; see also Payne, 2006). Further, Black male defendants accused of murdering a White victim are more likely to receive the death sentence if their facial features are more "stereotypically Black" (e.g., wider nose, darker skin; Eberhardt, Davies, Purdie-Vaughns, & Johnson, 2006). Such studies, however, have failed to include female targets, which would provide the necessary comparison to test fully the subordinate male target hypothesis.

Evidence from outside the laboratory is also consistent with the hypothesis that minority men are treated particularly harshly. In the United States, young African American men are more likely to be imprisoned than in college, whereas African American women attend college at relatively high rates (see Sidanius & Pratto, 1999). Or consider historical violence toward African Americans, such as the approximately 3,500 lynchings that took place between the 1880s and 1960s in the United States. Most victims were men who had been accused of having had sex, or simply of desiring to have sex, with White women. For instance, in 1955, Emmet Till, a 14-year-old African American, was lynched in Mississippi merely for having whistled at a White woman on the street. The sexualized nature of the charges in many lynchings provides anecdotal support for the notion that male–male intergroup violence originates in a competition not only for resources but for sexual access to women.

In sum, social dominance theory points out that patriarchy not only oppresses and controls women but reserves its greatest violence for the oppression of men in subordinated groups. Although male dominance benefits some men (those who achieve higher status individually or as part of a dominant group), hierarchies are pyramids in which those few at the top stand on the many at the bottom. Social dominance theory locates the distal causes of men's tendency toward violent competition with their fellow men in evolutionary (sexual selection) forces. This theory, however, also posits that more proximal social structural factors are responsible for maintaining group-based oppression, such as the ideologies that societies generate to legitimize current hierarchies. As discussed in Chapter 2, some social structural theorists (e.g., Wood & Eagly, 2002) downplay or reject aspects of the evolutionary argument, viewing the social structural causes of patriarchy as a sufficient explanation for male violence. We turn to these structural, and resulting cultural, explanations in the next section.

Social Structural and Cultural Causes of Male–Male Violence

In spite of disagreements about whether patriarchy stems mainly from biological versus cultural evolution (see Chapter 2), both evolutionary and social structural theorists agree that how a society is structured can mitigate or exacerbate patriarchy and the male violence it generates. Recall from Chapter 2 that foraging (or hunter–gatherer) societies exhibit less hierarchy, whereas agricultural and industrial societies, which generate a surplus, tend toward greater hierarchy. When societies begin to generate wealth that can be amassed (e.g., grain that can be stored, manufactured goods), male–male competition increases; war, conquest, and colonization often follow (see Wood & Eagly, 2002).

The structural basis for a society's wealth can also influence male aggressiveness and ideologies about the use of violence, according to Nisbett (1993). Specifically, societies that relied on herding may develop ideologies that promote male aggression more strongly than societies that rely on farming. Because their stock is mobile, herders experience greater vulnerability to raiding than farmers. Raiders can easily swoop in and steal sheep or cattle; by contrast, a farmer's land, although it may be forcefully and permanently conquered, cannot be stolen in the night. The increased danger herders face may generate greater male vigilance to threat as well as a concern with having a tough reputation and a propensity to seek revenge, both of which signal "If you raid me, you will pay, so don't even think about it."

Thus, herding societies are hypothesized to develop a culture of honor (Nisbett, 1993). For men, the ideology of honor represents concern, above all, with one's reputation as tough and unwilling to back down from a fight or a threat. Cultures that emphasize male honor, which is similar to the notion of machismo, socialize boys to defend their reputations aggressively. This, in turn, leads to a greater propensity for interpersonal violence to protect one's reputation and resources that can extend to intergroup violence in support of defending the honor of an in-group, such as one's family, tribe, clan, or nation.

Cultures that valorize male honor tend to have a specific kind of geography (e.g., dry plains more suited to grazing than to farming) that led to herding economies; see Vandello & Cohen, 2003). This includes many cultures in the Mediterranean (e.g., Spain, Greece, Italy) and the Middle East (e.g., among Arabs, such as the nomadic Bedouin). Further, cultures formed by immigrants from herder societies, such as Latin and South America, which were colonized by herders from the Iberian penninsula, tend to replicate culture of honor values. Within the United States, Nisbett (1993) notes that European immigrants to the southern United States during the 17th and 18th centuries came mainly from the borderlands of Scotland and Ireland. Unlike the Puritan farmers who settled in the North, Southerners were from herding societies with culture of honor values. Statistically controlling for a host of other variables associated with violence (e.g., poverty), men from the southern compared with the northern United States are more likely to commit violence (Nisbett, 1993). This difference is especially pronounced for violence in response to provocations that can be viewed as insults to a man's honor or property.

To investigate how culture of honor norms relate to reactive violence, Cohen, Nisbett, Bowdle, and Schwartz (1996) recruited as participants in a study male undergraduates who were raised in morthern versus southern states. Each participant was asked to carry a survey he had completed to a table at the end of a narrow hallway, which required him to squeeze by a male confederate. The confederate, apparently working at an open file cabinet, had to close the drawer and stand up against the cabinet to allow the participant to pass. When the participant made the return trek seconds later, the confederate slammed the file drawer shut, bumped the participant's shoulder, and said, "Asshole," before heading into a nearby room, locking the door behind him as a precautionary measure! Bystander confederates observed the participants' reactions (facial expressions and behavior) without knowing whether the participant was a Southerner or Northerner.

How did the male participants react to being insulted? The majority of northern men (67%) appeared to show more amusement than anger over the "asshole" incident. By contrast, the majority of southern men (85%) showed precisely the opposite pattern: more anger than amusement. One southern participant went so far as to not only go after the confederate but to rattle the knob of the locked door of the room to which he had retreated.

Such reactive aggression corresponds to a general cultural attitude that supports, even demands, male violence in response to insulted honor or threatened property as necessary to maintaining one's manhood. For instance, in Florida (and, increasingly, other southern states), a homeowner can legally kill a home intruder without having to prove that the intruder was an immediate threat. As one Florida man put it, "I have a right to keep my house safe." This man shot, but fortunately did not kill, an unarmed neighbor, who stopped by to argue about how many garbage bags city ordinances permitted at the curb. Although the neighbor merely made it to the doorstep and was shot not once but twice, because the incident occurred in the shooter's home, the neighbor was deemed an "intruder." The shooter escaped prosecution for what would, in all northern states, constitute attempted murder (Liptak, 2006). Similarly, until the 1970s, a man in Texas could legally defend his honor by shooting his wife's lover if he caught them having sex (Nisbett, 1993).

Polling data from the North and South (Cohen & Nisbett, 1994) reveal important differences in attitudes about male violence. Opposition to gun control is stronger in the South, where people typically view guns as necessary for self-protection. In response to hypothetical scenarios in which a man's honor is at stake (e.g., an insult about one's manliness), Southerners view violence as a more appropriate, even necessary, response. These attitudes extend beyond notions of the permissibility of particular forms of interpersonal violence to include honor-based intergroup violence. In particular, Southerners generally show stronger support for the idea of war in the service of defending national honor (Nisbett, 1993). Thus, at least some of the conservative southern "red state" versus liberal northern "blue state" divide in the United States relates to the South's greater endorsement of culture of honor norms.

Given that most people in the South are no longer herders, why do culture of honor norms persist? Even if obsolete, norms can become strongly embedded in a culture, passed along by socializing boys to live up to ideals dictating how to "be a man." For example, Southerners more commonly believe that a boy should handle bullying by fighting back (Nisbett, 1993). Further, cultural norms influence people's expectations about when violence is likely to or should occur. For example, when asked to estimate the likelihood that a typical man on their campus would react violently to another man's provocation (e.g., rudely cutting in line), men on a southern (vs. a northern) college campus estimated that their peers would be more likely to punch the other man (Vandello, Cohen, & Ransom, in press). Interestingly, men from both regions thought that their peers would react more violently than they themselves would. This was particularly true of southern men. Thus, culture of honor norms may be perpetuated by exaggerated expectations about male violence that, in turn, may pressure men to act aggressively even if they would not otherwise be inclined to do so.

Culture of honor norms bear a strong similarity to ambivalently sexist ideologies, especially benevolent sexism. Honor norms suggest that men fight, in part, to protect the honor of women, particularly their intimate partners or relatives. Women's honor is quite different than men's, requiring modesty and sexual purity, whereas men's honor requires independence and toughness (Vandello & Cohen, 2003). Thus, culture of honor norms appear to include benevolently sexist ideals of "pure," loyal women and of the heroic men who protect them. This includes protecting women not only from physical violence but from insults to their reputations and other men's sexual advances. For instance, most southern men asked to imagine one of their male friends making sexually suggestive comments to their girlfriend viewed this as an insult to honor that would justify a violent reaction (Cohen & Nisbett, 1994).

Although it may seem as though women benefit from such gallantry, we later show how culture of honor values increase aggression toward women in relationships by setting up benevolently sexist ideals that elicit punishment when women fail to meet them. In some cultures, these punishments include socially sanctioned murders, known as honor killings. These killings, perpetrated by husbands or other male family members, occur when a wife, sister, or daughter, has "stained" the men's honor (Baker, Gregware, & Cassidy, 1999; see later discussion).

In sum, the structure of a society's economy (herding as opposed to farming) can intensify sexist ideologies of male honor that demand physical toughness and aggression in response to perceived insults by other men. These norms echo prescriptive male ideals that are prevalent, albeit in less extreme forms, even in cultures that do not put a premium on male honor (Pleck, 1981; Pleck, Sonenstein, & Ku, 1993; see Chapter 5). Similar to evolutionary theory, the culture of honor approach suggests that competition for resources and men's desire to demonstrate control over their mates' sexuality can result in male–male aggression. Unlike evolutionary theory, however, the culture of honor approach emphasizes social structure and cultural ideology as sources of male aggression. Even if, as evolutionary theory posits, men are inherently prone to defend resources and mates aggressively, how readily such threats trigger aggression depends on social norms. Further, ideologies about gender and honor, although originally fostered by social structural conditions, can perpetuate themselves via socialization practices long after structural conditions change. Thus far, we have concentrated on how evolutionary and social structural theories explain male–male violence and merely hinted at how they address the violence that men commit toward women. We turn to this issue in the next section.

Violence in Relationships

We began this chapter noting that men both commit and are victimized by the most severe acts of violence at much higher rates than women. In daily life, women face a significantly lower risk for violence by strangers than men. Sexual violence—rape and sexual assault—represents the glaring exception, victimizing women at much greater rates than men. Regardless of the type of violence, however, threats to women most often come not from strangers but from men with whom they have close relationships, particularly romantic partners (although also, in honor cultures, male relatives). Even rape and sexual assault are perpetrated more frequently by male acquaintances and romantic partners than by strangers (Frieze, 2005). Thus, male aggression toward women generally occurs within sexual relationships or takes an explicitly sexual form. Further, even when violence toward women is not in itself a sexual assault, it may well stem from sex-related motives, such as jealousy. As with male–male aggression, we first consider evolutionary and then social structural explanations concerning the motives and circumstances that elicit relationship violence.

The Evolution of Male–Female Violence: Paternity, Fidelity, and Sexual Jealousy

Because women represent a sexual resource for men, evolutionary theory suggests that men should not typically seek to kill women; if men's motivation is to produce offspring, killing potential child bearers is (literally) counterproductive (Buss, 2005). Thus, the fact that male-initiated murder much more frequently targets men rather than women fits the evolutionary view. Evolutionary theory does not predict, however, that any and all male violence toward women will be inhibited, but rather that such violence will tend to stop short of murder.

The evolutionary view suggests that men's violence toward women occurs with the aim of controlling women's sexual behavior. More specifically, a man enhances his reproductive success not only by dominance over male competitors but also by his ability to ensure that he invests resources only in his own, and not other men's, offspring. Men's paternity uncertainty hypothetically created evolutionary pressures toward strong vigilance over mates' sexual fidelity and a related tendency to experience intense sexual jealousy when a female mate "strays" (Daly et al., 1982). The threat of violence represents one tool men use to ensure a mate's fidelity. Sexual jealousy, however, is an intense emotion that can create frustration-induced rage, resulting in severe violence toward female partners, including murder (Buss, 2005; Daly & Wilson, 1990).

By contrast, women have no uncertainty about the maternity of their children. This does not imply that women lack jealousy. Rather, because women rely on their mate's investment of resources in joint offspring, evolutionary theorists suggest that women evolved to experience jealousy at the prospect of a mate becoming emotionally invested in another woman (and her offspring), toward whom he might redirect his resources. Women may tolerate a male partner's sexual infidelity so long as they believe that there is little likelihood of an emotional investment in "the other woman" (Buss, 2005).

In short, evolutionary theorists argue that men evolved an obsessive concern with "mate guarding" to prevent male interlopers from having sex with their partners and to discourage their partners from choosing to have sex with other men. By contrast, this approach suggests that women experience relatively less concern about sexual infidelity by a male partner than emotional infidelity, which might lead the male partner to redirect his resources. In support of these differing motives, men report more distress than women in response to imagining sexual infidelity (one's romantic partner having sex with someone else but not being emotionally involved), whereas women report more distress than men when imagining emotional infidelity (one's romantic partner falling in love with someone else but not having had sex with the other person; Buunk, Angleitner, Oubaid, & Buss, 1996). These findings have been replicated by examining people's responses to actual incidents of infidelity in their past (Edlund, Heider, Scherer, Farc, & Sagarin, 2006).

Jealousy, of course, can, and all too often does, result in relationship violence enacted by both sexes. Serious violence, however, remains more the province of men, and, consistent with evolutionary theory, sexual jealousy is the most frequently reported motive for men who commit serious violence, such as murder, toward their female intimate partners (Wilson & Daly, 1996). Men who murder their spouses often have previously threatened their partners in an attempt to prevent infidelity or abandonment, suggesting an underlying motivation to control (Wilson & Daly, 1996). Less serious acts of male violence within relationships may reflect men's attempts to restrict their partner's autonomy, thereby lessening the possibility that she will find another partner or leave the relationship. Women, in turn, may stay in the relationship because they fear greater violence if they attempt to leave (Frieze, 2005).

In sum, the evolutionary approach suggests that paternity uncertainty led to evolved tendencies among men to seek control over female partners' sexual behavior and to experience strong sexual jealousy. These tendencies, in turn, can lead to violence toward female partners suspected of infidelity. By contrast, women are assumed to have evolved the tendency to experience jealousy when mates appear likely to invest resources elsewhere. Although evidence supports the predicted sex differences in what elicits jealousy, the issue is complicated by findings that are inconsistent with evolutionary theory's predictions (e.g., DeSteno, Bartlett, Braverman & Salovey, 2002; DeSteno, Valdesolo, & Bartlett, 2006; C. R. Harris, 2003). Moreover, sex differences in the causes of jealousy may have social origins as a by-product of patriarchy. When men monopolize resources, women become more dependent on men as providers, increasing women's motivation to maintain the flow of resources from male partners. An equally plausible social structural explanation, then, suggests that social circumstances create sex differences in jealousy by placing women in a position of dependence on their partner's resources. In the next section, we consider how social structural factors, such as patriarchy, can account for violence toward women.

Social Structural and Cultural Causes of Male–Female Violence

Although sexual jealousy represents an important cause of male violence toward women within close relationships, rates of relationship violence vary considerably across cultures (Archer, 2006), suggesting that social variables play an important role. In this section, we examine how social structural variables (e.g., the degree of gender hierarchy) and related ideologies (e.g., ambivalent sexism and culture of honor norms) affect the prevalence and forms of violence toward women. We expand here on the notion raised in Chapter 2 that sexist social structures and ideologies create a "protection racket," promising women that their male intimates will keep them safe from other men, but ultimately leaving women more vulnerable to violence within intimate relationships. If this is so, more gender-traditional, as opposed to egalitarian, societies ought to exhibit a higher rate of violence against women by male intimates.

Power Differences, Sexist Ideologies, and Relationship Violence

Cultural variations in rates of relationship violence by men toward women correlate strongly with sex differences in status and power (Archer, 2006; Vandello & Cohen, 2006; Yodanis, 2004). Societies where women generally have higher status, resources, and power also have lower rates of wife abuse. By contrast, in societies where women have low status, few resources, and little social power, women face a heightened risk of violence from their husbands. More specifically, using data from more than 50 nations, Archer (2006) found that women's self-reports of the degree of physical violence within their current relationship correlated –.69 with the United Nations' Gender Empowerment Measure (GEM), which assesses the degree to which women have obtained positions of high status, power, or authority within a nation. Thus, women's lack of power in a society predicts an increased likelihood of relationship violence (see also Vandello & Cohen, 2006).

As we showed in Chapter 2, women's lack of structural power in a society goes hand in hand with cultural values and ideologies that justify traditional gender roles. For instance, across national samples, the GEM is negatively correlated with both women's and men's endorsement of ambivalently sexist ideologies (Glick et al., 2000, 2004). Sexist ideologies, in turn, offer justifications for male violence toward female relationship partners who violate gender prescriptions, such as when a wife disobeys her husband or is suspected of infidelity. Recall that ambivalently sexist ideologies reflect a "carrot-and-stick" approach in which benevolent sexism promises protection for women who act in line with traditional ideals. Benevolent sexism itself may not directly support violence against women. For example, after statistically controlling for hostile sexism, benevolent sexism did not correlate with ideological support for wife abuse in a cross-cultural comparison of samples from Brazil and Turkey (Glick, Sakalli-Ugurlu, Ferreira, & de Souza, 2002). This suggests that benevolent sexism was neither protective nor harmful in itself. However, hostile sexism (which positively correlates with BS, predicted more tolerance of wife abuse (e.g., agreeing that "some women seem to ask for beatings from their husbands"). In short, the protection that benevolent sexism promises to women remains contingent: If they fail to fulfill prescriptive ideals of feminine modesty, loyalty, obedience, and fidelity, benevolent sexism gives way to hostile sexism.

Honor Killings

In some cultures, honor beliefs, which may represent an extreme version of ambivalent sexism, socially permit and encourage male violence toward female relationship partners, including murder. In cultures of honor, men's ability to maintain control over the women in their families, including sisters and daughters, affects their honor (Vandello & Cohen, 2003). Thus, a woman's sexual purity or fidelity determines not only her own honor but the honor of men in her family. For instance, Vandello and Cohen (2003) compared attitudes in Brazil, an honor culture, and among Northerners in the United States, who typically do not subscribe to honor beliefs. Brazilians, but not U.S. participants, perceived a husband less positively (e.g., less trustworthy and manly) if his wife was said to be unfaithful, suggesting that her infidelity ruined his honor. Further, if the man reacted to her infidelity by hitting his wife, Brazilians saw him as more manly than if he merely yelled at her (whereas U.S. participants saw it the other way around). For Brazilians, a wife's infidelity stained the man's honor, which was only reclaimed through violence toward her.

As we noted earlier, "honor" is an extremely gendered term: Men gain honor through autonomy and toughness (e.g., "I bow to no man"), whereas women gain honor through purity, self-sacrifice, and deference to their fathers, brothers, and husbands. In some cultures, women risk being killed for failing to live up to ideals of feminine purity, modesty, and deference (Baker et al., 1999; Vandello & Cohen, 2003). Honor killings are still socially approved in places such as rural Pakistan, Afghanistan, and Turkey (see Baker et al., 1999). They usually occur as a result of a perceived sexual impropriety, such as extramarital or premarital sex, which "stains" the honor of a woman's husband or family. The decision to kill is often made by a group of men within the family, who may appeal to local authorities for an official sentence of death. Honor killings are often carried out in especially brutal ways, including stoning or burning, and the men who commit them may face little risk of prosecution. Indeed, in some countries, honor killings are not simply tolerated but enforced by laws and carried out by legal authorities.

In such cultures, even the mere allegation of female sexual impropriety can damage male relatives' reputations. In cases of rape, women may be blamed for failing to protect their honor or as somehow having invited the attack. Women's disobedience also stains men's honor; fathers sometimes kill daughters who marry a man of their own, rather than their father's, choosing. Similarly, people view husbands as justified for killing a wife who seeks a divorce.

The gender-traditional cultures in which honor killings take place exhibit strong endorsement of benevolently sexist ideals (Glick et al., 2000, 2004), illustrating how benevolent sexism offers sharply limited and contingent protection. Women in cultures of honor must concede control of their lives, especially their sexuality, to men to secure or to "deserve" protection from male violence. Even then, the mere hint of sexual impropriety or defiance can elicit violence from male intimates. Finally, the protection offered to compliant women may be restricted only to those from the same social group (e.g., tribe, clan, ethnic or religious group). During intergroup conflict, mass rapes of women in enemy groups may occur. Wartime rape is discussed in more detail later.

Cultures that emphasize honor also tend to justify more mundane forms of male aggression to control women within relationships and also encourage women to endure such violence. For example, in one study by Vandello and Cohen (2003), both male and female participants individually witnessed an apparent confrontation between romantic partners. While the participant completed a questionnaire in a hallway and ostensibly waited for an "acquaintance study" to begin, a female confederate arrived with a male confederate, apparently her boyfriend. The female confederate told her boyfriend that, after completing the study, she had to go to "John's place to pick up a few things." The boyfriend grabbed her arm, dragged her down the hallway, and aggressively berated her about going to a former boyfriend's house. He demanded the car keys and forcibly took them from her hand. Finally, he shoved her against the wall when she tried to take the keys back and stalked off. Afterward, the female confederate sat down next to the participant, explaining, "That was my fiancé," followed by scripted self-blame and contrition ("I guess it was kind of my fault" and "He really cares about me.") or resistance ("I'm getting so damn tired of this" and "I should just give him his keys *and* his ring back").

Participants included individuals who were raised in the northern versus southern United States, as well as Hispanic participants (who, like Southerners, tend to endorse honor ideals). Participants rated the female confederate after she reacted to the male confederates' staged attempt to control her. Northerners reported liking the woman better when she reacted with defiance toward her fiancé. By contrast, Southern and Hispanic participants liked her better when she evinced contrition and loyalty to her fiancé. In fact, Southerners and Hispanics interpreted contrition and loyalty as a kind of strength (e.g., she put her relationship above herself), whereas Northerners saw this behavior as a sign of weakness (e.g., she is dependent). Further, when participants talked with the confederate, Southerners and Hispanics tended to advise her to tolerate her fiancé's behavior and stay in the relationship, whereas Northerners did not. Thus, culture of honor values not only provide ideological support for male aggression, but social approval for women who "stand by their man," remaining loyal and committed even in the face of violence.

In sum, when it comes to the most serious forms of aggression against women, the very cultures that promise women paternalistic protection (i.e., that most strongly endorse benevolent sexism and notions of defending women's "honor") promote aggression against women who stray from narrowly defined feminine ideals. In cultures of honor, benevolently sexist ideals trap women into a narrow range of behaviors, and those who do not comply can face severe and violent punishment. This illustrates how sexist ideologies, however sweet they may appear on the surface, reflect a system designed to control women. Socially shared notions of "honor" do not simply encourage, but demand, men's aggression in response to women's perceived indiscretions or disobedience.

Relationship Violence in More Egalitarian Cultures

In more egalitarian cultures, social norms that prohibit violence toward women and laws that treat relationship aggression as a serious social problem reduce violence within relationships. Rather than demanding violence toward disobedient women, egalitarian social norms discourage it. For example, a survey of Americans concerning the circumstances that justify hitting a wife or girlfriend revealed very low levels of approval for relationship violence (Simon, Anderson, Crosby, Shelley, & Sacks, 2001). Even in cases where the partner "hit first," fewer than 15% of respondents thought a man could justify hitting a female partner. The figure drops to less than 10% in matters relating to "disciplining" the partner to keep her in line. Interestingly, Americans find it more acceptable for a woman to hit back or otherwise use physical aggression against a male partner than the reverse. While even low levels of approval for relationship violence create problems, these figures stand in stark contrast to earlier findings in the United States, such as a 1970 survey in which 25% of men approved of a husband slapping a wife under some circumstances (Stark & McEvoy, 1970). This suggests significant changes in attitudes toward relationship violence during a period when American women gained more social power (e.g., by working outside the home) and the justice system began to more aggressively enact and enforce laws against domestic violence.

In addition to lower tolerance for male violence, considerably more gender symmetry in relationship violence exists in egalitarian societies, especially for the most common, milder forms of aggression. Gender symmetry (i.e., equal rates of violence by male and female partners) emerged as a finding in the 1980s when researchers began to use the Conflict Tactics Scale (CTS; Straus et al., 1980). The CTS is a self-report questionnaire that measures the frequency with which respondents perceive themselves and their partners to engage in various conflict tactics, including physical aggression of various levels of severity (e.g., slapping, throwing objects, pushing, punching, choking). Studies using the CTS find that both sexes frequently report using lesser forms of aggression (although not typically violence that could cause significant injury or death). In fact, when mundane forms of violence (e.g., pushing and throwing objects) occur in relationships, women tend to report using them more frequently than their male partners (Archer, 2006).

Keep in mind, however, that men remain more likely to commit serious relationship violence. Given that there is little social approval for such behavior within egalitarian societies, serious relationship violence may occur mainly among men who have an unusually aggressive personality. Studies show that men who engage in physical abuse tend to have a high need for power in combination with low verbal ability or expressiveness (Anderson & Umberson, 2001; Umberson, Anderson, Williams, & Chen, 2003). This suggests that abusive men want to control their partners and resort to violence because they do not have the communication skills to exert influence through nonviolent means. Other abusive men simply have chronically violent personalities, engaging in aggression in all aspects of their lives, both within and outside of their romantic relationships (Lawson et al., 2003; Stith & Hamby, 2002).

Overall, in nations where women have gained more social status, resources, and power, men less frequently resort to relationship violence. This probably occurs because of a lack of social and ideological support for violence against women as well as women's greater economic independence, which gives women more freedom to leave abusive partners. Furthermore, the feminist movement and women's political power have fostered organizations (e.g., women's shelters) and laws (e.g., domestic abuse laws) that help to prevent violence. This suggests that having a developed economy that gives women more opportunity to gain economic independence, status, and power can help to undermine the coercive violence that often pervades and controls the lives of women in less developed nations. Nonetheless, even within the most gender-egalitarian cultures, women remain in danger from romantic partners who still too often resort to violence in an effort to control them. However, when such violence is not socially sanctioned, severe abuse tends to be committed by only a minority of chronically violent men.

Sexual Violence: Sexual Assault and Rape

This section focuses on the most extreme form of sexual violence: rape (see Chapter 8 for information about sexual harassment). In addition to controversy over the causes of rape, theorists disagree even about how to define it. Some propose defining rape as unwanted sexual intercourse as a result of physical coercion or the overt threat of physical harm (e.g., Palmer, 1991); others include "psychological coercion," which can encompass feeling pressured to have sex without any explicit threat (Frieze, 2005).

Because of these varying definitions, both by researchers and participants, as well as a general reluctance to report rape, prevalence estimates of rape vary widely. For instance, in one study, fewer than half of the women who indicated that they had been coerced into specific sexual activities that met the researchers' definition of rape actually labeled the incident as "rape" (Fisher, Cullen, & Turner, 2000). Another complication is that women show particular reluctance to label coercive sex as rape when it occurs within a romantic relationship or marriage (Frieze, 1983). Thus, it is not surprising that estimates of the percentage of women who have been victims of rape range from 5% to 44% (see Frieze, 2005, for a review). As with other forms of violence toward women, women face greater risk of being raped by acquaintances and intimate partners than by strangers (Wilson & Leith, 2001), although the latter type of rape more often involves a weapon and results in additional injury (Rozee, 1999).

Despite the lower prevalence of stranger rapes, women particularly fear experiencing this type of assault (Hickman & Muehlenhard, 1997). This fear itself has extremely important implications illustrated by a simple exercise: Pause now and list the precautions you regularly take, or think about taking, to avoid being a victim of sexual violence. If you are male, your list is probably short or nonexistent (and perhaps even the request to make one was greeted with a guffaw). If you are female, however, the list is probably quite long. Women's fear of sexual assault represents a critical component of the protection racket that reinforces male dominance, driving women into the arms of male protectors to reduce their vulnerability to sexual assault by strangers. As with the other topics reviewed here, evolutionary and social structural explanations for rape and sexual assault illuminate the motivations and circumstances that increase or decrease the likelihood of these behaviors.

Evolutionary Explanations of Rape

A controversial view (Thornhill & Thornhill, 1983) holds that rape represents an adaptive male reproductive strategy, especially for men who otherwise fail to attract mates. Keep in mind that viewing rape as "adaptive" in no way implies a moral justification. Rather, this claim merely asserts that sexually coercive behavior yielded an increased number of offspring for men who engaged in it, either as a supplement to or a replacement for having a long-term mate. However, other evolutionary theorists (for a review, see Palmer, 1991) dispute the idea of rape as adaptive, noting that rape tends to result in offspring less frequently than consensual sex and that those offspring are less likely to be nurtured to adulthood, making them less likely to pass on the rapist's genes. Thus, other evolutionary theorists view rape and sexual coercion more as a by-product of evolved sex differences in sexuality. For instance, because of men's lower reproductive investment, evolutionary theory suggests that men evolved to be less choosy than women when selecting mating partners (especially short-term partners), have stronger sex drives, and generally be more aggressive (Palmer, 1991). These traits all make it more likely that men will seek to vigorously pursue sexual opportunities, engaging in assertive tactics that can easily shade over into coercion.

Certainly, rape is not some sort of biological imperative. At the same time, the extreme version of the cultural view of rape as unrelated to sexual motives, but only as a form of violence used to reinforce men's power, is equally untenable. Although it may be politically correct to view rape as being "all about power" and "having nothing to do with sex," this misses the point that rape combines power and sex motives. For example, rapists almost exclusively target women of reproductive age; women between the ages of 13 and 25 years are at greatest risk (Palmer, 1991). Further, men who become sexually aroused by violent pornography tend also to report having used coercion to obtain sex (Lohr, Adams, & Davis, 1997), and rapists self-report sexual motives for engaging in rape (Ellis, 1989). Finally, at least a subset of men who report using coercive strategies to obtain sex appear have unusually strong sex drives (Christopher & Sprecher, 2000).

In sum, although the idea of rape as adaptive creates controversy even among evolutionary theorists, evolved sex differences in both sexuality and aggressiveness may foster men's propensity to resort to coercive and aggressive tactics to obtain sex. However, although rape appears to occur in all societies, the rates of occurrence vary a great deal, indicating the importance of the social factors to which we now turn.

Social Structural Explanations for Rape

Like violence against women within romantic relationships (e.g., wife abuse), sexual assaults occur more frequently in cultures where women have lower status and power (Yodanis, 2004). This supports the notion that rape both reflects and maintains male dominance (Brownmiller, 1975). For instance, even within the United States, states where women have higher status (in terms of such factors as level of education and income) have a lower incidence of rape (Baron & Straus, 1989). Using cross-national comparisons involving 27 (mainly European) nations, ranging from Albania to the United Kingdom, Yodanis (2004) examined whether women had experienced sexual violence in the past 5 years, including such assaults as groping. National differences in women's likelihood of experiencing sexual assaults correlated with indicators of women's general educational and occupational attainment in their nation. Occupational attainment was a particularly strong predictor, with a –.83 correlation to sexual violence rates.

Although the Yodanis (2004) study did not specifically examine rape, it yielded results consistent with studies showing that rape occurs with greater frequency in cultures or areas where women have less power (Sanday, 1981; Whiley, 2001). Also, the Yodanis study is intriguing because women's fear of sexual violence was also assessed. Women were asked two questions about their fearfulness of going out after dark, which tends to be strongly associated with fear of stranger rape. In every nation, women expressed more fear than men, on average five times more. Furthermore, women's fearfulness was specifically predicted by their experiences with sexual violence and not by their experiences with nonsexual physical violence.

These data support the hypothesis that experiencing even mild forms of sexual violence, including being grabbed or groped, generates fear of rape among women. Such fear, in turn, may not only lead women to restrict their behavior but to seek male protectors and to endorse benevolently sexist beliefs. Indeed, American women expressed greater endorsement of benevolent sexism after they were told that a national survey revealed that men held relatively hostile views toward women (Fischer, 2006). This at least indirectly supports the protection racket hypothesis: When women generally fear men, they endorse paternalistic sexist ideologies that promise male protection in exchange for female compliance with traditional roles.

The fear of sexual violence helps to explain why, even though men face a much greater risk of violent assault or murder, women typically report more fear of being assaulted. The fear of stranger rape powerfully influences women's outlook, despite the reality that male acquaintances or intimates more frequently perpetrate sexual assaults. Rape, like terrorism, can affect people who have not been directly victimized. The fear of rape can alter women's attitudes and behaviors, coercing them into accepting ideologies that reinforce and elicit male paternalism in the hope of avoiding being the victim of male sexual aggression.

Although power differences on a societal level render women more vulnerable to rape, researchers have also found evidence that power and power-related motives directly predict individual men's propensity to commit sexual assaults. Dominant or powerful men are more likely to commit sexual assaults in the workplace (e.g., to sexually harass women; Rudman & Borgida, 1995) as well as within intimate relationships (Tang, 1999). Additionally, for some men, having power over a woman appears automatically to elicit sexual attraction and, in turn, to increase the likelihood of unwanted sexual attention (Bargh & Raymond, 1995). Thus, at both the macro (cultural) and micro (individual) levels, sexual violence relates to men's assertion of dominance.

Although gaining more power and status within society protects women to some extent, within specific social contexts, sexual assault can reflect men's attempt to resist changes in the balance of power and status. Recall from Chapter 8 that sexual harassment in the workplace occurs more frequently when women first begin to enter previously all-male domains. For instance, the women who first began working at the Eveleth Mines in northern Minnesota in the 1970s faced brutal harassment from male coworkers (Bingham & Gansler, 2002). More recently, when The Citadel, a private military academy, admitted women in the 1990s, allegations of widespread sexual assault followed. Based on the academy's own study, in 2005 about 20% of female cadets reported experiencing sexual assaults, even after a decade of female admissions (Smith, 2006). When women begin directly to compete with men in previously male domains, sexist men view these women as competitors who do not merit paternalistic protection (because benevolent sexism is contingent on women staying "in their place"). Instead, women who try to "act like men" can elicit a backlash designed to intimidate and push them out, often in the form of sexual assault. Keep in mind, however, that over the long run, increases in women's status and power as well as increasing numbers within a workplace reduce women's risk of sexual assault and harassment.

Wartime Rape

War dramatically increases the incidence of rape. Paternalistic protection does not seem to extend to women in occupied enemy territory. Accounts of mass rape of women in enemy groups appear in ancient texts, such as the Bible and *The Iliad*, as well as in modern reports

(Gottschall, 2004). Because wartime rapes remain largely unreported to authorities, the precise extent of occurrence is unknown, but estimates suggest a staggering increase in rape when armies invade. For instance, when the Soviets invaded Berlin at the end of World War II, estimates of the number of rapes that occurred range from 10,000 to hundreds of thousands (Brownmiller, 1975; Grossman, 1999).

Explanations for wartime rape include viewing it as a deliberate strategy to demoralize the enemy, "emasculating" men in the opposing group by demonstrating that they cannot protect their wives, sisters, and daughters (Gottschall, 2004). Wartime rape probably occurs as a result of a host of factors, including soldiers' habituation to violence, a transfer of physiological arousal (even fear can increase sexual arousal; Dutton & Aron, 1974), and the tendency to view members of enemy groups as not warranting the human rights accorded to members of one's own group or nationality. Finally, in a war zone or occupied country, perpetrators face little risk of punishment, freeing soldiers to act on impulse.

In sum, one type of violence committed by men almost exclusively targets women: sexual assault. This form of attack represents a volatile mix of sex and power motives. Women face much greater risk of sexualized violence in cultures where power and status differences between the sexes most favor men. Despite women's generally stronger fear of potential rape by a stranger, however, most sexual violence is committed by acquaintances or intimates, except during wartime when women in occupied territories are often treated as spoils of war.

Chapter Summary

This chapter reviewed the causes of male–male violence and violence in relationships. Men commit violence at much higher rates than women, although this sex difference is less pronounced for milder forms of relationship violence, at least in more egalitarian nations. When it comes to the most brutal violence, however, men remain the most frequent perpetrators. Both evolutionary and social structural explanations offer insight into why men are more frequent victims as well as perpetrators of nonsexual violence. Both approaches suggest that male–male violence occurs as a result of competition for resources, status, and power at an individual and a group level (e.g., between men from different tribes, ethnicities, and cultures). Women, to some extent, remain protected from nonsexual violence, remaining on the sidelines and traditionally representing one of the prizes to be "won" by men who dominate other men.

Women are more likely to be victims of serious male violence within close relationships. Additionally, sexual violence, whether committed by strangers or intimates, predominantly victimizes women. Evolutionary theorists attribute men's propensity toward sexual violence to evolved sex differences in sexuality and aggressiveness. By contrast, social structural theorists emphasize how men's social power increases the likelihood of sexual violence. At both societal and individual levels, when women lack power and status, they experience a greater likelihood of being victimized by sexual assault; wartime rape is an extreme example. Although sexual assault can occur as part of a backlash against female vanguards who challenge male power or who enter previously male domains, women become less vulnerable as they gain more power and better representation in specific domains (e.g., formerly male-dominated workplaces). The fear of sexual assault, however, remains a strong impediment to women's quest for equality, leading many women to restrict their independence and embrace the protective promises of benevolent sexism to avoid being victims of sexual violence. Ironically and tragically, this strategy ultimately leaves women vulnerable to violence within relationships from the very men they have chosen to protect them.

CHAPTER 12

Progress, Pitfalls, and Remedies

The object of this Essay is to explain as clearly as I am able, grounds of an opinion that I have held from the very earliest period... That the principle which regulates the existing social relations between the two sexes—the legal subordination of one sex to the other—is wrong in itself, and now one of the chief hindrances to human improvement; and that it ought to be replaced by a principle of perfect equality, admitting no power or privilege on the one side, nor disability on the other.

—JOHN STUART MILL (1869/1975)

Writing in the 19th century, John Stuart Mill professed the radical view for his time that the subjugation of women was morally wrong. He further argued that although there were compelling arguments against oppressing women, the crux of the problem lay in the consensus that men's dominance was legitimate. At the beginning of the 21st century, Mill's opinion is no longer antithetical to the popular view. Toiling against institutions and customs that were deeply rooted in sexism, women have managed to doggedly but peaceably revolutionize gender relations.

Is the "gender revolution" soon to be complete in the industrialized world, with women achieving complete parity with men on indicators

285

of power and social influence? Or has the revolution stalled, reached its limits, or begun to backslide? We suggested in Chapter 1 that, given the many contradictions in contemporary gender relations, an astute observer could just as easily construct a convincing case for either side in this debate. The chapters that followed presumably provided a great deal of fodder for both points of view in that each chapter examined both changes to and continuities in traditional gender relations.

In the current chapter, we review arguments focusing on the United States (and, by extension, other highly developed Western nations that are similarly situated) concerning whether complete gender equality is just on the horizon or whether serious obstacles will sharply limit further progress. In short, we attempt to pull together what we have covered in the preceding chapters to suggest which direction the future might take and why. However, prognosticating about the future is a notoriously dicey business, as anyone who has seen old exhibits that predicted the "World of Tomorrow" (i.e., today) with stunning inaccuracy. Thus, while we lay out the arguments about where the future might take gender relations and provide our best guesses, we offer no firm conclusions about which paths are most likely. We will, however, end this chapter (and therefore the book) with suggestions about interventions—by individuals, schools, business organizations, and government—that can influence which paths might be taken and how rapidly further change may occur.

The "Progress Is Inevitable" View

The Women's Movement has been dubbed "the only successful revolution of the twentieth century" (Denby, 1996, p. 392). In many ways, this seems true. Compared with other subordinated or stigmatized groups (e.g., African Americans, homosexuals), women (particularly White women) have made remarkable progress. For example, nearly 50% of today's medical and law school graduates are female, and 40% of MBA degrees are granted to women, placing many more qualified women in the "pipeline" for elite jobs (Ely & Meyerson, 2000).

Gender Inequality Is "Fated to End"

Some authors suggest that complete gender equality is on the cusp of being achieved, predicting that it will emerge within the next two to five generations. Most prominently, the sociologist Robert Max Jackson

(2006) confidently asserts that gender inequality, at least in industrialized nations such as the United States, is "fated to end" (p. 240). In his view, a number of potent social and economic forces are pushing inevitably in this direction. While acknowledging that progress has not always been smooth, Jackson argues that when one examines the progress that has been made over the past 200 years, a steady march toward gender equality is abundantly clear.

Specifically, the historical trend over the past two centuries has been consistently in the direction of increased equality on a host of important dimensions that are summarized in Table 12.1, taken from Jackson (2006). Consider the changes in the treatment of women in the United States over the past 200 years. Women were only granted legal rights to control their own income and property in the 19th century, leading to formal political equality in terms of the right to vote in the early 20th century and then to legislation designed to protect their equal rights in education and the workplace in the late 20th century. On the family front, women could not initiate divorce except in extraordinary circumstances in the 19th century, were increasingly allowed to do so (although with difficulty) in the early 20th century, and since the late 20th century have been completely free to divorce without having to prove maltreatment by their husbands or suffer the social stigma that used to attach to "divorcees." On the education and job front, almost no women were admitted to universities or allowed into high-status professions in the 19th century, then women gained increasing access to college (but rarely professional schools) and to limited professions in the early 20th century, and women are now earning graduate degrees at rates comparable to those of men as well as entering many previously male professional fields. Jackson argues that there is little reason to suspect that this large-scale trend will fail to continue or reverse.

Jackson (2006) also argues that trends toward gender equality are driven by larger social and economic forces that render opposition to gender equality less prevalent and less effective. Chief among these are "structural changes intrinsic to modern society [that] have transformed interests and redistributed social power in ways such that people and organizations pursuing their own individual interests and adapting to ordinary circumstances increasingly choose strategies inconsistent with the preservation of gender inequality" (p. 225). For example, the modern business environment exerts pressures on firms not to discriminate against women. Hypothetically, if Firm A offers women lower wages, then Firm B will hire their most talented women away, theoretically putting Firm A at a competitive disadvantage and making it more likely to

TABLE 12.1. Women's Changing Status in American Society

	19th century	Late-19th to mid-20th century	Mid-20th century to present	Future changes needed for equality
Legal and political status	Formal legal equality instituted	Formal political equality instituted	Formal economic equality instituted	Equity in high political offices
Economic opportunity	Working-class jobs appear for single women only	Some jobs for married women and for educated women	All kinds of jobs available to all kinds of women	Equity in male-dominated fields and high-status jobs
Higher education	A few women enter public universities and new women's colleges	Increasing college; little graduate or professional	Full access at all levels	Equal presence in prestigious fields
Divorce	Almost none; made available for dire circumstances	Increasingly available but difficult	Freely available and accepted	Equity after divorce
Sexuality and reproductive control	Repressive sexuality; little reproductive control	Positive sexuality but double standard; increasing reproductive control	High sexual freedom and reproductive control	End sexual harassment and threat of rape
Cultural image	Virtuous domesticity and subordination	Educated motherhood; capable for employment and public service	Careers, marital equality	End perception of sexes as inherently different

Note. From Jackson (2006). Copyright 2006 by Russell Sage Foundation. Reprinted by permission.

go out of business. A free labor market coupled with meritocratic individualism means that discrimination is bad for business. In other words, in Jackson's view, the United States and other industrialized nations are committed to the notion that society should be a meritocracy where individual talent, not group membership, matters.

Thus, Jackson argues that the many social changes toward greater gender quality have been inexorably driven by modern changes in how economies work and society is structured. Because these forces remain in place and, if anything, may be accelerating, the trend toward gender equality should continue. And as women increasingly inhabit high-status roles in business, government, and other organizations, the stereotype of women as less agentic than men should lessen (recall the dynamic stereotype work by Diekman & Eagly, 2000, reviewed in Chapter 5).

Relatedly, Eagly and Carli (2007) argue that modern business practices have fostered demand for a less autocratic, more participative style of leadership that is favorable to women. They note that the social consensus (e.g., in business organizations) concerning which qualities are required for leadership has changed as a result of a modern environment that requires more adaptable organizations in which individuals are inspired by their leaders rather that merely told what to do. As described in Chapter 8, inclusiveness and mentoring are the qualities that women have long been socialized to have; not only do they foster employee morale, but hiring female leaders (e.g., executives and board members) is related to increased profit margins for business organizations. As a result, women should be able to make use of these skills to increase their chances of rising through the ranks in contemporary organizations.

Greater Equality in Intimate Heterosexual Relationships

Changes in the public sphere (e.g., how modern economies and business work) have also been part of the engine driving change in the private sphere of marriage. For instance, as the need for two salaries has provided greater incentive for married women to move into (or stay in) the workforce, even after having children, social attitudes have increasingly accommodated this change. With women accounting for nearly 60% of the labor market, the career woman with a family is no longer an anomaly. Further, as women have gained increasing economic independence and clout, they have correspondingly gained more power within marriage. Gender equality in the public sphere creates more favorable conditions for women in the private realm of heterosexual relationships. For instance, recall that in nations where women are better represented in high-power public roles (e.g., in business, government), they are also less likely to be victims of domestic abuse (see Chapter 11).

Although there is still evidence of a great deal of ambivalence about women's sexuality in contemporary society, attitudes have come a long way since the days when women were punished for having sex out of wedlock and wives were expected to merely tolerate, but not to enjoy, sex. There is an increased emphasis on educating women about their bodies, acknowledgment of women's sexual needs, a wealth of books and Internet sites that specialize in discussing previously taboo topics about female sexuality, and an increased interest among men in learning how to please their partners (Hite, 2006; Kerner, 2004; Douglass & Douglass, 1997).

Additionally, although our focus in this book has been on heterosexual relations, sexism and heterosexism go hand in hand (Pharr, 1988). Thus, another barometer of increasingly favorable attitudes toward gender equality is the greater social acceptance of homosexuality. Despite recent referenda against civil unions or gay marriage in many states, the overall trend is for increasing acceptance of homosexuals, especially among younger people, suggesting a continuing trend toward less stigmatization (Herek, 2002). Acceptance of homosexuals signals greater tolerance for behavior that deviates from traditional gender prescriptions. As we discussed in Chapter 7, people avoid violating gender prescriptions partly because they fear being labeled as homosexual. Although this is particularly true for men, recall that "lesbian-bating" haunts powerful women and has diminished heterosexual women's interest in feminism. To the extent that lesbians and gays are no longer stigmatized, everyone's fear of behaving "out of line" with gender prescriptions should be lessened, which is further good news for gender vanguards.

Men Benefit from Advocating for Increasing Gender Equality

The struggle for African Americans' civil rights greatly depended on Whites' support. Similarly, the successful protection and enlargement of women's rights is greatly accelerated if men are also on board or, at the very least, do not constantly throw obstacles in women's path, as has often been the case in the past. For example, opponents of women's suffrage predicted dire consequences should women be allowed to vote. In 1914, the Nebraska Men's Association Opposed to Woman Suffrage issued a statement warning that "if woman suffrage should become universal ... this country would be in danger of ... insurrections." Of course, women got the vote and the predicted insurrections never happened. Because changes toward equality continue to occur without the social world collapsing, men have become more likely to accept gender equality. Although men in the United States continue to show significantly more gender-traditional attitudes than women, data from the 1970s onward show that they also have become less sexist over time (e.g., Twenge, 1997a).

Further, women have an advantage in leveraging social change that other subordinated groups do not: highly intimate interdependence with the dominant group. As a result, not only are women in a better position to influence men, but heterosexual interdependence gives men some important incentives to support gender equality. For instance, many men count on the income that an employed wife adds to their marital assets, allowing the couple to be more financially secure. It also seems likely that as men are increasingly raised by mothers who had careers, are married to women with careers, and raise their daughters expecting them to have careers, they will be more likely to identify with women's concerns about discrimination at work. Thus, men are likely to become more sensitized to both the costs and the subtleties of sex discrimination (e.g., as their wives relate their experiences at work over the dinner table), becoming more supportive of working women's rights as they witness firsthand the emotional and financial costs of discrimination. In short, because individual men's interests are intertwined with the interests of their female romantic partners and other women to whom they are close, intimate heterosexual interdependence should propel an increase in male support for gender equality.

Similarly, because gender equity issues are human equity issues, especially when it comes to the balance between work and family, men may realize that they stand to gain from female-friendly changes in how work is structured. For example, consider the Family and Medical Leave Act (FMLA) of 1993, which requires employers to provide time off for parents of newborns or when they need to act as caretakers for an ill family member (child, spouse, or parent). This legislation came about because of women's participation in the workforce; as many families adjusted to not having a full-time caretaker to handle these duties on her own, there has been increasing political pressure for workplaces to accommodate family needs. Thus, the influx of women into the workforce is changing corporations' old assumptions that (previously mostly male) employees would always put business first and family second.

Thus, the FMLA benefits men, enabling them to be better fathers and to respond to family emergencies. It also provides legal recourse when employers discriminate against male as well as female caretakers. For example, consider the case of former Maryland State Trooper Kevin Knussman. As a White male, church-going Baptist, and conservative Republican, he does not fit the stereotype of someone who would lodge a sex discrimination suit, but he did, and he won. Knussman sought the leave to which he was entitled under FMLA when his wife had life-threatening complications during a pregnancy. He was denied by a personnel manager, who said, "Unless your wife is in a coma or dead, you can't be the primary caregiver" (Press, 2007, p. 39). Thus, the FMLA, as the name of the act implies, is not merely a woman's issue but a family, and therefore a man's, issue.

Further, many men may welcome changes in the workplace that promise a more balanced and personally satisfying way of life than the traditional male role of "working like a dog" to support a family while seldom getting a chance to enjoy family life. For example, *The Wall Street Journal* (Lattman, 2007) reported on a new organization (Law Students Building a Better Legal Profession) founded by Stanford University law students that aims to create a better work–life balance by protesting the 90 hour-plus work week that high-powered law firms typically demand. These future lawyers are explicitly willing to trade off salary for a career that does not preclude having a personal life. With support from 125 classmates at the top law schools in the nation, the organization e-mailed partners and recruiters at the top 100 law firms, urging them to reform their practices. The founders of this student organization are both men. The long working hours demanded in some high-powered jobs (most prominently the legal and medical professions) have been a deterrent to many women, who worry that pursuing such a career may prohibit them from having children during their prime child-bearing years. It is worth noting that at least some men now also view these work demands not only as unattractive but potentially open to reform. If they succeed, they not only will strike a blow for a happier work–life balance but also will indirectly promote gender equality in their profession.

A better balance between work and family life would allow men to reap the benefits of more time with their children. Although stereotypes of women's maternal instincts suggest that they experience greater attachment to their children, most fathers also experience strong attachment to their newborns (Bader, 1995). Fathers are often just as invested in child rearing as mothers (Renshaw, 2005) but are pressured not to take time away from work for parenting. That the FMLA is designed to apply equally to fathers and mothers promises some remedy. However, many current laws presume traditional roles, giving mothers greater rights (e.g., in child custody cases; Carbone, 2000; Mendelson, 1997). Greater gender equality should also entail reforms that grant more parental rights to fathers.

In sum, a number of factors, ranging from the structure and dynamism of the modern economy to the benefits that increasing equality has not just for women but also for men suggest a continued march toward gender equality. The arguments outlined thus far highlight powerful forces for continued change. At the same time, other authors have suggested that there are significant counterforces that these arguments fail to address that will retard the pace of progress unless continuing collective efforts promote an egalitarian future. We review these arguments in the next section.

Continuing Counterforces to Gender Equality

On some fronts, changes in gender relations have been sluggish (Valian, 1999) and, despite Jackson's linear argument (see Table 12.1), do not fit a narrative of steady progress because each advance elicits a counterreaction of backlash (Faludi, 1991). In this view, American women have been through revolutions before, but the more things change, the more they stay the same. For instance, the dramatic advances women experienced in the early 20th century—the right to vote, opportunities to work in male-dominated jobs during World War II, and relaxed sexual double standards during the Roaring Twenties—seemed to dissipate in the 1950s and early 1960s. Can we trust, then, that later advances will "stick"? In some ways, everything old seems new again as gender issues once believed to be settled crop up in new forms in fierce social debates, including recent claims that women's careers harm their families, when the scientific evidence supports the many benefits that work has for women and for their families (see Chapter 8). Additionally, although women have flooded into the paid workforce, there is still considerable gender segregation in the workplace, and women remain underrepresented in the occupations that confer the highest financial and social rewards (Catalyst, 2006; England, 2006). Further, women continue to carry the bulk of family responsibilities even if they work full time (see Chapter 8).

Although the optimistic view discussed previously dismisses these concerns as a myopia that fails to see the bigger trends, there is evidence not only that progress has been uneven, but that there are subtle and insidious counterforces to progress that remain quite strong in their effects. While acknowledging past progress toward equality, Ridgeway (2006) argues that gender is too deeply embedded as an "organizing principle" of social interaction for continued change toward full equality to be considered inevitable. She suggests that powerful social forces continue to preserve inequality, although in a reduced form compared with the past, and claims that Jackson's (2006) optimistic view ignores the power of stereotypes, gender biases, and status differences to retard further progress.

We have stressed here that stereotypical beliefs about gender are highly essentialistic (i.e., they presume that men and women innately differ). These notions are not vanquished and continue to provide popular justifications for gender inequality. When people believe that sex differences are caused by immutable forces, they are more likely to use gender stereotypes as a guide for their own actions (Dar-Nimrod & Heine, 2006; Prentice & Miller, 2006) as well as when they interpret other people's behavior (Hegarty & Pratto, 2004). In addition to these continuing beliefs, there are important remaining structural impediments to further progress in gender equality, reviewed next.

Occupational Segregation Remains High

England (2006) notes that although many women have moved into previously male white-collar professions (e.g., law, medicine) and lower to middle levels of management in large numbers, gender segregation strongly persists among blue-collar jobs. Similarly, jobs associated with caretaking (e.g., child care, nursing) are still female domains with very few men. Recall that predominantly female occupations are stereotyped as requiring feminine traits, such as nurturance and warmth, whereas male-dominated occupations are associated with masculine traits (Cejka & Eagly, 1999). Thus, to the extent that sex segregation in the job market remains strong, it acts to reinforce traditional stereotypes.

As England (2006) points out, men do not generally seem to want to pour into traditionally feminine jobs. This probably represents a combination of low pay and prestige in these jobs plus the derision that men expect if they violate the masculine role (e.g., by going into nursing or day care as a career). You are not likely to run into a male maid cleaning your hotel room anytime soon. Thus, although women have been fairly successful at moving into more prestigious, formerly all-male, white-collar jobs, there is much less progress in large segments of the job market. As a result, whereas upper-class women are likely to be viewed as increasingly agentic (taking on the stereotypically masculine traits of high-powered roles), women who are less well situated may be more likely to be stuck in the rut of being perceived in line with traditional gender stereotypes.

Stereotypes, Positive Prescriptions, and Backlash Continue to Retard Progress

As we have emphasized throughout this book, gender schemas and stereotypes are pervasive, acting like an invisible force field that shapes people's own behaviors, as well as their interpretations of others' behavior, in myriad ways. Like a cultural virus, stereotypes pressure people to act in ways that perpetuate the disease. Social pressures to "perform gender" remain strong, and just as strong are inner voices that echo the cultural message. The result is a slow pace of change. On the one hand, gender stereotypes are changing, with the movement of women into the workplace affecting female stereotypes more so than male stereotypes (Diekman & Eagly, 2000). On the other hand, gender prescriptions regarding the ideal woman and man continue to reflect their traditional social roles as primary caretaker and provider, respectively (Prentice & Carranza, 2002).

More specifically, although women are no longer encouraged to downplay their intelligence, we have noted that prescriptions for feminine sensitivity, modesty, and warmth remain in force (see Chapter 5). There is likely to be little pressure for social change on this dimension because niceness is a favorable prescription that does not overtly resemble "sexism" in most people's eyes. Although we are not arguing that women need to be "colder," the niceness prescription handicaps women as they compete with men in the workplace. The problem is that holding women to a higher (and, perhaps more importantly, men to a lower) standard of niceness prevents women from promoting themselves effectively, exercising authority in a directive fashion, or criticizing subordinates without paying the high price of social rejection that can lead to negative performance evaluations and hiring discrimination (see Chapter 8). Moreover, behaviors that are linked to status enhancement and dominance (e.g., taking control and arrogance) are highly proscribed for women while tolerated for men (Prentice & Carranza, 2002). Thus, women are still hampered when it comes to achieving powerful positions or leadership roles.

Indeed, the strongest backlash effects seem to be directed at powerful women (see Chapter 7). As we write this chapter, Senator Hillary Clinton is the first competitive female presidential candidate in U.S. history, and polling suggests that a majority of Americans believe a woman would be as good at the job as a man (Marshall, 2005). At the same time, there are rumors that Senator Clinton is sexually frigid and a likely lesbian (e.g., Klein, 2005). An Internet search for images of powerful

women (such as Madeline Albright, Hillary Clinton, and Condoleezza
Rice) reveals many that caricature them as monsters or demean them
through what has been colorfully dubbed "political pornography," sexualized images in which a powerful woman is shown getting her "come-
uppance" (Remnick, 2005, p. 30). As noted in Chapter 9, women who
challenge male dominance risk being subjected to ridicule designed to
question their suitability as romantic partners for men.

In general, media portrayals rarely seem to show women successfully wielding power. On the contrary, powerful women are often portrayed as cold, neurotic, psychologically imbalanced, or dangerous.
Consider Meryl Streep in *The Devil Wears Prada* (a cold, manipulative
tycoon whose husband divorces her), Glenn Close in *Damages* (a fierce
and ruthless litigator who terrorizes her associates), or Calista Flock-
hart in *Ally McBeal* (a neurotic Boston lawyer subject to hallucinatory
fits). The brilliant police detective Helen Mirren portrayed in *Prime
Suspect* seemed a promising exception, but she ultimately descended
into alcoholism. The tendency to dramatize powerful women as
manipulative schemers helps to explain why women who are merely
described as successful leaders are often perceived (without cause) to
be hostile, cold, and socially unskilled (Heilman et al., 1995; 2004;
Phelan et al., 2007). Such hostile images of powerful women seem to
be more common than more positive portrayals, such as the intelligent
women featured in *The West Wing* or HBO's film *Iron Jawed Angels*,
which focused on the activists who struggled to win suffrage for American women.

Benevolent Sexism and Paternalism

The negative effects of prescriptions for feminine niceness are related
to a broader problem that has only recently been named and studied:
benevolent sexism (Glick & Fiske, 1996). Benevolent sexism is a subtle
but important impediment to continuing gender inequality that is part
of a system that rewards women for remaining in traditional roles and
punishes them (with hostile sexism) if they stray from those roles (Glick
et al., 1997). Benevolent sexism is the ideological representation of
paternalism. The behavioral manifestations of paternalism, such as the
tendency to allocate greater praise but fewer tangible rewards to women
compared with men (Vescio et al., 2005), represent a previously ignored
form of discrimination. Both the ideological and behavioral manifestations of paternalism are likely to prove difficult to combat because
they are associated with subjectively positive emotions and actions. It

may seem trivial to some when a boss calls a subordinate "sweetie" but perhaps not to the woman who realizes that she is being subtly (even if unintentionally) demeaned and dismissed.

Legal remedies for paternalistic behavior seem unlikely. Imagine trying to pursue a lawsuit because your boss called you by affectionate pet names. Unless this was accompanied by overt sexual harassment, no lawyer would take the case. Further, because many women welcome benevolently sexist behavior from men, it will be particularly difficult to motivate collective action to oppose it. In the short run, individual women can benefit by deliberately eliciting benevolently sexist behavior from men. To take some mundane examples, a woman who insists that a date open doors for her and pay for dinner or feigns hysteria to get a man to catch a mouse may get what she wants in the immediate situation. Unfortunately, however, she has also reinforced gender stereotypes and paternalistic condescension.

Romantic Relationships and Family

We have argued (in Chapter 9) that traditional ideologies about heterosexual romance are intertwined with benevolent sexism. Thus, to the extent that people enact these traditional scripts in their romantic lives, they also reinforce paternalistic assumptions. Again, we are not criticizing romantic love itself but rather are pointing out the ways in which cultural scripts about romantic love can reinforce traditional gender roles and ideologies that work against female independence. These traditional love roles emphasize men as active and women as passive. To question these love roles is taken by many people as an attack on love itself.

As Firestone (1970) noted, "The panic felt at any threat to love is a good clue to its political significance. Women and love are underpinnings. Threaten them and you threaten the very structures of culture" (p. 21). Popular programs and films targeting women seem to be laced with an undercurrent of fear that women's independence will result in losing men's love (e.g., *Sex in the City, Bridget Jones' Diary*). To step out of line is to risk ending up single and alone. It is as though scriptwriters have inhaled *Newsweek*'s fabrication that a woman unmarried by age 35 has a greater chance of being killed by a terrorist than finding a husband (see Chapter 8).

Traditional romantic ideologies imply that women must choose between success in their public lives or romantic fulfillment in their private lives (i.e., that they must sacrifice ambition in order to be loved).

Socializing women to believe that their basic function is to be loving and nurturing while men are free to pursue power in all its guises relegates women to low-status roles and leaves them outside of the primary spheres of influence and power. This is not to suggest that loving and nurturing are wrong, but only to ask why women are expected to do the lion's share of it. But questioning this arrangement invites hostility from traditionalists because the alternative—viewing women as persons in their own right—would require that men equally shoulder the burden of caring for others and afford women an equal voice in governing their private and public worlds.

The optimistic view that complete gender inequality is inevitable misses the point that many women find traditional roles attractive in romantic and family relationships. Traditional romantic ideology puts an acceptable shine on male dominance by casting it as something that benefits women: They are loved and protected by their knights in shining armor. And just as changes in public sphere drive changes in the private sphere, the reverse also occurs. Women still do often sacrifice careers (or at least the fast track) for romance and family, much more than men do. Recall also that socializing women to expect that "one day their prince will come" creates implicit beliefs that are associated with power avoidance, such as choosing less lucrative careers and eschewing leadership roles (Rudman & Heppen, 2003). Women are also still subtly socialized to put more emphasis on family than career. Even female college students aiming for careers automatically implicitly identify with motherhood more than education (Devos, Diaz, Viera, & Dunn, 2007). When explicitly asked which was more important to them, these women adamantly claimed it was education. But when their responses were less controlled, they leaned toward the maternal role. This suggests that cultural notions of what women are "best suited for" permeate deeply into women's identities, despite their explicit goals.

Further, England (2006) argues that Jackson's (2006) optimistic argument does not give enough weight to the influence of gender roles at home. She notes that while women have made tremendous gains in the workplace, on the home front women still do most of the domestic and caregiving labor (see Chapter 8). This not only diminishes the time women have for their careers or themselves but feeds into the continuation of core aspects of traditional stereotypes. Although perceptions of women's agency may increase as they move into previously male work roles, stereotypes that women are warmer and more nurturing are likely to remain (Diekman & Eagly, 2000). Because these stereotypes are associated with family roles and values, they are also likely to remain prescriptive.

Complacency and Antifeminism

One danger of the optimistic argument that full gender equality is "fated" to come about is that this view could breed complacency and a lack of action. To be fair, Jackson (2006), who presents the most optimistic view of gender equality's inevitability, still explicitly assumes that part of the reason this will occur is due to women's continuing efforts to resist any form of oppression. Also, as we have discussed, there are a multitude of factors that Jackson's argument either dismisses or misses that may well retard further progress unless people act diligently to overcome them. Complete equality is not likely to occur if people fail to act because they believe that progress will take care of itself or that gender equality has already been fully achieved.

Although most college-age adults support the goal of gender equality, we have pointed out that young women and men tend to dissociate from feminists, the pioneering champions of this cause. Recall that (in Chapter 9) we reviewed research showing that people see feminism as a threat to romantic love and the province of "man-hating lesbians" despite evidence that feminist attitudes appear to promote healthier and more satisfying heterosexual relationships (Rudman & Phelan, 2007). Additionally, some authors have suggested that we are now in a "postfeminism" era, in which women's interest in collective power has been replaced by an interest in self-empowerment (Riger, 1993; Zucker, 2004). For example, some women are hostile toward feminism because they view it as a movement for victims or for women who cannot achieve success based on their own merit (Rich, 2005). Others have suggested that feminism is now subsumed in the language of choice, such that women can be either vanguards or traditionalists; as long as they choose their life's path, it counts as feminist (Hirschman, 2006; Taylor, 1992), a view that may mask the subtle forces that reward women for choosing to limit their public lives. Thus, many women appear to believe that the problem of inequality has been solved, that they can best advance on their own steam, or that activism on behalf of further change will harm their relationships with men. These beliefs inhibit women from taking collective action, reducing the likelihood of future progress, and perhaps even threatening the erosion of gains that have already been made.

Fortunately, the perceived conflict between obtaining personal fulfillment and taking collective action to promote gender equality is illusory. Greater equality generally benefits heterosexual relationships for both partners (Rudman & Phelan, 2007). By exercising their collective power, women have also increased their personal power, both in the public and private realms of work and relationships. For the Women's Movement to continue to exert influence, however, it will need to counter the erroneous perception that feminism harms heterosexual relationships. As Naomi Wolfe puts it, "You are not sleeping with the enemy if he is not your enemy."

Because further progress toward gender equality will depend on individuals and organizations actively pursuing it, the next section considers interventions that are likely to help. We focus, in particular, on steps that can be taken within organizations (e.g., businesses, schools), by individuals, and by the government (e.g., through legislation and the legal system).

Remedies

The price of liberty is eternal vigilance.
—THOMAS JEFFERSON

I believe eternal vigilance can be institutionalized.
—RALPH NADER

Organizational Solutions

The ranks of professional women in America grow annually, but their presence in the upper echelons of power remains scant (see Chapter 8). With 63 million women working in the United States, why have so few managed to break through to the top? We have argued that contributing factors include sexist hostility toward powerful women and benevolence toward traditionalists. In addition, many more women than men are expected to downsize their ambitions to afford more time with their families. How might these problems be addressed?

One solution is for businesses and organizations to provide women and men with greater flexibility in the workplace to alleviate problems related to work–family balance. Some corporations already serve as exemplary role models in this regard (e.g., Hewlitt-Packard, IBM, and JPMorgan Chase; see Archambeau, 2006), but many have not yet established family-friendly norms. Studies show that companies perceived as progressive and gender fair benefit from having more satisfied and productive employees (Grover & Crooker, 1995; Kinicki, Carson, & Bohlander, 1992; Koys, 1991). When the Johns Hopkins School of Medicine revised its meeting schedule to better accommodate women (so that meetings were no longer scheduled in the evenings or on weekends), both men and women responded favorably (Fried et al., 1996). Worker satisfaction and productivity gains aside, institutions have an obligation to humanize their policies, to send the message that all employees have personal and family lives that require reasonable accommodation.

Organizations can also institute policies that recognize how implicit gender biases can create discriminatory hiring and promotion practices. In a dramatic example, U.S. orchestras were once extremely male dominated. When they switched to a blind audition policy (in which musicians play behind a screen), many more women were hired; in fact, a blind audition increases a woman's odds of winning an orchestra chair by 250% (Goldin & Rouse, 2000). More generally, it would be helpful if organizational decision makers were educated about their own biases. Most people do not understand that even if they are well-meaning individuals who want to be fair, they can be biased without realizing it. Simply knowing about the effects of implicit gender biases can help decision makers better monitor the fairness of their decisions.

Organizations can also reduce discrimination by making sure that they recruit a more diverse pool of applicants. Both male and female decision makers rate a female manager's qualifications more positively when at least 25% of the other candidates in the pool are female (Heilman, 1980). Policies that explicitly seek to increase the number of women in leadership positions also reduce discrimination simply because the job is no longer assumed to be masculine. Increasing the number of powerful women in organizations opens the door for others (Valian, 1999) and tempers the tendency for female leaders to be viewed as illegitimate (Ely, 1994).

Both genders possess implicit sex stereotypes that impinge on women's ability to lead (Nosek et al. 2002a; Rudman, Greenwald, & McGhee, 2001; Rudman & Kilianski, 2000). However, providing an atmosphere rich with female mentors decreases women's implicit sex stereotypes. After a single year, women attending an all-female college showed less implicit stereotyping of men as leaders (and women as followers) compared with a comparable cohort attending a coeducational college, an effect that was fully explained by the number of female professors and administrators on campus (Dasgupta & Asgari, 2004). This advantage of attending an all-female school could presumably be extended to mixed-sex colleges if more administrators and professors were female. Indeed, some dramatic changes are occurring at the top of the educational hierarchy. For the first time in its history, Harvard University now has a female president, following in the footsteps of Princeton University, University of Michigan, University of Pennsylvania, and Duke University, among others. Nonetheless, only 19% of college presidents are women, up from 10% in 1986 (Jacobson, 2002). Thus, female university presidents remain rare, even though women now attend college in unprecedented numbers.

Finally, gender bias can be embedded in the structure of an organization, in what is known as institutional sexism. But discriminatory acts are carried out by individuals who both adapt to and shape the culture of a workplace. In recognition of this fact, many organizations have embraced diversity education (e.g., sexual harassment training) as a catalyst for overcoming discrimination. However, its effects have not been well investigated (Paluck, 2006). For example, a survey found that 81% of U.S. colleges and universities have used diversity workshops, but none of these institutions had evaluated their outcome (McCauley, Wright, & Harris, 2000). One study found that college students greatly benefited when they volunteered for in-depth diversity training (Rudman, Ashmore, & Gary, 2001), but such training's effects on nonvolunteers may not be as positive. This is a potentially serious problem because people forced to undergo diversity training may perceive a threat to their freedom of expression or be offended by the implication that they are biased. The impact of enforced diversity education is not a trivial one; there is some evidence that it leads to anger and increased prejudice (Plant & Devine, 2001). In other words, diversity training can backfire if it is not conducted well (Roberson, Kulik, & Pepper, 2001, 2003). Much more systematic research is needed before we can be confident about when or whether diversity training is effective. Unfortunately, the rush to add such training has often led to a proliferation of poorly designed programs. At present, the scant research in this area has targeted programs designed to improve racial, more than gender, fairness (Ely & Thomas, 2001; Roberson et al., 2003).

Personal Solutions

As we write this chapter, there have been a number of publicized instances in which American celebrities have been ostracized for making anti-Semitic, racist, or anti-gay comments in public. In each case, a familiar script of contrition follows: The individual apologizes profusely, meets with leading representatives of the offended group, volunteers to undergo therapy, or claims that he or she has now "seen the light" and will never offend again. However disingenuous this may sometimes seem on the part of the offender, the fact that once commonplace prejudices are now socially unacceptable indicates progress. But sexist remarks tend not to elicit the same kind of ostracism that other forms of prejudice do. It is difficult to imagine celebrities, much less ordinary men and women, apologizing for stereotypic jokes about the other sex, a sign that the "gender war" is culturally sanctioned (Thomas & Esses, 2004).

We have noted that, in contrast to many other stereotypes, people are less vigilant about (and less ashamed of) gender stereotyping (Czopp & Monteith, 2003). In part, this is due to the historical treatment of women as lower in status than men, and most people tend to blithely follow traditions for good or ill. Gender norms are so embedded in how we interact with others that we become unaware that they are, in fact, cultural norms rather than "natural facts."

A prominent theme of this book concerns the invisible nature of sexism. Because it permeates nearly every cultural corner, it is difficult to see and its benevolent aspects can mask its malevolent effects. Because sex stereotypes and attitudes reflect well-entrenched ideologies and habits, resisting them involves vigilance and considerable effort. But there are a number of strategies that can help to combat their application to decisions and behaviors. The first step is to become aware of stereotypes, and the second is to become motivated to correct them (Wilson & Brekke, 1994). That is, it is necessary for people to know the contents of their minds and to believe that they do not have "permission" to use stereotypes, preferably because they personally believe it is wrong to do so (Yzerbyt, Schadron, Leyens, & Rocher, 1994). In addition, people can become aware of expectancy effects and confirmation biases that unfold during social interactions and that reinforce sex stereotypes (see Chapter 6). Adopting the goal to be accurate and seeking evidence that might disprove expectations can counteract confirmation bias (Chen, Shecter, & Chaiken, 1996; Neuberg, 1989). Striving to disconfirm hunches is a powerful logical tool for unmasking false beliefs.

Another factor we have stressed is how subjectively favorable but paternalistic attitudes and behaviors contribute to gender inequality in ways that often pass unnoticed. Thus, a critical step is awareness of how even apparently positive stereotypical assumptions can end up having negative effects. Benevolent sexism is prejudice in drag—prettied up, but sexism nonetheless. Paternalistic behavior can slip out all too easily (e.g., the pat on the head to a female subordinate at work). We hope that increasing awareness of why paternalism is problematic may help both men and women to resist its seductive appeal.

It is important, however, that the motivation to control stereotyping does not result in attempts to merely suppress or deny awareness of stereotypes. Suppression causes stereotypes to "rebound" more strongly once they are no longer guarded against (Macrae et al., 1994). The problem with suppression can be illustrated by the command "Do not think of a white bear!"; most likely, this has called the forbidden object to mind, and attempts to suppress the image are likely to fail (Wegner, 1989). This is similar to the experience of dieters who attempt to avoid thinking about food: The more they try to do so, the more thoughts of food intrude. It is better to acknowledge that automatic stereotyping effects are likely to occur and to seek to compensate for them rather than to deny their existence. To do so, perceivers must take the time and devote the necessary mental effort to compensate for stereotypes' automatic influence (e.g., Bodenhausen, 1990; Devine, 1989; Fiske & Von Hendy, 1992; Sinclair & Kunda, 1999).

Unfortunately, because of their covert nature, people are largely unaware of their implicit sex stereotypes. These associations can cause us to involuntarily use gender stereotypes, even when our explicit beliefs are gender fair (Rudman & Glick, 2001; Rudman & Kilianski, 2000). However, individuals can benefit from what has been dubbed "(un)consciousness raising" (Banaji, 2001, p. 136). We routinely ask our students to visit the Project Implicit Web site to test their own gender biases (*https://implicit.harvard.edu/implicit/*). For example, they can test their associations between gender and academic majors (e.g., science vs. humanities) or between gender and roles (e.g., career vs. homemaker). Students' reactions range from revelation ("I had no idea!") to chagrin ("Don't tell my mom about this—she's a physicist!"), but they provide an opening to discuss the pervasive influence of culture on individual minds.

Even people who vigilantly guard against being sexist are likely to possess implicit gender stereotypes because there is no bright line between society and the self (Banaji, 2001). Individuals do not exist in a vacuum, but in cultural, organizational, and social contexts that influence their thoughts and behavior much more so than most people realize. Breaking the "sexism habit" requires both vigilance and a willingness to question cultural norms. Becoming aware of implicit biases is the first step toward being able to compensate for them, so that our individual judgments and actions become less contaminated (T. D. Wilson & Brekke, 1994).

Legal Remedies

For the first time in history, the personal and political injustices that women have faced for millennia are "actionable offenses" in many modern cultures. What used to be "facts of life" for women, injustices to be borne without complaint, are now illegal behaviors. Sex discrimination, sexual harassment, acquaintance rape, and domestic violence are newly coined legal terms that provide for their prosecution.

Title VII of the Civil Rights Act of 1964 protects American women in the labor market, making sex discrimination unlawful with regard to hiring, termination, promotion, compensation, job training, or any other condition of employment. It also prohibits employment decisions based on sex stereotypes regarding abilities, traits, or performance. Further, Title VII prohibits discrimination regardless of whether it is intentional or the result of ostensibly neutral job policies that disproportionately exclude individuals on the basis of sex. According to the U.S. Equal Employment Opportunity Commission's (EEOC) Web site, in 2006 "the EEOC received 23,247 charges of sex-based discrimination, resolved 23,364 sex discrimination charges, and recovered $99.1 million in monetary benefits for aggrieved parties (not including monetary benefits obtained through litigation)." Because the EEOC handles only a minority of complaints, this represents a small number of the actual lawsuits that were filed, but the numbers provide a sense of the tremendous costs to employers for sex-based discrimination. To the extent that corporations are attentive to avoiding legal liability, making sex discrimination "bad for business" through continuing legal reform is likely to have a large impact.

Although the prototypical lawsuit likely conjures the image of a woman being denied employment or promotion because of her perceived lack of ability to do a "man's" job, we have stressed that even when women prove themselves to be highly competent in male-dominated occupations, they can be discriminated against for not acting as a woman should. That is, masterful women can suffer backlash for being "insufficiently feminine." When Ann Hopkins, the highly successful accountant described in Chapter 7, was denied promotion because she was told she needed a "course in charm school," she took her case to the Supreme Court and won. A judge who ruled in her favor argued that "an employer who objects to aggressiveness in women but whose positions require this trait places women in an intolerable Catch-22: out of job if they behave aggressively and out of a job if they don't. Title VII lifts women out of this bind" (*Price-Waterhouse v. Hopkins*, 1989, p. 1791).

Because of *Hopkins*, there is legal precedent to sue on the basis of backlash effects, which undoubtedly affect many women. However, the fact that successful women encounter social barriers as they reach for high-level positions because of a conflict between role demands to act as leaders and gender demands to "be nice" is not yet widely recognized. Indeed, the presence of benevolent sexism can harm a woman's chances for a successful suit. Paternalism involves acts that can seem affectionate and positive but are condescending and actively harm women at work.

Consider the case of Shelley Weinstock, a chemistry professor who was denied tenure despite a favorable faculty vote, external funding, and glowing letters of recommendation because an *ad hoc* committee considered her scholarship to be weak. Her evaluators assumed a patronizing tone, referring to her only by her first name and describing her as "perfectly nice," "caring," and "nurturing." These stereotypically feminine qualities were used to highlight Weinstock's perceived intellectual weakness (assimilating her into the stereotype of women as "nice but not competent"). After Weinstock filed an appeal that was reviewed by a panel of justices, the panel issued a summary judgment that dismissed her case out of hand. The court's majority rejected the claim of sex discrimination, ruling that "any reasonable person of either sex would like to be considered 'nice'" and pointing out that, unlike Hopkins, the plaintiff "faced no ... carping" about her perceived femininity (*Weinstock v. Columbia University*, 2000, p. 8).

One appellate judge protested that Weinstock deserved her day in court. Citing the patronizing tone of the *ad hoc* tenure committee, the dissenting justice wrote:

> This case presents the mirror image of Hopkins. The decision to deny tenure was based—ironically—on Weinstock's perceived success at projecting a stereotypically "feminine" image at work. She was described as gentle and caring, "nice," a "pushover," and nurturing. Unfortunately ... a stereotypically "feminine" person is not viewed in a male dominated field as a driven, scientifically-minded, competitive academic researcher. The inappropriate focus on Weinstock's "feminine" qualities in the tenure process led [her evaluators] to discount her "masculine" success as a researcher and professor. While Hopkins was punished for failing to perform a "feminine" role,

Weinstock was punished for performing it too well ... Hopkins was punished because her "masculinity" appeared inconsistent with gendered stereotypes of how women should look and behave; Weinstock was punished because her "femininity" appeared inconsistent with "masculine" success as a researcher. Yet if she had chosen to project a more "masculine" image, she could very well have suffered the same fate as Hopkins. (*Weinstock v. Columbia University*, 2000, p. 17)

Thus, although the dissenting judge recognized the dilemma faced by women in traditionally masculine occupations, the court's majority missed the influence of positive female stereotyping (and its undercurrent of paternalism) because it appears to benefit "any reasonable person." The result is a system-level barrier to gender equity stemming from judges relying on the commonly held opinion that benevolent views of women as "nice" do no harm. Taken together, the examples of *Weinstock* and *Hopkins* demonstrate that career women may be damned if they act femininely and damned if they don't. These cases serve as concrete examples of how sexism in the workplace can shape shift, with evaluators switching their focus to a woman's niceness when it undermines her competence and to her assertiveness when it undermines her interpersonal skills.

On the positive side, Hopkins's legal victory was predicated on the testimony of research scientists, particularly Susan Fiske, an expert in sex stereotyping and discrimination (Fiske, Bersoff et al., 1991). A large body of evidence demonstrating how stereotypes influence social judgments and decision making helped to persuade the Supreme Court that Hopkins' double bind constituted sex discrimination. In addition, evidence that priming men to view women as sexual objects (e.g., through hostile work environments) can lead to sexual harassment (Rudman & Borgida, 1995) helped the female miners we described in Chapter 8 win their class action suit (*Jenson v. Eveleth Taconite Mining Co.*, 1993). In this way, social scientists can provide social framework testimony that helps plaintiffs seek remedies for discrimination (Borgida & Fiske, 2008). Scientific evidence may someday help to convince the courts that benevolent sexism impedes gender equality. This is likely to take some time; theorists have only recently expanded their definition of prejudice to include the soft bigotry of paternalism (Dovidio, Glick, & Rudman, 2005; Glick et al., 2000), and research in this area is new. However, the evidence collected thus far makes a persuasive case that patronizing discrimination is a largely invisible barrier to gender equity that should be unmasked and dismantled.

Gender Inequality in the Rest of the World

It is important to remember that all of the arguments and remedies presented thus far concern the progress that has been and that still needs to be made to achieve gender equality in a U.S. context. For the most part, research on gender equality suggests that one can, in very broad terms, extend these arguments to most other highly developed nations. That said, we have focused this chapter on a debate that excludes very large swathes of the globe for which there is little research information. This lack of information is beginning to be addressed through cross-cultural research collaborations and has been a focus for research conducted by the United Nations (e.g., the United Nations Development Programme; see *www.undp.org*). From what is currently known about gender inequality in less developed parts of the world, it is clear that the picture is considerably less rosy than even the pessimistic view about progress in the industrialized West. For example, the U.N.'s Gender Empowerment Measure shows strong indications of persistent gender inequality in many regions.

More specifically, in some regions a combination of poverty and the increasing popularity of rigid, fundamentalist religious views has stalled or even reversed progress toward gender equality. For example, the religiously inspired revolution in Iran overthrew a monarchy but replaced it with an authoritarian theocracy that overtly oppresses women. Other Middle Eastern nations, such as Saudi Arabia, have attempted to placate religious fundamentalists by imposing social laws that restrict women or allowing religious organizations to impose their own restrictions. The picture is similar in some northern African nations, where conservative Islam is also prevalent. Although Western nations can point to how far women have come, in other parts of the world women are still being subjected to female circumcision and honor killings (see Chapters 10 and 11).

Although gender equality in western and, especially, northern Europe shows strong progress, eastern Europe has not evinced as much change. In the former Soviet Union, the demise of the communist system has not always led to favorable effects for women; there is evidence that gender-role attitudes have become more traditional in places such as Russia and Poland (Swim, Becker, Pruitt, & Lee, in press). In the relatively collectivist nations of East Asia, traditional gender roles and a relative absence of women in positions of power are still entrenched problems. Collectivist values, which put the group above the individual, when combined with traditional notions of gender roles, create strong resistance to change. Many South American nations also combine collectivism with traditional notions about gender (e.g., machismo; see Swim et al., in press, for a global review of gender attitudes research).

There are signs that when collectivist, gender-traditional nations become highly industrialized they experience pressure to address problems related to gender inequality. For example, as Japanese companies have become global, they have had to adapt to Western concerns with gender issues, such as curtailing the sexual harassment of female employees. In Japan, sexual harassment was, until quite recently, widely tolerated with no legal recourse for women. But it has now become a recognized problem that can create legal liabilities and has led to landmark awards in some high-profile cases (e.g., Maynard, 2006). Thus, some of the factors Jackson (2006) points to may also be starting to create movement toward increased gender equality in nations that have previously imposed highly traditional roles on women. However, it is also quite possible that the gender revolution will continue to bypass many parts of the globe, leading to a polarized world in which the "haves" are much closer to achieving gender parity while the "have nots" remain stuck in both poverty and gender traditionalism.

Conclusion

John Stuart Mill (1869/1975) argued that gender equality, including the education of women, was necessary to prepare people for democratic societies. He believed that hierarchical, paternalist cultures in which women are dependent on men were a hindrance to human improvement and antithetical to a modern society based on self-determination. History has borne him out. Cross-nationally, the countries that have the greatest female empowerment are those with the strongest economic indicators and democratic freedoms. If democratic societies foster global harmony and peace, then women's issues should be everyone's concern.

Like Mill, we have argued that gender equality is good not only for women but for all people, men included. As we have stressed throughout this book, prescriptive gender roles restrict men's as well as women's choices and behavior. Increasingly, individual women and men have begun to question these restrictions and seek greater personal freedom to fulfill their lives in a manner that best matches their own interests, talents, and unique personality. On a personal note, we hope that this book has rendered gender biases more visible, provided insight into the underlying coherence of many apparent contradictions and cross-currents in gender relations, and helped readers to more clearly see how gender structures their own lives.

In the end, it is evident that after millennia of standing in men's shadows, there has been dramatic progress in women's status. The wheels of progress, however, do not always turn smoothly as they grind against the forces of tradition. And progress is much more evident in some parts of the world than others. Speaking movingly about African Americans shortly before he died, Lyndon B. Johnson said, "Let no one delude himself that his work is done ... While the races may stand side by side, Whites stand on history's mountain, and Blacks stand in history's hollow. We must overcome unequal history before we overcome unequal opportunity" (Brinkley, 2006, p. 11). The same words apply to women, who stand in "history's hollow," so that to overcome unequal opportunity, unequal history must be conquered.

References

Abbey, A. (1991). Misperception as an antecedent of acquaintance rape: A consequence of ambiguity in communication between women and men. In A. Parrot & L. Bechhofer (Eds.), *Acquaintance rape: The hidden crime* (pp. 96–111). New York: Wiley.

Abele, A. E., & Wojciszke, B. (2007). Agency and communion from the perspective of self vs. others. *Journal of Personality and Social Psychology, 93,* 751–763.

Abrams, D., Viki, G. T. N., Masser, B., & Bohner, G. (2003). Perceptions of stranger and acquaintance rape: The role of benevolent and hostile sexism in victim blame and rape proclivity. *Journal of Personality and Social Psychology, 84,* 111–125.

Abu-Lughod, L. (1986). *Veiled sentiments: Honor and poetry in a Bedouin society.* Berkeley: University of California Press.

Allen, M. (1996, September 22). Defiant V.M.I. to admit women, but will not ease rules for them. *New York Times,* pp. 1, 36.

Allen, T. D. (2006). Rewarding good citizens: The relationship between citizenship behavior, gender, and organizational rewards. *Journal of Applied Social Psychology, 36,* 120–143.

Allen, T. D., & Rush, M. C. (2001). The influence of ratee gender on ratings of organizational citizenship behavior. *Journal of Applied Social Psychology, 31,* 2561–2587.

Allport, G. W. (1979). *The nature of prejudice.* Cambridge, MA: Perseus Books. (Original work published 1954)

Amanatullah, E. (2007). *The influence of injunctive gender stereotypes on perceivers' evaluations and targets' behaviors in value claiming negotiations and situational moderation by representation role.* Unpublished doctoral dissertation, Columbia University, New York.

Amar, A. F. (2006). Women's experience of stalking: Mental health symptoms and changes in routines. *Archives of Psychiatric Nursing, 20,* 108–116.

Amato, P. R., & Previti, D. (2003). People's reasons for divorcing: Gender, social class, the life course, and adjustment. *Journal of Family Issues, 24*, 602–626.

American Psychological Association, Task Force on the Sexualization of Girls. (2007). *Report of the APA Task Force on the Sexualization of Girls.* Washington, DC: Author. Retrieved from *www.apa.org/pi/wpo/sexualization.html*

Anderson, K. L., & Umberson, D. (2001). Gendering violence: Masculinity and power in men's account of sexual violence. *Gender and Society, 15*, 358–380.

Antilla, S. (2002). *Tales from the boom-boom room: Women vs. Wall Street.* Princeton, NJ: Bloomberg Press.

Archambeau, K. (2006). *Climbing the corporate ladder in high heels.* Franklin Lakes, NJ: Career Press.

Archer, J. (2000). Sex differences in physical aggression to partners: A meta-analytic review. *Psychological Bulletin, 126*, 651–680.

Archer, J. (2006). Cross-cultural differences in physical aggression between partners: A social role analysis. *Personality and Social Psychology Review, 10*, 133–153.

Archer, J. (2007). *Does sexual selection explain human sex differences in aggression?* Unpublished manuscript, University of Central Lancashire.

Archer, J., & Coyne, S. M. (2005). An integrated review of indirect, relational, and social aggression. *Personality and Social Psychology Review, 9*, 212–230.

Ariely, D., & Lowenstein, G. (2006). The heat of the moment: The effect of sexual arousal on sexual decision making. *Journal of Behavioral Decision Making, 19*, 87–98.

Aron, A., Fisher, H., Mashek, D. J., Strong, G., Li, H., & Brown, L. L. (2005). Reward, motivation, and emotion systems associated with early-stage intense romantic love. *Journal of Neurophysiology, 94*, 327–337.

Aron, A., Paris, M., & Aron, E. N. (1995). Falling in love: Prospective studies of self-concept change. *Journal of Personality and Social Psychology, 69*, 1102–1112.

Aron, E. N., & Aron, A. (1997). Extremities of love: The sudden sacrifice of career, family, dignity. *Journal of Social and Clinical Psychology, 16*(2), 200–212.

Aronson, J., Lustina, M. J., Good, C., Keough, K., Steele, C. M., & Brown, J. (1999). When White men can't do math: Necessary and sufficient factors in stereotype threat. *Journal of Experimental Social Psychology, 35*, 29–46.

Asch, S. E. (1952). Effects of group pressures upon the modification and distortion of judgments. In G. E. Swanson, T. M. Newcomb, & E. L. Hartley (Eds.), *Readings in social psychology* (pp. 393–410). New York: Holt, Reinhart & Winston.

Asch, S. E. (1955). Opinions and social pressure. *Scientific American, 193*(5), 31–35.

Ashmore, R. D., Del Boca, F. K., & Bilder, S. M. (1995). Construction and validation of the Gender Attitude Inventory, a structured inventory to assess multiple dimensions of gender attitudes. *Sex Roles, 32*, 753–785.

Atwater, L. E., Carey, J. A., & Waldman, D. A. (2001). Gender and discipline in the workplace: Wait until your father gets home. *Journal of Management, 27*, 537–561.

Aubrey, J. S. (2004). Sex and punishment: An examination of sexual consequences and the sexual double standard in teen programming. *Sex Roles, 50,* 505–514.

Auster, C. J., & Ohm, S. C. (2000). Masculinity and femininity in contemporary American society: A reevaluation using the Bem Sex-Role Inventory. *Sex Roles, 43,* 499–528.

Averill, J. (1985). The social construction of emotion: With special reference to love. In K. J. Gergen & K. Davis (Eds.), *The social construction of the person* (pp. 89–101). New York: Springer-Verlag.

Babcock, L., & Laschever, S. (2003). *Women don't ask: Negotiation and the gender divide.* Princeton, NJ: Princeton University Press.

Bader, A. P. (1995). Engrossment revisited: Fathers are still falling in love with their newborn babies. In J. L. Shapiro, J. Lee, M. J. Diamond, & M. Greenberg (Eds.), *Becoming a father: Contemporary, social, developmental, and clinical perspectives* (pp. 224–233). New York: Springer.

Bailey, J. M., & Pillard, R. C. (1991) A genetic study of male sexual orientation. *Archives of General Psychiatry, 48,* 1089–1096.

Bailey, J. M., & Zucker, K. J. (1995). Childhood sex-typed behavior and sexual orientation: A conceptual analysis and quantitative review. *Developmental Psychology, 31,* 43–55.

Baize, H. R., & Schroeder, J. E. (1995). Personality and mate selection in personal ads: Evolutionary preferences in a public mate selection process. *Journal of Social Behavior and Personality, 10,* 517–536.

Bakan, D. (1966). *The duality of human existence: An essay on psychology and religion.* Chicago: Rand McNally.

Baker, N. V., Gregware, P. R., & Cassidy, M. A. (1999). Family killing fields: Honor rationales in the murder of women. *Violence Against Women, 5,* 164–184.

Banaji, M. R. (2001). Implicit attitudes can be measured. In H. L. Roediger, J. S. Nairne, I. Neath, & A. M. Surprenant (Eds.), *The nature of remembering: Essays in honor of Robert G. Crowder* (pp. 117–150). Washington, DC: American Psychological Association.

Banaji, M. R., & Greenwald, A. G. (1995). Implicit gender stereotyping in judgments of fame. *Journal of Personality and Social Psychology, 68,* 181–198.

Banaji, M. R., & Hardin, C. D. (1996). Automatic stereotyping. *Psychological Science, 7,* 136–141.

Banaji, M. R., Hardin, C. D., & Rothman, A. J. (1993). Implicit stereotyping in person judgment. *Journal of Personality and Social Psychology, 65,* 272–281.

Bannerjee, R., & Lintern, V. (2000). Boys will be boys: The effect of social evaluation concerns on gender-typing. *Social Development, 9,* 397–408.

Bargh, J. A., & Raymond, P. (1995). The naïve misuse of power: Nonconscious sources of sexual harassment. *Journal of Social Issues, 51,* 85–96.

Bargh, J. A., Raymond, P., Pryor, J. B., & Strack, F. (1995). Attractiveness of the underling: An automatic power-sex association and its consequences for sexual harassment and aggression. *Journal of Personality and Social Psychology, 68,* 768–781.

Barker, G. T. (2005). *Dying to be men: Youth, masculinity, and social exclusion.* New York: Taylor & Francis.

Barnett, R. C., & Baruch, G. K. (1987). Social roles, gender, and psychological distress. In R. C. Barnett, L. Biener, & G. K. Baruch (Eds.), *Gender and stress* (pp. 122–141). New York: Free Press.

Baron, L., & Straus, M. A. (1989). *Four theories of rape in American society.* New Haven, CT: Yale University Press.

Bartels, A., & Zeki, S. (2000). The neural basis of romantic love. *NeuroReport, 17*(11), 3829–3834.

Bartlett, F. A. (1932). *A study in experimental and social psychology.* New York: Cambridge University Press.

Bartol, K. M., & Butterfield, D. A. (1976). Sex effects in evaluating leaders. *Journal of Applied Psychology, 61,* 446–454.

Basow, S. A., Phelan, J. E., & Capotosto, L. (2006). Gender patterns in college students' choices of their best and worst professors. *Psychology of Women Quarterly, 30,* 25–35.

Baumeister, R. F. (1989). *Masochism and the self.* Hillsdale, NJ: Erlbaum.

Baumeister, R. F. (2000). Gender differences in erotic plasticity: The female sex drive as socially flexible and responsive. *Psychological Bulletin, 126,* 347–374.

Baumeister, R. F., & Bratslavsky, E. (1999). Passion, intimacy, and time: Passionate love as a function of change in intimacy. *Personality and Social Psychology Review, 3,* 49–67.

Baumeister, R. F., Catanese, K. R., & Vohs, K. D. (2001). Is there a gender difference in strength of sex drive? Theoretical views, conceptual distinctions, and a review of relevant evidence. *Personality and Social Psychology Review, 5,* 242–273.

Baumeister, R. F., & Vohs, K. D. (2004). Sexual economics: Sex as a female resource for exchange in heterosexual relationships. *Personality and Social Psychology Review, 8,* 339–362.

Bay-Cheng, L. Y., & Zucker, A. N. (2007). Feminism between the sheets: Sexual attitudes among feminists, nonfeminists, and egalitarians. *Psychology of Women Quarterly, 31,* 157–163.

Belkin, L. (2000, July 23). Your kids are their problem [Electronic version] *New York Times Magazine,* pp. 30–35, 42, 56, 60–63.

Belkin, L. (2003, October 26). The opt-out revolution [Electronic version]. *New York Times Magazine,* pp. 42–58.

Bell, D., & Klein, R. (1996). *Radically speaking: Feminism reclaimed.* Victoria, Australia: Spinifex Press.

Belsey, C. (1994). *Desire: Love stories in Western culture.* Oxford, UK: Blackwell.

Bem, S. L. (1974). The measurement of psychological androgyny. *Journal of Consulting and Clinical Psychology, 42,* 155–162.

Bem, S. L. (1981). Gender schema theory: A cognitive account of sex-typing. *Psychological Review, 88,* 354–364.

Bem, S. L. (1989). Genital knowledge and gender constancy in preschool children. *Child Development, 60,* 649–662.

Bennett, S. (1982). Student perceptions of and expectations for male and female instructors: Evidence relating to the question of gender bias in teaching evaluations. *Journal of Educational Psychology, 74,* 170–179.

Berdahl, J. L. (2007a). Harassment based on sex: Protecting social status in the context of gender hierarchy. *Academy of Management Review, 32*(2), 641–658.

Berdahl, J. L. (2007b). The sexual harassment of uppity women. *Journal of Applied Psychology, 92*, 425–437.

Berger, J., Webster, M., Jr., Ridgeway, C. L., & Rosenholtz, S. J. (1986). Status cues, expectations, and behaviors. In E. Lawler (Ed.), *Advances in group processes* (Vol. 3, pp. 1–22). Greenwich, CT: JAI Press.

Bernard, J. (1972). *The future of marriage.* New York: Bantam Books.

Berscheid, E., Dion, K., Walster, E., & Walster, G. W. (1971). Physical attractiveness and dating choice: A test of the matching hypothesis. *Journal of Experimental Social Psychology, 7*, 173–189.

Berscheid, E. (1991). The emotion-in-relationships model: Reflections and update. In W. Kessen, A. Ortony, & F. I. M. Craik (Eds.), *Memories, thoughts, and emotions: Essays in honor of George Mandler* (pp. 323–335). Hillsdale, NJ: Erlbaum.

Berscheid, E., & Reis, H. T. (1998). Attraction and close relationships. In D. T. Gilbert & S. T. Fiske (Eds.), *The handbook of social psychology* (Vol. 2, pp. 193–281). New York: McGraw-Hill.

Berscheid, E., Snyder, M., & Omoto, A. M. (1989). The Relationship Closeness Inventory: Assessing the closeness of interpersonal relationships. *Journal of Personality and Social Psychology, 57*, 792–807.

Berscheid, E., & Walster, E. (1978). *Interpersonal attraction* (2nd ed.). New York: Random House.

Bertrand, M., & Hallock, K. (2001). The gender gap in top corporate jobs. *Industrial and Labor Relations Review, 55*(1), 3–21.

Bianchi, S. M. (2000). Maternal employment and time with children: Dramatic change or surprising continuity? *Demography, 47*, 401–414.

Bianchi, S. M., & Casper, L. (2002). American families. *Population Bulletin, 455*(4), 1–44.

Bianchi, S. M., Milkie, M. A., Sayer, L. C., & Robinson, J. P. (2000). Is anyone doing the housework? Trends in the gender division of household labor. *Social Forces, 79*, 191–228.

Biernat, M. (2003). Toward a broader view of social stereotyping. *American Psychologist, 58*, 1019–1027.

Biernat, M., & Fuegen, K. (2001). Shifting standards and the evaluation of competence: Complexity in gender-based judgment and decision making. *Journal of Social Issues, 57*, 707–724.

Biernat, M., & Kobrynowicz, D. (1997). Gender- and race-based standards of competence: Lower minimum standards but higher ability standards for devalued groups. *Journal of Personality and Social Psychology, 72*, 544–557.

Biernat, M., & Ma, J. E. (2005). Stereotypes and the confirmability of trait concepts. *Personality and Social Psychology Bulletin, 31*, 483–495.

Biernat, M., & Wortman, C. B. (1991). Sharing of home responsibilities between professionally employed women and their husbands. *Journal of Personality and Social Psychology, 60*, 844–860.

Bigler, R. S. (1997). Conceptual and methodological issues in the measurement of children's sex typing. *Psychology of Women Quarterly, 21*, 53–59.

Bigler, R. S. (1999). Psychological interventions designed to counter sexism in children: Empirical limitations and theoretical foundations. In W. B. Swann, Jr., L. A. Gilbert, & J. Langlois (Eds.), *Sexism and stereotypes in modern society: The gender science of Janet Taylor Spence* (pp. 129–151). Washington, DC: American Psychological Association.

Bingham, C., & Gansler, L. L. (2002). *Class action: The story of Lois Jenson and the landmark case that changed sexual harassment law.* New York: Random House.

Blackwell, D. L., & Lichter, D. T. (2004). Homogamy among dating, cohabiting, and married couples. *Sociological Quarterly, 45,* 719–737.

Blair, I. V., & Banaji, M. R. (1996). Automatic and controlled processes in stereotype priming. *Journal of Personality and Social Psychology, 70,* 1142–1163.

Blair, S. L., & Lichter, D. T. (1991). Measuring the division of household labor: Gender segregation of housework among American couples. *Journal of Family Issues, 12,* 91–113.

Blanchard, R., McConkey, J. G., Roper, V., & Steiner, B. W. (1983). Measuring physical aggressiveness in heterosexual, homosexual, and transsexual males. *Archives of Sexual Behavior, 12,* 511–524.

Blau, F. D., & Kahn, L. M. (2007). The gender pay gap: Have women gone as far as they can? *Academy of Management Perspectives, 21,* 7–23.

Blinde, E. M., & Taub, D. E. (1992). *Women athletes as falsely accused deviants: Managing the lesbian stigma. Sociological Quarterly, 33,* 521–533.

Bodenhausen, G. V. (1990). Stereotypes as judgmental heuristics: Evidence of circadian variations in discrimination. *Psychological Science, 1,* 319–322.

Bodenhausen, G. V. (1993). Emotions, arousal, and stereotypic judgments: A heuristic model of affect and stereotyping. In D. M. Mackie & D. L. Hamilton (Eds.), *Affect, cognition, and stereotyping* (pp. 13–38). New York: Academic Press.

Bogardus, E. S. (1927). Race, friendliness, and social distance. *Journal of Applied Sociology, 11,* 272–287.

Bolino, M. C., & Turnley, W. H. (2003). Counternormative impression management, likeability, and performance ratings: The use of intimidation in an organization setting. *Journal of Organizational Behavior, 23,* 237–250.

Bombardieri, M. (2005, April 8). Summers displays new understanding of women's careers. [Electronic version] *The Boston Globe.*

Borgida, E., & Fiske, S. T. (Eds.). (2008). *Beyond common sense: Psychological science in the courtroom.* Malden, MA: Blackwell.

Bosson, J. K., Prewitt-Freilino, J. L., & Taylor, J. N. (2005). Role rigidity: A problem of identity misclassification? *Journal of Personality and Social Psychology, 89,* 552–565.

Bosson, J. K., Taylor, J. N., & Prewitt-Freilino, J. L. (2006). Gender role violations and identity misclassification: The roles of audience and actor variables. *Sex Roles, 55,* 13–24.

Bowles, H. R., Babcock, L., & Lai, L. (2007). Social incentives for gender differences in the propensity to initiate negotiations: Sometimes it does hurt to ask. *Organizational Behavior and Human Decision Processes, 103*(1), 84–103.

Bowles, H. R., Babcock, L., & McGinn, K. L. (2005). Constraints and triggers: Situational mechanics of gender in negotiation. *Journal of Personality and Social Psychology, 89,* 951–965.

Bowman, C. G. (1993). Street harassment and the informal ghettoization of women. *Harvard Law Review, 106,* 517–580.

Boyce, L. A., & Herd, A. M. (2003). The relationship between gender role stereotypes and requisite military leadership characteristics. *Sex Roles, 49,* 365–378.

Branscombe, N. R., Crosby, P., & Weir, J. A. (1993). Social inferences concerning male and female homeowners who use a gun to shoot an intruder. *Aggressive Behavior, 19,* 113–124.

Brehm, S., & Brehm, J. W. (1981). *Psychological reactance: A theory of freedom and control.* New York: Academic Press.

Brehm, S. S. (1998). *Intimate relationships.* New York: McGraw-Hill.

Brett, J. F., Atwater, L. E., & Waldman, D. A. (2005). Effective delivery of workplace discipline: Do women have to be more participatory than men? *Group and Organization Management, 30,* 487–513.

Brescoll, V., & Uhlmann, E. L. (in press). Can angry women get ahead? Status conferral, gender, and workplace emotion expression. *Psychological Science.*

Brewer, M. B. (1988). A dual-process model of impression formation. In T. K. Srull & R. W. Wyer, Jr. (Eds.), *Advances in social cognition* (Vol. 1, pp. 1–36). Hillsdale, NJ: Erlbaum.

Brewer, M. B. (1991). The social self: On being the same and different at the same time. *Personality and Social Psychology Bulletin, 17,* 475–482.

Brewer, M. B. (1999). The psychology of prejudice: Ingroup love or outgroup hate? *Journal of Social Issues, 55,* 429–444.

Brinkley, A. (2006, August 20). The making of a war president. *New York Times Book Review,* pp. 10–11.

Brooks, D. (2005, October 16). Mind over muscle. *New York Times,* p. 12.

Brooks, D. (2006, June 11). The gender gap at school [Electronic version]. *New York Times.*

Brooks-Gunn, J., & Ruble, D. N. (1986). Men's and women's attitudes and beliefs about the menstrual cycle. *Sex Roles, 14,* 287–299.

Brownmiller, S. (1975). *Against our will.* New York: Simon & Schuster.

Brumberg, J. J. (1997). *The body project: An intimate history of American girls.* New York: Vintage Books.

Buckley, L. M., Sanders, K., Shih, M., Kallar, S., & Hampton, C. (2000). Obstacles to promotion? Values of women faculty about career success and recognition. *Academic Medicine, 75,* 283–288.

Bukowski, W. M., Gauze, C., Hoza, B., & Newcomb, A. F. (1993). Differences and consistency between same-sex and other-sex peer relationships during early adolescence. *Developmental Psychology, 29,* 255–263.

Bumpass, L. L., & Sweet, J. A. (1989). National estimates of cohabitation. *Demography, 26,* 615–625.

Burgess, D., & Borgida, E. (1999). Who women are, who women should be: Descriptive and prescriptive stereotyping in sex discrimination. *Psychology, Public Policy, and Law, 5,* 665–692.

Burns, A. (2002). Women in love and men at work: The evolving heterosexual couple? *Psychology, Evolution and Gender, 4,* 149–172.

Buschman, J. K., & Lenart, S. (1996). "I am not a feminist, but ... ": College women, feminism, and negative experiences. *Political Psychology, 17,* 59–75.

Buss, D. M. (1989). Sex differences in human mate preferences: Evolutionary hypotheses tested in 37 cultures. *Brain and Behavioral Sciences, 12,* 1–14.

Buss, D. M. (2003). *Evolutionary psychology: The new science of the mind* (2nd ed.). Boston: Allyn & Bacon.

Buss, D. M. (2005). *The murderer next door: Why the mind is designed to kill.* New York: Penguin Press.

Buss, D. M., Abbott, M., Angleitner, A., Biaggio, A., Blanco-Villasenor, A., Bruchon-Schweitzer, M., et al. (1990). International preferences in selecting mates: A study of 37 cultures. *Journal of Cross-Cultural Psychology, 21,* 5–47.

Bussey, K., & Bandura, A. (1999). Social cognitive theory of gender development and differentiation. *Psychological Review, 106,* 617–713.

Butler, D., & Geis, F. L. (1990). Nonverbal affect responses to male and female leaders. Implications for leadership evaluations. *Journal of Personality and Social Psychology, 58,* 48–59.

Buttner, E. H., & McEnally, M. (1996). The interactive effect of applicant gender, influence tactics, and type of job on hiring recommendations. *Sex Roles, 34,* 581–592.

Buunk, A. P., Angleitner, Oubaid, A., & Buss, D. M. (1996). Sex differences in jealousy in evolutionary and cultural perspective: Tests from the Netherlands, Germany, and the United States. *Psychological Science, 7,* 359–363.

Byrne, D. (1971). *The attraction paradigm.* New York: Academic Press.

Cabrera, S. F., & Thomas-Hunt, M. C. (2007). "Street cred" and the executive woman: The effects of gender differences in social networks on career advancement. In S. Correll (Ed.), *Advances in group processes* (Vol. 24, pp. 123–147). New York: Elsevier.

Cahill, B., & Adams, E. (1997). An exploratory study of early childhood teachers' attitudes toward gender roles. *Sex Roles, 36,* 517–529.

Campbell, A., Shirley, L., Heywood, C., & Crooke, C. (2000). Infants' visual preference for sex-congruent babies, children, toys and activities: A longitudinal study. *British Journal of Developmental Psychology, 18,* 479–498.

Caporeal, L. R. (2001). Evolutionary psychology: Toward a unifying theory and hybrid science. *Annual Review of Psychology, 52,* 607–628.

Caporeal, L. R. (2004). Bones and stones: Selection for sociality. *Journal of Cultural and Evolutionary Psychology, 2,* 195–211.

Caporeal, L. R., & Baron, R. M. (1997). Groups as the mind's natural environment In J. A. Simpson & D. T. Kenrick (Eds.), *Evolutionary social psychology* (pp. 317–343). Mahwah, NJ: Erlbaum.

Carbone, J. (2000). *From partners to parents: The second revolution in family law.* New York: Columbia University Press.

Carli, L. L. (1990). Gender, language, and influence. *Journal of Personality and Social Psychology, 59,* 941–951.

Carli, L. L. (2001). Gender and social influence. *Journal of Social Issues, 57,* 725–741.

Carli, L. L., LaFleur, S. J., & Loeber, C. C. (1995). Nonverbal behavior, gender, and influence. *Journal of Personality and Social Psychology, 68,* 1030–1041.

Carlson, J., & Hatfield, E. (1992). *The psychology of emotion.* Fort Worth, TX: Hold, Rinehart, & Winston.

Carpenter, S., & Banaji, M. R. (1998, April). *Implicit attitudes and behavior toward female leaders.* Paper presented at the annual meeting of the Midwestern Psychological Association, Chicago, IL.

Carpenter, S., & Trentham, S. (1998). Subtypes of women and men: A new taxonomy and categorical analysis. *Journal of Social Behavior and Personality, 13,* 679–696.

Carpenter, S., & Trentham, S. (2001). Should we take the gender out of gender subtypes? The effects of gender, evaluative valence, and context on the organization of person subtypes. *Sex Roles, 45,* 455–480.

Carranza, E. (2004). *Is what's good for the goose derogated in the gander? Reactions to masculine women and feminine men.* Unpublished doctoral dissertation, Princeton University.

Carroll, J. L., Volk, K. D., & Hyde, J. S. (1985). Differences between males and females in motives for engaging in sexual intercourse. *Archives of Sexual Behavior, 14,* 131–139.

Cartland, B. (1999). *The little pretender.* Columbus, MS: Genesis Press.

Catalyst. (2001). *Women in financial services: The word on the street.* New York: Catalyst.

Catalyst. (2004). *The bottom line: Connecting corporate performance and gender diversity.* New York: Catalyst.

Catalyst. (2006). *2005 Catalyst census of women corporate officers and top earners of the Fortune 500.* New York: Catalyst.

Cejka, M. A., & Eagly, A. H. (1999). Gender-stereotypic images of occupations correspond to the sex segregation of employment. *Personality and Social Psychology Bulletin, 25,* 413–423.

Chaiken, S., Liberman, A., & Eagly, A. H. (1989). Heuristic and systematic information processing within and beyond the persuasion context. In J. S. Uleman & J. A. Bargh (Eds.), *Unintended thought* (pp. 212–252). New York: Guilford Press.

Chen, S., Shechter, D., & Chaiken, S. (1996). Getting at the truth or getting along: Accuracy- versus impression-motivated heuristic and systematic processing. *Journal of Personality and Social Psychology, 71,* 262–275.

Cherry, F., & Deaux, K. (1978). Fear of success versus fear of gender-inappropriate behavior. *Sex Roles, 4,* 97–101.

Christopher, E. S., & Sprecher, S. (2000). Sexuality in marriage, dating, and other relationships: A decade review. *Journal of Marriage and the Family, 62,* 999–1017.

Cialdini, R. B., & Trost, M. R. (1998). Social influence: Social norms, conformity and compliance. In D. T. Gilbert, S. T. Fiske, & G. Lindzey (Eds.), *The handbook of social psychology* (4th ed., Vol. 2, pp. 151–192). New York: McGraw-Hill.

Clausell, E., & Fiske, S. T. (2005). When do subgroup parts add up to the stereotype whole? Mixed stereotype content for gay male subgroups explains overall ratings. *Social Cognition, 23,* 161–181.

Clayton, S. D., & Crosby, F. J. (1992). *Justice, gender, and affirmative action.* Ann Arbor, MI: University of Michigan Press.

Cohen, C. (1981). Person categories and social perception: Testing some boundaries of the processing effect of prior knowledge. *Journal of Personality and Social Psychology, 40,* 441–452.

Cohen, D., & Nisbett, R. E. (1994). Self-protection and the culture of honor: Explaining southern homicide. *Personality and Social Psychology Bulletin, 20,* 551–567.

Cohen, D., Nisbett, R. E., Bowdle, B., & Schwartz, N. (1996). Insult, aggression, and the Southern culture of honor: An "experimental ethnography." *Journal of Personality and Social Psychology, 70,* 945–960.

Cole, J. R., & Singer, B. (1991). A theory of limited differences: Explaining the productivity puzzle in science. In H. Zuckerman, J. R. Cole, & J. T. Bruer (Eds.), *The outer circle: Women in the scientific community* (pp. 277–310). New York: Norton.

Collins-Standley, T., Gan, S., Yu, J. J., & Zillman, D. (1996). Choice of romantic, violent, and scary fairy-tale books by preschool girls. *Child Study Journal, 26,* 279–302.

Coltrane, S. (1996). *Family man: Fatherhood, housework, and gender equity.* Oxford, UK: Oxford University Press.

Coltrane, S., & Adams, M. (1997). Work-family imagery and gender stereotypes: Television and the reproduction of difference. *Journal of Vocational Behavior, 50,* 323–347.

Conte, A. (1990). *Sexual harassment in the workplace: Law and practice.* New York: Wiley.

Coontz, S. (2005). *Marriage, a history: From obedience to intimacy or how love conquered marriage.* New York: Viking.

Conway, M., Pizzamiglio, M. T., & Mount, L. (1996). Status, communality, and agency: Implications for stereotypes of gender and other groups. *Journal of Personality and Social Psychology, 71,* 25–38.

Correll, J., Park, B., Judd, C. M., & Wittenbrink, B. (2002). The police officer's dilemma: Using ethnicity to disambiguate potentially threatening individuals. *Journal of Personality and Social Psychology, 83,* 1314–1329.

Costrich, N., Feinstein, L., Kidder, L., Marecek, J., & Pascale, L. (1975). When stereotypes hurt: Three studies of penalties for sex-role reversals. *Journal of Experimental Social Psychology, 11,* 520–530.

Coutts, L., & Berg, D. H. (1993). The portrayal of the menstruating woman in menstrual product advertisements. *Health Care for Women International, 14,* 179–191.

Crandall, C. S., & Stangor, C. (2005). Conformity and prejudice. In J. F. Dovidio, P. Glick, & L. A. Rudman (Eds.), *On the nature of prejudice: Fifty years after Allport* (pp. 295–309). Malden, MA: Blackwell.

Crawford, M. (1988). Gender, age, and the social evaluation of assertion. *Behavior Modification, 12,* 549–564.

Crawford, M., & Popp, D. (2003). Sexual double standards: A review and methodological critique of two decades of research. *Journal of Sex Research, 40,* 13–26.

Crick, N. R. (1996). The role of overt aggression, relational aggression, and prosocial behavior in the prediction of children's future social adjustment. *Child Development, 67,* 2317–2327.

Crocker, J., & McGraw, K. M. (1984). What's good for the goose is not good for the gander: Solo status as an obstacle to occupational achievement for males and females. *American Behavioral Scientist, 27*(3), 357–369.

Crombie, G., & DesJardins, M. J. (1993, March). *Predictors of gender: The relative importance of children's play, games, and personality characteristics.* Paper presented at the Society for Research in Child Development, New Orleans, LA.

Crosby, F. J. (1982). *Relative deprivation and working women.* New York: Oxford University Press.

Crosby, F. J. (1984). The denial of personal discrimination. *American Behavioral Scientist, 27,* 371–386.

Crosby, F. J. (1991). *Juggling: The unexpected advantages of balancing career and home for women and their families.* New York: Free Press.

Crosby, F. J., Cordova, D. I., & Jaskar, K. (1993). On the failure to see oneself as disadvantaged: Cognitive and emotional components. In M. A. Hogg & D. Abrams (Eds.), *Group motivation: Social psychological perspectives* (pp. 87–104). Hertfordshire, UK: Harvester Wheatsheaf.

Crosby, F. J., Williams, J., & Biernat, M. (2004). The maternal wall. *Journal of Social Issues, 60,* 675–682.

Cuddy, A. J. C., Fiske, S. T., & Glick, P. (2004). When professionals become mothers, warmth doesn't cut the ice. *Journal of Social Issues, 60,* 701–718.

Czopp, A. M., & Monteith, M. J. (2003). Confronting prejudice (literally): Reactions to confrontations of racial and gender bias. *Personality and Social Psychology Bulletin, 29,* 532–544.

Dall'Ara, E., & Maass, A. (2000). Studying sexual harassment in the laboratory: Are egalitarian women at higher risk? *Sex Roles, 41,* 681–704.

Daly, M., & Wilson, M. (1988). *Homicide.* New York: Aldine de Gruyter.

Daly, M., & Wilson, M. (1990). Killing the competition: Female/female and male/male homicide. *Human Nature, 1,* 81–107.

Daly, M., & Wilson, M. (1994). Evolutionary psychology of male violence. In J. Archer (Ed.), *Male violence* (pp. 253–288). London: Routledge.

Daly, M., Wilson, M., & Weghorst, S. J. (1982). Male sexual jealousy. *Ethology and Sociobiology, 3,* 11–27.

Darley, J. M., Fleming, J. H., Hilton, J. L., & Swann, W. B. (1988). Dispelling negative expectancies: The impact of interaction goals and target characteristics on the expectancy confirmation process. *Journal of Experimental Social Psychology, 24,* 19–36.

Darley, J. M., & Gross, P. H. (1983). A hypothesis-confirming bias in labeling effects. *Journal of Personality and Social Psychology, 44,* 20–33.

Dar-Nimrod, I., & Heine, S. J. (2006). Exposure to scientific theories affects women's math performance. *Science, 314,* p. 435.

Darwin, C. (1871). *The descent of man and selection in relation to sex.* London: Murray.

Dasgupta, N., & Asgari, S. (2004). Seeing is believing: Exposure to counter-stereotypic women leaders and its effect on the malleability of automatic gender stereotyping. *Journal of Experimental Social Psychology, 40,* 642–658.

Daubman, K. A., Heatherington, L., & Ahn, A. (1992). Gender and the self-presentation of academic achievement. *Sex Roles, 27,* 187–204.

Davey, A. G. (1977). Racial awareness and social identity in young children. *Mental Health and Society, 4,* 255–262.

Davies, P. G., Spencer, S. J., Quinn, D. M., & Gerhardstein, R. (2002). Consuming images: How television commercials that elicit stereotype threat can restrain women academically and professionally. *Personality and Social Psychology Bulletin, 28,* 1615–1628.

Davies, P. G., Spencer, S. J., & Steele, C. M. (2005). Clearing the air: Identity safety moderates the effects of stereotype threat on women's leadership aspirations. *Journal of Personality and Social Psychology, 88,* 276–287.

Davis, C. M., Blank, J., Lin, H., & Bonillas, C. (1996). Characteristics of vibrator use among women. *Journal of Sex Research, 33,* 313–320.

Davis, K. E., Coker, A. L., & Sanderson, M. (2002). Physical and mental health effects of being stalked for men and women. *Violence and Victims, 17*(4), 429–443.

Dean, C. (2005, May 4). The National Academy of Sciences elects 19 women, a new high. *New York Times.* Retrieved October 17, 2007, from *www.nytimes. com/2005/05/04/science/04women.html*

Deaux, K. (1995). How basic can you be? The evolution of research on gender stereotypes. *Journal of Social Issues, 51,* 11–20.

Deaux, K., & Emswiller, T. (1974). Explanations of successful performance on sex-linked tasks: What is skill for the male is luck for the female. *Journal of Personality and Social Psychology, 29,* 80–85.

Deaux, K., & Hanna, R. (1984). Courtship in the personals column: The influence of gender and sexual orientation. *Sex Roles, 11,* 363–375.

Deaux, K., & LaFrance, M. (1998). Gender. In D. T. Gilbert, S. T. Fiske, & G. Lindzey (Eds.), *The handbook of social psychology* (4th ed., Vol. 1, pp. 788–827). New York: McGraw-Hill.

Deaux, K., & Lewis, L. L. (1984). The structure of gender stereotypes: Interrelationships among components and gender label. *Journal of Personality and Social Psychology, 46,* 991–1004.

Deaux, K., Winton, W., Crowley, M., & Lewis, L. L. (1985). Level of categorization and the content of stereotypes. *Social Cognition, 3,* 145–167.

De Beauvoir, S. (1952). *The second sex.* New York: Alfred A. Knopf.

Denby, D. (1996). *Great books.* New York: Touchstone.

Dennison, S. M., & Stewart, A. (2006). Facing rejection: New relationships, broken relationships, shame, and stalking. *International Journal of Offender Therapy and Comparative Criminology, 50*(3), 324–337.

Derlega, V. J., & Chaiken, A. L. (1976). Norms affecting self-disclosure in men and women. *Journal of Consulting and Clinical Psychology, 44,* 376–380.

De Rougemont, D. (1956). *Love in the Western world.* Princeton, NJ: Princeton University Press.

DeSteno, D., Bartlett, M. Y., Braverman, J., & Salovey, P. (2002). Sex differences in jealousy: Evolutionary mechanism or artifact of measurement? *Journal of Personality and Social Psychology, 83,* 1103–1116.

DeSteno, D., Valdesolo, P., & Bartlett, M. Y. (2006). Jealousy and the threatened self: Getting to the heart of the green-eyed monster. *Journal of Personality and Social Psychology, 91,* 626–641.

Deutsch, F. M. (1999). *Halving it all: How equally shared parenting works.* Cambridge, MA: Harvard University Press.

Deutsch, F. M., Lussier, J. B., & Servis, L. J. (1993). Husbands at home: Predictors of paternal participation in childcare and housework. *Journal of Personality and Social Psychology, 65,* 1154–1166.

Deutsch, M., & Gerard, H. (1955). A study of normative and informational social influences upon individual judgment. *Journal of Abnormal and Social Psychology, 51,* 629–636.

Devine, P. G. (1989). Stereotypes and prejudice: Their automatic and controlled components. *Journal of Personality and Social Psychology, 56,* 5–18.

Devos, T., Diaz, P., Viera, E., & Dunn, R. (2007). College education and motherhood as components of self-concept: Discrepancies between implicit and explicit assessments. *Self and Identity, 6,* 256–277.

De Waal, F. B. M., & Lanting, F. (1997). *Bonobo: The forgotten ape.* Berkeley, CA: University of California Press.

Diekman, A. B., & Eagly, A. H. (2000). Stereotypes as dynamic constructs: Women and men of the past, present, and future. *Personality and Social Psychology Bulletin, 26,* 1171–1188.

Diekman, A. B., & Goodfriend, W. (2006). Rolling with the changes: A role-congruity perspective on gender norms. *Psychology of Women Quarterly, 30,* 369–383.

Diekman, A. B., Goodfriend, W., & Goodwin, S. (2004). Dynamic stereotypes of power: Perceived change and stability in gender hierarchies. *Sex Roles, 50,* 201–215.

Diekman, A. B., McDonald, M., & Gardner, W. L. (2000). Love means never having to be careful: The relationship between reading romance novels and safe sex behavior. *Psychology of Women Quarterly, 24,* 179–188.

Dillon, S. (2005, January 18). Harvard chief defends his talk on women. *New York Times,* p. A16.

Dion, K. K., & Dion, K. L. (1985). Personality, gender, and the phenomenology of love. In P. R. Shaver (Ed.), *Self, situations, and behavior: Review of personality and social psychology* (Vol. 6, pp. 209–239). Beverly Hills, CA: Sage.

DiPietro, J. (1981). Rough and tumble play: A function of gender. *Developmental Psychology, 17,* 50–58.

Dodge, K. A., Gilroy, F. D., & Fenzel, L. M. (1995). Requisite management characteristics revisited: Two decades later. *Journal of Social Behavior and Personality, 10,* 253–264.

Douglass, M., & Douglass, L. (1997). *The sex you want: A lover's guide to women's sexual pleasure.* New York: Marlow.

Douvan, E., & Adelson, J. (1966). *The adolescent experience.* New York: Wiley.

Dovidio, J. F., Glick, P., & Rudman, L. A. (Eds.) (2005). *On the nature of prejudice: Fifty years after Allport.* Malden, MA: Blackwell.

Dovidio, J. F., Kawakami, K., & Gaertner, S. L. (2002). Implicit and explicit prejudice and interracial interactions. *Journal of Personality and Social Psychology, 82,* 62–68.

Dovidio, J. F., Kawakami, K., Johnson, C., Johnson, B., & Howard, A. (1997). On the nature of prejudice: Automatic and controlled processes. *Journal of Experimental Social Psychology, 33,* 510–540.

Driscoll, R., Davis, K. E., & Lipetz, M. E. (1972). Parental interference and romantic love: The Romeo and Juliet effect. *Journal of Personality and Social Psychology, 24,* 1–10.

Duncombe, J., & Marsden, D. (1993). Love and intimacy: The gender division of emotion and "emotion work." *Sociology, 17,* 221–241.

Dunn, S., & Morgan, V. (1987). Nursery and infant school play patterns: Sex-related differences. *British Educational Research Journal, 13,* 271–281.

Dutton, D. G., & Aron, A. P. (1974). Some evidence for heightened sexual attraction under conditions of high anxiety. *Journal of Personality and Social Psychology, 30,* 510–517.

Dworkin, A. (1987). *Intercourse.* New York: Free Press.

Eagly, A. H. (1987). *Sex differences in social behavior: A social role interpretation.* Hillsdale, NJ: Erlbaum.

Eagly, A. H., & Carli, L. L. (2007). *Through the labyrinth: The truth about how women become leaders.* Boston, MA: Harvard Business School Press.

Eagly, A. H., & Diekman, A. B. (2005). What is the problem? Prejudice as an attitude-in-context. In J. F. Dovidio, P. Glick, & L. A. Rudman (Eds.), *On the nature of prejudice: Fifty years after Allport* (pp. 19–35). Malden, MA: Blackwell.

Eagly, A. H., Johannesen-Schmidt, M. C., & van Engen, M. L. (2003). Transformational, transactional, and laissez-faire leadership styles: A meta-analysis comparing women and men. *Psychological Bulletin, 129,* 569–591.

Eagly, A. H., & Karau, S. J. (2002). Role congruity theory of prejudice toward female leaders. *Psychological Review, 109,* 573–598.

Eagly, A. H., Karau, S. J., & Makhijani, M. G. (1995). Gender and the effectiveness of leaders: A meta-analysis. *Psychological Bulletin, 117,* 125–145.

Eagly, A. H., Makhijani, M. G., & Klonsky, B. G. (1992). Gender and the evaluation of leaders: A meta-analysis. *Psychological Bulletin, 111,* 3–22.

Eagly, A. H., & Mladinic, A. (1989). Gender stereotypes and attitudes toward women and men. *Personality and Social Psychology Bulletin, 15,* 543–558.

Eagly, A. H., & Mladinic, A. (1993). Are people prejudiced against women? Some answers from research on attitudes, gender stereotypes and judgments of competence. In W. Stroebe & M. Hewstone (Eds.), *European review of social psychology,* (Vol. 5, pp. 1–35). New York: Wiley.

Eagly, A. H., & Steffen, V. J. (1984). Gender stereotypes stem from the distribution of women and men into social roles. *Journal of Personality and Social Psychology, 46,* 735–754.

Eagly, A. H., & Wood, W. (1999). The origins of sex differences in human behavior: Evolved dispositions versus social roles. *American Psychologist, 54,* 408–423.

Eagly, A. H., Wood, W., & Diekman, A. (2000). Social role theory of sex differences and similarities: A current appraisal. In T. Eckes & H. M. Trautner (Eds.), *The developmental social psychology of gender* (pp. 123–174). Mahwah, NJ: Erlbaum.

Eberhardt, J. L., Davies, P. G., Purdie-Vaughns, V. J., & Johnson, S. L. (2006). Looking deathworth: Perceived stereotypicality of Black defendants predicts capital-sentencing outcomes. *Psychological Science, 17,* 383–386.

Eccles, J. S. (1984). Sex differences in achievement patterns. In T. Sonderegger (Ed.), *Nebraska symposium on motivation* (Vol. 32, pp. 98–132). Lincoln: Nebraska University Press.

Eckes, T. (2002). Paternalistic and envious gender stereotypes: Testing predictions from the stereotype content model. *Sex Roles, 47*, 99–114.

Edlund, J. E., Heider, J. D., Scherer, C. R., Farc, M. M., & Sagarin, B. J. (2006). Sex differences in jealousy in response to actual infidelity experiences. *Evolutionary Psychology, 4*, 462–470.

Eisenberger, N. I., Lieberman, M. D., & Williams, K. D. (2003). Does rejection hurt? An fMRI study of social exclusion. *Science, 302*, 290–292.

Ellis, H., & Symonds, J. A. (1897). *Sexual inversion*. Bedford Row, UK: Wilson and Macmillan.

Ellis, L. (1989). *Theories of rape: Inquiries into the causes of sexual aggression*. New York: Hemisphere.

Ely, R. J. (1994). The effects of organizational demographics and social identity on relationships among professional women. *Administrative Science Quarterly, 39*, 203–238.

Ely, R. J., & Meyerson, D. E. (2000). Theories of gender in organizations: A new approach to organizational analysis and change. In A. Brief & B. M. Staw (Eds.), *Research in organizational behavior* (Vol. 22, pp. 103–151). New York: Elsevier.

Ely, R. J., & Thomas, D. A. (2001). Cultural diversity at work: The moderating effects of work group perspectives on diversity. *Administrative Science Quarterly, 46*, 229–273.

England, P. (2006). Toward gender equality: Progress and bottlenecks. In F. D. Blau, M. B. Brinton, & D. B. Grusky (Eds.), *The declining significance of gender?* (pp. 245–264). New York: Russell Sage.

Enserink, M. (2005, June 10). Let's talk about sex—and drugs. *Science, 308*, 1578–1580.

Epstein, D. (1996). *Cultures of schooling, cultures of sexuality*. New York: American Educational Research Association.

Esser, J. K., & Lindoerfer, J. S. (1989). Groupthink and the space shuttle Challenger accident: Toward a quantitative case analysis. *Journal of Behavioral Decision Making, 2*, 167–177.

Etaugh, C., & Duits, T. (1990). Development of gender discrimination: Role of stereotypic and counter-stereotypic gender cues. *Sex Roles, 23*, 215–222.

Fabes, R. A., Martin, C. L., & Hanish, L. D. (2003). Young children's play qualities in same-, other-, and mixed-sex peer groups. *Child Development, 3*, 921–932.

Fagot, B. I. (1995). Changes in thinking about early sex role development. *Developmental Review, 5*, 83–98.

Fagot, B. I., Hagen, R., Leinbach, M. D., & Kronsberg, S. (1985). Differential reactions to assertive and communicative acts of toddler boys and girls. *Child Development, 56*, 1499–1505.

Fagot, B. I., Leinbach, M. D., & Hagen, R. (1986). Gender labeling and the adoption of gender-typed behavior. *Developmental Psychology, 22*, 440–443.

Fagot, B. I., Leinbach, M. D., & O'Boyle, C. (1992). Gender labeling, gender stereotyping, and parenting behaviors. *Developmental Psychology, 28*, 225–230.

Fagot, B. I., Rodgers, C. S., & Leinbach, M. D. (2000). Theories of gender socialization. In T. Eckes & H. M. Trautner (Eds.), *The developmental social psychology of gender* (pp. 65–89). Mahwah, NJ: Erlbaum.

Fairchild, K., & Rudman, L. A. (in press). Everyday stranger harassment and women's objectification. *Social Justice Research*.

Faith, M., & Schare, M. L. (1993). The role of body image in sexually avoidant behavior. *Archives of Sexual Behavior, 22*, 345–356.

Faludi, S. (1991). *The undeclared war against American women*. New York: Crown.

Fan, X., Chen, M., & Matsumoto, A. R. (1997). Gender differences in mathematics achievement: Findings from the *National Education Longitudinal Study of 1988*. *Journal of Experimental Education, 65(3)*, 229–242.

Fazio, R. H., & Hilden, L. E. (2001). Emotional reactions to a seemingly prejudiced response: The role of automatically activated racial attitudes and motivation to control prejudiced reactions. *Personality and Social Psychology Bulletin, 27*, 538–549.

Fazio, R. H., & Olson, M. A. (2003). Implicit measures in social cognition research: Their meaning and use. *Annual Review of Psychology, 54*, 297–327.

Federal Bureau of Investigation. (2007). *Uniform crime reports*. Retrieved August 27, 2007, from *http://www.fbi.gov/ucr/ucr.htm*.

Fein, E., & Schneider, S. (1995). *The rules: Time-tested secrets for capturing the heart of Mr. Right*. New York: Warner Books.

Feingold, A. (1988). Matching for attractiveness in romantic partners and same-sex friends: A meta-analysis and theoretical critique. *Psychological Bulletin, 104*, 226–235.

Feingold, A., & Mazella, R. (1998). Gender differences in body image are increasing. *Psychological Science, 9*, 32–37.

Fidell, L. S. (1975). Empirical verification of sex discrimination in hiring practices in psychology. In R. K. Unger & F. L. Denmark (Eds.), *Woman: Dependent or independent variable?* (pp. 774–782). New York: Psychological Dimensions.

Finkelson, L., & Oswalt, R. (1995). College date rape: Incidence and reporting. *Psychological Reports, 77*, 526.

Fiorentine, R. (1988). Sex differences in success expectancies and causal attributions: Is this why fewer women become physicians? *Social Psychology Quarterly, 51*, 236–249.

Firestone, S. (1970). *The dialectic of sex: The case for a feminist revolution*. New York: Farrar, Straus, & Giroux.

Fischer, A. R. (2006). Women's benevolent sexism as a reaction to hostility. *Psychology of Women Quarterly, 30*, 410–416.

Fisher, B. S., Cullen, E. T., & Turner, M. G. (2000). *The sexual victimization of college women*. Washington, DC: National Institute of Justice.

Fisher, H. (1992). *The anatomy of love: A natural history of adultery, monogamy, and divorce*. London: Simon & Schuster.

Fisher, W. A., Branscombe, N. R., & Lemery, C. R. (1983). The bigger the better? Arousal and attributional responses to erotic stimuli that depict different size penises. *Journal of Sex Research, 19*, 377–396.

Fiske, A. P., Haslam, N., & Fiske, S. T. (1991). Confusing one person with another: What errors reveal about the elementary forms of social relations. *Journal of Personality and Social Psychology, 60*, 656–674.

Fiske, S. T. (1998). Stereotyping, prejudice, and discrimination. In D. T. Gilbert, S. T. Fiske, & G. Lindzey (Eds.), *Handbook of social psychology* (4th ed., Vol. 2, pp. 357–411). New York: McGraw-Hill.

Fiske, S. T. (2005). Social cognition. In J. F. Dovidio, P. Glick, & L. A. Rudman (Eds.), *On the nature of prejudice: Fifty years after Allport* (pp. 36–53). Malden, MA: Blackwell.

Fiske, S. T., Bersoff, D. N., Borgida, E., Deaux, K., & Heilman, M. E. (1991). Social science research on trial: Use of sex stereotyping research in Price Waterhouse v. Hopkins. *American Psychology, 46,* 1049–1060.

Fiske, S. T., Cuddy, A. J. C., Glick, P., & Xu, J. (2002). A model of (often mixed) stereotype content: Competence and warmth respectively follow from perceived status and competition. *Journal of Personality and Social Psychology, 82,* 878–902.

Fiske, S. T., & Glick, P. (1995). Ambivalence and stereotypes cause sexual harassment: A theory with implications for organizational change. *Journal of Social Issues, 51,* 97–115.

Fiske, S. T., & Neuberg, S. L. (1990). A continuum model of impression formation from category-based to individuating processes: Influences of information and motivation on attention and interpretation. In M. P. Zanna (Ed.), *Advances in experimental social psychology* (Vol. 23, pp. 1–74). San Diego, CA: Academic Press.

Fiske, S. T., & Stevens, L. E. (1993). What's so special about sex? Gender stereotyping and discrimination. In S. Oskamp & M. Costanzo (Eds.), *Gender issues in contemporary society: Applied social psychology annual* (pp. 173–196). Newbury Park, CA: Sage.

Fiske, S. T., & Von Hendy, H. M. (1992). Personality feedback and situational norms can control stereotyping processes. *Journal of Personality and Social Psychology, 62,* 577–596.

Fitzgerald, L. F., Drasgow, F., Hulin, C. L., Gelfand, M. J., & Magley, V. J. (1997). Antecedents and consequences of sexual harassment in organizations: A test of an integrated model. *Journal of Applied Psychology, 82(4),* 578–589.

Fitzgerald, L. F., Gelfand, M. J., & Drasgow, F. (1995). Measuring sexual harassment: Theoretical and psychometric advances. *Basic and Applied Social Psychology, 17,* 425–445.

Fitzgerald, L. F., Hulin, C. L., & Drasgow, F. (1995). The antecedents and consequences of sexual harassment in organizations: An integrated model. In G. P. Keita & J. J. Hurrell (Eds.), *Job stress in a changing workforce: Investigating gender, diversity, and family issues* (pp. 55–73). Washington, DC: American Psychological Association.

Flannery, K. A., & Watson, M. W. (1993). Are individual differences in fantasy play related to peer acceptance levels? *Journal of Genetic Psychology, 154,* 407–416.

Foschi, M. (2000). Double standards for competence: Theory and research. *Annual Review of Sociology, 26,* 21–42.

Foster, C. A., & Campbell, W. K. (2005). The adversity of secret relationships. *Personal Relationships, 12,* 125–143.

Francken, A. B., van de Wiel, H. B. M., van Driel, M. F., & Weijmar Schultz, W.

C. M. (2002). What importance do women attribute to size of the penis? *European Urology, 42,* 426–431.

Franke, K. M. (1997). What's wrong with sexual harassment? *Stanford Law Review, 49,* 691–772.

Frankforter, S. A. (1996). The progression of women beyond the glass ceiling. *Journal of Social Behavior and Personality, 11,* 121–132.

Franklin, K., & Herek, G. (2003). Violence toward homosexuals. In S. Plous (Ed.), *Understanding prejudice and discrimination* (pp. 384–401). New York: McGraw Hill.

Fredrickson, B. L., & Roberts, T. A. (1997). Objectification theory: Toward understanding women's lived experiences and mental health risks. *Psychology of Women Quarterly, 21,* 173–206.

Fredrickson, B. L., Roberts, T. A., Noll, S. M., Quinn, D. M., & Twenge, J. M. (1998). That swimsuit becomes you: Sex differences in self-objectification, restrained eating, and math performance. *Journal of Personality and Social Psychology, 75,* 269–284.

French, J. R. P., Jr., & Raven, B. (1959). The bases of social power. In D. Cartwright (Ed.), *Studies in social power* (pp. 150–167). Ann Arbor: University of Michigan.

Freud, S. (2000). *Three essays on the theory of sexuality.* New York: Basic Books. (Original work published 1905)

Fried, L. P., Francomano, C. A., MacDonald, S. M., Wagner, E. M., Stokes, E. J., Carbone, K. M., et al. (1996). Career development for women in academic medicine: Multiple interventions in a department of medicine. *Journal of the American Medical Association, 276,* 898–905.

Frieze, I. H. (1983). Investigating the causes and consequences of marital rape. *Signs, 8,* 532–553.

Frieze, I. H. (2005). *Hurting the one you love: Violence in relationships.* Belmont, CA: Wadsworth.

Frieze, I. H., Olson, J. E., & Russell, J. (1991). Attractiveness and income for men and women in management. *Journal of Applied Social Psychology, 21*(13), 1039–1057.

Frisco, M. L., & Williams, K. (2003). Perceived housework equity, marital happiness, and divorce in dual-earner households. *Journal of Family Issues, 24,* 51–73.

Frone, M. R., Russell, M., & Cooper, M. L. (1992). Antecedents and outcomes of work-family conflict: Testing a model of the work–family interface. *Journal of Applied Psychology, 77,* 65–78.

Furnham, A., & Mak, T. (1999). Sex-role stereotyping in television commercials: A review and comparison of fourteen studies done on five continents over 25 years. *Sex Roles, 41,* 413–437.

Galinsky, A. D., Gruenfeld, D. H., & Magee, J. C. (2003). From power to action. *Journal of Personality and Social Psychology, 85,* 453–466.

Garcia-Retamero, R., & López-Zafra, E. (2006). Prejudice against women in male-congenial environments: Perceptions of gender role congruity in leadership. *Sex Roles, 55,* 51–61.

Gardner, C. B. (1995). *Passing by: Gender and public harassment.* Berkley: University of California Press.

Garst, J., & Bodenhausen, G. V. (1997). Advertising's effects on men's gender role attitudes. *Sex Roles, 36,* 551–572.

Gavey, N., & McPhillips, K. (1999). Subject to romance: Heterosexual passivity as an obstacle to women initiating condom use. *Psychology of Women Quarterly, 23,* 349–367.

Geer, J. H., & Robertson, G. G. (2005). Implicit attitudes in sexuality: Gender differences. *Archives of Sexual Behavior, 34,* 671–677.

Geis, F. L. (1993). Self-fulfilling prophecies: A social-psychological view of gender. In A. E. Beall & R. J. Sternberg (Eds.), *The psychology of gender* (pp. 5–54). New York: Guilford Press.

Geis, F. L., Brown, V., Jennings, J., & Porter, N. (1984). TV commercials as achievement scripts for women. *Sex Roles, 10,* 513–525.

Gelman, S. A., Collman, P., & Maccoby, E. E. (1986). Inferring properties from categories versus inferring categories from properties: The case of gender. *Child Development, 57,* 396–404.

Gelman, S. A., & Taylor, M. G. (2000). Gender essentialism in cognitive development. In P. H. Miller & E. Scholnick (Eds.), *Toward a feminist developmental psychology* (pp. 169–190). New York: Routledge.

Gerhart, B., & Rynes, S. (1991). Determinants and consequences of salary negotiations by male and female MBA graduates. *Journal of Applied Psychology, 76,* 256–262.

Gilligan, C. (1982). *In a different voice.* Cambridge, MA: Harvard University Press.

Giordano, P. C. (2003). Relationships in adolescence. *Annual Review of Sociology, 29,* 257–281.

Giordano, P. C., Longmore, M. A., & Manning, W. D. (2006). Gender and the meanings of adolescent romantic relationships: A focus on boys. *American Sociological Review, 71*(2), 260–287.

Glass, S. P., & Wright, T. L. (1992). Justifications for extramarital relationships: The association between attitudes, behaviors, and gender. *Journal of Sex Research, 29,* 361–387.

Glick, P. (1991). Trait-based and sex-based discrimination in occupational prestige, occupational salary, and hiring. *Sex Roles, 25,* 351–378.

Glick, P., Diebold, J., Bailey-Werner, B., & Zhu, L. (1997). The two faces of Adam: Ambivalent sexism and polarized attitudes toward women. *Personality and Social Psychology Bulletin, 23,* 1323–1334.

Glick, P., & Fiske, S. T. (1996). The Ambivalent Sexism Inventory: Differentiating hostile and benevolent sexism. *Journal of Personality and Social Psychology, 70,* 491–512.

Glick, P., & Fiske, S. T. (1999). The Ambivalence Toward Men Inventory: Differentiating hostile and benevolent beliefs about men. *Psychology of Women Quarterly, 23,* 519–536.

Glick, P., & Fiske, S. T. (2001). Ambivalent sexism. In M. P. Zanna (Ed.), *Advances in experimental social psychology* (Vol. 33, pp. 115–188). Thousand Oaks, CA: Academic Press.

Glick, P., Fiske, S. T., Mladinic, A., Saiz, J., Abrams, D., Masser, B., et al. (2000). Beyond prejudice as simple antipathy: Hostile and benevolent sexism across cultures. *Journal of Personality and Social Psychology, 79,* 763–775.

Glick, P., Gangl, C., Gibb, S., Klumpner, S., & Weinberg, E. (2007). Defensive reactions to masculinity threat: More negative affect toward effeminate (but not masculine) gay men. *Sex Roles, 57*, 55–59.

Glick, P., Lameiras, M., Fiske, S. T., Eckes, T., Masser, B., Volpato, C., et al. (2004). Bad but bold: Ambivalent attitudes toward men predict gender inequality in 16 nations. *Journal of Personality and Social Psychology, 86*, 713–728.

Glick, P., Larsen, S., Johnson, C., & Branstiter, H. (2005). Evaluations of sexy women in low and high status jobs. *Psychology of Women Quarterly, 29*, 389–395.

Glick, P., Sakalli-Ugurlu, N., Ferreira, M. C., & de Souza, M. A. (2002). Ambivalent sexism and attitudes toward wife abuse in Turkey and Brazil. *Psychology of Women Quarterly, 26*, 291–296.

Glick, P., Wilk, K., & Perreault, M. (1995). Images of occupations: Components of gender and status in occupational stereotypes. *Sex Roles, 32*, 564–582.

Glick, P., Zion, C., & Nelson, C. (1988). What mediates sex discrimination in hiring decisions? *Journal of Personality and Social Psychology, 55*, 178–186.

Glomb, T. M., Richman, W. L., Hulin, C. L., Drasgow, F., Schneider, K. T., & Fitzgerald, L. F. (1997). Ambient sexual harassment: An integrated model of antecedents and consequences. *Organizational Behavior and Human Decision Processes, 71(3)*, 309–328.

Goffman, E. (1959). *The presentation of self in everyday life.* Garden City, NY: Anchor Books.

Goldberg, P. (1968). Are women prejudiced against women? *Transaction, 5*, 316–322.

Goldberg, P. A., Gottesdiener, M., & Abramson, P. R. (1975). Another put-down of women? Perceived attractiveness as a function of support for the feminist movement. *Journal of Personality and Social Psychology, 32*, 113–115.

Golden, C., & Rouse, C. (2000). Orchestrating impartiality: The impact of "blind" auditions on female musicians. *American Economic Review, 90(4)*, 715–742.

Goldenberg, J. L., Pyszczynski, T., Greenberg, J., & Solomon, S. (2000). Fleeing the body: A terror management perspective on the problem of human corporeality. *Personality and Social Psychology Review, 4*, 200–218.

Goldenberg, J. L., Pyszczynski, T., Greenberg, J., Solomon, S., Kluck, B., & Cornwell, R. (2001). I am not an animal: Mortality salience, disgust, and the denial of human creatureliness. *Journal of Experimental Psychology, 130*, 427–435.

Goldenhar, L. M., Swanson, N. G., Hurrell, J. J., Jr., Ruder, A., & Deddens, J. (1998). Stressors and adverse outcomes for female construction workers. *Journal of Occupational Health Psychology, 3*, 19–32.

Goodwin, S. A., Fiske, S. T., Rosen, L. D., & Rosenthal, A. M. (2002). The eye of the beholder: Romantic goals and impression biases. *Journal of Experimental Social Psychology, 38*, 232–241.

Gorner, P. (2006, April 19). Survey of 29 nations shows male-centered cultures least satisfied [Electronic version]. *Chicago Tribune.*

Gottman, J. M. (1993). A theory of marital dissolution and stability. *Journal of Family Psychology, 7*(1), 57–75.

Gottman, J. M., & Parker, J. (1984). *Conversations of friends.* New York: Cambridge University Press.

Gottman, J. M., & Silver, N. (1999). *The seven principles for making marriage work.* New York: Crown.

Gottschall, J. (2004). Explaining wartime rape. *Journal of Sex Research, 41,* 129–136.

Gough, H. G., & Heilbrun, A. B., Jr. (1980). *Adjective check list manual.* Palo Alto, CA: Consulting Psychologists Press.

Gould, R. J., & Slone, C. G. (1982). The "feminine modesty" effect: A self-presentational interpretation of sex differences in causal attribution. *Personality and Social Psychology Bulletin, 8,* 477–485.

Goy, R. W., Bercovitch, F. B., & McBrair, M. C. (1988). Behavioral masculinization is independent of genital masculinization in prenatally androgenized female rhesus macaques. *Hormones and Behavior, 22,* 552–571.

Grabe, S., Routledge, C., Cook, A., Andersen, C., & Arndt, J. (2005). In defense of the body: The effect of mortality salience on female body objectification. *Psychology of Women Quarterly, 29,* 33–37.

Graglia, C. F. (1998). *Domestic tranquility: A brief against feminism.* Dallas, TX: Spence.

Gray, J. (1992). *Men are from Mars, women are from Venus: The classic guide to understanding the opposite sex.* New York: HarperCollins.

Graziano, W. G., Jensen-Campbell, L. A., Todd, M., & Finch, J. F. (1997). Interpersonal attraction from an evolutionary perspective: Women's attraction to dominant and prosocial men. In J. A. Simpson & D. T. Kenrick (Eds.), *Evolutionary social psychology* (pp. 141–167). Mahwah, NJ: Erlbaum.

Green, R. J., Ashmore, R. D., & Manzi, R., Jr. (2005). The structure of gender type perception: Testing the elaboration, encapsulation, and evaluation framework. *Social Cognition, 23,* 429–464.

Greene, R. (2003). *The art of seduction.* New York: Penguin Books.

Greenwald, A.G., & Banaji, M.R. (1995). Implicit social cognition: Attitudes, self-esteem, and stereotypes. *Psychological Review, 102,* 4–27.

Greenwald, A. G., Banaji, M. R., Rudman, L. A., Farnham, S. D., Nosek, B. A., & Mellott, D. S. (2002). A unified theory of implicit attitudes, stereotypes, self-esteem, and self-concept. *Psychological Review, 109,* 3–25.

Greenwald, A. G., McGhee, D. E., & Schwartz, J. L. K. (1998). Measuring individual differences in implicit cognition: The Implicit Association Test. *Journal of Personality and Social Psychology, 74,* 1464–1480.

Greenwald, A. G., Oakes, M. A., & Hoffman, H. G. (2003). Targets of discrimination: Effects of race on responses to weapons holders. *Journal of Experimental Social Psychology, 39,* 399–405.

Greenwald, A. G., Poehlman, T. A., Uhlmann, E., & Banaji, M. R. (in press). Measuring and using the Implicit Association Test: III. Meta-analysis of predictive validity. *Journal of Personality and Social Psychology.*

Groesz, L. M., Levine, M. P., & Murnen, S. K. (2002). The effect of experimental presentation of thin media images on body satisfaction: A meta-analytic review. *International Journal of Eating Disorders, 31*(1), 1–16.

Grossman, A. (1999). A question of silence: The rape of German women by Soviet occupying soldiers. In N. Dombrowski (Ed.), *Women and war in the twentieth century* (pp. 116–137). New York: Garland.

Grossman, T. (2002). Pre-homosexual childhoods: An empirical study of gender role conformity among homosexual men. *Zeitschrift fur Sexualforschung, 15,* 98–119.

Grossman, L. (2006, September 4). The secret love lives of teenage boys. *Time, 168*(10), 40–41.

Grote, N. K., Naylor, K. E., & Clark, M. S. (2002). Perceiving the division of family work to be unfair: Do social comparisons, enjoyment, and competence matter? *Journal of Family Psychology, 16,* 510–522.

Grover, S. L., & Crooker, K. J. (1995). Who appreciates family-responsive human resource policies: The impact of family-friendly policies on the organizational attachment of parents and non-parents. *Personnel Psychology, 48,* 271–288.

Gupta, A. S., & Lynn, D. B. (1972). A study of sexual behavior in females. *Journal of Sex Research, 8,* 207–218.

Gupta, U., & Singh, P. (1982). Exploratory study of love and liking and types of marriages. *Indian Journal of Applied Psychology, 19,* 92–97.

Gutek, B. A. (1985). *Sex and the workplace: Impact of sexual behavior and harassment on women, men, and organizations.* San Francisco: Jossey-Bass.

Gutek, B. A., & Done, R. S. (2001). Sexual harassment. In R. K. Unger (Ed.), *Handbook for the psychology of women and gender* (pp. 367–387). New York: Wiley.

Gutek, B. A., & Morasch, B. (1982). Sex-ratios, sex-role spillover, and sexual harassment of women at work. *Journal of Social Issues, 38,* 55–74.

Guy, M. E., & Newman, M. A. (2004). Women's jobs, men's jobs: Sex segregation and emotional labor. *Public Administration Review, 64,* 289–298.

Haddock, G., & Zanna, M. P. (1994). Preferring "housewives" to "feminists": Categorization and the favorability of attitudes toward women. *Psychology of Women Quarterly, 18,* 25–52.

Haddock, S. A., Zimmerman, T. Z., Ziemba, S. J., & Current, L. R. (2001). Ten adaptive strategies for work and family balance: Advice from successful families. *Journal of Marital and Family Therapy, 27,* 445–458.

Hafner, J. (1993). *The end of marriage.* London: Random House.

Haidt, J., McCauley, C. R., & Rozin, P. (1994). Individual differences in sensitivity to disgust: A scale sampling seven domains of disgust elicitors. *Personality and Individual Differences, 16,* 701–713.

Hall, J. A., & Carter, J. D. (1999). Gender-stereotype accuracy as an individual difference. *Journal of Personality and Social Psychology, 77,* 350–359.

Haney, C., Banks, C., & Zimbardo, P. (1973). Interpersonal dynamics in a simulated prison. *International Journal of Criminology and Penology, 1,* 69–97.

Harriet, R. C., & Rivers, C. (1996). *She works/he works: How two-income families are happier, healthier, and better-off.* San Francisco: Harper.

Harris, A. C. (1994). Ethnicity as a determinant of sex role identity: A replication study of item selection for the Bem Sex Role Inventory. *Sex Roles, 31,* 241–273.

Harris, C. R. (2003). Factors associated with jealousy over real and imagined infidelity: An examination of the social-cognitive and evolutionary perspectives. *Psychology of Women Quarterly, 27*(4), 319–329.

Harris, J. R. (1998). *The nurture assumption.* New York: Free Press.

Harris, M. (1993). The evolution of human gender hierarchies: A trial formulation. In B. D. Miller (Ed.), *Sex and gender hierarchies* (pp. 57–79). New York: Cambridge University Press.

Harris, M. B. (1994). Gender of subject and target as mediators of aggression. *Journal of Applied Social Psychology, 24,* 453–471.

Harrison, K., & Fredrickson, B. L. (2003). Women's sport media, self-objectification, and mental health in black and white adolescent females. *Journal of Communication, 53,* 216–232.

Haslam, N., Rothschild, L., & Ernst, D. (2000). Essentialist beliefs about social categories. *British Journal of Social Psychology, 39,* 113–127.

Haslett, B. J., Geis, F. L., & Carter, M. R. (1992). *The organizational woman: Power and paradox.* Westport, CT: Ablex.

Hatfield, E., & Rapson, R. L. (1993). *Love, sex, and intimacy: Their psychology, biology, and history.* New York: HarperCollins College.

Hatfield, E., & Rapson, R. L. (1996). *Love and sex: Cross-cultural perspectives.* Needham Heights, MA: Allyn & Bacon.

Hatfield, E., & Rapson, R. L. (2006). Passionate love, sexual desire, and mate selection: Cross-cultural and historical perspectives. In P. Noller & J. A. Feeney (Eds.), *Close relationships: Functions, forms and processes* (pp. 227–243). Hove, UK: Psychology Press/Taylor & Francis.

Haugaard, J. J., & Seri, L. G. (2003). Stalking and other forms of intrusive contact after the dissolution of adolescent dating or romantic relationships. *Violence and Victims, 18*(3), 279–297.

Heatherington, L., Daubman, K. A., Bates, C., Ahn, A., Brown, H., & Preston, C. (1993). Two investigations of "female modesty" in achievement situations. *Sex Roles, 29,* 739–754.

Heaton, T. B, & Blake, A. M. (1999). Gender differences in determinants of marital disruption. *Journal of Family Issues, 20,* 25–45.

Hebl, M. R., King, E., Glick, P., Singletary, S. L., & Kazama, S. M. (2007). Hostile and benevolent reactions toward pregnant women: Complementary interpersonal punishments and rewards that maintain traditional roles. *Journal of Applied Psychology, 92,* 1499–1511.

Heer, F. (1962). *The medieval world: Europe, 1100–1350.* New York: New American Library.

Hegarty, P., & Pratto, F. (2004). The differences that norms make: Empiricism, social constructionism, and the interpretation of group differences. *Sex Roles, 50,* 445–453.

Heilman, M. E. (1980). The impact of situational factors on personnel decisions concerning women: Varying the sex composition of the applicant pool. *Organizational Behavior and Human Performance, 26,* 286–295.

Heilman, M. E. (1983). Sex bias in work settings: The lack of fit model. *Research in Organizational Behavior, 5,* 269–298.

Heilman, M. E. (2001). Description and prescription: How gender stereotypes prevent women's ascent up the organizational ladder. *Journal of Social Issues, 57,* 657–674.

Heilman, M. E., & Blader, S. L. (2001). Assuming preferential selection when the admissions policy is unknown: The effects of gender rarity. *Journal of Applied Psychology, 86,* 188–193.

Heilman, M. E., Block, C. J., & Martell, R. F. (1995). Sex stereotypes: Do they influence perceptions of managers? *Journal of Social Behavior and Personality, 10,* 237–252.

Heilman, M. E., & Chen, J. J. (2005). Same behavior, different consequences: Reactions to men's and women's altruistic citizenship behavior. *Journal of Applied Psychology, 90,* 431–441.

Heilman, M. E., & Haynes, M. C. (2005). No credit where credit is due: Attributional rationalization of women's success in male-female teams. *Journal of Applied Psychology, 90,* 905–916.

Heilman, M. E., & Okimoto, T. G. (2007). Averting penalties for women's success: Rectifying the perceived communality deficiency. *Journal of Applied Psychology, 92,* 81–92.

Heilman, M. E., & Stopek, M. H. (1985). Being attractive, advantage or disadvantage? Performance-based evaluations and recommended personnel actions as a function of appearance, sex, and job type. *Organizational Behavior and Human Decision Processes, 35,* 202–215.

Heilman, M. E., Wallen, A. S., Fuchs, D., & Tamkins, M. M. (2004). Penalties for success: Reactions to women who succeed at male gender-typed tasks. *Journal of Applied Psychology, 89,* 416–427.

Heim, P. (1990). Keeping the power dead even. *Journal of American Medical Women's Association, 45,* 232–243.

Hendrick, C., & Hendrick, S. S. (1988). Lovers wear rose colored glasses. *Journal of Social and Personal Relationships, 5,* 161–183.

Hendrick, S. S., & Hendrick, C. (1992). *Liking, loving and relating* (2nd ed.). Belmont, CA: Thomson Brooks/Cole.

Hendrick, S. S., & Hendrick, C. (1995). Gender differences and similarities in sex and love. *Personal Relationships, 2,* 55–65.

Herek, G. M. (1989). Hate crimes against lesbians and gay men: Issues for research and policy. *American Psychologist, 44,* 948–955.

Herek, G. M. (1993). Sexual orientation and military service: A social science perspective. *American Psychologist, 48,* 538–549.

Herek, G. M. (2002). Gender gaps in public opinions about lesbians and gay men. *Public Opinion Quarterly, 66,* 40–66.

Hewitt, S. A. (2002). *Creating a life: Professional women and the quest for children.* New York: Miramax Books.

Hickman, S. E., & Muehlenhard, C. L. (1997). College women's fears and precautionary behaviors related to acquaintance rape and stranger rape. *Psychology of Women Quarterly, 21,* 527–547.

Hill, C. T., Rubin, Z., & Peplau, L. A. (1979). Breakups before marriage: The end of 103 affairs. In G. Levinger & O. C. Moles (Eds.), *Divorce and separation* (pp. 64–82). New York: Basic Books.

Hirschman, L. R. (2006). *Get to work: A manifesto for women of the world.* New York: Viking.

Hite, S. (1987). *Women and love: A cultural revolution in progress.* New York: Alfred A. Knopf.

Hite, S. (1991). *The Hite report on love, passion, and emotional violence.* London: Optima.

Hite, S. (2003). *The Hite report: A nationwide study of female sexuality.* New York: Seven Stories Press. (Original work published 1976)

Hite, S. (2006). *The Shere Hite reader: New and selected writings on sex, globalization, and private life.* New York: Seven Stories Press.

Hochschild, A. (1989). *The second shift: Working parents and the revolution at home.* New York: Viking.

Hoff-Summers, C. (2000). *The war against boys: How misguided feminism is harming our young men.* New York: Touchstone.

Hoffman, C., & Hurst, N. (1990). Gender stereotypes: Perception or rationalization? *Journal of Personality and Social Psychology, 58,* 197–208.

Holland, D. C., & Eisenhart, M. A. (1990). *Educated in romance: Women, achievement, and college culture.* Chicago: University of Chicago Press.

Holland, D. C., & Skinner, D. (1987). Prestige and intimacy: The cultural models behind Americans' talk about gender types. In D. C. Holland & N. Quinn (Eds.), *Cultural models in language and thought* (pp. 78–111). Cambridge, UK: Cambridge University Press.

Holt, C. L., & Ellis, J. B. (1998). Assessing the current validity of the Bem Sex-Role Inventory. *Sex Roles, 39,* 929–941.

Hosseini, K. (2003). *The kite runner.* New York: Riverhead Books.

Howes, C. (1988). Peer interactions of young children. *Monographs of the Society for Research in Child Development,* 53(1), Serial No. 217.

Hu, W. (2007, January 14). Equal cheers for boys and girls draw some boos [Electronic version]. *New York Times.*

Huddy, L., & Terkildsen, N. (1993). The consequences of gender stereotypes for women candidates at different levels and types of office. *Political Research Quarterly, 46,* 503–525.

Huffman v. Pepsi-Cola Bottling Co. of Minneapolis-St. Paul, et al., 1994, Hennepin County Trial Court, File # MC 92-10995.

Hyde, J. S. (2005). The gender similarities hypothesis. *American Psychologist, 60,* 581–592.

Hyde, J. S., Fennema, E., & Lamon, S. J. (1990). Gender differences in performance in mathematics: A meta-analysis. *Psychological Bulletin, 107,* 139–155.

Ibarra, H. (1997). Paving an alternative route: Gender differences in managerial networks. *Social Psychology Quarterly, 60,* 91–102.

Ickes, W., Snyder, M., & Garcia, S. (1997). Personality influences on the choice of situations. In R. Hogan, J. A. Johnson, & S. R. Briggs (Eds.), *Handbook of personality psychology* (pp. 165–195). San Diego, CA: Academic Press.

Impett, E. A., & Peplau, L. A. (2003). Sexual compliance: Gender, motivational, and relationship perspectives. *Journal of Sex Research, 40,* 87–100.

Impett, E. A., & Tolman, D. L. (2006). Late adolescent girls' sexual experiences and sexual satisfaction. *Journal of Adolescent Research, 21,* 628–646.

Isaacson, W. (1983, August 15). Trying to make amends [Electronic verison]. *Time Magazine.* http://www.time.com/time/magazine/article/0,9171,949711-4,00.html

Isay, R. (1999). Gender in homosexual boys: Some developmental and clinical considerations. *Psychiatry: Interpersonal and Biological Processes, 62,* 187–194.

Jacklin, C. N., & Maccoby, E. E. (1978). Social behavior at 33 months in same-sex and mixed-sex dyads. *Child Development, 49,* 557–569.

Jackman, M. R. (1994). *The velvet glove: Paternalism and conflict in gender, class, and race relations.* Berkeley: University of California Press.

Jackman, M. R. (1999). Gender, violence, and harassment. In J. Saltzman Chafetz (Ed.), *Handbook of the sociology of gender* (pp. 275–317). New York: Springer.

Jackman, M. R. (2001). License to kill: Violence and legitimacy in expropriative intergroup relations. In J. T. Jost & B. Major (Eds.), *The psychology of legitimacy: Emerging perspectives on ideology, justice, and intergroup relations* (pp. 437–467). New York: Cambridge University Press.

Jackson, R. (1990). The Chinese foot-binding syndrome: Observations and sequelae of wearing ill-fitting shoes. *International Journal of Dermatology, 29,* 322–328.

Jackson, R. M. (1998). *Destined for equality: The inevitable rise of women's status.* Cambridge, MA: Harvard University Press.

Jackson, R. M. (2006). Opposing forces: How, why, and when will gender equity disappear. In F. D. Blau, M. B. Brinton, & D. B. Grusky (Eds.), *The declining significance of gender?* (pp. 215–243). New York: Russell Sage.

Jacobs, J. A. (1992). Women's entry into management: Trends in earnings, authority and values among salaried mangers. *Administrative Science Quarterly, 37,* 282–301.

Jacobs, J. E., & Eccles, J. S. (1992). The impact of mothers' gender-role stereotypic beliefs on mothers' and childrens' ability perceptions. *Journal of Personality and Social Psychology, 63,* 932–944.

Jacobson, J. (June 27, 2002). Parity and the presidency. *The Chronicle of Higher Education.* Retrieved October 17, 2007, from http://chronicle.com/jobs/2002/06/2002062701c.htm

Janis, I. L. (1982). *Groupthink: Psychological studies of policy decisions and fiascos.* Boston: Houghton Mifflin.

Janoff-Bulman, R., & Wade, M. B. (1996). The dilemma of self-advocacy for women: Another case of blaming the victim? *Journal of Social and Clinical Psychology, 15,* 445–446.

"Japan tries women-only train cars to stop groping." (2005, June 10). Retrieved June 14, 2005, from http://abcnews.go.com/GMA/International/story?id=803965&GMA=true

Jeffreys, S. (2005). *Beauty and misogyny: Harmful cultural practices in the West.* New York: Routledge.

Jensen-Campbell, L. A., Graziano, W. G., & West, S. (1995). Dominance, prosocial orientation, and female preferences: Do nice guys really finish last? *Journal of Personality and Social Psychology, 68*, 427–440.

Jenson v. Eveleth Taconite Mining Co., 824 F. Supp. 847 (D. Minn 1993).

Johnson, L. B. (1991). Job strain among police officers: Gender comparisons. *Police Studies, 14*, 12–16.

Johnson, S. M. (2003). The revolution in couple therapy: A practitioner-scientist perspective. *Journal of Marital and Family Therapy, 29*, 365–384.

Jost, J. T., & Banaji, M. R. (1994). The role of stereotyping in system-justification and the production of false-consciousness. *British Journal of Social Psychology, 33*, 1–27.

Jost, J. T., Burgess, D., & Mosso, C. (2001). Conflicts of legitimation among self, group, and system: The integrative potential of system-justification theory. In J. T. Jost & B. Major (Eds.), *The psychology of legitimacy: Emerging perspectives on ideology, justice, and intergroup relations* (pp. 363–388). New York: Cambridge University Press.

Jost, J. T., & Kay, A. C. (2005). Exposure to benevolent sexism and complementary gender stereotypes: Consequences for specific and diffuse forms of system justification. *Journal of Personality and Social Psychology, 88*, 498–509.

Jost, J. T., Pelham, P. W., & Carvallo, M. R. (2002). Non-conscious forms of system justification: Implicit and behavioral preferences for high status groups. *Journal of Experimental Social Psychology, 38*, 586–602.

Judd, C. M., & Park, B. (2005). Group differences and stereotype accuracy. In J. F. Dovidio, P. Glick, & L. A. Rudman (Eds.), *On the nature of prejudice: Fifty years after Allport* (pp. 123–138). Malden, MA: Blackwell.

Judd, C. M., Park, B., Ryan, C. S., Brauer, M., & Kraus, S. (1995). Stereotypes and ethnocentrism: Interethnic perceptions of African American and White American college samples. *Journal of Personality and Social Psychology, 69*, 460–481.

Judge, T. A., & Piccolo, R. F. (2004). Transformational and transactional leadership: A meta-analytic test of their relative validity. *Journal of Applied Psychology, 89*, 901–910.

Kamen, P. (2002). *Her way: Young women remake the sexual revolution*. New York: Broadway.

Kanter, R. M. (1977). *Men and women of the corporation*. New York: Basic Books.

Karpf, A. (2006). *The human voice*. London: Bloomsbury.

Kelley, H. H. (1952). The two functions of reference groups. In G. E. Swanson, T. M. Newcomb, & E. L. Hartley (Eds.), *Readings in social psychology* (pp. 410–414). New York: Holt.

Keltner, D., Gruenfeld, D. H., & Anderson, C. (2003). Power, approach, and inhibition. *Psychological Review, 110*, 265–284.

Kenrick, D. T., Gutierres, S. E., & Goldberg, L. L. (1989). Influence of popular erotica on judgments of strangers and mates. *Journal of Experimental Social Psychology, 25*, 159–167.

Kenrick, D. T., & Simpson, J. A. (1997). Why social psychology and evolutionary psychology need one another. In J. A. Simpson & D. T. Kenrick (Eds.), *Evolutionary social psychology* (pp. 1–20). Mahwah, NJ: Erlbaum.

Kerner, I. (2004). *She comes first: A thinking man's guide to pleasuring a woman.* New York: Regan Books.

Kessler-Harris, A. (2002). *In pursuit of equity: Women, men, and the quest for economic citizenship in 20th century America.* New York: Oxford University Press.

Kidder, D. L., & Parks, J. M. (2001). The good soldier: Who is s(he)? *Journal of Organizational Behavior, 22,* 939–959.

Kilianski, S. E., & Rudman, L. A. (1998). Wanting it both ways: Do women approve of benevolent sexism? *Sex Roles, 39,* 333–352

Kimmel, M. (1995). *Manhood in America: A cultural history.* New York: Free Press.

Kinicki, A. J., Carson, K. P., & Bohlander, G. W. (1992). Relationship between an organization's actual human resource efforts and employee attitudes. *Group and Organization Management, 17,* 135–152.

Kipnis, L. (2006). *The female thing: Dirt, sex, envy, vulnerability.* New York: Pantheon.

Kite, M. E., & Deaux, K. (1987). Gender belief systems: Homosexuality and the implicit inversion theory. *Psychology of Women Quarterly, 11,* 83–96.

Kite, M. E., & Whitely, B. E., Jr. (1996). Sex differences in attitudes toward homosexual persons, behaviors, and civil rights: A meta-analysis. *Personality and Social Psychology Bulletin, 22,* 336–353.

Klein, E. (2005). *The truth about Hillary: What she knew, when she knew it, and how far she'll go to become president.* New York: Sentinel.

Knudson-Martin, C., & Mahoney, A. R. (1996). Gender dilemma and myth in the construction of marital bargains: Issues for marital therapy. *Family Process, 35,* 137–153.

Knudson-Martin, C., & Mahoney, A. R. (1998). Language and processes in the construction of equality in new marriages. *Family Relations, 47,* 81–91.

Knudson-Martin, C., & Mahoney, A. R. (2005). Moving beyond gender: Processes that create relationship equality. *Journal of Marital and Family Therapy, 31,* 235–246.

Koch, S. C. (2005). Evaluative affect display toward male and female leaders of task-oriented groups. *Small Group Research, 36,* 678–703.

Koenig, A. M., & Eagly, A. H. (2005). Stereotype threat in men on a test of social sensitivity. *Sex Roles, 52,* 489–496.

Kohlberg, L. (1966). A cognitive-developmental analysis of children's sex role concepts and attitudes. In E. E. Maccoby (Ed.), *The development of sex differences* (pp. 82–173). Palo Alto, CA: Stanford University Press.

Konrad, A., Ritchie, J. E., Jr., Lieb, P., & Corrigall, E. (2000). Sex differences and similarities in job attribute preferences: A meta-analysis. *Psychological Bulletin, 126,* 593–641.

Kottak, C. P. (2004). *Cultural anthropology* (10th ed.). New York: McGraw-Hill.

Kowalski, R. M., & Chapple, T. (2000). The social stigma of menstruation: Fact or fiction? *Psychology of Women Quarterly, 24,* 74–80.

Koys, D. J. (1991). Fairness, legal compliance, and organizational commitment. *Employee Responsibilities and Rights Journal, 4,* 283–291.

Kunda, Z., & Oleson, K. C. (1995). Maintaining stereotypes in the face of disconfirmation: Constructing grounds for subtyping deviants. *Journal of Personality and Social Psychology, 68,* 565–579.

Kunda, Z., & Sherman-Williams, B. (1993). Stereotypes and the construal of individuating information. *Personality and Social Psychology Bulletin, 19*, 90–99.

Kunda, Z., & Spencer, S. J. (2003). When do stereotypes come to mind and when do they color judgment? A goal-based theoretical framework for stereotype activation and application. *Psychological Bulletin, 129*, 522–544.

Kunda, Z., & Thagard, P. (1996). Forming impressions from stereotypes, traits and behaviors: A parallel-constraint satisfaction theory. *Psychological Review, 103*, 284–308.

La Freniere, P., Strayer, F. F., & Gauthier, R. (1984). The emergence of same-sex affiliative preferences among preschool peers: A developmental/ethological perspective. *Child Development, 55*, 1958–1965.

La Rocco, C. (2007, August 5). Often on point but rarely in charge. *New York Times*, p. 29.

Lambert, T. A., Kahn, A. S., & Apple, K. J. (2003). Pluralistic ignorance and hooking up. *The Journal of Sex Research, 40*, 129–133.

Landau, M. J., Goldenberg, J. L., Greenberg, J., Gillath, O., Solomon, S., Cox, C., et al. (2006). The siren's call: Terror management and the threat of men's sexual attraction to women. *Journal of Personality and Social Psychology, 90*, 129–146.

Lane, J. D., & Wegner, D. M. (1995). The cognitive consequences of secrecy. *Journal of Personality and Social Psychology, 69*, 237–253.

Langford, W. (1999). *Revolutions of the heart: Gender, power, and the delusions of love*. London: Routledge.

Langlois, J. H., Roggman, L. A., & Reiser-Danner, L. A. (1990). Infants' differential responses to attractive and unattractive faces. *Developmental Psychology, 26*, 153–159.

Larson, R., & Richards, M. H. (1991). Daily companionship in late childhood and early adolescence: Changing developmental contexts. *Child Development, 62*, 284–300.

Lattman, P. (2007, August 28). You say you want a big-law revolution. *Wall Street Journal Online*. Retrieved from October 17, 2007, *http://blogs.wsj.com/law/2007/04/03/you-say-you-want-a-big-law-revolution*

Laumann, E. O., Paik, A., Glasser, D. B., Kang, J. H., Wang, T., Levinson B., et al. (2006). A cross-national study of subjective sexual well-being among older women and men: Findings from the Global Study of Sexual Attitudes and Behaviors. *Archives of Sexual Behavior, 35*, 145–161.

Laumann, E. O., Paik, A., & Rosen, R. C. (1999). Sexual dysfunction in the United States: Prevalence and predictors. *Journal of the American Medical Association, 281*(6), 537–544.

Lavie-Ajayi, M. (2005). "Because all real women do": The construction and deconstruction of "female orgasmic disorder." *Sexualities, Evolution and Gender, 7*, 57–72.

Lavine, H., Sweeney, D., & Wagner, S. H. (1999). Depicting women as sex objects in television advertising: Effects on body dissatisfaction. *Personality and Social Psychology Bulletin, 25*, 1049–1058.

Lawson, D. M., Weber, D., Beckner, H. M., Robinson, L., Marsh, N., & Cool,

A. (2003). Men who use violence: Intimate violence versus non-intimate violence profiles. *Violence and Victims, 18,* 259–277.

Leacock, E. (1978). Women's status in egalitarian society: Implications for social evolution. *Current Anthropology, 19,* 247–275.

Leary, M. R., & Baumeister, R. F. (2000). The nature and function of self-esteem: Sociometer theory. In M. P. Zanna (Ed.), *Advances in experimental social psychology* (Vol. 32, pp. 1–62). New York: Academic Press.

Leary, M. R., Kowalski, R. M., Smith, L., & Phillips, S. (2003). Teasing, rejection, and violence: Case studies of the school shootings. *Aggressive Behavior, 29,* 202–214.

Leary, M. R., Twenge, J. M., & Quinlivan, E. (2006). Interpersonal rejection as a determinant of anger and aggression. *Personality and Social Psychology Review, 10,* 111–132.

Lederer, W. (1968). *The fear of women.* New York: Grune & Stratton.

Lee, P. A. (1996). Survey report: Concept of penis size. *Journal of Sex and Marital Therapy, 22,* 131–135.

Lefevre, J., Kulak, A., & Heymans, S. (1992). Factors influencing the selection of university majors varying in mathematical content. *Canadian Journal of Behavioral Sciences, 24,* 276–289.

Leibold, J. M., & McConnell, A. R. (2002). *The consequences of powerlessness on aggression and on attraction toward women in sexually aggressive men.* Unpublished manuscript, Miami University.

Leibold, J. M., & McConnell, A. R. (2004). Women, sex, hostility, power, and suspicion: Sexually aggressive men's cognitive associations. *Journal of Experimental Social Psychology, 40,* 256–263.

Lemon, K. D. (2001). *Domestic violence law* (2nd ed). St. Paul, MN: West Group.

Lenahan, P. (2003). *Anabolic steroids and other performance enhancing drugs.* New York: Taylor & Francis.

Lennon, M. C., & Rosenfield, S. (1994). Relative fairness and the division of housework. *American Journal of Sociology, 10,* 506–531.

Leonhardt, D. (2006, December 24). Gender pay gap, once narrowing, is stuck in place [Electronic verison]. *New York Times.* Retrieved October 17, 2007, from *www.nytimes.com/2006/12/24/business/24gap.html*

Lerner, M. J. (1980). *The belief in a just world: A fundamental delusion.* New York: Plenum.

LeVay, S. (1993). *The gay brain.* Cambridge, MA: MIT Press.

LeVay, S. (1996). *Queer science.* Cambridge, MA: MIT Press.

Lever, J., Frederick, D. A., & Peplau, L. A. (2006). Does size matter? Men's and women's views on penis size across the lifespan. *Psychology of Men & Masculinity, 7,* 129–143.

Levy, G. D., Zimmerman, B., Barber, J., Martin, N., & Malone, C. (1998, May). *Preverbal awareness of gender roles in toddlers.* Paper presented at the meeting of the American Psychological Society, Washington, DC.

Lewin, T. (2006, July 9). At colleges, women are leaving men in the dust [Electronic version]. *New York Times.* Retrieved October 17, 2007, from *www.nytimes.com/2006/07/09/education/09college.html*

Lin, C. A. (1998). Uses of sex appeals in prime-time television commercials. *Sex Roles, 38,* 461–475.

Lin, M. H., Kwan, V. S. Y., Cheung, A., & Fiske, S. T. (2005). Stereotype content model explains prejudice for an envied outgroup: Scale of anti-Asian American stereotypes. *Personality and Social Psychology Bulletin, 31,* 34–47.

Lips, H. M. (1988). *Sex and gender.* Mountain View, CA: Mayfield.

Lips, H. M. (1991). *Women, men, and power.* Mountain View, CA: Mayfield.

Lips, H. M. (2003). The gender pay gap: Concrete indicator of women's progress toward equality. *Analyses of Social Issues and Public Policy, 3,* 87–109.

Liptak, A. (2006, August 7). 15 states expand right to shoot in self-defense. *New York Times.* Retrieved October 17, 2007, from *www.nytimes.com/2006/08/07/ us/07shoot.html*

Locksley, A., Borgida, E., Brekke, N., & Hepburn, C. (1980). Sex stereotypes and social judgment. *Journal of Personality and Social Psychology, 39,* 821–831.

Logan, T. K., Walker, R., Jordan, C. E., & Leukefeld, C. G. (2006). Justice system options and responses. In T. K. Logan, R. Walker, C. E. Jordan, & C. G. Leukefeld (Eds.), *Women and victimization: Contributing factors, interventions, and implications* (pp. 161–194). Washington, DC: American Psychological Association.

Lohr, B. A., Adams, H. E., & Davis, J. M. (1997). Sexual arousal to erotic and aggressive stimuli in sexually coercive and noncoercive men. *Journal of Abnormal Psychology, 106,* 230–242.

Lovdal, L. (1989). Sex role messages in television commercials: An update. *Sex Roles, 21,* 715–724.

Lyness, K. S., & Judiesch, M. K. (1999). Are women more likely to be hired or promoted into management positions? *Journal of Vocational Behavior, 54,* 158–173.

Lyness, K. S., & Thompson, D. E. (1997). Above the glass ceiling? A comparison of matched samples of female and male executives. *Journal of Applied Psychology, 82,* 359–375.

Lytton, H., & Romney, D. M. (1991). Parents' differential socialization of boys and girls: A meta-analysis. *Psychological Bulletin, 109,* 267–296.

Maass, A., Cadinu, M., Guarnieri, G., & Grasselli, A. (2003). Sexual harassment under social identity threat: The computer harassment paradigm. *Journal of Personality and Social Psychology, 85,* 853–870.

Maccoby, E. E. (1998). *The two sexes: Growing up apart, coming together.* Cambridge, MA: Harvard University Press.

Maccoby, E. E. (2002). Gender and group process: A developmental perspective. *Current Directions in Psychological Science, 11,* 54–58.

Maccoby, E. E., & Jacklin, C. N. (1987). Gender segregation in childhood. In E. H. Reese (Ed.), *Advances in child development and behavior* (Vol. 20, pp. 239–287). New York: Academic Press.

MacKinnon, C. A. (1987). *A feminist theory of the state.* Cambridge, MA: Harvard University Press.

MacMillan, R., Nierobisz, A., & Welsh, S. (2000). Experiencing the streets: Harassment and perceptions of safety among women. *Journal of Research in Crime and Delinquency, 37,* 306–322.

Macrae, C. N., Milne, A. B., & Bodenhausen, G. V. (1994). Stereotypes as energy saving devices: A peek inside the cognitive toolbox. *Journal of Personality and Social Psychology, 66,* 37–47.

Madon, S. (1997). What do people believe about gay males? A study of stereotype content and strength. *Sex Roles, 17*, 663–685.

Magley, V. J., Hulin, C. L., Fitzgerald, L. F., & DeNardo, M. (1999). Outcomes of self-labeling sexual harassment. *Journal of Applied Psychology 84(3)*, 390–402.

Maines, R. P. (1999). *The technology of the orgasm: "Hysteria," the vibrator, and women's sexual satisfaction.* Baltimore, MD: Johns Hopkins University Press.

Major, B. (1987). Gender, justice, and the psychology of entitlement. In P. Shaver & C. Hendricks (Eds.), *Sex and gender: Review of personality and social psychology* (Vol. 7, pp. 124–148). Newbury Park, CA: Sage.

Major, B. (1993). Gender, entitlement, and the distribution of family labor. *Journal of Social Issues, 49*, 141–159.

Manis, M., Biernat, M., & Nelson, T. F. (1991). Comparison and expectancy processes in human judgment. *Journal of Personality and Social Psychology, 61*, 203–211.

Manning, W. D., Longmore, M. A., & Giordano, P. C. (2005). Adolescents' involvement in non-romantic sexual activity. *Social Science Research, 34*, 384–407.

Marazziti, D., & Canale, D. (2004). Hormonal changes when falling in love. *Psychoneuroendocrinology, 29(7)*, 931–936.

Marks, M. J., & Fraley, R. C. (2005). The sexual double standard: Fact or fiction? *Sex Roles, 52*, 175–186.

Marques, J. M., & Yzerbyt, V. Y. (1988). Judgmental extremity towards ingroup members in inter- and intra-group situations. *European Journal of Social Psychology, 18*, 287–292.

Marshall, L. (2005, December 9). Geena in 2008. *Dissident Voice.* Retrieved October 17, 2007, from *www.dissidentvoice.org/Nov05/Marshall1109.htm*

Martell, R. F., Lane, D. M., & Emrich, C. G. (1996). Male-female differences: A computer simulation. *American Psychologist, 51*, 157–158.

Martell, R. F., Parker, C., Emrich, C. G., & Crawford, M. S. (1998). Sex stereotyping in the executive suite: "Much ado about something." *Journal of Social Behavior and Personality, 13*, 127–138.

Martin, C. L. (1990). Attitudes and expectations about children with nontraditional and traditional gender roles. *Sex Roles, 22*, 151–165.

Martin, C. L. (1999). A developmental perspective on gender effects and gender concepts. In W. B. Swann, Jr., J. H. Langlois, & L. A. Gilbert (Eds.). *Sexism and stereotypes in modern society: The gender science of Janet Taylor Spence* (pp. 45–73). Washington DC: American Psychological Association.

Martin, C. L., & Fabes, R. A. (1997, April). *Building gender stereotypes in the preschool years.* Paper presented at the meetings of the Society for Research in Child Development. Washington, DC.

Martin, C. L., & Fabes, R. A. (2001). The stability and consequences of young children's same-sex peer interactions. *Developmental Psychology, 37*, 431–446.

Martin, C. L., & Ruble, D. (2004). Children's search for gender cues: Cognitive perspectives on gender development. *Current Directions in Psychological Science, 13*, 67–70.

Martin, C. L., Ruble, D. N., & Szkyrbalo, J. (2002). Cognitive theories of early gender development. *Psychological Bulletin, 128*, 903–933.

Martin, E. (1987). *The woman in the body: A cultural analysis of reproduction*. Boston, MA: Beacon Press.

Martin, J., & Meyerson, D. (1988). Women and power: Conformity, resistance, and disorganized coaction. In R. M. Kramer & M. A. Neale (Eds.), *Power and influence in organizations* (pp. 311–348). Thousand Oaks, CA: Sage.

Martin, K. A., Luke, K. P., & Verduzco-Baker, L. (2007). The sexual socialization of young children: Setting the agenda for research. In S. Correll (Ed.), *Advances in group processes* (Vol. 24, pp. 231–260). New York: Elsevier.

Masters, W. H., & Johnson, V. E. (1979). *Homosexualities in perspective*. Boston: Little, Brown.

Maume, D. J. (1999). Glass ceilings and glass escalators: Occupational segregation and race and sex differences in managerial promotions. *Work and Occupations, 26*, 483–509.

Maushart, S. (2001). *Wifework: What marriage really means for women*. New York: Bloomsbury.

Maynard, M. (2006, August 6). Automaker reaches settlement in sexual harassment suit [Electronic version]. *New York Times*. Retrieved October 17, 2007, from *www.nytimes.com/2006/08/05/business/worldbusiness/05harass/html*

McCauley, C. R., Wright, M., & Harris, M. E (2000). Diversity workshops on campus: A survey of current practice at U.S. colleges and universities. *College Student Journal, 34*, 100–114.

McConahay, J. B. (1986). Modern racism, ambivalence, and the Modern Racism Scale. In J. F. Dovidio & S. L. Gaertner (Eds.), *Prejudice, discrimination, and racism* (pp. 91–126). Orlando, FL: Academic Press.

McConnell, A. R., & Leibold, J. M. (2001). Relations among the Implicit Association Test, explicit attitudes, and discriminatory behavior. *Journal of Experimental Social Psychology, 37*, 435–442.

McGinn, D. (2006, June 5). Marriage by the numbers. *Newsweek*, pp. 40–48.

McIlwee, J. S., & Robinson, J. G. (1992). *Women in engineering: Gender, power, and workplace culture*. Albany: State University of New York Press.

McKenzie-Mohr, D., & Zanna, M. P. (1990). Treating women as sexual objects: Look to the (gender schematic) male who has viewed pornography. *Personality and Social Psychology Bulletin, 16*, 296–308.

McKinley, N. M. (2002). Feminist perspectives and objectified body consciousness. In T. F. Cash & T. Pruzinsky (Eds.), *Body image: A handbook of theory, research, and clinical practice* (pp. 55–64). New York: Guilford Press.

McKinley, N. M., & Hyde, J. S. (1996). The objectified body consciousness scale. *Psychology of Women Quarterly, 20*, 181–215.

McLoyd, V. C. (1983). The effects of structure of play objects on the pretend play of low-income preschool children. *Child Development, 54*, 626–635.

McNulty, J. K., & Karney, B. R. (2004). Positive expectations in the early years of marriage: Should couples expect the best or brace for the worst? *Journal of Personality and Social Psychology, 86*, 729–743.

Meany, M. J., Stewart, J., & Beatty, W. W. (1985). Sex differences in social play: The socialization of sex roles. In J. S. Rosenblatt, C. Beer, C. M. Busnell, & P. Stater (Eds.), *Advances in the study of behavior* (Vol. 15, pp. 1–58). New York: Academic Press.

Medin, D. L., & Ortony, A. (1989). Psychological essentialism. In S. Vosnaidou

& A. Ortony (Eds.), *Similarity and analogical reasoning* (pp. 179–195). Cambridge, UK: Cambridge University Press.

Melton, H. C. (2007). Predicting the occurrence of stalking in relationships characterized by domestic violence. *Journal of Interpersonal Violence, 22,* 3–25.

Mendelson, R. (1997). *A family divided: A divorced father's struggle with the child custody industry.* Amherst, NY: Prometheus Books.

Mernissi, F. (1987). *Beyond the veil: Male-female dynamics in a modern Muslim society.* Cambridge, MA: Schenkman.

Mero, J. (2007, August). Fortune 500 women CEOs [Electronic version]. *Fortune.* Retrieved October 17, 2007, from *http://money.cnn.com/galleries/2007/fortune/0704/gallery.F500_womenceos.fortune/*

Merton, R. K. (1948). The self-fulfilling prophecy. *Antioch Review, 8,* 193–210.

Mill, J. S. (1975). *The subjection of women.* Oxford, UK: Oxford University Press. (Original work published 1869)

Millett, K. (1970). *Sexual politics.* New York: Doubleday.

Mischel, W. (1966). A social learning view of sex differences in behavior. In E. E. Maccoby (Ed.), *The development of sex differences* (pp. 56–81). Stanford, CA: Stanford University Press.

Misciagno, P. S. (1997). *Rethinking feminist identification: The case for de facto feminism.* Westport, CT: Praeger.

Monteith, M. J. (1993). Self-regulation of prejudiced responses: Implications for progress in prejudice-reduction efforts. *Journal of Personality and Social Psychology, 65,* 469–485.

Monteith, M. J., Deneen, N. E., & Tooman, G. D. (1996). The effect of social norm activation on the expression of opinions concerning gay men and Blacks. *Basic and Applied Social Psychology, 18,* 267–288.

Monteith, M. J., & Voils, C. I. (2001). Exerting control over prejudiced responses. In G. B. Moskowitz (Ed.), *Cognitive social psychology: The Princeton symposium on the legacy and future of social cognition* (pp. 375–388). Mahwah, NJ: Erlbaum.

Montenegro, X. (2004, May). The divorce experience: A study of divorce at midlife and beyond [Electronic version]. *AARP Magazine.* Retrieved October 17, 2007, from *www.aarp.org/research/reference/publicopinions/aresearch_import_867.html*

Mor Barak, M. E., Cherin, D. A., & Berkman, S. (1998). Organizational and personal dimensions in diversity management: Ethnic and gender differences in employee perceptions. *Journal of Applied Behavioral Sciences, 34,* 82–104.

Moore, G. E. (1903). *Principia ethica.* Cambridge, UK: Cambridge University Press.

Morry, M. M., & Staska, S. L. (2001). Magazine exposure: Internalization, self-objectification, eating attitudes, and body satisfaction in male and female university students. *Canadian Journal of Behavioral Science, 33,* 269–279.

Mosher, D. L., & Sirkin, M. (1984). Measuring a macho personality constellation. *Journal of Research in Personality, 18,* 150–163.

Moya, M., Glick, P., Expósito, F., de Lemus, S., & Hart, J. (2007). It's for your own good: Benevolent sexism and women's reactions to protectively justified restrictions. *Personality and Social Psychology Bulletin, 33*, 1421–1434.

Muehlenkamp, J. J., & Saris-Baglama, R. N. (2002). Self-objectification and its psychological outcomes for college women. *Psychology of Women Quarterly, 26*, 371–379.

Murray, H. A. (1938). *Explorations in personality.* New York: Oxford University Press.

Murray, S. L., & Holmes, J. G. (1997). A leap of faith? Positive illusions in romantic relationships. *Personality and Social Psychology Bulletin, 23*, 586–604.

Murray, S. L., Holmes, J. G., & Griffin, D. W. (1996). The benefits of positive illusions: Idealization and the construction of satisfaction in close relationships. *Journal of Personality and Social Psychology, 70*, 79–98.

Mussweiler, T., & Förster, J. (2000). The sex → aggression link: A perception-behavior dissociation. *Journal of Personality and Social Psychology, 79*, 507–520.

Muth, J. L., & Cash, T. F. (1997). Body-image attitudes: What difference does gender make. *Journal of Applied Social Psychology, 27*, 1438–1452.

Myers, D. (2005). *Social psychology* (8th ed.). New York: McGraw-Hill.

National Institute of Child Health and Human Development. (2005). *Child care and child development: Results from the NICHD study of early child care and youth development.* New York: Guilford Press.

Neuberg, S. L. (1989). The goal of forming accurate impressions during social interactions: Attenuating the impact of negative expectancies. *Journal of Personality and Social Psychology, 56*, 374–386.

Nieva, V. E, & Gutek, B. A. (1981). *Women and work: A psychological perspective. New* York: Praeger.

Nisbett, R. E. (1993). Violence and U.S. regional culture. *American Psychologist, 48*, 441–449.

Noar, S. M., & Morokoff, P. J. (2002). The relationship between masculinity ideology, condom attitudes, and condom use stage of change: A structural equation modeling approach. *International Journal of Men's Health, 1*, 43–58.

Noelle-Neumann, E. (1993). *Spiral of silence: Public opinion–Our social skin* (2nd ed.). Chicago: University of Chicago Press.

Noer, M. (2006, August 22). Don't marry career women [Electronic version]. Forbes.com. Retrieved August 23, 2006, from *http://www.forbes.com/ Marriage-Careers-Divorce_cx_mn_land.html*

Noll, S. M., & Fredrickson, B. L. (1998). A mediational model linking self-objectification, body shame, and disordered eating. *Psychology of Women Quarterly, 22*, 623–636.

Norton, K. I., Olds, T. S., Olive, S., & Dank, S. (1996). Ken and Barbie at life size. *Sex Roles, 34*, 287–294.

Nosek, B. A., Banaji, M. R., & Greenwald, A. G. (2002a). Harvesting implicit group attitudes and beliefs from a demonstration web site. *Group Dynamics: Theory, Research, and Practice, 6*, 101–115.

Nosek, B. A., Banaji, M. R., & Greenwald, A. G. (2002b). Math = male, me =

female, therefore math ≠ me. *Journal of Personality and Social Psychology, 83,* 44–59.

Noseworthy, C. M., & Lott, A. (1984). The cognitive organization of gender-stereotypic categories. *Personality and Social Psychology Bulletin, 10,* 474–481.

Nossiter, A. (1997, March 11). A cadet is dismissed and 9 are disciplined for Citadel harassment. *New York Times,* p. A15.

Oakes, P. J., & Turner, J. C. (1980). Social categorization and intergroup behaviour: Does minimal intergroup discrimination make social identity more positive? *European Journal of Social Psychology, 10,* 295–302.

Offermann, L. R., & Gowing, M. K. (1990). Organizations of the future: Changes and challenges. *American Psychologist, 45,* 95–108.

Oliver, M. B., & Hyde, J. S. (1993). Gender differences in sexuality: A meta-analysis. *Psychological Bulletin, 114,* 29–51.

Olson, J. E., & Frieze, I. H. (1987). Income determinants for women in business. In A. H. Stromberg, L. Larwood, & B. A. Gutek (Eds.), *Women and work: An annual review* (Vol. 2., pp. 173–206). Thousand Oaks, CA: Sage.

Omark, D. R., Omark, M., & Edelman, M. (1973). Formation of dominance hierarchies in young children. In T. R. Williams (Ed.), *Psychological anthropology* (pp. 289–316). The Hague, the Netherlands: Mouton.

Orenstein, P. (2006, December 24). What's wrong with Cinderella? [Electronic version]. *New York Times Magazine.* Retrieved October 17, 2007, from *www. nytimes.com/2006/12/24/magazine/24princess.t.html?_r=1*

Osman, S. L. (2003). Predicting men's rape perceptions based on the belief that "no" really means "yes." *Journal of Applied Social Psychology, 33,* 683–692.

Ostrom, T. M., & Sedikides, C. (1992). Out-group homogeneity effects in natural and minimal groups. *Psychological Bulletin, 112,* 536–552.

Painter, S. (1940). *French chivalry: Chivalric ideas and practices in medieval France.* Baltimore, MD: Johns Hopkins Press.

Palmer, C. T. (1991). Human rape: Adaptation or byproduct? *Journal of Sex Research, 28,* 365–385.

Paluck, E. L. (2006). Diversity training and intergroup contact: A call to action research. *Journal of Social Issues, 62,* 577–595.

Panteli, N., Stack, J., & Ramsay, H. (2001). Gendered patterns in computing work in the late 1990s. *New Technology, Work and Employment, 16,* 3–11.

Paquette, J. A., & Underwood, M. K. (1999). Gender differences in adolescents' experiences of peer victimization: Social and physical aggression. *Merrill-Palmer Quarterly, 45,* 242–266.

Parker, S. K., & Griffin, M. A. (2002). What is so bad about a little name-calling? Negative consequences of gender harassment for overperformance demands and distress. *Journal of Occupational Health Psychology, 7,* 195–210.

Payne, B. K. (2006). Weapon bias: Split-second decisions and unintended stereotyping. *Current Directions in Psychological Science, 15,* 287–291.

Peeters, G. (1983). Relational and informational patterns in social cognition. In W. Doise & S. Moscovici (Eds.), *Current issues in European social psychol-*

ogy (pp. 201–237). Cambridge, UK: Maison des Sciences de l'Homme and Cambridge University Press.

Peplau, L. A., & Gordon, S. L. (1985). Women and men in love: Gender differences in close heterosexual relationships. In V. E. O'Leary, R. K. Unger, & B. S. Wallston (Eds.), *Women, gender, and social psychology* (pp. 257–292). Hillsdale, NJ: Erlbaum.

Perkins, H. W., & DeMeis, D. K. (1996). Gender and family effects on the "second shift" domestic activity of college-educated young adults. *Gender and Society, 10,* 78–93.

Peter, K., & Horn, L. (2005). *Gender differences in participation and completion of undergraduate education and how they have changed over time* (NCES 2005–169). Washington, DC: U.S. Government Printing Office.

Peters, T. (1988). Restoring American competitiveness: Looking for new models of organizations. *Academy of Management Executive, 2,* 103–109.

Pfeffer, J. (1989). A political perspective on careers: Interests, networks, and environments. In M. B. Arthur, D. T. Hall, & B. S. Lawrence (Eds.), *Handbook of career theory* (pp. 380–396). New York: Cambridge University Press.

Pharr, S. (1988). *Homophobia: A weapon of sexism.* Little Rock, AR: The Women's Project.

Phelan, J. E., Moss-Racusin, C. A., & Rudman, L. A. (2007). *Competent yet out in the cold: Shifting standards reflect backlash toward agentic women.* Manuscript submitted for publication.

Philaretou, A. G., Allen, K. R. (2003). Macro and micro dynamics of male sexual anxiety: Theory and intervention. *International Journal of Men's Health, 2,* 201–220.

Phillips, G., & Over, R. (1992). Adult sexual orientation in relation to memories of childhood gender conforming and nonconforming behaviors. *Archives of Sexual Behavior, 21,* 543–558.

Pierce, K. (1990). A feminist theoretical perspective on the socialization of teenage girls through *Seventeen* magazine. *Sex Roles, 23,* 491–500.

Pietropinto, A. (1986). Misconceptions about male sexuality. *Medical Aspects of Human Sexuality, 20,* 80–85.

Pinel, E. C. (2002). Stigma consciousness in intergroup contexts: The power of conviction. *Journal of Experimental Social Psychology, 76,* 114–128.

Pittinsky, T. L., Shih, M., & Ambady, N. (2000). Will a category cue affect you? Category cues, positive stereotypes and reviewer recall for applicants. *Social Psychology of Education, 4,* 53–65.

Plaks, J. E., Stroessner, S. J., Dweck, C. S., & Sherman, J. W. (2001). Person theories and attention allocation: Preferences for stereotypic versus counterstereotypic information. *Journal of Personality and Social Psychology, 80,* 876–893.

Plant, E. A., & Devine, P. G. (1998). Internal and external motivation to respond without prejudice. *Journal of Personality and Social Psychology, 75,* 811–832.

Plant, E. A., & Devine, P. G. (2001). Responses to other-imposed pro-Black pressure: Acceptance or backlash? *Journal of Experimental Social Psychology, 37,* 486–501.

Pleak, R. (1999). Ethical issues in diagnosing and treating gender-dysphoric children and adolescents. In M. Rottnek (Ed.), *Sissies and tomboys: Gender nonconformity and homosexual childhood* (pp. 34–51). New York: University Press.

Pleck, J. H. (1981). *The myth of masculinity.* Cambridge, MA: MIT Press.

Pleck, J. H. (1992). Families and work: Small changes with big implications. *Qualitative Sociology, 15*(4), 427–432.

Pleck, J. H., Sonenstein, F. L., & Ku, L. C. (1993). Masculinity ideology and its correlates. In S. Oskamp & M. Costanzo (Eds.), *Gender issues in contemporary society* (pp. 85–110). Newbury Park, CA: Sage.

Plomin, R., & Daniels, D. (1987). Why are children in the same family so different from one another? *Behavioral and Brain Sciences, 10,* 1–60.

Pollack, W. (1998). *Real boys: Rescuing our sons from the myths of boyhood.* New York: Henry Holt.

Pollard, P. (1992). Judgements about victims and attackers in depicted rapes: A review. *British Journal of Social Psychology, 31,* 307–326.

Powers, T. A., & Zuroff, D. C. (1988). Interpersonal consequences of overt self-criticism: A comparison with neutral and self-enhancing presentations of self. *Journal of Personality and Social Psychology, 54,* 1054–1062.

Powlishta, K. K. (1995a). Gender bias in children's perceptions of personality traits. *Sex Roles, 32,* 17–28.

Powlishta, K. K. (1995b). Intergroup processes in childhood: Social categorization and sex role development. *Developmental Psychology, 31,* 781–788.

Powlishta, K. K., Serbin, L. A., Doyle, A. B., & White, D. R. (1994). Gender, ethnic, and body type biases: The generality of prejudice in childhood. *Developmental Psychology, 30,* 526–536.

Pratto, F., Stallworth, L. M., Sidanius, J., & Siers, B. (1997). The gender gap in occupational role attainment: A social dominance approach. *Journal of Personality and Social Psychology, 72,* 37–53.

Prentice, D. A., & Carranza, E. (2002). What women and men should be, shouldn't be, are allowed to be, and don't have to be: The contents of prescriptive gender stereotypes. *Psychology of Women Quarterly, 26,* 269–281.

Prentice, D. A., & Miller, D. T. (2006). Essentializing differences between women and men. *Psychological Science, 17,* 129–135.

Press, E. (2007, July 29). Family-leave values. *New York Times Magazine,* pp. 37–41.

Price-Waterhouse v. Hopkins, 109 S. Ct. 1775 (1989).

Pryor, J. B. (1995). The psychosocial impact of sexual harassment on women in the U.S. military. *Basic and Applied Social Psychology, 17,* 581–603.

Pryor, J. B., Giedd, J. L., & Williams, K. B. (1995). A social psychological model for predicting sexual harassment. *Journal of Social Issues, 51,* 69–84.

Pryor, J. B., Hesson-McInnis, M. S., Hitlan, R. T., Olson, M., & Hahn, E. J. (2001). *Antecedents of gender harassment: Analysis of person and situation factors.* Unpublished manuscript.

Pryor, J. B., LaVite, C., & Stolle, L. (1993). A social psychological analysis of sexual harassment: The person/situation interaction. *Journal of Vocational Behavior, 42,* 68–83.

Pugh, M. D., & Wahrman, R. (1983). Neutralizing sexism in mixed-sex groups:

Do women have to be better than men? *American Journal of Sociology, 88,* 746–762.

Pugliesi, K. (1999). The consequences of emotional labor: Effects on work stress, job satisfaction, and well-being. *Motivation and Emotion, 23,* 125–154.

Quinn, D. M., Kallen, R. W., & Christie, C. (2006). Body on my mind: The lingering effect of state self-objectification. *Sex Roles, 55,* 869–874.

Radway, J. (1987). *Reading the romance.* London: Verso.

Ragins, B. R., & Sundstrom, E. (1989). Gender and power in organizations: A longitudinal perspective. *Psychological Bulletin, 105,* 51–88.

Remnick, D. (2005, July 4). Political porn. *The New Yorker,* pp. 29–30.

Rennison, C. M. (2003). *Intimate partner violence: 1993–2001.* Washington, DC: U. S. Bureau of Justice. Retrieved October 17, 2007, from *http://www.ojp. usdoj.gov/bjs/pub/pdf/ipv01.pdf*

Renshaw, D. C. (2005). Fathering today. *Family Journal: Counseling and Therapy for Couples and Families, 13,* 7–9.

Renzetti, C. M. (1987). New wave or second stage? Attitudes of college women toward feminism. *Sex Roles, 16,* 265–277.

Reskin, B. F., & Padovic, I. (1994). *Women and men at work.* Thousand Oaks, CA: Pine Ridge Press.

Reskin, B. F., & Padovic, I. (2002). *Women and men at work* (2nd ed.). Thousand Oaks, CA: Pine Forge Press.

Reskin, B. F., & Ross, C. E. (1995). Jobs, authority, and earnings among managers: The continuing significance of sex. In J. A. Jacobs (Ed.), *Gender inequality at work* (pp. 127–151). Thousand Oaks, CA: Sage.

Rich, E. (2005). Young women, feminist identities and neo-liberalism. *Women's Studies International Forum, 28,* 495–508.

Richardson, L. (1988). Secrecy and status: The social construction of forbidden relationships. *American Sociological Review, 53,* 209–219.

Richeson, J. A., & Ambady, N. (2001). Who's in charge? Effects of situational roles on automatic gender bias. *Sex Roles, 44,* 493–512.

Ridge, R. D., & Reber, J. S. (2002). "I think she's attracted to me": The effect of men's beliefs on women's behavior in a job interview scenario. *Basic and Applied Social Psychology, 24,* 1–14.

Ridgeway, C. L. (2001a). Gender, status, and leadership. *Journal of Social Issues, 57,* 627–655.

Ridgeway, C. L. (2001b). The emergence of status beliefs: From structural inequality to legitimizing ideology. In J. T. Jost & B. Major (Eds.), *The psychology of legitimacy: Emerging perspectives on ideology, justice, and intergroup relations* (pp. 257–277). Cambridge, UK: Cambridge University Press.

Ridgeway, C. L. (2006). Gender as an organizing force in social relations: Implications for the future of inequality. In F. D. Blau, M. B. Brinton, & D. B. Grusky (Eds.), *The declining significance of gender?* (pp. 265–287). New York: Russell Sage.

Riger, S. (1993). What's wrong with empowerment? *American Journal of Community Psychology, 21,* 279–292.

Rimer, S. (2005, April 15). For women in the sciences, the pace of progress at top universities is slow. *New York Times,* p. A15.

Rivadeneyra, R., & Ward, L. M. (2005). From Ally McBeal to Sábado Gigante: Contributions of television viewing to the gender role attitudes of Latino adolescents. *Journal of Adolescent Research, 20*, 453–475.

Roberson, L., Kulik, C. T., & Pepper, M. B. (2001). Designing effective diversity training: Influence of group composition and trainee experience. *Journal of Organizational Behavior, 22*, 871–885.

Roberson, L., Kulik, C. T., & Pepper, M. B. (2003). Using needs assessment to resolve controversies in diversity training design. *Group and Organization Management, 28*, 148–174.

Roberts, S. (2006, October 15). It's official: To be married means to be outnumbered [Electronic version] *New York Times*. Retrieved October 17, 2007, from *www.nytimes.com/2006/10/15/us/15census.html?ex=1176609600&en=9 9c95d1dd848dcb2&ei=5087&excamp=mkt_at2*

Roberts, T. A. (2004). Female trouble: The menstrual self-evaluation scale and women's self-objectification. *Psychology of Women Quarterly, 28*, 22–26.

Roberts, T. A., & Gettman, J. Y. (2004). Mere exposure: Gender differences in the negative effects of priming a state of self-objectification. *Sex Roles, 51*, 17–27.

Roberts, T. A., Goldenberg, J. L., Power, C., & Pyszczynski, T. (2002). "Feminine protection": The effects of menstruation on attitudes towards women. *Psychology of Women Quarterly, 26*, 131–139.

Ronner, A. D. (2005). *Homophobia and the law*. Washington, DC: American Psychological Association.

Roos, P. A., & Gatta, M. L. (1999). The gender gap in earnings: Trends, explanations, and prospects. In G. Powell (Ed.), *Handbook of gender and work* (pp. 95–123). Thousand Oaks, CA: Sage.

Rose, S., & Frieze, I. H. (1989). Young singles' scripts for a first date. *Gender and Society, 3*, 258–268.

Rose, S., & Frieze, I. H. (1993). Young singles' contemporary dating scripts. *Sex Roles, 28*, 499–509.

Rose, S. M. (2002). *Lesbian love and relationships*. Binghamton, NY: Harrington Park.

Rosenbloom, S. (2007, February 1). And for my princess, a pedicure [Electronic version]. *New York Times*. Retrieved October 17, 2007, from *http://www. nytimes.com/2007/02/01/fashion/01girls.html*

Rosenblum, G. D., & Lewis, M. (1999). The relations among body image, physical attractiveness, and body mass in adolescence. *Child Development, 70*, 50–64.

Rosener, J. B. (1990). Ways women lead. *Harvard Business Review, 68*, 119–125.

Rosenthal, R., & Jacobson, L. (1968). *Pygmalion in the classroom*. New York: Holt, Rinehart & Winston.

Rosenthal, R., & Rubin, D. B. (1978). Interpersonal expectancy effects: The first 345 studies. *Behavioral and Brain Sciences, 3*, 377–415.

Rozee, R. (1999). Stranger rape. In M. A. Paludi (Ed.), *The psychology of sexual victimization: A handbook* (pp. 97–115). Westport, CT: Greenwood Press.

Rozin, P., Haidt, J., McCauley, C., Dunlop, J., & Ashmore, M. (1999). Individual differences in disgust sensitivity: Comparisons and evaluations of paper-and-pencil versus behavioral measures. *Journal of Research in Personality, 33*, 330–351.

Rubin, J. Z., Provenzano, F. J., & Luria, Z. (1974). The eye of the beholder: Parents' views on the sex of newborns. *American Journal of Orthopsychiatry, 44*, 512–519.

Ruble, D. N., & Ruble, T. L. (1982). Sex stereotypes. In A. G. Miller (Ed.), *In the eye of the beholder: Contemporary issues in stereotyping* (pp. 188–252). New York: Praeger.

Rudman, L. A. (1998). Self-promotion as a risk factor for women: The costs and benefits of counterstereotypical impression management. *Journal of Personality and Social Psychology, 74*, 629–645.

Rudman, L. A. (2004). Sources of implicit attitudes. *Current Directions in Psychological Science, 13*(2), 80–83.

Rudman, L. A. (2005). Rejection of women? Beyond prejudice as antipathy. In J. F. Dovidio, P. Glick, & L. A. Rudman (Eds.), *On the nature of prejudice: Fifty years after Allport* (pp. 106–120). Malden, MA: Blackwell.

Rudman, L. A., Ashmore, R. D., & Gary, M. L. (2001). "Unlearning" automatic biases: The malleability of implicit stereotypes and prejudice. *Journal of Personality and Social Psychology, 81*, 856–868.

Rudman, L. A., & Borgida, E. (1995). The afterglow of construct accessibility: The behavioral consequences of priming men to view women as sexual objects. *Journal of Experimental Social Psychology, 31*, 493–517.

Rudman, L. A., & Fairchild, K. (2004). Reactions to counterstereotypic behavior: The role of backlash in cultural stereotype maintenance. *Journal of Personality and Social Psychology, 87*, 157–176.

Rudman, L. A., & Fairchild, K. (2007). The *F* word: Is feminism incompatible with beauty and romance? *Psychology of Women Quarterly, 31*, 125–136.

Rudman, L. A., Feinberg, J. M., & Fairchild, K. (2002). Minority members' implicit attitudes: Ingroup bias as a function of group status. *Social Cognition, 20*, 294–320.

Rudman, L. A., & Glick, P. (1999). Feminized management and backlash toward agentic women: The hidden costs to women of a kinder, gentler image of middle-managers. *Journal of Personality and Social Psychology, 77*, 1004–1010.

Rudman, L. A., & Glick, P. (2001). Prescriptive gender stereotypes and backlash toward agentic women. *Journal of Social Issues, 57*, 732–762.

Rudman, L. A., & Goodwin, S. A. (2004). Gender differences in automatic in-group bias: Why do women like women more than men like men? *Journal of Personality and Social Psychology, 87*, 494–509.

Rudman, L. A., Greenwald, A. G., & McGhee, D. E. (2001). Implicit self-concept and evaluative implicit gender stereotypes: Self and ingroup share desirable traits. *Personality and Social Psychology Bulletin, 27*, 1164–1178.

Rudman, L. A., Greenwald, A. G., Mellott, D. S., & Schwartz, J. L. K. (1999). Measuring the automatic components of prejudice: Flexibility and generality of the Implicit Association Test. *Social Cognition, 17*(4), 1–29.

Rudman, L. A., & Heppen, J. B. (2003). Implicit romantic fantasies and women's interest in personal power: A glass slipper effect? *Personality and Social Psychology Bulletin, 29*, 1357–1370.

Rudman, L. A., & Kilianski, S. E. (2000). Implicit and explicit attitudes toward female authority. *Personality and Social Psychology Bulletin, 26*, 1315–1328.

Rudman, L. A., & Phelan, J. E. (in press). Backlash effects for counterstereotypical behavior in organizations. In A. Brief & B. M. Staw (Eds.), *Research in organizational behavior*. New York: Elsevier.

Rudman, L. A., & Phelan, J. E. (2007). The interpersonal power feminism: Is feminism good for relationships? *Sex Roles: A Journal of Research, 57*(11–12), 787–799.

Ryan, M. K., & Haslam, S. A. (2005). The glass cliff: Evidence that women are over-represented in precarious leadership positions. *British Journal of Management, 16*, 81–90.

Sabo, D., Kupers, T. A., & London, W. (2001). *Prison masculinities*. Philadelphia, PA: Temple University Press.

Sabo, D., Miller, K. E., Melnick, M. J., Farrell, M. P., & Barnes, G. M. (2002). Athletic participation and the health risks of adolescent males: A national study. *International Journal of Men's Health, 1*, 173–193.

Sacchetti, M. (2006, June 13). Harvard staff grants aim boost to diversity [Electronic version]. *The Boston Globe*. Retrieved October 17, 2007, from *http://www.boston.com/news/local/articles/2006/06/13/harvard_staff_grants_aim_to_boost_diversity/*

Sailer, P., Yau, E., & Rehula, V. (2002). Income by gender and age from information returns. *Statistics of Income Bulletin, 21*, 83–102.

Salholz, E. (1986, June 2). The marriage crunch. *Newsweek*, p. 55.

Salzman, P. C. (1999). Is inequality universal? *Current Anthropology, 40*, 31–44.

Sanchez, D. T., Crocker, J., & Boike, K. R. (2005). Doing gender in the bedroom: Investing in gender norms and the sexual experience. *Personality and Social Psychology Bulletin, 31*, 1445–1455.

Sanchez, D. T., Kiefer, A. K., & Ybarra, O. (2006). Sexual submissiveness in women: Costs for sexual autonomy and arousal. *Personality and Social Psychology Bulletin, 32*, 512–524.

Sanchez, L. (1994). Gender, labor allocations, and the psychology of entitlement within the home. *Social Forces, 73*, 533–553.

Sanday, P. R. (1981). The socio-cultural context of rape: A cross-cultural study. *Journal of Social Issues, 37*, 5–27.

Sandnabba, N. K., & Ahlberg, C. (1999). Parents' attitudes and expectations about children's cross-gender behavior. *Sex Roles, 40*, 249–263.

Savin-Williams, R. C., & Cohen, K. M. (2004). Homoerotic development during childhood and adolescence. *Child and Adolescent Psychiatric Clinics of North America, 13*, 529–549.

Schachter, S. (1951). Deviation, rejection, and communication. *Journal of Abnormal Social Psychology, 46*, 190–207.

Schmader, T. (2002). Gender identification moderates stereotype threat effects on women's math performance. *Journal of Experimental Social Psychology, 38*, 194–201.

Schmitt, D. P., Shackelford, T. K., & Buss, D. M. (2001). Are men really more "oriented" toward short-term mating than women? A critical review of theory and research. *Psychology, Evolution and Gender, 3*, 211–239.

Schneider, K. T., Swan, S., & Fitzgerald, L. F. (1997). Job-related and psychological effects of sexual harassment in the workplace: Empirical evidence from two organizations. *Journal of Applied Psychology, 82(3)*, 401–415.

Schofield, V. W. (1981). Complementary and conflicting identities: Images of interaction in an interracial school. In S. A. Asher & J. M. Gottman (Eds.), *The development of children's friendships* (pp. 53–90). New York: Cambridge University Press.

Schooler, D., & Ward, L. M. (2006). Average Joes: Men's relationships with media, real bodies, and sexuality. *Psychology of Men and Masculinity, 7*, 27–41.

Serbin, L. A., Sprafkin, C., Elman, M., & Doyle, A. B. (1984). The early development of sex differentiated patterns and social influence. *Canadian Journal of Social Science, 14*, 350–363.

Sergios, P., & Cody, J. (1986). Importance of physical attractiveness and social assertiveness skills in male homosexual dating behavior and partner selection. *Journal of Homosexuality, 12*, 71–84.

Sharabany, R., Gershoni, R., & Hofman, J. E. (1981). Girlfriend and boyfriend: Age and sex differences in intimate friendship. *Developmental Psychology, 17*, 800–808.

Sharps, M. J., Price, J. L., & Williams, J. K. (1994). Spatial cognition and gender: Instructional and stimulus influences on mental image rotation performance. *Psychology of Women Quarterly, 18*, 413–425.

Sherfey, M. J. (1973). *The nature and evolution of female sexuality.* New York: Vintage.

Shih, M., Pittinsky, T. L., & Ambady, N. (1999). Stereotype susceptibility: Identity salience and shifts in quantitative performance. *Psychological Science, 10*, 80–83.

Sidanius, J., & Pratto, F. (1999). *Social dominance: An intergroup theory of social hierarchy and oppression.* Cambridge, UK: Cambridge University Press.

Siegal, M. (1987). Are sons and daughters treated more differently by fathers than mothers? *Developmental Review, 7*, 183–209.

Siegel, S. J. (1986). The effect of culture on how women experience menstruation: Jewish women and *mikvah. Woman and Health, 10*, 63–74.

Sigel, R. (1996). *Ambition and accommodation: How women view gender relations.* Chicago: University of Chicago Press.

Simon, T. R., Anderson, M., Crosby, M. P., Shelley, G., & Sacks, J. J. (2001). Attitudinal acceptance of intimate partner violence among U.S. adults. *Violence and Victims, 16*, 115–126.

Sinclair, L., & Kunda, Z. (1999). Reactions to a Black professional: Motivated inhibition and activation of conflicting stereotypes. *Journal of Personality and Social Psychology, 77*, 885–904.

Sinclair, L., & Kunda, Z. (2000). Motivated stereotyping of women: She's fine if she praised me but incompetent if she criticized me. *Personality and Social Psychology Bulletin, 26*, 1329–1342.

Sinclair, S., Huntsinger, J., Skorinko, J., & Hardin, C. D. (2005). Social tuning of the self: Consequences for the self-evaluations of stereotype targets. *Journal of Personality and Social Psychology, 89*, 160–175.

Six, B., & Eckes, T. (1991). A closer look at the complex structure of gender stereotypes. *Sex Roles, 24*, 57–71.

Skow, J. (1989, August 7). The myth of male housework. *Time*, p. 62.

Skrypnek, B. J., & Snyder, M. (1982). On the self-perpetuating nature of stereotypes about women and men. *Journal of Experimental Social Psychology, 18*, 277–291.

Slater, T. (2006, September 1). Teaching gender issues to inmates. *The Chronicle of Higher Education*, p. B5.

Smith, B. (2006, August 23). *Female cadets report assaults at Citadel.* ABC News.

Smith, D. S. (1995). *Undressing infidelity: Why more wives are unfaithful.* Cincinnati, OH: Adams Media.

Smith, J. E., Waldorf, V. A., & Trembath, D. L. (1990). "Single White male looking for thin, very attractive …" *Sex Roles, 23*, 675–685.

Smith, J. L., & White, P. H. (2002). An examination of implicitly activated, explicitly activated, and nullified stereotypes on mathematical performance: It's not just a women's issue. *Sex Roles, 47*, 179–191.

Smuts, B. (1995). The evolutionary origins of patriarchy. *Human Nature, 6*, 1–32.

Snow, L. F., & Johnson, S. M. (1978). Myths about menstruation: Victims of our folklore. *International Journal of Women's Studies, 1*, 64–72.

Snowberger, A. (1997, October 7). "Christian" promise keepers: A wolf in sheep's clothing? [Electronic version]. The George-Anne Opinions Page. Available at *http://www.stp.georgiasouthern.edu/George-Anne/arc3/fal97/1007opn.html*.

Snyder, M. (1981). Seek and ye shall find: Testing hypotheses about other people. In E. T. Higgins, C. P. Herman, & M. P. Zanna (Eds.), *Social cognition: The Ontario Symposium on Personality and Social Psychology* (Vol. 1, pp. 277–303). Hillsdale, NJ: Erlbaum.

Snyder, M. (1984). When belief creates reality. In L. Berkowitz (Ed.), *Advances in experimental social psychology* (Vol. 18, pp. 247–305). New York: Academic Press.

Snyder, M., & Haugen, J. (1994). Why does behavioral confirmation occur? A functional perspective on the role of the perceiver. *Journal of Experimental Social Psychology, 30*, 218–246.

Snyder, M., & Swann, W. B., Jr. (1978). Behavioral confirmation in social interaction: From social perception to social reality. *Journal of Experimental Social Psychology, 14*, 148–162.

Snyder, M., Tanke, E. D., & Berscheid, E. (1977). Social perception and interpersonal behavior: On the self-fulfilling nature of social stereotypes. *Journal of Personality and Social Psychology, 35*, 656–666.

Sommers, C. H. (2000). *The war against boys: How misguided feminism is harming our young men.* New York: Simon & Schuster.

Spaulding, C. (1970). The romantic love complex in American culture. *Sociology and Social Research, 55*, 82–100.

Spence, J. T. (1993). Women, men, and society: *Plus ça change, plus c'est la même chose.* In S. Oskamp & M. Costanzo (Eds.), *Gender issues in contemporary society* (pp. 3–18). Newbury Park, CA: Sage.

Spence, J. T. (1999). Thirty years of gender research: A personal chronicle. In W. B. Swann, J. H. Langlois, & L. A. Gilbert (Eds.), *Sexism and stereotypes in modern society: The gender science of Janet Taylor Spence* (pp. 255–289). Washington, DC: American Psychological Association.

Spence, J. T., & Buckner, C. E. (2000). Instrumental and expressive traits, trait stereotypes, and sexist attitudes: What do they signify? *Psychology of Women Quarterly, 24,* 44–62.

Spence, J. T., & Helmreich, R. L. (1972). The Attitudes Toward Women Scale: An objective instrument to measure attitudes toward the rights and roles of women in contemporary society (Ms. No. 153). *JSAS Catalog of Selected Documents in Psychology, 2,* 66–67.

Spencer, S. J., Steele, C. M., & Quinn, D. M. (1999). Stereotype threat and women's math performance. *Journal of Experimental Social Psychology, 35,* 4–28.

Spiro, M. (1997). *Gender ideology and psychological reality: An essay on cultural reproduction.* New Haven, CT: Yale University Press.

Sprecher, S. (1989). The importance to males and females of physical attractiveness, earning potential, and expressiveness in initial attraction. *Sex Roles, 21,* 591–607.

Sprecher, S., Aron, A., Hatfield, E., Cortese, A., Potapova, E., & Levitskaya, A. (1994). Love: American style, Russian style and Japanese style. *Personal Relationships, 1*(4), 349–369.

Sprecher, S., & Metts, S. (1989). Development of the "Romantic Beliefs Scale" and examination of the effects of gender and gender-role orientation. *Journal of Social and Personal Relationships, 6,* 387–411.

Sprecher, S., Regan, P. C., & McKinney, K. (1998). Beliefs about the outcomes of extramarital sexual relationships as a function of the gender of the "cheating spouse." *Sex Roles, 38,* 301–311.

Sroufe, L. A., Bennet, C., England, M., Urban, J., & Shulman, S. (1993). The significance of gender boundaries in preadolescence: Contemporary correlates and antecedents of boundary violation and maintenance. *Child Development, 64,* 455–466.

Stangor, C., Lynch, L., Duan, C., & Glass, B. (1992). Categorization of individuals on the basis of multiple social features. *Journal of Personality and Social Psychology, 62,* 207–218.

Stangor, C., Sechrist, G., & Jost, J. T. (2001). Changing racial beliefs by providing consensus information. *Personality and Social Psychology Bulletin, 27,* 484–494.

Stark, R., & McEvoy, J. (1970). Middle class violence. *Psychology Today, 4,* 52–65.

Steele, C. M. (1997). A threat in the air: How stereotypes shape intellectual identity and performance. *American Psychologist, 52,* 613–629.

Steele, C. M. (1998). Stereotyping and its threat are real. *American Psychologist, 53,* 680–681.

Steele, C. M., & Aronson, J. (1995). Stereotype threat and the intellectual test performance of African Americans. *Journal of Personality and Social Psychology, 69,* 797–811.

Steele, C. M., Spencer, S. J., & Aronson, J. (2002). Contending with group image: The psychology of stereotype and social identity threat. In M. P. Zanna (Ed.), *Advances in experimental social psychology* (Vol. 34, pp. 379–440). San Diego, CA: Academic Press.

Steil, J. (1997). *Marital equality: Its relationship to the well-being of husbands and wives.* Newbury Park, CA: Sage.

Steinpreis, R. E., Anders, K. A., & Ritzke, D. (1999). The impact of gender on the review of the curricula vitae of job applicants and tenure candidates: A national empirical study. *Sex Roles, 47,* 587–599.

Stephan, W. G., & Stephan, C. W. (2000). An integrated threat theory of prejudice. In S. Oskamp (Ed.), *Reducing prejudice and discrimination* (pp. 23–45). Mahwah, NJ: Erlbaum.

Stevens, C. K., Bavetta, A. G., & Gist, M. E. (1993). Gender differences in the acquisition of salary negotiation skills: The role of goals, self-efficacy, and perceived control. *Journal of Applied Psychology, 78,* 723–735.

Stith, S. M., & Hamby, S. L. (2002). The anger management scale: The development and preliminary psychometric properties. *Violence and Victims, 17,* 383–402.

Stockdale, M. S., Visio, M., & Batra, L. (1999). The sexual harassment of men: Evidence for a broader theory of sexual harassment and sex discrimination. *Psychology, Public Policy, and Law, 5,* 630–664.

Stone, E. A., Goetz, A. T., & Shackelford, T. K. (2005). Sex differences and similarities in preferred mating arrangements. *Sexualities, Evolution and Gender, 7,* 269–276.

Stone, J., Lynch, C., Sjomeling, M., & Darley, J. M. (1999). Stereotype threat effects on Black and White athletic performance. *Journal of Personality and Social Psychology, 77,* 1213–1227.

Story, L. (2005, September 20). Many women at elite colleges set career path to motherhood. [Electronic version]. *New York Times,* Retrieved October 17, 2007, from *http://www.nytimes.com/2005/09/20/national/20women.html*

Straus, M. A., Gelles, R. J., & Steinmetz, S. K. (1980). *Behind closed doors: Violence in the American family.* Garden City, NY: Doubleday.

Stroessner, S. J. (1992). Target-based determinants of social categorization: Extensions of the "White male norm" hypothesis. *Dissertation Abstracts International, 54*(2-B), p. 1153.

Stroh, L. K., Brett, J. M., & Reilly, A. H. (1996). Family structure, glass ceiling, and traditional explanations for the differential rate of turnover of female and male managers. *Journal of Vocational Behavior, 49,* 99–118.

Stroh, L. K., Langlands, C. L., & Simpson, P. A. (2004). Shattering the glass ceiling in the new millennium. In M. S. Stockdale & F. J. Crosby (Eds.), *The psychology and management of workplace diversity* (pp. 147–167). Malden, MA: Blackwell.

Sussman, A. (May 23, 2006). *In Rio rush hour, women relax in single sex trains.* Retrieved May 24, 2006, from *http://www.womensenews.org/article.cfm?aid =2750*

Swain, J. (2000). The money's good, the fame's good, the girls are good: The role of playground football in the construction of young boys' masculinity in junior school. *British Journal of Sociology of Education, 21*, 95–109.

Swim, J. K. (1994). Perceived versus meta-analytic effect sizes: An assessment of the accuracy of gender stereotypes. *Journal of Personality and Social Psychology, 66*, 21–36.

Swim, J. K., Aikin, K. J., Hall, W. S., & Hunter, B. A. (1995). Sexism and racism: Old-fashioned and modern prejudices. *Journal of Personality and Social Psychology, 68*, 199–214.

Swim, J. K., Becker, J., Pruitt, E. R., & Lee, E. (in press). Sexism reloaded: Worldwide evidence for its endorsement, expression, and emergence in multiple contexts. In H. Landrine & N. Russo (Eds.), *Bringing diversity to feminist psychology*. Washington, DC: American Psychological Association.

Swim, J. T., Borgida, E., Maruyama, G., & Myers, D. G. (1989). Joan McKay vs. John McKay: Do gender stereotypes bias evaluations? *Psychological Bulletin, 105*, 409–429.

Swim, J. K., Ferguson, M. J., & Hyers, L. L. (1999). Avoiding stigma by association: Subtle prejudice against lesbians in the form of social distancing. *Basic and Applied Social Psychology, 21*, 61–68.

Swim, J. K., & Sanna, L. J. (1996). He's skilled, she's lucky: A meta-analysis of observers' attributions for women's and men's successes and failures. *Personality and Social Psychology Bulletin, 22*, 507–519.

Tajfel, H. (1981). *Social identity and intergroup relations*. Cambridge, UK: Cambridge University Press.

Tajfel, H., & Jahoda, G. (1966). Development in children of concepts about their own and other countries: A cross-national study. In *Proceedings of the XVIII International Congress of Psychology, Moscow, Symposium, 36*, 17–33.

Tajfel, H., & Turner, J. C. (1979). An integrative theory of intergroup conflict. In W. G. Austin & S. Worchel (Eds.), *The social psychology of intergroup relations* (pp. 33–48). Monterey, CA: Brooks-Cole.

Tallis, F. (2005). Crazy for you. *The Psychologist, 18*, 72–74.

Tang, C. S. K. (1999). Marital power and aggression in a community sample of Hong Kong Chinese families. *Journal of Interpersonal Violence, 14*, 586–602.

Tannen, D. (1990). *You just don't understand: Women and men in conversation*. New York: Morrow.

Tannen, D. (1994). *Talking from 9 to 5: Women and men in the workplace: Language, sex, and power*. New York: Morrow.

Tavris, C., & Wade, C. (1984). *The longest war* (2nd ed.) San Diego, CA: Harcourt Brace Jovanovich.

Taylor, J. K. (1992). *Reclaiming the mainstream: Individualist feminism rediscovered*. Amherst, NY: Prometheus Books.

Taylor, M. G. (1996). The development of children's beliefs about social and biological aspects of gender differences. *Child Development, 67*, 1555–1571.

Taylor, S. E., Fiske, S. T., Etcoff, N. L., & Ruderman, A. (1978). Categorical bases of person memory and stereotyping. *Journal of Personality and Social Psychology, 36*, 778–793.

Taywaditep, K. J. (2001). Marginalization among the marginalized: Gay men's anti-effeminacy attitudes. *Journal of Homosexuality, 42,* 1–28.

Thomas, C. A., & Esses, V. M. (2004). Individual differences in reactions to sexist humor. *Group Processes and Intergroup Relations, 7,* 89–100.

Thomas, M. A. (2002). *I believe in the cause, but not in the word: Women's ambivalence toward liberal feminism.* Unpublished manuscript, Lawrence University.

Thompson, S. K. (1975). Gender labels and early sex role development. *Child Development. 46,* 339–347.

Thompson, E. H., & Pleck, J. H. (1986). The structure of male role norms. *American Behavioral Scientist, 29,* 531–543.

Thorne, B. (1986). Girls and boys together … but mostly apart: Gender arrangements in elementary schools. In W. W. Hartup & Z. Rubin (Eds.), *Relationships and development* (pp. 167–184). Hillsdale, NJ: Erlbaum.

Thorne, B. (1993). *Gender play: Girls and boys in school.* New Brunswick, NJ: Rutgers University Press.

Thorne, B. (1997). Children and gender: Constructions of difference. In M. M. Gergen & S. N. Davis (Eds.), *Toward a new psychology of gender: A reader* (pp. 185–201). London: Routledge.

Thorne, B., & Luria, Z. (1986). Sexuality and gender in children's daily world. *Social Problems, 33,* 176–190.

Thornhill, R., & Thornhill, L. N. W. (1983). Human rape: An evolutionary analysis. *Ethology and Sociobiology, 4,* 137–173.

Tiggemann, M., & Kuring, J. K. (2004). The role of body objectification in disordered eating and depressed mood. *British Journal of Clinical Psychology, 43,* 299–311.

Tomaskovic-Devey, D. (1995). Sex composition and gendered earnings inequality: A comparison of job and occupational models. In J. A. Jacobs (Ed.), *Gender inequality and work* (pp. 23–56). Thousand Oaks, CA: Sage.

Tougas, F., Brown, R., Beaton, A. M., & Joly, S. (1995). Neosexism: Plus ça change, plus c'est pariel. *Personality and Social Psychology Bulletin, 21,* 842–849.

Touhey, J. C. (1974). Effects of additional women professionals on ratings of occupational prestige and desirability. *Journal of Personality and Social Psychology, 29,* 86–89.

Trautner, H. M., Ruble, D. N., Cyphers, L., Kirsten, B., Behrendt, R., & Hartmann, P. (2005). Rigidity and flexibility of gender stereotypes in childhood: Developmental or differential? *Infant and Child Development, 14,* 365–381.

Trivers, R. L. (1972). Parental investment and sexual selection. In B. Campbell (Ed.), *Sexual selection and the descent of man 1871–1971* (pp. 136–179). Chicago: Aldine.

Twenge, J. M. (1997a). Attitudes toward women, 1970–1995: A meta-analysis. *Sex Roles, 31,* 35–52.

Twenge, J. M. (1997b). "Mrs. His Name": Women's preferences for married names. *Psychology of Women Quarterly, 21,* 417–429.

Twenge, J. M. (2001). Changes in women's assertiveness in response to status and roles: A cross-temporal meta-analysis, 1931–1993. *Journal of Personality and Social Psychology, 81,* 133–145.

Uhlmann, E. L., & Cohen, G. L. (2005). Constructed criteria: Redefining merit to justify discrimination. *Psychological Science, 16,* 474–480.

Umberson, D., Anderson, K. L., Williams, K., & Chen, M. D. (2003). Relationship dynamics, emotion state, and domestic violence: A stress and masculinities perspective. *Journal of Marriage and the Family, 65,* 233–247.

Unger, R., & Crawford, M. (1996). *Women and gender: A feminist psychology* (2nd ed.). New York: McGraw-Hill.

Unger, R. K., Hilderbrand, M., & Madar, T. (1982). Physical attractiveness and assumptions about social deviance: Some sex-by-sex comparisons. *Personality and Social Psychology Bulletin, 8,* 293–301.

United Nations Development Programme. (2005). *Human development report 2005.* New York: Oxford University Press.

U. S. Bureau of Justice Statistics. (2007). *Crime and victims.* Retrieved August 27, 2007, from *http://www.ojp.usdoj.gov/bjs/*

U.S. Bureau of Labor Statistics. (2006). *Household data: Monthly household data* (Table A-19: Employed persons by occupation, sex, and age). Retrieved May 4, 2006, from *ftp://ftp.bls.gov/pub/suppl/empsit.cpseea19.txt*

U.S. Bureau of Labor Statistics. (2007). *Tables from employment and earnings: Annual averages, household data. http://www.bls.gov/cps/*

U.S. Census Bureau (2005). Bicentennial edition: Historical statistics of the United States. *http://www.census.gov/prod/www/abs/statab.html.*

U. S. Census Bureau. (2007a). Earnings in the past 12 months (2005). Retrieved July 13, 2007 from *http://factfinder.census.gov*

U. S. Census Bureau. (2007b). *Historical income–Families Table F-22. Married couple families with wives' earnings greater than husbands' earnings: 1981–2005.* Retrieved July 13, 2007, from *http://www.census.gov/hhes/www/income/histinc/f22.html*

U. S. General Accounting Office. (2001, October). *Women in management: Analysis of selected data from the current population survey (GAO-02-156).* Retrieved May 4, 2006, from *http://www.equality2020.org/women.pdf.*

Valian, V. (1999). *Why so slow? The advancement of women.* Cambridge, MA: MIT Press.

Vandello, J. A., Bosson, J. K., Cohen, D., Burnaford, R. M., & Wasti, S. A. (2007). *Precarious manhood and aggression.* Manuscript submitted for publication.

Vandello, J. A., & Cohen, D. (2003). Male honor and female fidelity: Implicit cultural scripts that perpetuate cultural violence. *Journal of Personality and Social Psychology, 84,* 997–1010.

Vandello, J. A., & Cohen, D. (2006). *Male violence against women as defense of honor: A cross-cultural analysis.* Unpublished manuscript, University of South Florida.

Vandello, J. A., Cohen, D., & Ransom, S. (in press). U.S. southern and northern differences in perceptions of norms about aggression: Mechanisms for the perpetuation of a culture of honor. *Journal of Cross-Cultural Psychology.*

Van Wyk, P. H. (1982). Relationship of time spent on masturbation assignments with orgasmic outcome in preorgasmic women's groups. *Journal of Sex Research, 18,* 33–40.

Vescio, T. K., Gervais, S. J., Snyder, M., & Hoover, A. (2005). Power and the creation of patronizing environments: The stereotype-based behaviors of the powerful and their effects on female performance in masculine domains. *Journal of Personality and Social Psychology, 88,* 658–672.

Vinokur, A. D., Pierce, P. F., & Buck, C. L. (1999). Work-family conflicts of women in the Air Force: Their influence on mental health functioning. *Journal of Organizational Behavior, 20,* 865–878.

von Baeyer, C. L., Sherk, D. L., & Zanna, M. P. (1981). Impression management in the job interview: When the female applicant meets the male (chauvinist) interviewer. *Personality and Social Psychology Bulletin, 7,* 45–51.

Vora, S. (2007, January 14). Money doesn't talk [Electronic version]. *New York Times.* Retrieved October 17, 2007, from *http://www.nytimes.com/2007/01/14/fashion/14CASH.html*

Wakin, D. J. (2005, July 10). Baltimore Symphony board backs choice of Marin Alsop. [Online Archive]. *New York Times.* Available at *http://www.nytimes.com/2005/07/20/arts/music/20also.html.*

Waller, W. W., & Hill, P. (1951). *The family: A dynamic interpretation.* New York: Dryden Press.

Walsh, M., Hickey, C., & Duffy, J. (1999). Influence of item content and stereotype situation and gender differences in mathematical problem solving. *Sex Roles, 41,* 219–240.

Walton, M., Fineman, R. M., & Walton, P. J. (1996). Why can't a woman be more like a man? A renaissance perspective on the biological basis for female inferiority. *Women and Health, 24,* 87–95.

Walton, M. D., Sachs, D., Ellington, R., Hazlewood, A., Griffin, S., & Bass, D. (1988). Physical stigma and the pregnancy role: Receiving help from strangers. *Sex Roles, 18,* 323–311.

Ward, L. M., Hansbrough, E., & Walker, E. (2005). Contributions of music video exposure to Black adolescents' gender and sexual schemas. *Journal of Adolescent Research, 20,* 143–166.

Weiner, T. (1994, March 28). Women, citing bias, may sue the C. I. A. *New York Times,* p. A10.

Wegner, D. M. (1989). *White bears and other unwanted thoughts: Suppression, obsession, and the psychology of mental control.* New York: Viking.

Wegner, D. M., Lane, J. D., & Dimitri, S. (1994). The allure of secret relationships. *Journal of Personality and Social Psychology, 66,* 287–300.

Weinstock v. Columbia University, 224 F.3d 33 (2nd Cir. 2000).

Wertheimer, A. (2003). *Consent to sexual relations.* Cambridge, UK: Cambridge University Press.

Westermack, E. A. (1903). *The history of human marriage.* London: Macmillan.

Wheeler, L., Reis, H. T., & Nezlek, J. (1983). Loneliness, social interaction, and sex roles. *Journal of Personality and Social Psychology, 45,* 943–953.

Wheeler, S. C., & Petty, R. E. (2001). The effects of stereotype activation on behavior: A review of possible mechanisms. *Psychological Bulletin, 127,* 797–826.

Whiley, R. B. (2001). The paradoxical relationship between gender inequality and rape: Toward a refined theory. *Gender and Society, 15,* 531–555.

Whissell, C. (1996). Mate selection in popular women's fiction. *Human Nature, 7*(4), 427–447.

White House Project. (2006). *Snapshots of current political leadership.* Retrieved May 4, 2006, from *http://www.thewhitehouseproject.org/v2/researchandreports/snapshots.html*

Whiting, B. B., & Edwards, C. P. (1988). *Children of different worlds: The formation of social behavior.* Cambridge, MA: Harvard University Press.

Wiederman, M. W. (1997). Extramarital sex: Prevalence and correlates in a national survey. *Journal of Sex Research, 34,* 167–174.

Wiener, R. L., & Gutek, B. A. (1999). Advances in sexual harassment research, theory, and policy. *Psychology, Public Policy, and Law, 5(3),* 507–518.

Wigfield, A., Harold, R. D., Freedman-Doan, C., Eccles, J. S., Yoon, K. S., Arbreton, A. J. A., & Blumenfeld, P. C. (1997). Change in children's competence beliefs and subjective task values across the elementary school years: A 3-year study. *Journal of Educational Psychology, 89(3),* 451–469.

Wilcox, D., & Hager, R. (1980). Toward realistic expectations for orgasmic response in women. *Journal of Sex Research, 16,* 162–179.

Wiley, M. G., & Eskilson, A. (1985). Speech style, gender stereotypes, and corporate success: What if women talk more like men? *Sex Roles, 12,* 993–1007.

Willer, R. (2005, August). *Overdoing gender: A test of the masculine overcompensation thesis.* Paper presented at the meeting of the American Sociological Association, Philadelphia, PA.

Williams, C. L. (1992). The glass escalator: Hidden advantages for men in the "female" professions. *Social Problems, 39,* 253–267.

Williams, C. L. (1995). *Still a man's world: Men who do women's work.* Berkeley: University of California Press.

Williams, J. C. (2000). *Unbending gender: Why family and work conflict and what to do about it.* New York: Oxford University Press.

Williams, J. E., & Best, D. L. (1990). *Measuring sex stereotypes: A multination study* (rev. ed.). Newbury Park, CA: Sage.

Williams, K. D. (2007). Ostracism. *Annual Review of Psychology, 58,* 425–452.

Williams, K. D., Bernieri, F., Faulkner, S., Grahe, J., & Gada-Jain, N. (2000). The Scarlet Letter Study: Five days of social ostracism. *Journal of Personality and Interpersonal Loss, 5,* 19–63.

Williams, K. D., Govan, C. L., Croker, V., Tynan, D., Cruickshank, M., & Lam, A. (2002). Investigations into differences between social and cyber ostracism. *Group Dynamics: Theory, Research, and Practice, 6,* 65–77.

Williams, R., & Wittig, M. A. (1997). "I'm not a feminist, but …": Factors contributing to the discrepancy between pro-feminist orientation and feminist social identity. *Sex Roles, 37,* 885–904.

Wilson, M. A., & Leith, S. (2001). Acquaintances, lovers, and friends: Rape within relationships. *Journal of Applied Social Psychology, 31,* 1709–1726.

Wilson, M. I., & Daly, M. (1996). Male sexual proprietariness and violence against wives. *Current Directions in Psychological Science, 5,* 2–7.

Wilson, T. D., & Brekke, N. (1994). Mental contamination and mental correction: Unwanted influences on judgments and evaluations. *Psychological Bulletin, 116,* 117–142.

Winslow, J. T., & Insel, T. R. (2004). Neuroendocrine basis of social recognition. *Current Opinion in Neurobiology, 14*(2), 248–253.

Wojciszke, B. (2005). Affective concomitants of information on morality and competence. *European Psychologist, 10,* 60–70.

Wojciszke, B., Bazinska, R., & Jaworski, M. (1998). On the dominance of moral categories in impression formation. *Personality and Social Psychology Bulletin, 24,* 1245–1257.

Wolf, N. (1991). *The beauty myth.* New York: William Morrow.

Wolff, K., Tsapakis, E. M., Winstock, A. R., Hartley, D., Holt, D., Forsling, M. L., & Aitchison, K. J. (2006). Vasopressin and oxytocin secretion in response to the consumption of ecstasy in a clubbing population. *Journal of Psychopharmacology, 20*(3), 400–410.

Wood, R. G., Corcoran, M. E., & Courant, P. N. (1993). Pay differences among the highly paid: The male-female earnings gap in lawyers' salaries. *Journal of Labor Economics, 11*(3), 417–441.

Wood, W., & Eagly, A. H. (2002). A cross-cultural analysis of the behavior of women and men: Implications for the origins of sex differences. *Psychological Bulletin, 128,* 699–727.

Yee, M., & Brown, R. (1994). The development of gender differentiation in young children. *British Journal of Social Psychology, 33,* 183–196.

Yodanis, C. L. (2004). Gender inequality, violence against women, and fear: A cross-national test of the feminist theory of violence against women. *Journal of Interpersonal Violence, 19,* 655–675.

Yoder, J. D. (2001). Making leadership work for women. *Journal of Social Issues, 57,* 815–828.

Yoder, J. D., & Schleicher, T. L. (1996). Undergraduates regard deviation from occupational gender stereotypes as costly for women. *Sex Roles, 34,* 171–188.

Yoder, J. D., Schleicher, T. L., & McDonald, T. W. (1998). Empowering token women leaders: The importance of organizationally legitimated credibility. *Psychology of Women Quarterly, 22,* 209–222.

Young, I. M. (1992). Breasted experience: The look and the feeling. In R. Weitz (Ed.), *The politics of women's bodies: Sexuality, appearance, and behavior* (pp. 125–136). Oxford, UK: Oxford University Press.

Yzerbyt, V. Y., & Cornielle, O. (2005). Cognitive processes: Reality constraints and integrity concerns in social perception. In J. F. Dovidio, P. Glick, & L. A. Rudman (Eds.), *On the nature of prejudice: Fifty years after Allport* (pp. 175–191). Malden, MA: Blackwell.

Yzerbyt, V. Y., Rocher, S., & Schadron, G. (1997). Stereotypes as explanations: A subjective essentialistic view of group perception. In R. Spears, P. J. Oakes, N. Ellemers, & S. A. Haslam (Eds.), *The social psychology of stereotyping and group life* (pp. 20–50). Oxford, UK: Blackwell.

Yzerbyt, V. Y., Rogier, A., & Fiske, S. T. (1998). Group entiativity and social attribution: On translating situational constraints into stereotypes. *Personality and Social Psychology Bulletin, 24,* 1089–1103.

Yzerbyt, V. Y., Schadron, G., Leyens, J., & Rocher, S. (1994). Social judgeability:

The impact of meta-informational cues on the use of stereotypes. *Journal of Personality and Social Psychology, 66,* 48–55.

Zammuner, V. L. (1993). Perception of male and female personality traits and behaviors by Dutch children. *Bulletin of the Psychonomic Society, 31,* 87–90.

Zanna, M. P., & Pack, S. J. (1975). On the self-fulfilling nature of apparent sex differences in behavior. *Journal of Experimental Social Psychology, 11,* 583–591.

Zernike, K. (2007, January 21). Why are there so many single Americans? [Electronic version]. *New York Times. http://www.nytimes.com/2007/01/21/weekinreview/21zernike.html*

Zucker, A. N. (2004). Disavowing social identities: What it means when women say, "I'm not a feminist but ..." *Psychology of Women Quarterly, 28,* 423–435.

Zucker, K. J., Bradley, S. J., & Sanikhani, M. (1997). Sex differences in referral rates of children with gender identity disorder. *Journal of Abnormal Child Psychology, 25,* 217–227.

Zvonkovic, A. M., Greaves, K. M., Schmeige, C. J., & Hall, L. D. (1996). The marital construction of gender through work and family decisions. *Journal of Marriage and the Family, 58,* 91–100.

Author Index

Subject Index

Abusive behavior in relationships, 224–225
Academic achievement, 75–76, 77, 134–135, 158–159
Achieved status, 162
Acquaintance rape, 234, 240, 279
Action figure, doll compared to, 61
Activities
  associations with gender, 111, 131
  preferences for, in childhood, 60–62
Adaptability to social and cultural influences, 14, 34–35
Adjective Check List, 88
Adolescence, romance in, 215–220
Affiliation motives, 140
Agentic mode of being
  description of, 82
  implicit attitudes and, 114–115
  stereotypes and, 86–88, 91–95
Agentic women
  backlash against, 128–130, 161–167, 295–296
  emotional and implicit reactions to, 167–168
  gender differences in backlash for, 169–170
  moderators of backlash for, 168–169
  self-concept and, 126–127
Aggression
  in childhood, 62–63
  fear of deviance, overperforming masculinity, and, 149–151
  heterosexual sex and, 235–237
  male–female, 224, 270–278
  male–male, 36, 262–270

same-sex physical, 17
sexual, 30, 31, 32, 219–220, 278–283
See also Violence
Agreeableness, and mate selection, 33–34
Agricultural societies, 32, 33, 35–36, 267
Alsop, Marin, 156, 169
Ambivalence
  ehormb and jumere analogy and, 25–27
  gender, violence, and, 260
  of sexes, 28
  toward sex, 239–240
  toward women's bodies, 240–242
  See also Ambivalent sexism theory
Ambivalence toward Men Inventory (AMI), 38–40, 48–52, 123
Ambivalent Sexism Inventory (ASI), 38–47
Ambivalent sexism theory
  inequality, resistance to, and, 46–47
  overview of, 23, 37–40
  protection racket and, 30–32, 48, 260, 279
  relationship violence and, 274
  romantic love and, 211–214
  stereotypes and, 90, 123
  See also Ambivalence toward Men Inventory; Ambivalent Sexism Inventory; Benevolent sexism; Hostile sexism
AMI (Ambivalence toward Men Inventory), 38–40, 48–52, 123
Anabolic steroids, 246
Antifeminism, 299
Arranged marriages, 208
The Art of Love (Ovid), 238–239
Ascribed status, 162

377